www.markworkman.com

One for the Road
How to Be a Music Tour Manager
By Mark Workman

United States Copyright Office Registration # TX0008393370
ISBN: 978-0615726113

General Information
Road Crew Books
info@markworkman.com

Book cover and logo design
by Eliran Kantor
www.elirankantor.com

Words of Praise
"Workman has provided priceless insight with his book which should be studied top-to-bottom by anyone looking to make their living in the business." **Blabbermouth.net**

"It's a virtual treasure trove of information for current or aspiring road crew members. I cannot fathom a single nugget of information that was left out of this book." **National Rock Review**

"Workman has written a 354-page book that not only shows the novice tour manager how to do the job correctly, but also provides a witty and entertaining read for anyone who just wants to know how a music tour is run." **Revolver Magazine**

Beware the man of one book.
—St. Thomas Aquinas

Without comedy, we have nothing.
—Anonymous

This book is dedicated to Nicolette Galbraith.
You endured so much, yet you still care.
I will always love you.

Thomas Ray Workman
1962-2010
Rest in peace, brother.
I will see you again on the other side
when this crusade of madness finally ends.

Jeffrey John Hanneman
1964-2013
In our memories you will forever reign.

TABLE OF CONTENTS

FOREWORD BY ALEX SKOLNICK

Take a very close look at any band that has achieved international recognition, and you'll find someone who has been an integral part of that band's development from offstage. For example, producer George Martin—as well as manager Brian Epstein, keyboardist Billy Preston and others— each earned the nickname "The Fifth Beatle." Led Zeppelin's longtime manager, Peter Grant, was considered an unofficial offstage band member.

The individuals mentioned above happen to be household names to any serious rock fan. But in most cases, a band's crucial team member is someone who is less widely known, especially in the genre of thrash metal, where compared to The Beatles and Led Zeppelin, the audience is, to quote from the mock rock documentary *This Is Spinal Tap*: "More selective." Yet whatever thrash metal may lack in terms of mainstream popularity—especially when compared to timeless rock royalty—it more than makes up for in terms of fan dedication. And if there is one name that should be better known to fans of this genre—or for that matter, any music fan interested in what takes place behind the scenes—it is Mark Workman.

As you read this, there may be thousands out there working on behalf of bands—emailing, calling, negotiating, and rousting them out of bed, etc....but scant few, if any, have had the insight, knowledge, humor, and intellect to write about this process effectively, until now. *One for the Road* is the perfect title for this series, and Mark Workman is the perfect author to create it.

A seasoned veteran of many a metal tour (a short list of credits includes Testament, Slayer, Anthrax, Megadeth, Machine Head, Danzig, Dio, and Mudvayne), Mark has long been the instigator of many repeated tour quotes and anecdotes. My own band, Testament, never had the good fortune of finding the right producer or manager early on—both positions would change hands several times. But in 1988, as touring began for our second album, *The New Order*, we found Mark, who'd become our first long-term trusted team member. He'd only signed on to that tour as LD (lighting director) and came across as an inconspicuous crew guy. But when our tour manager suddenly jumped ship, it was Mark who grabbed the reigns and took over the job as TM, while continuing as LD.

As I write this, my own memoir, *Geek to Guitar Hero*, is being published. I mention this not in the interest of self-promotion, but because it directly relates to this book. Mark

Workman is the sole person who has an entire chapter devoted to him, based on our original nickname for him: *Sergeant Slaughter.*

"Without a doubt, the most memorable and dominant personality in the history of the band is Mark Workman. It pretty much started on the day he took over as tour manager. With a fierce directness, strict work ethic and leadership skills to match, Mark was the only one able to get us checked in and out of hotels, to interviews, or wherever else we needed to be on time. As our first lighting director (LD), his demeanor had been that of an unassuming crewmember who kept to himself. But as tour manager, he transformed us from an out-of-control nursery school to an army barracks."

From the day he hopped on board that bus in 1988 till the time of my own departure in the early 90's, from the reunion shows of the mid-00's to the 2012 release, *Dark Roots of Earth* (our first to crack the Billboard top 15) and several points in between, Mark has been a part of the soul of our band's organization. He has helped get the live show where it needs to be, both on a visual and organizational level, and helped guide us through that crucial early period when things easily could have gone sour. Sure, there'd be times where he and the band would drift apart (as is true of my own situation with the band). There'd be times when his demons would get the better of him (as detailed near the end of the book). But Mark has always come back, like a prizefighter that refuses to go down for the count.

While we're on that subject, Mark's dedication to the road and metal music mirrors that of his other passion—professional boxing—for which he is a boxing writer with essays posted by BoxingScene, Fox Sports, and others. When a band gets offstage, it's a bit like the period in between rounds during a boxing match, where the fighter is in the corner, talking to no one but his trainer. The band sits alone in the dressing room, allowing the breathing to return to normal, the sweating to dissipate, and the dizziness of constant movement to subside. No guests and other well-wishers are allowed backstage during this sacred time. Mark is like the trainer—the first non-band member to walk through the door—a welcome presence, letting the band know just how the show went—what worked, what didn't, if it was a great night or just so-so.

Having shared buses and dressing rooms with Mark since our first tour together in 1988, I've long found him to be the rare person who says what he means and does what he says he's going to do. He will tell a band what they *need* to hear and not what they *want* to hear. He's also a constant source of dark comedy with an acerbic wit and abrasive humor. That spirit shines through in these pages. Faint of heart, take heed: Mark does not mince words.

While he occasionally causes shock and insult, Mark always keeps things from getting boring. His harsh mannerisms, brutal honesty and fierce directness are not for everyone.

Those who do not have a thick skin be warned (and while you're at it, this might be a good time to reconsider a career in the music business). Whether in the Testament camp (bandspeak for organization), or others, Mark is the source of more tour stories than the musicians themselves.

This book, and the eventual companion editions, will no doubt become an invaluable asset to anyone who thinks they have what it takes to run a tight ship on tour. This will be the guide that many tour vets wish they'd had when starting out. Reading it, one can imagine what might have happened if Charles Bukowski or Hunter S. Thompson had been a fight fan who spent his life as a member of the road crew for some of the world's fastest heavy metal bands and wrote about it. I will not be the least surprised to see *One for the Road: ~~How to~~ Be a Music Tour Manager* become a must read among road crews for many years to come.

The road is a great equalizer. Not being prepared for its pitfalls, curveballs, "clusterfucks" (a favorite term of Mark's), and other unpredictable factors has contributed to many a mental breakdown among tour personnel, regardless of age, gender, cultural background, or musical genre. This book will encourage potential tour managers to realize just what they are getting themselves into and come to the tour adequately prepared. Conversely, it will also force those who do not have what it takes to come to their senses and, it is hoped, get out with their dignity still intact.

Alex Skolnick
www.alexskolnick.com

INTRODUCTION

This is a book for beginners.

I almost quit writing this book three times, but I don't believe you're *out* after three strikes any more than I believe cats only have nine lives—the little bastards live forever. If I believe in nothing else in this life, I believe in resurrection and new beginnings. Trust me; I'm living, pulsing proof of it.

Writing this book became more frustrating with each successive draft, and I simply couldn't figure out why my middle finger seemed to be constantly pulled against its will to my computer's delete button like a planchette on a Ouija board.

Captain Howdy, that isn't very nice!

Is there an exorcist in the house?

Then it struck me like an uppercut from "Iron" Mike Tyson; the problem was clear to a blind man. As I edited each chapter, I wearily waded through a rigid how-to book that highlighted the positives and downplayed the negatives of being a music tour manager. To put it simply: this book was so full of happy horseshit, you needed a manure collector to get rid of it all.

I made up my mind, right then and there, to tell it like it is: the good, the bad, the ugly, and the monstrously horrible. I offer no phony sales pitch; no mysterious insider secrets will be revealed, and no false promises of an exciting new career are guaranteed or your money back. Not that this book ever contained any of those shameful things—it didn't—but it was stiffer than a crone's arthritic fingers and had about as much humor as a handbook on autopsy practice.

My book was reborn.

I hope you have a sense of humor. Yes, there is job discrimination in the music business; tour managers born without a thick funny bone need not apply. You won't last without one.

This is a book for those of you hoping to become a tour manager in the music business, and for new tour managers already working on the road who are still struggling to learn how to do the job correctly.

The music tour manager is at the top of the road crew totem pole. It's a very high-paying job. Top tour managers earn thousands of dollars a week. It's also one of the few jobs on a band's road crew where you don't need to have any technical or musical skills—but brains do help.

If you want to be a tour manager in the music business, this is the book to read. It will also benefit sound engineers, lighting directors, backline technicians, and production assistants who want to move up the career ladder or do double-duty to earn more money. It will also benefit day-to-day staff at music management companies. You can't be strong support to the road manager when you don't know what the road manager does—or should be doing—every day.

New tour managers without any training, flying by the seat of their pants and praying for success, will find this book a valuable guide that will teach them how to perform the job correctly. It will also help new road managers who are about to do their first tour overseas. The information in this book will even benefit new bands that can't afford a tour manager yet and have to do the job themselves. It's also for those of you who just want to know more about how a music tour is run.

Qualified tour managers for music groups are needed more than ever now. With the music business going through dramatic changes, touring is the primary way many bands make a living. Because of this, good tour managers are in great demand.

I've spent thirty years traveling the world as a tour manager and lighting designer in the music business. My list of past and present clients include many popular bands, such as Slayer, Megadeth, Anthrax, Testament, Machine Head, Danzig, Mudvayne, Dio, Queens of the Stone Age, Soulfly, Keel, Steeler, and many others. I've always worked in the heavy metal genre, but it doesn't matter what type of bands you intend to work with. Everything in this book applies to any kind of music tour.

In the following pages I'll show you everything a new tour manager needs to know to get started in the music business; how to successfully organize and complete your first music tour; and how to build a successful career as a music tour manager.

Part 1 tells you how I got started as a tour manager and why I wrote this book.

Part 2 teaches you how to organize a concert tour and:

> create a complete and accurate tour budget;
>
> hire the best road crew;
>
> lease the right tour bus and safest driver;
>
> book hotels and air travel the right way;
>
> create a proper backstage pass system and where to get it made;
>
> deal with foreign artist tax for your band;
>
> apply for overseas visas and work permits for your entourage;
>
> create a tour book and the vital information it should contain;
>
> coordinate trucking and air cargo;

hire sound and lighting systems for your tour;

understand tour riders and contracts;

prepare ATA carnets and equipment manifests;

get backdrops, scrims and stage sets made;

prepare your tour accounting and a lot more.

Part 3 shows you how to get organized and properly advance each show and:

what you should know about stage plots and input charts;

preparing your pre-advance package;

making a proper advance sheet;

how to advance each show;

advancing your cash requirements and much more.

Part 4 guides you through an entire show day and shows you:

what it takes to be a tour manager running a music tour;

the mechanics of how to do press, meet-and-greets, and in-stores;

the proper way to do your guest list each day;

the right way to handle venue security;

how to do your daily tour accounting correctly;

how to do your show settlement each night;

important information about merchandising, foreign currencies, and more.

Part 5 shows you how to:

promote yourself so you can build your successful career;

find your first job as a tour manager;

and the road hazards to avoid.

I'll soon begin my thirtieth year in the music business, and I'm a college dropout from a small town in southern Virginia. I didn't have a book like this when I started out, but I found a way to make my career in the music business a reality. I'm glad that I can finally give you the information and advice that was not available to me when I started my career many years ago.

If you finish this book feeling you've gained enough knowledge and confidence to actually move forward and try to become a professional tour manager in the music business, then I've accomplished my ultimate goal in writing these words for you.

PART ONE

THE BEGINNING

HOW I STARTED IN THE MUSIC BUSINESS

For three decades, I've traveled the world working as a tour manager and lighting designer for many popular rock bands. During these travels, I've met countless people who have asked me how they can become a music tour manager.

Their question has always been a difficult one for me to answer. There are no actual schools that teach you how to become a music tour manager. I was self-taught through a lot of trial and error. I didn't have a book like this to give me the knowledge that I needed. I wrote this book so the beginning of your career will be much easier than mine was.

In 1983, I began my career as a lighting designer for the heavy metal band Steeler. I worked as a lighting designer for five years before I accepted my first gig working double-duty as a tour manager/lighting designer for the heavy metal band Leatherwolf.

Many people have asked me what made me want to become a tour manager. The answer is a simple one: I wanted to make as much money as possible on every tour that I did, and the ambitious control freak inside me also had me believing that *my way* was the better way.

Doing two jobs on a tour is a good way to make more money, as long as you can do both jobs effectively. There are also more tours for those who can perform two jobs because it saves the band money.

To be a good tour manager, you must be highly motivated, possess a strong work ethic, and be good at time management. You also have to be a strong leader. Road managers must be computer literate and own a laptop, compact printer, and Microsoft Office. You need to be reasonably proficient in using Word and Excel. Tour managers also need to be good enough with numbers to do basic accounting and have a fundamental knowledge of accounting software such as Quicken. You must also own some kind of smart phone, like a Blackberry or iPhone, and have an email address. Communication is everything in this business.

If you don't have a valid passport, you should apply for one now. You cannot have a criminal record. No manager will hire anyone with a criminal past that will prevent them from entering other countries. We travel the world for a living.

In 1979, I left the mountains of West Virginia on a Trailways bus with $150 to my name and went twenty-four hundred miles to Los Angeles to find a way into the music business. I was only nineteen years old. I had never traveled anywhere before, and I didn't know a single soul in California.

I found a job working at a porn distributor in Hollywood, eventually ended up running the place, got the bright idea to start bootlegging porn video tapes, got sued for a million dollars and came very close to ending up in a hole in the desert, got out of that by the skin of my teeth, met Ron Keel in Steeler, started a merch company for Steeler, then became their lighting designer, and a career was born.

Even at that young age, I knew that if I didn't make the move then, I never would. I also knew that I was determined to build a career in the music business. I desired—demanded—something more for me than working in the coal mines, a job that I was actually doing in West Virginia at that time. I had no intention of spending the next fifty years of my life working in some dark, cold hole in the ground and dying of black lung like my grandfather did. I wanted wine, women, and song all over the world, and I was damn well going to have it.

I had confidence in me that some people said bordered on complete lunacy. I believed in myself, and I refused to give up. I also refused to listen to all of the negative reasons from unmotivated people why I would never succeed.

Four years later, I made it happen. You, too, can do the same. You just have to believe it.

PART TWO

ORGANIZING THE TOUR

GATHERING VITAL INFORMATION

If you've taken a gig with a new client, the first thing you must do is gather information about their organization. You can't start organizing a tour until you know you know who's on it, unless you're psychic.

I always send an email to the band's manager requesting the information that I need. Much of this information will be going into the front pages of the tour book, so you're going to need it all. You'll also need contact information for the band members and any road crew members who already work for the band.

Below is a list of some of the information that I might request from the manager:

- Name, cell phone number, and email address for all band members.
- Name, cell phone number, and email address for all road crew members currently working for the band.
- Company name, address, office telephone number, cell phone number, and work email address for the manager. He might have a private email address that he may not want published in the front of a tour book. Ask about this.
- Name, company name, address, office telephone number, cell phone number, and email address for the business manager (accountant).
- Name, company name, address, office telephone number, cell phone number, and email address for the booking agent.
- Name, company name, address, office telephone number, cell phone number, and email address for record company and contact info for any reps that I'll be working with, including any independent publicists the band may be hiring.
- Name, company name, address, office telephone number, cell phone number, and email address for the merchandising company and their company rep that I'll be working with. Name, cell phone number, and email address for the tour's merch seller.
- Does the band have a bus company they prefer to work with? If so, please send the same contact info.
- Does the band use a travel agent? If so, please send the same contact info.

- Name, company name, address, office telephone number, cell phone number, and email address for any other vendors and their reps that the band insists on using.
- Name, address, and telephone number of the band rehearsal studio where their gear will be picked up to start the tour.
- What is the hotel situation for the band and crew? Do they share rooms or have single rooms on days off, or do they only buy shower rooms? Please send any rooming list preferences that may exist.

Every band and tour is different. If you've taken a gig knowing that the band is going to be traveling in a van, then you don't need to ask the manager about bus company contact information. Tailor your information requests to your tour's specific needs. Start the flow of information between you and the manager. You probably won't think of everything you need in the first email, but you'll begin organizing the tour.

Ask for more information as you think of it, but don't send the manager emails all day long. Compile a list of things you need and send the manager an email at the end of the day. They have better things to do than wade through a dozen emails that could've easily been reduced down to one.

Make an email address book for your new client and enter all of the applicable email addresses as you receive them. There will be many times when you'll be sending out emails to everyone in the organization. Enter all of their cell phone numbers into your smart phone. Get set up right away so you can communicate with everyone involved.

Start a constant flow of communication with everyone in your organization. If no one ever hears from you, it's only a matter of time before the manager starts to wonder if you're getting anything done. Constant communication will set him at ease, and his confidence in you will grow quickly.

WORKING WITH THE TEAM

》》 The Manager

The band's personal manager is at the top of the totem pole for those who work for the band. The tour manager works under him. Unlike the tour manager, who works for a weekly salary, the manager usually gets a commission for the work he does for the band. Through the years, the standard management commission has been 20 percent of the band's gross income, but because the music business is rapidly changing, many bands are trying to change this old model that they feel is unfair. Every management agreement is different; it's all in what the band negotiates with their manager.

The manager is the overseer of every aspect of the band's career. The buck stops with the manager. It's his job to make sure the booking agent is getting the band the biggest tours and earning the highest income possible from each show and that there's forward progress in building the band's popularity around the world by playing everywhere possible on the planet.

The manager supervises the business manager (accountant) to make sure that she is doing her job, such as filing the appropriate paperwork to reduce artist taxes for the band, filing the band's income taxes on time, paying band and crew salaries on time, paying the band's bills on time, creating regular income and expense reports for the band and manager, and, of course, paying the manager's commission when it's due.

The manager is also in constant contact with the record company to make sure the band's new music is being promoted properly, that it's on sale everywhere possible, and that the band is getting press from every avenue possible. He works with the band's business manager to make sure that the band's royalty statements from the record company and publishing company are correct and that those royalties are paid on time. He supervises anything and everything involving the band's business with these companies. He's also constantly looking for new income streams for the band.

The manager works with the record company publicist—and any independent publicist that may be hired—to make sure the band is getting as much publicity, including interviews and reviews, as possible to increase their exposure in the worldwide marketplace.

Some tour managers get it in their head that they don't work for the manager because the band hired them and pays their salary. Trust me; you work for the manager. If you start butting heads with the band's manager, it's only a matter of time before you'll find yourself unemployed. No band is going to lose a good manager—one they have a legal contract with—over a road manager, no matter how much the band likes you or how well you do your job. Don't ever put yourself in such a hopeless position.

Good road managers who plan to last with the band need to not only become valuable assets to the band but also to the manager. You must get to the point where the manager can stop worrying about what's going on out there on the road so he can spend his time doing his job. No manager wants to spend his every waking hour doing your job for you or mopping up the messes you've created because you don't know what you're doing or you're not making the effort to do it right. Take a lot of the worry from his shoulders, and you'll find yourself employed much longer.

One of the most important things for you to do for any manager is to keep him highly informed, but don't fill up his email box every day with trivial matters that he doesn't need to know about unless he specifically asks for it. Copy him on important emails that contain essential information he needs to know, not emails to the bus company about the broken toilet on the bus, unless you're not getting anywhere with the bus company and you need to get the manager involved.

I've worked for some managers who just let me do my job, and I only heard from them regarding important matters that I needed to know about. I prefer the non-micro-managing manager who lets me get the job done but is there for me to drop the hammer on someone when I need his wrath.

When you're organizing a tour, if you reply to the manager's emails in a timely manner with the information he requests and send him a reasonably detailed weekly update on what you've gotten done, most of them will be happy with this and feel confident that you're getting the tour organized on time. Not doing this, of course, will get them worried, and they'll be on your back constantly as their confidence in you wanes.

Once you're on the road, as long as you send the manager your nightly report, and the others on the team aren't complaining that you're not doing your job, the manager will be the least of your worries. He just wants to be kept highly informed while you're doing your job to the best of your ability.

❯❯ The Business Manager

The most important thing to do when dealing with the band's business manager is to make sure your accounting is correct and sent to her on a regular basis. Without your accounting, she can't add this information into her master accounting and send her reports to the band and manager on time.

The best way to get the manager on the warpath against you is to cause the business manager to complain that you're not sending your road reports in on time or that you're not sending them at all. The business manager will also quickly lose faith in you if your weekly road reports show that you're out there spending a lot more money than what was budgeted. You're going to be on the path to unemployment if you're so sloppy that you're actually sending in road reports with errors on them. You must account for every single penny you pick up and spend in your road reports.

Being a road manager is an odd job. Sometimes you have to tell your employer, the band, that they can't spend their own money. Often with new bands that lack experience, you'll find yourself in uncomfortable situations where they're arguing with you why they can't spend their own money.

Most bands understand right away that they have to save every dime to make the budget work so they can stay on the road and build a career. However, a band can sometimes lose sight of the big picture, and you suddenly become the bad guy who has to say no to them when they want to spend money on something that's not in their budget.

I normally work with established bands that understand the important concept of sticking to the tour budget, but some of them are so successful that they can afford to spend some of their earnings on luxuries that help to make life on the road a bit less painful. In a situation like this, do what they tell you to do; it's their money. Don't argue with them.

You should still keep the business manager and manager informed about these unbudgeted expenditures. If they have a problem with it, they can speak directly to the band about it. Don't allow yourself to get caught in a firestorm over these things and lose your job.

❯❯ The Booking Agent

Most booking agents will probably never admit this, but the best road manager is the one they never hear from except for their nightly report.

For a busy booking agent, there's nothing worse than having a road manager blowing up his email box or, even worse, ringing his phone off the hook, complaining that the promoter didn't get the band's favorite brand of beer and how they're threatening to cancel the show over it—God forbid you've actually been psychotic enough to copy the manager on these ridiculous emails.

Painting the painful picture a bit darker, it becomes even more miserable for the booking agent when the road manager expects him to start calling the promoter to get something done about it. I'm sorry, but if you can't even solve such a minor problem without involving the booking agent and manager, then, let me think, maybe, umm, quite possibly, you're in the wrong fucking *job*!

A smart road manager will avoid this kind of situation more than a groupie with herpes simplex. It's your job to solve problems with the promoter. Emailing the booking agent every five minutes about production matters that he can't do anything about only makes him begin to wish the band would hire a new road manager—and, believe me, it will only be a matter of time before he begins to express those deep and sincere wishes to the manager.

If the catering budget for the show is maxed out and the promoter can't afford anything more, then you need to deal with it and explain this reality to your band. Most of them will understand if you explain the situation to them correctly. If the show is selling badly and the promoter is losing a lot of money, you'll have no choice in the matter.

If the PA and lighting system is inadequate and the band's deal is cut based upon the agreement that they use house production, then you must use the house production and make it work if the promoter is unwilling to rent better gear. None of this should've come as a shock if you advanced the show properly. Don't waste your agent's valuable time ranting and raving about things he cannot change.

Don't misunderstand me; if you're being blatantly screwed over by the promoter because you advanced and confirmed one thing but now you're getting something completely different and the show is selling well and you've done all you can do, then that is the time to get the booking agent involved. Just don't call him until you've exhausted every possibility of solving the problem on your own; and leave the manager out of it until all hope is lost. He's more interested in hearing how you solved the problem on your own.

A top booking agent usually has a lot of clients and does a lot of business with the promoters, so he has leverage that you don't have and can often get a bad situation turned good pretty quickly. It's just important that you try and solve these problems with the promoter before getting the agent involved. Be polite and professional and remind the promoter of what you agreed on during the advance, and more times than not, you'll solve an issue and never have to bother the booking agent with it.

You should also know that the promoters are also sending the agents their own nightly report, so do everything you can to make sure the promoter's report to the agent is a positive one about you. Be professional and courteous and leave the venue each night with the promoter having had a positive experience working with you and the band. Even if he's lost money, he's more likely to take a chance on the band the next time. You don't want the band's booking agent to get constant complaints from promoters about you because it will eventually get back to the manager. Handle your business and represent your band properly.

>> The Record Company

It can be an overwhelming experience working with a large record company if you're an inexperienced tour manager. There can be many people in a multitude of departments contacting you on a regular basis. There may be one rep that handles the band's radio promotion, another rep that deals with print publications, another one that deals with online media, a different rep that handles television show appearances, and then you may have reps in each city coming to the venue to make sure all of this press goes as planned.

On some smaller labels, you might only hear from one press person who is dealing with each aspect of press, and you may never see any local reps at the shows except when you play in the town where the record company is located. Personally, I prefer it when a label rep comes down to deal with all of the press people, especially when it's a busy press day.

If you're on tour in Europe and the U.K., you'll often have label reps in the different territories to help you handle press each day. It's important to build a good relationship with all of the label reps because they're coming to the venue to help make your day easier.

You'll find that if you give the record label a list of press protocol before they begin to book press for the tour, your life will be easier each day. Don't let them start booking everything under the sun at any time they choose and then complain when you realize that it's impossible to get all of it done. Their job is to get the band the most press possible, but sometimes you have to pull in the reigns a bit when what they're expecting of the band is unrealistic and simply too much for them to handle.

You may have to get the manager involved if you're having problems with this, but many managers may approve the press schedules before they even get to you. However, I've worked with some managers that approved the press but left it to me to sort out the schedule. If you send the press team at the record company a specified protocol for how you want press done, they'll usually follow it if it makes sense; and if they have an important interview that falls outside of that protocol, they'll ask you and the band to make an exception.

I'll normally speak with the leader of the band who makes the decisions and find out how they like to do press if it's an act I've never worked with before, and then I'll send an email to the label explaining how we'd like to do press each day. Keep in mind that if the band has been around a while, they may already have their ways of doing things. If you're new to them, they're going to be less likely to do things your way until you prove yourself and show them that your way is the better way.

Below are some of the usual points that I'll cover—keeping in mind that each band is different in what they want:

The band prefers to do phone and in-person interviews between 1:00 and 3:30 p.m. in the time zone that we're in because we have sound check every day at 4:00 p.m., sharp.

The band prefers to start meet-and-greets at 5:30 p.m., right after dinner. If a meet-and-greet cannot happen at this time, it must be done right after doors open, but we'd prefer to avoid this whenever possible. If this isn't possible, then the band will do the meet-and-greet approximately thirty minutes after the show is over.

The band prefers to do photo shoots ten minutes before they go on stage so they're dressed in their stage clothes. For any special photo shoots for individual band members for musician-specific publications, such as guitar or drum magazines, the band members can do these photo shoots between 1:00 and 3:30 p.m.

The band prefers not to do press of any kind on days off unless it can only be done on that day and is too important to turn down.

Please do not book every interview with the singer; spread them out across the other band members unless the interviewer specifically requests the interview to be done with the band's singer.

As you can see, we've given the press team some guidelines to follow when booking the press. Make sure the manager has been copied on these guidelines so he's not approving press at the wrong time because you haven't' made him aware of the band's requested guidelines.

Once the press team starts sending you their requests for each city, it'll be a lot more organized and done more to the band's liking because you've sent them these guidelines, and it'll make your life much easier.

We'll cover more about press, in-stores, and meet-and-greets in the applicable chapter, but you'll quickly find that most of your interaction with the record company will be in regards to press-related matters.

»» The Independent Publicist

Some bands will hire—or talk the record company into hiring—an independent publicist to work their album in addition to the work the record label's press team is doing. Sometimes this is paid for directly by the band, or the record company will pay for it as a recoupable expense that must be repaid out of any royalties the band will receive. Sometimes a smaller record label that has a small promotion staff will hire the independent publicist to help work the record.

On occasion, this can be a headache because you're getting press from not only the label's people but from the independent publicist, too, and sometimes those schedules may conflict. I always try to ask that all of the press go through one final person, either the independent publicist or someone at the label, before it comes to me so it can be rearranged if there is a conflict.

I don't want to waste a lot of time going through multiple press sheets and back and forth with everyone involved trying to sort out conflicting interviews. A tour manager's job is to see that the press gets done after it's been approved and confirmed. This is why it's best for one person to combine all of the press coming in from the different departments and solve any scheduling conflicts before it comes to the manager and tour manager for final approval.

Sometimes this can cause some political drama if the independent publicist is hired directly by the band and not the label. Press people at the label sometimes don't like it when an independent publicist has been hired by the band. Some of them take it personally because they feel the band doesn't believe they know how to do their jobs, causing them to be uncooperative with the independent publicist. On the other hand, some of them appreciate it and look at it as much-needed help.

If you can't get them to agree to filter all of the press through one person, then you'll just have to deal with going over multiple press sheets to resolve the scheduling conflicts if the management company isn't doing it.

Having an independent publicist usually means you're going to have a lot more press each day. My old friend Maria Ferrero at Adrenaline PR is one of the best publicists in the music business, and the very best for heavy music. She and her staff are experts at publicizing heavy music, and they do an excellent job.

No matter how many people are involved with the band's daily press schedule, always remember how important it is to get it done correctly. Your band could have the greatest record of all time, but if there's no press about it they're going to sell zilch.

PREPARING AN ACCURATE TOUR BUDGET

When organizing a tour, one of the most important things to do is create the tour budget. With a new band, the tour budget will be a simple one because the group will be touring on limited resources.

Even if the manager tells you that it's unnecessary to do a tour budget, do it anyway. You need the experience of creating one. You don't want to find yourself in a situation on your next tour where the manager insists on a tour budget and you have no idea how to create one.

Some management companies insist on doing their own tour budgets. These are often bigger management firms that have a lot of experience in doing tour budgets. It's also possible that they've had bad experiences in the past with road managers who submitted tour budgets that ended up being inaccurate and thousands of dollars over budget. Sometimes the band's business manager may help create the tour budget. I always prefer to do the tour budget myself.

The manager and business manager should always make sure that the budget is realistic and no mistakes have been made. Three heads are better than one. Make sure they have approved the budget for your protection, and get their approval sent via email so you have a record of it.

There are a few differences in creating a tour budget for a U.S./Canada tour versus a tour of the U.K. and Europe. The United States, the countries of Europe, the United Kingdom, and Canada are the countries where bands tour most often, so we're going to examine a U.S. budget and a Europe budget. You must learn the differences between them.

If we were going into Canada on this U.S. tour, we'd include those tour dates in this same U.S. budget. On a tour of Europe, if we were going into the U.K., we'd add those shows into the same Europe budget.

Below is a tour budget for a twenty-five day U.S. tour that I created using an Excel spreadsheet that I built. Microsoft Excel is easy to learn, and there are many free tutorials online that will teach you how to use the program so you can build a similar budget spreadsheet if you don't already know how.

All of the documents and spreadsheets in this book are from a fictitious band that I created called Skinny Girl Riot. I did this because none of my clients, past or present, would appreciate me putting their confidential information in this book.

I came up with the name Skinny Girl Riot when I was trying to think of a new name for an emo band that I was managing back in 2006. Yes, it was a misguided time of madness that I did actually believe in. And, no, I had never heard of the Skinny Girl Diet when I came up with the name. I don't even know if that brand even existed back then. The band didn't like the name anyway or anything else resembling victory. The sweet stench of success frightened them to death.

The Skinny Girl Riot entourage is traveling on one tour bus with a fifteen-foot trailer. Look it over and you'll see some of the expense categories in a tour budget. The band and crew salaries and the band's guarantees (show fees) are all fabricated. Arena tours will have more expense categories, while a small van tour will have fewer categories.

The first category is band salaries. On a tour with a new band, there will usually be nothing but zeros in that category. At this early stage of their career, the band is barely earning enough money—if anything at all—to pay for road expenses, so they pay themselves nothing until the day arrives when their company is showing a profit and they can pay themselves a salary.

Most new bands rely on their merchandising profits to pay their road expenses until they earn enough from their shows to pay the bills. The days of a risky baby band getting tour support from the record company are pretty much over. Tour support is a loan from the record company to subsidize the band's touring expenses. This money almost always has to be paid back and is usually deducted from the band's royalties.

The next category in this budget is crew salaries. Your first tour will probably be a van tour with a new band, so you'll most likely be entering many zeros in that category. You may not have any crew members at all.

It's rare that a new band is carrying more than one or two crew members on a van tour. The first reason is limited money in the budget. The second reason is limited room in the van. These crew members are often friends of the band who are hoping to hitch themselves onto something they hope is going somewhere. They are often working for free or next to nothing, learning while making an investment in the band, in hopes that they'll one day be paid a salary when the band can afford it—sort of an intern-type situation.

Skinny Girl Riot Tour Budget--USA 2012							
Expenses							
						Total Expenses	**$179,197.18**
	Daily Rate	**Days**	**Total**		**Daily Rate**	**Days**	**Total**
Band salaries				**Hotels**			
Stevie Starbright--vocals	$500.00	25	$12,500.00	Bus driver (1)	$100.00	33	$3,300.00
Frankie Fabulous--guitar	$500.00	25	$12,500.00	Band shower room (1)	$100.00	4	$400.00
Jimmy Giant--guitar	$500.00	25	$12,500.00	Crew shower room (1)	$100.00	4	$400.00
Mikey Massive--bass	$500.00	25	$12,500.00	Truck driver	$0.00		$0.00
Tommy Twosticks--drums	$500.00	25	$12,500.00		$0.00		$0.00
Totals	**$2,500.00**		**$62,500.00**	**Totals**	**$300.00**		**$4,100.00**
Crew Salaries				**Air Travel**			
Bobby Blinder--TM/LD	$400.00	25	$10,000.00	Airfares for band (5)	$300.00	5	$1,500.00
Lance Loudnoise--PM/FOH	$400.00	25	$10,000.00	Airfares for crew (7)	$300.00	7	$2,100.00
Tony Tonedeaf--Monitors	$250.00	25	$6,250.00	Excess baggage	$500.00	1	$500.00
Ricky Racket--SM/guitar tech	$250.00	25	$6,250.00	**Totals**	**$1,100.00**		**$4,100.00**
Jerry Spazon--guitar tech	$200.00	25	$5,000.00	**Local transportation**			
Kyle Klown--drum tech	$200.00	25	$5,000.00	Bus driver taxis	$40.00	25	$1,000.00
Penny Tightpants--PA	$150.00	25	$3,750.00	Airport vans	$150.00	2	$300.00
	$0.00		$0.00	**Totals**	**$190.00**		**$1,300.00**
Totals	**$1,850.00**		**$46,250.00**	**Trucking**			
Per Diems				Truck rental & mileage	$0.00		$0.00
Band per diems (5)	$30.00	125	$3,750.00	Truck driver salary	$0.00		$0.00
Crew per diems (7)	$30.00	175	$5,250.00	Truck fuel	$0.00		$0.00
	$0.00		$0.00	Truck wash & supplies	$0.00		$0.00
Totals	**$60.00**		**$9,000.00**	Truck tolls	$0.00		$0.00
Tour Bus				**Totals**	**$0.00**		**$0.00**
Tour bus & trailer rental	$450.00	33	$14,850.00	**Miscellaneous**			
Bus driver salary	$215.00	33	$7,095.00	Backline rental	$0.00		$0.00
Bus driver overdrives	$215.00	2	$430.00	Sound rental	$0.00		$0.00
Bus Fuel	$225.60	33	$7,444.80	Lighting rental	$0.00		$0.00
Bus wash & clean linen	$125.00	5	$625.00	Radios rental	$15.00	28	$420.00
Generator services	$45.00	8	$360.00	Tips	$100.00	1	$100.00
Engine service, final cleaning	$1,330.60	1	$1,330.60	FedEx/DHL charges	$50.00	4	$200.00
Bus supplies	$150.00	4	$600.00	Show supplies	$200.00	4	$800.00
Tolls	$250.00	1	$250.00	Office supplies	$25.00	4	$100.00
Double-driver costs	$0.00		$0.00	Itineraries & passes	$1,300.00	1	$1,300.00
Driver per diem	$0.00		$0.00	Backdrops, scrims	$6,000.00	1	$6,000.00
Satellite TV and WIFI	$0.00		$0.00	TM/PM tour advance fees	$400.00	4	$1,600.00
Driver bus cleaning fee	$0.00		$0.00	FICA payroll tax (7.65%)	$0.00		$8,441.78
Totals	**$3,006.20**		**$32,985.40**	**Totals**	**$8,090.00**		**$18,961.78**

Skinny Girl Riot Tour Budget--USA 2012				
Income				
			Total income	**$280,000.00**
Date	**Venue/City/State**	**Guarantee**	**Production Contribution**	**Total**
4/1/2012	Club 1--San Francisco, CA	$20,000.00	$0.00	$20,000.00
4/2/2012	Club 2--Los Angeles, CA	$20,000.00	$0.00	$20,000.00
4/3/2012	Club 3--San Diego, CA	$15,000.00	$0.00	$15,000.00
4/4/2012	Club 4--Phoenix, AZ	$15,000.00	$0.00	$15,000.00
4/5/2012	Club 5--Albuquerque, NM	$10,000.00	$0.00	$10,000.00
4/7/2012	Club 6--El Paso, TX	$15,000.00	$0.00	$15,000.00
4/8/2012	Club 7--San Antonio, TX	$10,000.00	$0.00	$10,000.00
4/9/2012	Club 8--Houston, TX	$15,000.00	$0.00	$15,000.00
4/10/2012	Club 9--Dallas, TX	$15,000.00	$0.00	$15,000.00
4/11/2012	Club 10--New Orleans, LA	$10,000.00	$0.00	$10,000.00
4/13/2012	Club 11--Tallahassee, FL	$12,000.00	$0.00	$12,000.00
4/14/2012	Club 12--Tampa, FL	$15,000.00	$0.00	$15,000.00
4/15/2012	Club 13--Orlando, FL	$12,000.00	$0.00	$12,000.00
4/16/2012	Club 14--Atlanta, GA	$15,000.00	$0.00	$15,000.00
4/17/2012	Club 15--Raleigh, NC	$12,000.00	$0.00	$12,000.00
4/19/2012	Club 16--Washington, DC	$15,000.00	$0.00	$15,000.00
4/20/2012	Club 17--Philadelphia, PA	$13,000.00	$0.00	$13,000.00
4/21/2012	Club 18--Hartford, CT	$9,000.00	$0.00	$9,000.00
4/22/2012	Club 19--Boston, MA	$12,000.00	$0.00	$12,000.00
4/23/2012	Club 20--New York, NY	$20,000.00	$0.00	$20,000.00
		$0.00	$0.00	$0.00
		$0.00	$0.00	$0.00
		$0.00	$0.00	$0.00
		$0.00	$0.00	$0.00
		$0.00	$0.00	$0.00
		$0.00	$0.00	$0.00
		$0.00	$0.00	$0.00
		$0.00	$0.00	$0.00
		$0.00	$0.00	$0.00
		$0.00	$0.00	$0.00
Totals		**$280,000.00**	**$0.00**	**$280,000.00**

Skinny Girl Riot Tour Budget--USA 2012	
Profit - Loss Summary	
Total tour expenses	$179,197.18
Promoter production contribution	$0.00
Total income	$280,000.00
Net income	$100,802.83
Management commission @ 15%	$42,000.00
Booking Agent Commission @ 10%	$28,000.00
Business Management Commission @ 5%	$14,000.00
Total commissions	$84,000.00
Artist tax	$0.00
Artist tax accountant fee	$0.00
Total profit (or loss)	$16,802.83

Someone once said, "You don't get what you deserve; you get what you negotiate." This statement couldn't be truer than in the music business. When you're first starting your career, you may have to work for low money or just a small per diem or even for free, but it's worth it to build a resume. This is how you build a career. Interns do it all the time in every kind of business. Everyone has to pay their dues—just like the band is doing—and you're getting valuable on-the-job training. Just get that first notch on your resume at any cost or sacrifice.

Next is the category for band and crew per diems. A per diem is a daily expense allowance that the band and crew are paid to cover their personal expenses on the road. Most businesses that have employees who travel for the company pay a per diem to the employee, although some bands cannot afford to pay per diem.

The average per diem is usually $25 to $35 a day per person for mid-level acts, but a newer band might only be paying $10 a day if that's all they can afford. Some American bands will pay one amount while on tour in North America and increase it to a higher amount when traveling overseas where the U.S. dollar doesn't go as far. The amount is up to the band and what they can afford. On this U.S. tour, per diems are $30 per person.

Our next category is the tour bus. This is probably the most involved category for the novice tour manager. Tour buses can be rented from a variety of companies to fit any tour budget. There are companies that have thirty-year-old Eagles for $200 a day up to brand new Prevost XL2's with slide-outs for $650 a day and higher. Older Van Hools, Prevost XLs, XL2s, and H3s can be had for $400 a day, depending on the time of year. Spring and summer is peak touring season, and better deals can be had in the winter when business is slower. I call wintertime the dead season, but it's usually our only real time off the road.

You should always get quotes from three different bus companies for the sake of comparison until you build a strong relationship with a bus company and fully understand pricing.

For this budget we've entered $400 a day for the bus rental and $50 a day for the trailer rental. The trailer almost always comes from the bus company. Next we've added $215 a day for the bus driver's salary, and this includes the extra money he earns for pulling a trailer. The driver always earns extra money for the additional work and headaches involved in pulling a trailer. If you're not using a trailer, the driver's salary would be about $25 a day less, depending on the company you're using.

The next entry in this category is bus driver overdrives. If the bus driver drives for more than four hundred and fifty miles or ten hours, whichever comes first, he gets an extra day of pay. This is called an overdrive. If a drive is so long that he goes beyond six hundred and fifty miles, or fourteen hours of driving, he earns two overdrives. This means that he got paid for three days of salary for that six hundred and fifty-one-mile drive. This will continue for each two-hundred-mile segment of driving, but no responsible road manager would allow a driver to go much farther than six hundred and fifty miles in one drive. It's just not safe. You'll usually average about two overdrives per week on a tour, depending on the routing. On this tour, we only have two overdrives on the entire tour because of good routing.

Next, we need to enter our estimated diesel fuel costs for the entire tour. You can find the estimated diesel costs on the bus company quote in the chapter, "Hiring the Right Bus Company and Driver," in Part Two of this book. There is also more information on how to calculate diesel fuel costs for your tour's vehicle. We've gotten our quote from the bus company, which includes the estimated fuel costs. Our estimated tour mileage is 9,306 miles. To cover you in the budget, estimate that the bus with a fully-loaded trailer will get five miles to the gallon. Estimate that the average cost of diesel fuel is $4 a gallon, for the sake of the estimate. This gives us a diesel fuel cost of $7,444.80. In the future, depending on where fuel prices go, you may change that estimated cost per gallon.

The satellite TV and WIFI charges are paid for by the band. Some bus companies charge extra for these services, while some others just build it into the quote. I always ask that it be built into the daily bus rental fee and not listed as a separate cost. For this budget, it's built into the daily coach rental fee.

Some bus drivers also expect to be paid for doing a regular interior bus cleaning. Frankly, I feel that this is part of their job, and I don't think the bus driver should be paid extra for doing this duty unless the people in your entourage are the biggest slobs that ever stumbled onto a tour bus. Ask about this when you book the bus. If you have to pay the driver for cleaning the bus, add it to the budget.

Engine service and end-of-tour cleaning costs are also listed on the quote. Just enter the amounts on the quote into the spreadsheet. The cost for the bus engine service is usually about ten cents a mile in the U.S. if you're pulling a trailer, and the end-of-tour bus cleaning is usually about $400 per bus. So we'll add $930.60 for the engine service and $400 for the end-of-tour bus cleaning, $1,330.60 total, to this category.

The bus generator has to be serviced by the driver every one hundred hours, approximately every four days. Depending on the bus company, the driver will usually get around $45 to $50 for each generator service. If the driver does the weekly bus wash himself instead of getting it done at a truck stop, he will usually get $55 for the bus wash and an extra $20 if there's a trailer to be washed. The cost of cleaning bus linens is usually about $50 a week if you choose to pay the driver for this service. Otherwise, you can wash them yourself. I always add $150 a week to the budget for bus supplies, such as cleaning products, trash bags, generator service items (oil, filters, and coolant) and engine oil and coolant. It can be more depending on the entourage and the bus.

Next, we see the category for hotels. On this tour, we're only booking two hotel rooms for the entourage on days off: a shower room for the band and a shower room for the crew. The bus driver gets a room every day of the tour. The shower rooms are for the band and crew to take showers, and everyone lives on the bus. Some groups will buy just one shower room on days off, while other bands cannot afford even one room.

The average tour will usually do five shows a week, and the other two days will be days off or long travel days, depending on the routing. If you don't have a complete list of tour dates when you start your tour budget, but you know that the tour is going to be four weeks long, it's best to just plug five shows and two days off a week into your budget until you get the final list of dates and income. Then you can revise the budget when you receive the final list of tour dates.

Successful bands may buy a hotel room for everyone in the entourage on days off, or the crew members will double up in rooms. Some bands will buy a hotel room for each band member and the tour manager every day, and they just arrive at the venue for sound check on show days. It all depends on what their budget can bear.

Skinny Girl Riot--USA Tour 2012						The Booking Factory Inc
Date	Venue/Address	Capacity	Support Act	Promoter	Phone	Email
4/1/2012	Club 1--San Francisco	1633	The Worst	Antitrust Suit, Inc, J. Slowhand	555-666-1369	paidbail@email.com
4/2/2012	Club 2--Los Angeles	992	The Worst	Antitrust Suit, Inc, J. Slowhand	555-666-1369	paidbail@email.com
4/3/2012	Club 3--San Diego	1100	The Worst	Antitrust Suit, Inc, J. Slowhand	555-666-1369	paidbail@email.com
4/4/2012	Club 4--Phoenix	1100	The Worst	Antitrust Suit, Inc, J. Slowhand	555-666-1369	paidbail@email.com
4/5/2012	Club 5--Albuquerque	1200	The Worst	Antitrust Suit, Inc, J. Slowhand	555-666-1369	paidbail@email.com
4/7/2012	Club 6--El Paso	1500	The Worst	Fun Concerts, Candy Cane	555-777-1238	sweets@email.com
4/8/2012	Club 7--San Antonio	1550	The Worst	Fun Concerts, Candy Cane	555-777-1238	sweets@email.com
4/9/2012	Club 8--Houston	1000	The Worst	Fun Concerts, Candy Cane	555-777-1238	sweets@email.com
4/10/2012	Club 9--Dallas	1400	The Worst	Fun Concerts, Candy Cane	555-777-1238	sweets@email.com
4/11/2012	Club 10--New Orleans	1450	The Worst	Fun Concerts, Candy Cane	555-777-1238	sweets@email.com
4/13/2012	Club 11--Tallahassee	1200	The Worst	Big Shows Inc, Jimmy Cash	555-303-3868	jcash@email.com
4/14/2012	Club 12--Tampa	1200	The Worst	Big Shows Inc, Jimmy Cash	555-303-3868	jcash@email.com
4/15/2012	Club 13--Orlando	1200	The Worst	Big Shows Inc, Jimmy Cash	555-303-3868	jcash@email.com
4/16/2012	Club 14--Atlanta	1300	The Worst	Big Shows Inc, Jimmy Cash	555-303-3868	jcash@email.com
4/17/2012	Club 15--Raleigh	1400	The Worst	Big Shows Inc, Jimmy Cash	555-303-3868	jcash@email.com
4/19/2012	Club 16--Washington, DC	1500	The Worst	Trouble LLC, Jack Horshack	555-444-2238	bigtrouble@email.com
4/20/2012	Club 17--Philadelphia	1200	The Worst	Trouble LLC, Jack Horshack	555-444-2238	bigtrouble@email.com
4/21/2012	Club 18--Hartford	1000	The Worst	Trouble LLC, Jack Horshack	555-444-2238	bigtrouble@email.com
4/22/2012	Club 19--Boston	1000	The Worst	Trouble LLC, Jack Horshack	555-444-2238	bigtrouble@email.com
4/23/2012	Club 20--New York	1000	The Worst	Trouble LLC, Jack Horshack	555-444-2238	bigtrouble@email.com

Many bands will never use a hotel on show days because of their tight budget. To them, it's a waste of money because they have a tour bus to spend the day on. The crew will rarely ever have a hotel room on show days unless it's a fly date and there's no tour bus to sleep on at night. There's really no reason for the crew to have hotel rooms on a show day because they're at the venue working all day and leave for the next city after the show is over and the gear is packed up.

In the U.S., the bus driver is contractually guaranteed to have his own hotel room each day. He does not share a room with anyone. You don't want the bus driver to show up at 2:00 a.m. with a five-hundred-mile drive ahead of him and find out that he's dead tired because some other driver kept him awake all evening snoring louder than Metallica's PA. This is very unsafe and should never happen. The bus drivers always have their own rooms for this reason.

On a mid-level U.S. tour, I usually budget $100 a room. Some cities, such as New York, Chicago, and Los Angeles, will be more expensive, but other smaller cities will be cheaper, and it usually evens out in the budget. In Europe and the U.K., things are more expensive when you consider the U.S. dollar against the British Pound and the Euro, so I will usually budget hotels at $150 per room over there.

Notice that the driver is in the budget for thirty-three days of hotel rooms, despite the fact that the tour is only twenty-five days long. The driver is picking up the entourage in San Francisco, but he had to drive from Los Angeles to get there. You'll have to pay for the driver's room for that day of "deadhead" to get to you. At the end of the tour in New York, the bus has to go back to Los Angeles, but he must drop off the band's gear in San Francisco first. The band has to pay for his hotels for the drive back home or pay him an acceptable hotel buyout for each day, but everything is negotiable.

A hotel buyout is simply money that you give to the bus driver instead of buying him a room. It's always an amount that is less than what you would've spent on a room for him. It puts money in his pocket and saves the band money. He may sleep on the bus while driving the empty bus across country or buy a dirt-cheap hotel room; that's up to the driver.

Hotel buyouts are for deadhead at the beginning and end of the tour. I don't recommend having a bus driver sleep on the bus every day during the tour for the same reasons previously stated above: he will never get any sleep and could become a dangerous driver.

Our next budget category to examine is airfares. If your band lives in San Francisco, for example, the booking agent may start and end the tour in California. This reduces a lot of deadhead costs on the bus if you're using a West Coast bus company. It also saves money on airfares at the beginning and end of the tour. You're also more likely to save money on airfares when you can hire road crew members who live in your same city if that's possible. Add up the total costs of all airfares needed at the beginning and end of your tour and enter them into your spreadsheet for this category. We'll cover more on this subject in the chapter, "Booking Air Travel," in Part Two of this book.

Our next expense category is local transportation. I usually plan ahead and determine if we'll need airport cars to pick up or drop off anyone at the airport at the beginning or end of the tour and determine the costs. On every show day of the tour, the bus driver will usually show up for bus call around 2:00 a.m. in a taxi because the venue's runner will probably be cut and gone home by that time. It really just depends on the tour and what time you're leaving each night. If you're headlining the tour, you probably won't be leaving until late, but if you're a support act, you can always leave a bit sooner, as long as the bus driver has had enough time to sleep. The cost of the bus driver's taxis needs to be put into the budget.

If you're on a club tour and going on late every night, you probably won't be leaving town until around 2:00 a.m., or even later if it's a short drive. On a bigger tour where there's an 11:00 p.m. union curfew, your band bus might be leaving early, and the runner may still be on call to pick up the band driver. But you might need your crew bus drivers picked up at 1:30 a.m. for a 2:00 a.m. bus call when the trucks are loaded and everyone has showered. If the runner has been cut and gone home by then, the driver will have to come in a taxi. Every tour is different, but you must plan for all of this and enter the appropriate numbers into the budget.

For a one-bus tour, I'll usually enter $40 a day for the driver's taxi fare. I always try to book the driver in hotels as close to the venue as possible to save on this expense, but sometimes the venue can be in a bad neighborhood. You don't want to book the driver in a hotel that's in a bad part of town for reasons that should be obvious to anyone.

The next category to deal with is trucking. On this tour, we have no truck because the band's gear and merchandise is traveling in the trailer, but if you should end up carrying so much gear and merch that it won't all fit into the trailer, you may need to rent a truck for the tour. This can be anything from a twenty-six-foot Ryder truck up to a semi, depending on how much gear the band is carrying. Even established acts these days are pulling trailers more often because of the high costs of a truck, driver, hotel and fuel.

If you're renting a Ryder truck, you'll need to enter into the budget the weekly rental fee for the truck, calculate any mileage charges that might apply, determine fuel costs, add a daily hotel room for the driver, and include the driver's salary and per diem if the driver is getting one.

If you have a semi, the driver will sleep in the cab at the front of the truck, so hotels won't be needed for him, but you'll usually have to pay him a hotel buyout on days off. His salary is built into the trucking company fee. All of these things will be listed on the trucking company's quote.

In the Miscellaneous category, add any backline rentals (guitar amps, guitar cabinets, drums, drum riser) that the band may require. If they're buying a new backdrop and scrims, add that into the budget. If they're renting or buying radios (walkie talkies), add that expense into the budget. Anything that might be needed should be added to the budget. Some managers may not want large purchases, such as a backdrop or stage props, added into the tour budget because they're items that will be used for every tour leg during the album cycle and are considered start-up costs. Just do what the manager and business manager ask you to do.

Add any production rentals into the budget. It's doubtful that a baby band is going to be carrying a sound or lighting system unless they've got a rich—and possibly insane—mommy or daddy betting the farm on their hopeful mammoth success. The band will most likely be in a van pulling a trailer, so they won't have any space for that kind of gear. They may be opening up for a larger band where all of these production needs are taken care of by the headliner. If they're doing their first headline club tour, they'll probably be using what the venue has to offer.

Some acts may begin to carry a small lighting package to supplement the house lighting rig and give their show some extra bang for the audience. Sometimes a band will carry a digital monitor console or a digital FOH (front-of-house) console to make them sound better. Some bands may carry a complete monitor system. Whatever it is that they're renting, you'll need to enter that weekly rental amount into the tour budget.

If your band becomes popular enough to carry full sound and lighting, there will also be a sound and lighting crew that comes along with it to set up that gear each day. Their salaries are always built into the sound and lighting company fees, but you may have to pay each crew member a per diem. So this expense must be budgeted for. The sound and lighting crew also increases the amount of hotels needed on days off. They also increase the airfare budget because the band is obligated to get them to and from their home base.

Depending on how many sound and lighting crew members are on the tour, you'll probably be forced into a second bus if you're beyond twelve people. The typical tour bus sleeps twelve, although I've seen slave barges in Europe that were equipped with as many as eighteen bunks. That leaves little room for a kitchen or sitting area for the entourage unless the bus is a double-decker, and even then it's still going to be tight for that many people. Hey, welcome to the music business.

The number of people on the tour will determine how many bunks you'll need and how many buses the band will have to lease. If this puts you into a second bus, the numbers will have to be changed in the bus rental category and all of the bus expenses that come with it. It's highly doubtful that you'll be worrying about multiple buses in the beginning of your career, but this is important information to learn and remember.

Add any tour advance fees that you or the production manager—this will probably also be you in the beginning—have negotiated with management for organizing the tour. The amount you'll get for organizing a tour varies depending on the band and their budget. One manager may agree to pay you two weeks of half-salary for organizing a six-week tour and another manager may beat you down to one week of half-salary for the same amount of work. Some managers will try to get you to do it for free because the band can't afford to pay you anything.

Don't ever ignore the process of negotiating your salary and tour advance fee, thinking the manager will do the right thing by you, and do the work while praying to finally get paid one day. You'll be on your knees for all eternity, waiting on the check. You get what you negotiate. If you've agreed to work for free, fair enough; but if you're supposed to get paid for the work, make sure you negotiate the exact terms with the manager.

The payroll tax entry is for the matching payroll tax that the band must pay for each employee. The Federal Insurance Contributions Act (FICA) tax is a matching tax that your employer must pay for you as an employee to help fund Social Security and Medicare in the United States. This is only for band members and road crew members who are U.S. citizens and pay taxes in this country. Use 7.65% of the total amount of band and crew salaries— including any fees paid to the tour manager or production manager for advancing the tour—to calculate the FICA tax amount. The business manager will tell you if this amount ever changes.

Sometimes a smaller act can't afford to pay the matching FICA tax, so they won't take any taxes out of your check each week. They'll pay you the gross salary amount, treating you as an independent contractor. At the end of the year, the business manager will send you IRS Form 1099 for your taxes if you're a U.S. citizen. While getting your full salary with no tax deductions may seem great each week, it's not so great at the end of the year when you get hit with a big tax bill if you haven't been making quarterly tax payments to cover your estimated tax obligation. Having the IRS haunting you is not a hell you want to be in. Trust me on this.

Include any other expenses, such as show supplies, office supplies, tour passes, itineraries, and FedEx charges for shipping your weekly road reports to the business manager, in the tour budget.

On the Income page of the budget, you will see a column called Production Contribution. When the band is playing in venues that don't have sound and lighting installed in them, the promoter will have to rent sound and lights locally. These expenses are paid for out of the show costs.

Having the promoter rent sound and lighting locally is not always the best thing for the show. You're usually better off carrying your own production because it will be the way the band wants it every night. In small secondary markets, there may only be one sound and lighting company in the area, or it could be the same company providing both sound and lighting. Sometimes they won't have the gear that you want, and you'll have to settle for what they have.

If the band insists on carrying full production, one of the ways to help pay for it is to get a production contribution from the promoter in every city. What you're essentially doing is getting the same amount of money from the promoter that he was already going to spend renting the sound and lighting locally.

If you're averaging five shows a week, these production contributions may cover a large part of the costs of sound and lighting and save the promoter a lot of headaches because he doesn't have to worry about coordinating the rental of this gear. He also doesn't have to worry about you and the band raising holy hell at him when the gear is not what you asked for.

The downside of carrying your own production is that the band will have to pay for the trucking costs to transport the gear from city to city and pay for the production crew and their related expenses. If the promoter is renting the gear locally, these expenses are minimal and are built into the fee that he pays to the local sound and lighting company.

If there's a production contribution negotiated by the band's booking agent, you'll want to enter this amount into the budget for each show. You're probably wondering why the booking agent doesn't just ask for a bigger guarantee for that show that includes the production contribution. Why does it have to be separate?

The manager and agent can't take a commission from a production contribution for sound and lighting from the promoter, but they can take a commission from an increased guarantee. This is why it's better for the band to separate the two.

The norm for decades has been for managers to earn 20 percent of the band's gross income right off the top, but bands are now realizing that after the cash starts rolling in, their managers are making a lot more money than the individual band members.

Today, bands are becoming a lot more astute as to how the music business actually works, and many of them are negotiating much different deals with managers. Some managers won't budge on their commission amount with a new baby band because they know that they may never make any money from them. It's a risky business, and time and effort is worth something.

Should the band become successful one day, it's always possible to negotiate the manager's commission down to a lower rate, such as 15, 10 or even 5 percent for a superstar act. Anything is possible. It's all about negotiating. Many bands are now negotiating partnership deals with managers that include contract clauses that stipulate the manager can never make more money than any partner band member.

Take a quick look at the numbers below in this simplified example:

Band's gross income from show guarantees for the year: $1,000,000
Manager's 20% commission: $200,000
Agent's 10% commission: $100,000
Business manager's 5% commission: $50,000
Net band income after all commissions: $650,000
Less road expenses: $300,000
Adjusted net band income: $350,000

These figures are simplified for the sake of an explanation, but as you can see, the band has $350,000 left over, and that's before tax deductions. After taxes, five band members are probably ending up with $50,000 each, while the manager is making four times as much as any individual band member. And this happens across all income streams, such as record sales, publishing, and merchandising. I think you can quickly see why musicians no longer like this "old math" and are becoming better trained in how their business works.

Don't misunderstand me: there are managers in this business who are worth every dime of commission they earn, but there are some who are nothing more than despicable vampires that do nothing but suck the financial life from their client as long as they can. Then they go on to their next trusting, unsuspecting victims, who are blinded by their own hopes and dreams.

The booking agent is the person who books all of the band's shows. They earn their 10 percent commission. It's in their best interest to negotiate the highest guarantees possible with the promoters because it only makes their commission larger.

Most agents are always there for the band and usually have your back when calamity strikes, while there are other agents who book the gig, take their commission, and forget you exist when you show up at the venue and discover that all you have is a boom box for a PA, a few porch lights for a lighting system, and a few crackers slathered in some mysterious brown shit masquerading as an edible dinner.

Business managers provide many services for their 5 percent of the gross. They do the band's monthly accounting and present reports to the band and manager, offer financial advice and planning, and do the band's taxes at the end of the year. They also deal with the complexities of foreign artist tax waivers and will even pay the band's personal bills for them each month. Some business managers will also work for a flat monthly fee or hourly fee instead of 5 percent of the gross, but the services they provide are usually limited to monthly business accounting and tax preparation.

You'll want to check with the band's manager to verify his commission and that of the booking agent and business manager. They could be different from the standard, and you'll need to change them in the spreadsheet's formula. Never assume anything.

Keep in mind that some managers may not want to tell you what they're getting. In that case, just leave it at 20 percent. The booking agent's commission is almost always 10 percent. The business manager is usually 5 percent or they're on a flat rate. If they're on a flat rate, ask the manager what number he'd like for you to enter into the budget for their services.

As you can see on the Profit–Loss Summary page, the tour is showing a profit of $16,802.83 in our budget. You probably won't see many budgets that actually earn money or break even in the beginning of your career, so have your personal thrill now.

As you receive the confirmed guarantees from the booking agent, you'll want to enter all of those amounts into the spreadsheet so the total income calculates correctly in the budget. If your U.S. tour includes any dates in Canada, most of the time your guarantees will be negotiated in U.S. dollars for a U.S. band. Convert any expenses that are in Canadian dollars into U.S. dollars before entering them into your budget or accounting.

At the time I'm writing this chapter, the Canadian dollar is again at parity (equal to) with the U.S. dollar. Whenever the Canadian dollar is at parity with the U.S. dollar, you can treat the expenses as if they were paid for with U.S. dollars.

Building budget spreadsheets using Excel isn't difficult to do once you learn how to use the program. There are templates that come with Excel, and there are many others that are available for free on the internet. You can use any of them to start your spreadsheets and then modify them to suit your needs, or you can just start from scratch and build your own.

The next thing we'll do is take a look at the differences between a U.K./Europe tour budget and the U.S. budget we just finished. Below is a U.K./Europe tour budget for Skinny Girl Riot on tour for twenty-nine days.

The band and crew salaries are the same. You'll notice that band and crew per diems have been increased by $5 a day per person to help cover the higher costs of traveling in Europe. Some bands won't increase the per diem amount when they go overseas because they don't have the budget for it, and some bands just don't feel it's necessary.

The next category is the bus rental. You'll immediately notice that we don't have a long breakdown of expenses for the bus like we did on the U.S. tour. Bus companies in Europe and the U.K. give you an "all-in quote" that covers everything from the bus rental fee to the driver's salary to fuel and oil to double-driver costs, if a double-driver is ever needed. With all of the new driver safety rules in Europe and the U.K., you're almost always going to need a double driver at some point on a long tour over there.

Skinny Girl Riot Tour Budget--U.K./Europe 2012							
Expenses							
						Total Expenses	$226,872.89
	Daily Rate	Days	Total		Daily Rate	Days	Total
Band salaries				**Hotels**			
Stevie Starbright--vocals	$500.00	29	$14,500.00	Bus driver (1)	$0.00		$0.00
Frankie Fabulous--guitar	$500.00	29	$14,500.00	Shower room (1)	$150.00	4	$600.00
Jimmy Giant--guitar	$500.00	29	$14,500.00	Crew shower room (1)	$150.00	4	$600.00
Mikey Massive--bass	$500.00	29	$14,500.00	Truck driver	$0.00		$0.00
Tommy Twosticks--drums	$500.00	29	$14,500.00		$0.00		$0.00
Totals	**$2,500.00**		**$72,500.00**	**Totals**	**$300.00**		**$1,200.00**
Crew Salaries				**Air Travel**			
Bobby Blinder--TM/LD	$400.00	29	$11,600.00	Airfares for band (5)	$1,000.00	5	$5,000.00
Lance Loudnoise--PM/FOH	$400.00	29	$11,600.00	Airfares for crew (7)	$1,171.43	7	$8,200.01
Tony Tonedeaf--Monitors	$250.00	29	$7,250.00	Excess baggage	$3,000.00	1	$3,000.00
Ricky Racket--SM/guitar tech	$250.00	29	$7,250.00	**Totals**	**$5,171.43**		**$16,200.01**
Jerry Spazon--guitar tech	$200.00	29	$5,800.00	**Local transportation**			
Kyle Klown--drum tech	$200.00	29	$5,800.00	Bus driver taxis	$0.00		$0.00
Penny Tightpants--PA	$150.00	29	$4,350.00	Airport vans	$400.00	1	$400.00
	$0.00		$0.00	**Totals**	**$400.00**		**$400.00**
Totals	**$1,850.00**		**$53,650.00**	**Trucking**			
Per Diems				Truck rental & mileage	$0.00		$0.00
Band per diems (5)	$35.00	145	$5,075.00	Truck driver salary	$0.00		$0.00
Crew per diems (7)	$35.00	203	$7,105.00	Truck fuel	$0.00		$0.00
	$0.00		$0.00	Truck wash & supplies	$0.00		$0.00
Totals	**$70.00**		**$12,180.00**	Truck tolls	$0.00		$0.00
Tour Bus				**Totals**	**$0.00**		**$0.00**
Tour bus & trailer rental	$46,250.00	1	$46,250.00	**Miscellaneous**			
Bus driver salary	$0.00		$0.00	Backline rental	$10,000.00	1	$10,000.00
Bus driver overdrives	$0.00		$0.00	Sound rental	$0.00		$0.00
Bus Fuel	$0.00		$0.00	Lighting rental	$0.00		$0.00
Bus wash & clean linen	$0.00		$0.00	Radios rental	$15.00	28	$420.00
Generator services	$0.00		$0.00	Tips	$100.00	1	$100.00
Engine service, final clean	$0.00		$0.00	FedEx/DHL charges	$100.00	4	$400.00
Bus supplies	$0.00		$0.00	Show supplies	$200.00	4	$800.00
Tolls	$0.00		$0.00	Office supplies	$25.00	4	$100.00
Double-driver costs	$0.00		$0.00	Itineraries & passes	$1,300.00	1	$1,300.00
Driver per diem	$0.00		$0.00	Backdrops, scrims	$0.00		$0.00
Satellite TV and WIFI	$0.00		$0.00	TM/PM tour advance fees	$400.00	4	$1,600.00
Driver bus cleaning fee	$0.00		$0.00	FICA payroll tax (7.65%)	$0.00		$9,772.88
Totals	**$46,250.00**		**$46,250.00**	**Totals**	**$12,140.00**		**$24,492.88**

31

Skinny Girl Riot Tour Budget--U.K./Europe 2012				
Income				
			Total income	**$366,000.00**
Date	**Venue/City/State**	**Guarantee**	**Production Contribution**	**Total**
5/1/2012	Venue 1--Berlin, Germany	€ 15,000.00	€ -	€ 15,000.00
5/2/2012	Venue 2--Hamburg, Germany	€ 15,000.00	€ -	€ 15,000.00
5/3/2012	Venue 3--Dortmund, Germany	€ 15,000.00	€ -	€ 15,000.00
5/4/2012	Venue 4--Frankfurt, Germany	€ 15,000.00	€ -	€ 15,000.00
5/5/2012	Venue 5--Munich, Germany	€ 15,000.00	€ -	€ 15,000.00
5/6/2012	Venue 6--Nuremberg, Germany	€ 15,000.00	€ -	€ 15,000.00
		€ 90,000.00	€ -	€ 90,000.00
	Total in U.S. $ (Euro rate: 1.25)	**$112,500.00**	**$0.00**	**$112,500.00**
5/8/2012	Venue 7--London, UK	£ 15,000.00	£ -	£ 15,000.00
5/9/2012	Venue 8--Bristol, UK	£ 10,000.00	£ -	£ 10,000.00
5/10/2012	Venue 9--Oxford, UK	£ 10,000.00	£ -	£ 10,000.00
5/11/2012	Venue 10--Birmingham, UK	£ 15,000.00	£ -	£ 15,000.00
5/12/2012	Venue 11--Nottingham, UK	£ 10,000.00	£ -	£ 10,000.00
5/13/2012	Venue 12--Liverpool, UK	£ 10,000.00	£ -	£ 10,000.00
		£ 70,000.00	£ -	£ 70,000.00
	Total in U.S. $ (GBP rate: 1.55)	**$108,500.00**	**$0.00**	**$108,500.00**
5/15/2012	Venue 13--Milan, Italy	$10,000.00	$0.00	$10,000.00
5/16/2012	Venue 14--Zurich, Switzerland	$10,000.00	$0.00	$10,000.00
5/17/2012	Venue 15--Lausanne, Switzerland	$10,000.00	$0.00	$10,000.00
5/18/2012	Venue 16--Lyon, France	$10,000.00	$0.00	$10,000.00
5/19/2012	Venue 17--Toulouse, France	$10,000.00	$0.00	$10,000.00
5/20/2012	Venue 18--San Sebastian, Spain	$10,000.00	$0.00	$10,000.00
5/22/2012	Venue 19--Barcelona, Spain	$15,000.00	$0.00	$15,000.00
5/23/2012	Venue 20--Madrid, Spain	$15,000.00	$0.00	$15,000.00
5/24/2012	Venue 21--Bordeaux, France	$10,000.00	$0.00	$10,000.00
5/25/2012	Venue 22--Paris, France	$15,000.00	$0.00	$15,000.00
5/25/2012	Venue 23--Brussels, Belgium	$15,000.00	$0.00	$15,000.00
5/26/2012	Venue 24--Amsterdam, Holland	$15,000.00	$0.00	$15,000.00
	Total in U.S. $	**$145,000.00**	**$0.00**	**$145,000.00**
Totals in U.S. $		**$366,000.00**	**$0.00**	**$366,000.00**

Skinny Girl Riot Tour Budget--U.K./Europe 2012	
Profit - Loss Summary	
Total tour expenses	$226,872.89
Promoter production contribution	$0.00
Total income	$366,000.00
Net income	$139,127.12
Management commission @ 15%	$54,900.00
Booking Agent Commission @ 10%	$36,600.00
Business Management Commission @ 5%	$18,300.00
Total commissions	$109,800.00
Artist tax	$36,600.00
Artist tax accountant fee	$0.00
Total profit (or loss)	($7,272.89)

Our bus quote has come in at 37,000 Euros. At the exchange rate of 1.25, our bus bill is $46,250 U.S. dollars. As you can see, that's a big jump from the $31,150.40 the bus cost for the U.S. tour. This tour is four days longer, but that's still a big increase in the bus budget.

The only other bus category you may have to enter is the bus driver's food allowance on the days off. You don't pay the driver a per diem, but with some bus companies, you're obligated to give him a food allowance on days off since he can't go into the venue catering room and eat like he does on a show day. This amount is usually about 15 GBP for British bus companies or 10 Euros for European bus companies for each day off, but may vary depending on the bus company. If your bus company requires a food buyout for the driver, it will usually be listed on their quote. Always ask if it's not.

The next category that is different is hotels. On this tour, we only have four days off, just like the U.S. tour. Due to the increased expenses of touring in Europe and the U.K., we're doing more shows to cover the cost of the tour. Again, we're only doing two shower rooms on days off for the entourage.

You'll notice that I've budgeted $150 per room for hotels in Europe and the U.K. because of the exchange rate for the U.S. dollar. A great website for getting up-the-minute currency exchange rates is XE.com, and they also have a good app for your smart phone.

Some bands don't bother with a shower room on days off on U.K./Euro tours; they just stop at a truck stop and use the showers there. Depending on the number of people in your entourage, the cost of the showers is usually cheaper than buying a shower room at a decent hotel, if you can even find one with bus parking. It also saves time because there are more showers, and many of these European and U.K. truck stops have restaurants, coin laundry, and a convenience store so you can buy food and drinks. Some of them also sell beer and wine.

Notice that there are no hotels for the bus driver on this tour. Bus drivers in the U.K. and Europe live on the bus. The driver has his own sleeping compartment in the bus. This saves the band money, and it's also good for bus security.

I still don't believe in bus drivers sleeping on the bus, but this is the way it's always been done in the U.K. and Europe. Even though the driver has his own sleeping compartment that isn't in the same area as the entourage's sleeping area, everyone still has to be quiet when he's sleeping or you'll be keeping him awake all day. It's not a perfect scenario, but that's the way they do things in that part of the world when it comes to tour buses.

Our next category to compare is airfares. As you can see, that number has increased significantly because we have to get the entire entourage to Amsterdam and back to San Francisco at the end of the tour. The tour bus is picking the band up at Amsterdam's Schiphol airport, and then they're driving to the first city of the tour in Berlin, Germany. When the tour ends in Amsterdam, the bus will drive them back to Schiphol airport so they can fly back home to San Francisco. This was the most economical plane ticket for the group and made the most sense, considering how the tour was routed. They also rented the tour bus from a company in Germany because the tour starts and ends in Europe. Each plane ticket cost $1,000. So, we've entered that amount times the twelve people in our entourage. We've also added $1,200 to crew airfares for domestic tickets for the four crew members who don't live in San Francisco.

We're allocating $3,000 for excess baggage charges for the trip over and back. The band will have to bring certain items, such as guitars, backdrop, scrims, show supplies and other assorted items that must be checked on the plane. Depending on how much gear and luggage you're checking on the plane, this amount can be even higher.

Next we go to local transportation. We have no bus driver taxi expenses to budget on this tour because the bus driver lives on the bus and doesn't go to a hotel every day. Since we'll need to get the entourage from the rehearsal studio to the airport at the beginning of the tour and back to the rehearsal studio from the airport at the end of the tour, we've entered $400 for the necessary airport vans.

Our next category is trucking. Like the U.S. tour, we're carrying our gear and merchandise in a trailer, so we have no trucking costs.

We're not shipping anything via air cargo because the band is renting all of their backline from a backline rental company in Germany, and the bus is picking it up and dropping it off at the end of the tour. So we have to add $10,000 in backline rental fees to the budget. We've brought our radios that we're renting in the U.S. with us on the plane, so we're paying the same rate as the four-week U.S. tour.

Our expenses for show supplies (guitar strings, guitar picks, drum heads, drum sticks, batteries, and gaffer tape) are the same for this four-week tour because we've brought the supplies with us on the plane.

We're not carrying any sound or lighting gear on this tour, so those categories remain zero.

Office supplies, tour books and passes cost the same as the U.S. tour because we bought them in the U.S. and brought them with us on the plane. We've doubled our number for FedEx charges because we're sending our accounting and hard receipts to the business manager each week from Europe and not from inside the United States. DHL is an alternate service to FedEx that you may be able to use if FedEx doesn't pick up in the city you're in.

The road manager gets the same fee to organize the tour. There's nothing in the budget for backdrops and scrims because these items were paid for out of the U.S. tour budget.

Let's now look at the Income page of the Europe budget. The booking agent has negotiated the U.K. shows in British Pounds, the German shows in Euros, and the rest of the shows in Europe in U.S. dollars. We're not carrying any production on this tour, so there are no production contributions from the promoters.

Our spreadsheet has already calculated the commissions for the manager, booking agent, and business manager. The bottom line is now showing a loss of $7,272.89. Even with more shows and more income than the U.S. tour, the U.K./Europe tour still lost a small amount of money due to the higher costs of touring over there. Some bands may subsidize a tour shortfall (loss) with some of their merchandising profits, but many groups don't like to do that because it may be the only profits they'll ever see.

Whenever any of the guarantees are negotiated in Euros or British Pounds, you must convert those guarantees into U.S. dollars in the Income page of the budget so that the numbers add up correctly. Be sure to go to a currency website, such as XE.com, to get the current exchange rates. Always make a note on the Income page of the exchange rates that you used as it stood on the day you completed the final version of the budget. Budgets for overseas tours can be precarious sometimes because the exchange rates of the U.S. dollar against the British pound and the Euro can go up or down during the course of a long tour, changing the budget's bottom line.

It's important to remember that a budget is an educated financial guide, not a prediction of the future. No tour manager or business manager can predict the rise and fall of any country's currency; we'd be billionaires if we could do that. Plus, something always seems to break down and must be replaced on a music tour, or a show is canceled for one reason or another. Tour managers aren't Nostradamus, able to predict every single thing that can happen on a tour, but we must try to create a tour budget that is as realistic as possible.

Many times the band's guarantees will be paid in British Pounds for the U.K. shows and Euros for the shows in Europe. Some booking agents will negotiate only U.S. dollars for every foreign show for an American band. The agent's deal sheets will list each show's guarantee. Take a look at the deal sheet below to familiarize yourself with it.

The Booking Factory Inc   **Date confirmed:** 2/1/2012
                                          Deal Sheet

Artist Skinny Girl Riot
Date of show Sunday, April 01, 2012

Venue Club 1	**Promoter** Antitrust Suit, Inc	
www.theclub1.com	J. Slowhand	
666 3rd St	777 3rd St	
San Francisco, CA 94107	San Francisco, CA 71717	
555-777-1439	paidbail@email.com	
Capacity 1633	**Phone** 555-666-1369	**Fax** 555-666-1368
Show advance Vince Vega	cell: 666-555-3838, vincent@promoter.net	

Terms $20,000.00 guarantee plus 85% over $36,777.00 net door receipts

Deposit $10,000.00	**Production** $0 (paid to artist)	**Tax on terms** 7%
Tickets		
1633 GA Advance $30.00		
GA DOS $30.00		
FMF $0.00 on top per ticket	**Charity** $0.00 on top per ticket	**Artist comps** 30
4-Pk FMF $0.00 on top per ticket	**Tax** 0.00%	**Tour comps** 35
Parking $0.00 on top per ticket	**Gross after tax** $48,990.00	

Doors open 7:00 PM	**Set Length** 60+ minutes	**Announce date** 2/8/2012
Showtime 8:00 PM	**Age limit** All ages	**On Sale Date** 2/15/2012
Performance 9:00 PM	**Radio** KASS	**Next show** Los Angeles
Curfew 11:00 PM	**Sponsors** None	**db Limit** N/A

Billing 100% headline billing, artist to close show
Merch rate 80/20 artist sells; 100% to artist on all music sales
Other artists The Worst
Miscellaneous Stage dimensions: 20' x 12' X 2'.

A barricade will be provided for this show.

Venue has two small dressing rooms.

Opening act will be paid $200.00 and receive 5 comps.

A state tax of 7% will be deducted from payment to artist. Please contact promoter for info on how to waive or reduce this tax. California companies are exempt from this tax.

The Booking Factory Inc

Deal Expense Sheet

Artist Skinny Girl Riot			**City** San Francisco, CA	
Date of show 4/1/2012			**Venue** Club 1	
Artist Guarantee	$ 20,000.00		Licenses/Permits ____ %	
Support act	$ 200.00		Loaders	
Production	$ 1,750.00		Medical	
Radio advertising			Parking	
Print advertising			Payroll	
Flyers			Rent ____ %	$ 1,000.00
Other advertising			Riggers	
Total advertising	$ 3,000.00		Roofing	
ASCAP/BMI ____ %	$ 576.00		Runners	$ 150.00
Barricade	$ 400.00		Security police	
Box office manager			Security private	$ 900.00
Box office rental	$ 200.00		Security t-shirt	
Catering	$ 1,000.00		Set up	
Chair rental			Spotlights	
Charge cards ____ $			Spot ops	
Clean up			Staff	
Curtain			Stagehands	$ 600.00
Door guards			Stage manager	$ -
Dressing room			Staging	
Electrician			Taxes	
Equipment			Telephone	
Exchange			Ticket commiss ____ %	$ 1,334.00
Firemen			Ticket printing	$ -
Floor cover			Ticket sellers	
Forklift			Ticket takers	
Furniture			Towels	$ 50.00
Generator			Transportation	
Ground support			Ushers	
House manager			Utilities	
House nut			Misc 1	
Immigration			Misc 2	
Insurance	$ 820.00		Misc 3	
Insurance ____ %			Misc 4	
Total fixed expenses	$ 31,980.00	**Notes**		
Total variables		No additional expenses will be accepted without prior approval.		
Expense total	$ 31,980.00			
Promoter profit 15%	$ 4,797.00			
Variable additions	$ 4,797.00			
Split point	$ 36,777.00			
Band will receive 85% @	$ 36,777.00			

On the Profit – Loss Summary page, you'll notice the addition of the payment to the U.K. tax accountant for their work related to the band's U.K. and European artist tax situation. Depending on the level of their income, a band will sometimes hire a U.K. tax accountant to reduce their artist tax for the U.K. and European countries where it applies. Some U.S. business managers have offices in London or other cities in Europe, in which case their business manager in that overseas office would handle the band's artist tax affairs. Some U.S. business managers may have someone on their staff that handles foreign artist tax.

Foreign artist tax is a complicated matter and will be covered more in that chapter. If a band hasn't hired a business manager yet—or doesn't want to pay for one—the band's manager will often hire a tax specialist in the U.K. to deal with these matters for them if the band's income is high enough to warrant it.

We've also entered the amount for the band's estimated foreign artist tax deductions. Until the U.K. tax accountant gives us a clearer picture of the foreign artist tax deductions, we'll put in a "guesstimate" of 10 percent of the gross income for the sake of the budget. Be sure to change this amount to the correct one when the tax accountant sends you the final artist tax deductions that will occur.

During his tour of the U.S. in 1883, Irish writer Oscar Wilde saw a sign on the wall of a Leadville, Colorado, saloon that said, "Don't shoot the piano player; he's doing the best he can." Sending a tour budget off to the band's manager can sometimes make you feel like a piano player in a room full of trigger-happy drunks with bad dispositions, especially when you've been hired at the last minute and the tour starts in a short period of time. But you're only presenting the reality of the situation. Tour managers aren't magicians. They can't change bad news into good news with a few taps on a computer keyboard.

You'll find yourself creating many versions of a budget until you finally get it down to where it's manageable and acceptable to the manager and the band. Often the band will have a bigger picture in mind—carrying production, crew bus, and stage set—until they see how much money they're going to lose with that big picture.

Some bands don't care how much money they're going to lose—they just want the big show—but the manager will sometimes fight them to cut some of the expenses and get the loss down to a more realistic and less painful number. You don't really have much choice but to sit back and wait until the band and their manager finish arguing over the cuts and decide what they're going to do. Then you can finish the final version of the budget and move forward organizing the tour.

Creating a realistic and accurate tour budget takes a little time and effort, but the task becomes much easier with experience. Once you've created a few tour budgets, you'll soon discover that you can quickly modify a budget from a previous tour and turn it into a new one for the tour you're currently organizing. Save everything in your computer for future use and reference.

HIRING THE BEST ROAD CREW

If you're working with a new band on their first tour, it's unlikely that the band will be able to afford much of a road crew. They might only have a few inexperienced friends helping out, but that's better than nothing in most cases.

There's no substitute for experience, but if you have no money to pay for a professional road crew, then you have no choice but to take whatever help you can get in the beginning.

Over the years, I've seen many new people working for new bands who have risen to the occasion and built a lasting career. They are people who are serious about making it in the music business and try to do the best job they possibly can.

A new band will be lucky to have more than one or two crew members on the road with them in the beginning because of their limited budget and room in the vehicle if they're traveling in a van or small motor home. Many new acts will hire a tour manager/sound engineer who can do both of these important jobs because it saves them money. Some bands might have a sound engineer that also sets up their backline gear, and the band will do their own tuning and guitar changes during the show; or they'll hire a road manager who is also the merch seller. It's really up to the band and what they feel is most important to them. Some bands may have a motivated band member who does the job of the tour manager until they can afford a real one.

Some support acts will pay the headliner's sound engineer to do sound for them every night of the tour. This is the cheaper option because they only have to pay the headliner's sound engineer a flat per-show rate, not a weekly salary and per diem; and it's one less body in the crowded van and one less plane ticket and hotel room to buy.

This can be a problem if your band decides to do headline shows on days off and the headliner's sound engineer does not want to spend his day off at some bar trying to mix your band through an antiquated PA with half of its speakers blown out. In this situation, you'll usually have to use the house sound engineer if you don't know any sound engineers in that town. Truthfully, the house sound engineer is sometimes the best option because they use that PA every week and know how to milk it for all it's worth without blowing it up completely.

Build relationships with crew members you know you can count on and bring them into your organization as soon as the budget permits. A new band isn't going to know too many professional crew members. They will look to you and the manager to solve this situation. Surround yourself with a good crew and your job will be a lot easier.

Get contact info from every crew person you meet if you believe they are rock-solid and have some potential. If you're the opening band for a bigger act, bond with the headliner's crew and get their contact info. Once your band can afford some crew, these people could be looking for work and might come on board, or they may have other crew friends they can recommend. Build a database in your laptop and keep all of the contact info for these crew members. You'll be glad you did when you're suddenly looking to fill a position.

There are a few crew websites that can be helpful to you. One website is Crewspace. com, a Facebook-type website for professional road crew members, but you have to be recommended by a current member to join. Most of the crew members that I know have Facebook and LinkedIn pages. Doing a search for professional crew members is easy, and becoming "friends" with them can't hurt.

Another good resource for hiring crew members is Bobnet. This is a free and informal service run by veteran tour accountant Bob Davis. It's grown into a popular way for managers, road managers, and production managers to fill road crew jobs. It's also very helpful for road crew members trying to find work.

Employers looking to fill spots on a tour will send Bob a job listing via email, and he then forwards it to the people in his large email address book. It brings together people looking to hire crew and crew members looking for a job. Like Crewspace, you need to be recommended by someone to get into the Bobnet email address book. Once you've done a few tours and meet some people in the business, ask one of them to email Bob Davis and see if he'll enter your email address in Bobnet. There are also other people in the business who send out these kinds of job listings.

A lot of gigs come down the Bobnet pipeline, including smaller, lower-paying tours that would be a great career building block for you in the beginning. Be smart and don't apply for jobs that you're not yet qualified for. The Bobnet emails are usually pretty specific about what they are looking for and the experience level required.

Once you're in Bobnet and you need to hire some crew, you'll usually get a response immediately. Many positions are filled in a matter of hours. You'll also want to create a different email address for any job posting you send to Bobnet. You don't want to use your own personal email address. It only takes a few minutes to set up a new Gmail email address for that job search. Once you've filled the position, you can delete the email address so you don't continue getting unwanted emails.

The one thing I've learned about reading a crew member's resume is to see if he has repeat clients. If you see a long resume where a person has never worked for the same band twice, that fact should send up red flags. This could mean that he's not being asked back for more tours with that client, and there's usually a reason for this. If you see that he's done multiple tours with numerous repeat clients, he's probably doing a good job. Even though this crew member has a lot of repeat clients, you should still check his references thoroughly if you don't know him.

You never know when you're reading a resume that's been embellished or is an outright fabrication. Most of the professional crew members out there are good people who do the right thing, but there are some bad ones. Watch out for them so you don't get stung by hiring them.

There may come a time when a crew member is fired or quits for a better gig in the middle of the tour with little or no notice at all, leaving you and the band hanging. When this happens and your usual suspects are not available, you may have no choice but to hire a crew person that you don't know.

Make sure to check with the camp of the last three bands this person has worked for, and I don't mean the last three one-offs (single shows), but the last three tours. Anyone trying to hide a drug or alcohol problem can make it through one show without being exposed, but they won't make it through an entire tour.

Get three references from your prospect and call as many people connected to those three tours as possible. Call the manager and any crew members that you might know that were on the tour and worked with this person. Call any band members that you might know that he worked for. Ask a lot of questions about him. Try to speak to both the manager and the tour manager. Sometimes you might get a completely different story from each of them.

Don't take one person's word as the gospel; check around. Ask questions about his performance and how he got along with the band and crew. Did he drink too much or use hard drugs? Was he reliable and representing the band in a positive way? Ask a lot of questions, and if you begin to hear conflicting answers from people, you'll know something's up. If everyone you speak to gives you the same story, you'll know you're hearing something close to reality.

I cannot stress enough how important it is to do a thorough check on crew members that you don't know. Your band cannot afford to waste money flying someone in just to find out after the first show that you've made a horrible mistake hiring that person. Flying him back home and flying in another person will get expensive quickly, and the band will be looking at you as the person who wasted money they didn't have to throw away.

After you've found the crew member that you want to hire, the next thing you have to deal with is their salary. I learned long ago that no matter how much money you think you're worth, you're only worth what the band can afford. There's nothing wrong with negotiating, but when it becomes crystal clear that the band can only afford to pay you X when you believe you're worth Y, you either agree to X and take the gig or you don't and stop wasting everyone's time.

Make it clear what the band can afford, and they'll either take it or they won't. Some people still won't get it and pass on the tour. There's nothing you can do with people like this. Go on to the next person on the list and stop wasting your time.

At this point in my career, I still take lighting designer gigs where I'm only doing the one job, and I have to negotiate my salary with the band's manager or the tour manager—often someone with less experience than me—and I still try to get what I feel I'm worth. I'm also experienced enough to have a pretty good idea what the prospective client can afford before I begin speaking about money with them, so I do know when we've hit the financial wall in the negotiations and it's time to either take what they're offering or go and find another gig.

I have old friends in this business that won't get off the couch unless they get every nickel of "their rate," and if the band can't pay it they'd rather stay at home. While I truly believe that we shouldn't cut our "going rate" so drastically that we're damn near a crew Walmart, devaluing ourselves in the marketplace to such a point that we hurt our own careers, I do believe that it's better to do a smaller tour and take a little less than what we're used to getting during a slow period than make nothing at all. I'd rather be on the road working than sitting at home making no money unless I just don't want to go on the road.

I don't mind bending on money a little bit with a band that I really like, especially if they're good people and show me courtesy and respect. And while I'm not about to do a van tour at this point in my career, I do believe in helping young acts with some promise. After all, today's baby bands are the future of this business.

There's a current trend in the music business where some acts are now paying the crew, and sometimes the band members, a show day rate and then a reduced rate on days off. Sometimes it's half salary on days off or even less. Many crew members balk at this and won't take the job because of it; their reason being that they cannot work for another band on those days off while traveling on your band's behalf, so they feel they should be paid full salary.

Personally, I agree with them. Whether this is wrong or right or fair or unfair, it's what some acts are now doing. For some bands, it's the only way to make the budget work and keep touring. In the end, you can either help the band to make their budget work or you go and find another gig. Me, I'm more inclined to stick around and help the band out, within reason, if they're good people and old clients. But I still have to make a living and can only do so much to help them.

Below is a brief description of the other most common crew positions on a tour. This is for the band's core crew that travels with them everywhere and does not include sound and lighting crew that can change every tour leg. On big arena and stadium tours, new positions are created out of thin air for almost anything if the band has the money to burn.

Sure, if you've got the money to blow, you can hire a nanny willing to read soothing bedtime stories to the singer's herd of spastic, vegan, insomniac Chihuahuas before the frazzled and fed-up bus driver quietly dropkicks them all out the tour bus door while speeding down the highway in the middle of the night.

Production manager: The production manager is responsible for performing the general advance of a show and is directly in charge of the road crew, while the tour manager is directly responsible for looking after the band. He makes sure that the show loads in on time; the sound, lighting, and stage set goes up on time; sound check happens on time; the support acts are set up on time in conjunction with the stage manager; and that the doors open on time. He is pretty much the go-to person for anything involving the production. On a smaller tour where the band isn't carrying production, the duties of the production manager are usually handled by the tour manager.

Stage manager: The stage manager is the person on stage that makes sure everything stays on schedule. He's there to deal with the local crew to make sure that everything is set up on time for sound check, and he directs the support acts on stage and keeps them on schedule. He makes sure that the trucks are unloaded and loaded quickly and efficiently at load-in and load-out. On many tours, this job may be done by one of the backline techs.

FOH sound engineer: The sound engineer is responsible for mixing the band's live sound through the PA every night. He'll place the microphones on the band's gear with the help of the sound and backline crew and is in charge of the band's overall sound.

Monitor engineer: The monitor engineer mixes the band's sound on stage. This is done through the monitor system, which is essentially a smaller PA on stage for the band so they can hear themselves and what the others are playing and singing. Some bands use conventional side fills, wedges, and drum fills, while many bands are now using in-ear monitors. This job is often a hot seat with difficult singers.

Lighting designer: The lighting designer designs, programs, and performs the light show each night. There are some lighting designers who only design and program a show and then hire a board operator to do the tour.

Guitar tech: The guitar tech is responsible for setting up the band's amps and cabinets; cleaning, re-stringing, and tuning the guitars; and making sure the entire guitar rig is maintained and always working properly. Many guitar techs will also activate the guitar player's effects cues on their foot pedals, allowing the guitarist more freedom on stage. Some tours will have one guitar tech for each guitar player and the bass player; and some bands will have one guitar tech doing everyone if they're on a tight budget.

Drum tech: The drum tech is responsible for setting up the drum kit and drum riser each day. He makes sure that new drum heads are always on the drum kit and tuned properly. He also makes sure that the kit is spotless and looks great each night and sets up any electronics that the drummer may use.

Production assistant: The production assistant does pretty much whatever the tour manager and/or production manager needs them to do. The list is never-ending. They do everything from setting up the band's wardrobe cases in the dressing room to making sure the band's catering is in the dressing room when it's supposed to be there and that it's all correct. They also do many other things, such as sending out the band's laundry each day so they have clean stage clothes each night. They post signs and day sheets all over the venue where needed. The production assistant is one of the most overworked people on the tour, but it's a good entry level position that doesn't require any technical knowledge or skills and is a good launching pad for those looking to work their way up to a tour manager position one day.

HIRING THE RIGHT BUS COMPANY AND DRIVER

Some bus companies have the best buses and spend a lot more money on the vehicle's interior, but when looking at comparable bus companies, the service and driver they provide makes the difference to me.

I spend more time obtaining information about the driver than I do about the bus. There are a lot of good bus companies, but there are also some bad ones. You need to avoid those companies. I'm not going to list any of them in this book because I don't want to end up in court. You'll just have to find out which ones they are by doing your own research.

Back in the old days, bus drivers would be out in the bars with the band and crew on days off, whoopin' it up just as much as we did. We thought that was cool at the time because we didn't know better. Then you grow up and realize you need a driver whose primary concern is your safety.

There's usually a reason some bus drivers work for the worst bus companies. Many of them have a bad history, and the good bus companies won't hire them anymore. There are veteran drivers who used to raise holy hell back in the old days but are rock-solid today. I'd rather have one of those drivers because he's been-there-done-that and is serious about his gig; but there are some who haven't learned that lesson yet.

If you're a new tour manager and don't already have a relationship with a bus company that you like and trust, ask a lot of questions about the prospective driver they want to send out to you. Ask the same questions you would ask when checking out any new crew member.

Probe the bus company about how long the driver has been working for them. If he's new to the company, they might not know a lot about him except what was in the resume he submitted. The bus company might have been lazy in checking him out, especially if it was peak season and they were hurting for drivers when they hired him.

Some drivers judge their stature in the business by the age of the bus they're driving. There are veterans who wouldn't be caught dead driving a thirty-year-old Eagle; they think it sends a message that they're not successful. Whether this is true or not doesn't matter.

46

There are many good drivers that have worked for the same bus company for a long time and just care about working. They'll go from a new bus to an old one, depending on the bus company's needs. They don't get wrapped up in the "quality of my bus determines the quality of me" thing.

Tour bus drivers work hard driving the bus and performing the regular maintenance that keeps it rolling down the road for you. Take care of your drivers. They hold your lives in their hands when they drive you every night.

I always try to use the same bus company because you build a loyal relationship. There have been numerous times over the years when Sandy Stein at Coast to Coast Coach in Lancaster, CA, has given me a good deal on a bus because he knew it was all that the band could afford. There have been times when he's given me a better bus than what we were paying for because he wanted to go the extra mile for the client. Try to build strong relationships with vendors; be loyal and they'll be the same with you. There are many great entertainer coach companies out there, and a simple Google search will yield a long list for you.

The average tour bus sleeps twelve people. Many of these buses can be converted to condo bunks, turning two bunks into a taller one. If the band has their own bus, they might convert the bunks into condo bunks. Condo bunks are taller and allow a person to sit up in them. Some bus companies will charge you a small fee for doing this conversion, and it's a task that's best done at the shop before the tour starts.

I've never spent much time dwelling on the make and model of a bus. I care about the quality of the interior, the amenities inside the bus, the curb appeal of the exterior, the quality of the driver, and a price that fits the band's budget.

Some road managers get too wrapped up in the age of the bus. Some of them won't even look at a bus if it is more than ten years old. When you're dealing with a quality company, the year of the bus is only a number on the registration card. Most of the good companies refurbish the interior of the bus as soon as it starts to show wear and tear. They keep the TVs, stereos, DVD players, satellite dishes, and appliances in good condition and swap them out when they get old. They replace the carpet and reupholster the furniture when they become worn, and always make sure that the exterior of the bus looks sharp with a new paint job and is without dents. But if the band is a superstar act with money to burn, they deserve a new bus if they choose.

One of the things I care most about is that the air conditioning system works well. There is nothing worse than touring in the summer and suffocating in your bunk and sweating like a pig while you're trying to sleep. If you can't sleep at night, how are you going to work all day? Ask about the bus's AC system and make sure it works well.

Don't just look at pictures of a bus on the company's website; those pictures could be five years old. Ask the bus company if the pictures are recent. If not, tell them you want to see new pictures of the bus. In this day and age, everyone has a quality digital camera on their phone, and someone can easily take new pictures of the bus and email them to you.

Ask them about the age of the amenities on the bus. Does the AC work really well if you're doing a summer tour? Ask if the heating system works well if you're touring in the dead of winter. Ask the bus company how long it's been since they remodeled the interior of the bus. Ask a lot of questions, and you won't get any surprises when the bus shows up on the first day of the tour. At that point, it's too late to do anything about it. If it is peak season and buses are scarce, you could find yourself stuck with a bus you don't like for the entire tour.

There are many independent operators in the tour bus business. Some of them are great veteran drivers with a lot of experience who have bought their own bus so they can have more control over their future. Many of them find their own work, while some of them utilize a larger bus company as their broker that finds them work and takes a commission from their earnings.

Some of these independent operators own a few buses and hire drivers to operate their vehicles. They're essentially a small, independent bus company. There are some advantages to using an owner-operator who owns and drives his own bus. When business is slow, some of them may be willing to work with you on the price because they own the vehicle and are also getting paid their driver salary.

Some of them may be willing to take a cut in their driver salary or lease fee just to get the bus leased so they can keep making the monthly mortgage payment. They might work with you on other things, such as their fees for generator services and washing the bus. It's really up to what you can negotiate with them. These drivers also tend to take better care of their buses because it's their property.

There are drawbacks to using an owner-operator. You never know if the owner is in financial trouble and making the mortgage payments on the bus. There have been incidents in the past where the repo man showed up and took a bus away because the owner hadn't been making the loan payments. It's not a pleasant experience seeing your entourage suddenly sitting on the curb, watching your tour bus being taken away.

You also need to consider what happens if the bus breaks down due to a major mechanical malfunction. Buses break down, no matter how well you take care of them, especially on a music tour where you're logging thousands of miles each week.

If an independent operator owns only one bus and it needs to go into the shop for a week, you could be in trouble. The next show could go down the toilet. The bigger bus companies that own dozens of buses will have another one on the way as soon as possible, and if all of their buses are rented out, they'll sublet another bus just to get you back on the road. If it takes overnight to get that bus to you, they'll most likely put your entourage up in a hotel until the other bus arrives.

If a show should go down the toilet and income is lost due to the breakdown, the bus company may or may not cover some of that loss. That's something to speak to them about before your manager signs the contract. If it's not in the contract, see if they'll add provisions to the contract that protect you in this event. If you have a good relationship with the company, they will usually do all they can to solve the problem and keep your future business.

When you're organizing a tour and trying to book a tour bus, always get a quote from three bus companies for the sake of comparison until you build a strong relationship with a bus company and know what buses cost. Always make sure that those three quotes are for a comparable bus or the comparison makes no sense; $400.00 a day for a 1988 Eagle and $400.00 a day for a 2004 Prevost XL2 is a no-brainer. You want the XL2. But you need to know that.

When they send you the quote, ask questions about anything that you don't understand. Don't be embarrassed to ask questions because you don't want them to know you're new. Trust me; they know you're new.

A good bus company wants to answer all of your questions and make sure you're clear on all expenses. The last thing they want is for you to suddenly find out in the middle of the tour that you have to pay for something that you didn't know about and budget for.

The next thing we're going to do is go over an actual bus quote, and I'll explain to you all of the things you need to be aware of.

The first thing you'll see on the quote is the drive mileages and drive times for the tour. The bus company was able to calculate these figures because I provided them the routing (list of tour dates). They don't need the routing to give you the weekly bus rate, but with it, they can give you a quote containing more details, such as estimated overdrives, fuel costs, and maintenance costs. For a European/U.K. tour, you must send them the routing because the quote is all-in, including the fuel costs, ferries, and driver salary. They cannot give you an exact quote without the complete tour routing.

You still need to double-check all of the mileages to make sure they're correct. You can use Mapquest.com or Googlemaps.com or software such as Microsoft's Streets and Trips. Whatever you use, make sure you check the mileages yourself.

Badass Busses							
Client Skinny Girl Riot				**Tour manager** Bobby Blinder			
Date 3/2/2012				**Vehicle** 1 Prevost XL2 with 15' trailer (pink!)			
Date	City	Next city	Miles	Time/Hrs	Fuel costs	Overdrives	Overdrives costs
3/31/2012	Los Angeles	San Francisco	382	6.37	$305.60		$0.00
4/1/2012				0.00	$0.00		$0.00
4/2/2012	San Francisco	Los Angeles	382	6.37	$305.60		$0.00
4/3/2012	Los Angeles	San Diego	120	2.00	$96.00		$0.00
4/4/2012	San Diego	Phoenix	355	5.92	$284.00		$0.00
4/5/2012	Phoenix	Albuquerque	466	7.77	$372.80	1	$215.00
4/6/2012	Albuquerque	El Paso	266	4.43	$212.80		$0.00
4/7/2012	**Travel/Day off**			0.00	$0.00		$0.00
4/8/2012	El Paso	San Antonio	552	9.20	$441.60		$0.00
4/9/2012	San Antonio	Houston	199	3.32	$159.20		$0.00
4/10/2012	Houston	Dallas	241	4.02	$192.80		$0.00
4/11/2012	Dallas	New Orleans	508	8.47	$406.40	1	$215.00
4/12/2012	New Orleans	Tallahassee	385	6.42	$308.00		$0.00
4/13/2012	**Travel/Day off**			0.00	$0.00		$0.00
4/14/2012	Tallahassee	Tampa	274	4.57	$219.20		$0.00
4/15/2012	Tampa	Orlando	84	1.40	$67.20		$0.00
4/16/2012	Orlando	Atlanta	438	7.30	$350.40		$0.00
4/17/2012	Atlanta	Raleigh	407	6.78	$325.60		$0.00
4/18/2012	Raleigh	Washington, DC	282	4.70	$225.60		$0.00
4/19/2012	**Travel/Day off**			0.00	$0.00		$0.00
4/20/2012	Washington, DC	Philadelphia	139	2.32	$111.20		$0.00
4/21/2012	Philadelphia	Hartford	211	3.52	$168.80		$0.00
4/22/2012	Hartford	Boston	102	1.70	$81.60		$0.00
4/23/2012	Boston	New York	225	3.75	$180.00		$0.00
4/24/2012	New York	San Francisco	2906	48.43	$2,324.80		$0.00
	San Francisco	Los Angeles	382	6.37	$305.60		$0.00
Totals			9306	155.10	$7,444.80	2	$430.00
Notes:	At the end of the tour, the bus will take the band's gear back to San Francisco.						
Tour dates	33	Overdrives	2	Gen service	8		
Mileage	9306	Overdrives costs	$430.00	Gen serv costs	$ 360.00		
Time/hrs	155.10	Driver salary	$7,095.00	Bus wash & linen	5		
Fuel usage	1861.20	Coach lease	$14,850.00	Wash, linen costs	$ 625.00		
Fuel costs	$7,444.80	Dish/WIFI	included				
Daily coach rate		$450.00					
Driver rate		$215.00					
Main engine service		$930.60					
End of tour cleaning costs		$400.00					
Total costs		**$32,135.40**					

You'll also notice that the estimated drive times are on the quote. I normally use 50 mph to determine how long a drive will take. Using this speed for long drives will compensate for traffic and fuel stops, and it almost always works out to be about this amount. Even if the driver cranks it and gets there sooner, it's better to be early than late.

Next on the quote are the estimated fuel costs for the tour. This will be helpful when you're creating your tour budget. Please refer to the chapter, "Trucking," in Part Two of this book for details on how to calculate diesel fuel costs for a truck and tour bus. It's done the same way for both types of vehicle. Ask your bus company how many miles per gallon their bus gets, and it will be pretty simple to calculate the diesel fuel costs. Always remember that the bus will get better mileage when it's not pulling a trailer loaded with gear.

The next things you see on the quote are the driver's estimated overdrives for the tour. You can always negotiate overdrives with the driver but put all of the overdrives in your tour budget to cover yourself. It's always better to have a bit of padding in the budget so you don't go over budget. It's better to come in under budget at the end of the tour than over budget.

Some drivers will bill you for an overdrive if they go one mile over four hundred and fifty miles. I don't put up with this and will call the bus company and complain over this kind of nonsense; and I'd never use that driver again. But once the driver is nearing fifty miles over the four hundred and fifty-mile mark, you'll probably have to pay the overdrive. You can always negotiate with the driver if the band is tight on money, and most good drivers will work with you on this. Some may not. In the end, I don't want a disgruntled driver up front, holding our lives in his hands, pissed off over a few hundred dollars.

At the bottom of the quote, you'll see all of the totals for the items we just discussed. You'll notice the bus company has put in the number of lease days for the bus. Check and make sure this is correct, including the deadhead days the driver has to travel to get to you at the beginning of the tour and to get the bus back to their shop after they've dropped you off at the end of the tour.

The driver's salary is listed on the quote. If you're not pulling a trailer on the tour, the driver's salary will usually be about $25 a day less. The driver gets an extra fee for pulling a trailer. Make sure the amount is correct on the quote; the bus company may assume that you're pulling a trailer if you haven't told them otherwise. Unless your band is an acoustic act and their gear will fit into the luggage bay of the bus, you will almost always be dragging a trailer.

Next on the quote are the weekly maintenance costs. The driver must service the generator on the bus every one hundred hours, roughly every four days. He changes the oil and oil filters, changes the air filter when it's needed, and checks the water, antifreeze, and belts. He gets about $50 every time he does a generator service. Check with the bus company for the correct amount; it varies slightly from company to company.

The exterior of the bus has to be washed once a week. The driver can have it done at a truck stop or he can do it himself. Either way, it's the band's expense, and you must pay for it. This is usually about $55 for the bus and an extra $20 if there's a trailer on the bus. If the driver gets the bus washed at a truck wash, such as Blue Beacon, the price can vary a bit, depending on the city, but it's usually in the $75 range.

There's a charge for washing the linen in the bunks each week. This is usually $50 a week but can vary from company to company. I've seen some bands not want to pay for this, so they just wash their own sheets and pillowcases when they see fit. It's up to you, but you certainly don't want to let the entourage go weeks without washing their linen, or bunk alley will begin to smell like a locker room. No one wants to live that way.

When the tour is over, you're contractually obligated to pay for an end-of-tour bus cleaning. This is usually about $400 per bus. You'll rarely get out of paying this charge. I've never seen a tour bus that wasn't upside down at the end of a tour. Your entourage's mess must be cleaned up before the bus can be rented to the next client.

There's also a charge for the main engine service. You will see this listed on the quote. The cost is usually about five or six cents a mile or ten cents a mile if the bus is pulling a trailer.

Make sure that the daily rental rate is correct on the quote and is what you originally discussed with the bus company. Sometimes mistakes are made. It's up to you to be sure that doesn't happen.

You'll also see the charges for satellite TV and WIFI. Some bus companies charge for this and some don't. Many build it into the daily rental rate. Either way, you're most likely paying for it because the bus company has to pay for it. The cost for the satellite TV programming is usually about $15 a day and wireless internet is usually about $10 per day for each bus.

It's a good habit to reset the wireless internet router every morning in the next city to get the best signal. Just unplug it for thirty seconds, and it should be fine unless you're in the middle of nowhere and the signal is weak. I always ask the driver to do this when he arrives in the next city each morning.

Most U.S. bus companies will disable the wireless internet when you go into Canada because the roaming charges are expensive. Plan on being without wireless internet while in Canada unless your band is willing to pay the roaming charges, or if your bus company does not have an internet service in Canada.

When your accountant pays the bus bill each week, they're usually only paying for the bus rental fee, main engine service charges and end-of-tour cleaning charges (both spread across all of the weekly payments), and satellite TV and WIFI costs. The rest of the expenses, including the driver's salary and overdrives (unless the band has the driver on payroll), fuel, oil, generator services, generator service supplies, and weekly bus linen cleaning fees have to be paid for in cash by you each week. So you need to plan ahead for that when estimating your weekly cash nut. Some bands will insist on putting the bus driver on payroll just like the road crew—and most of the drivers will complain about this— but they really have no choice in the matter if that's what the band wants to do.

Normally, you will give the driver $1,000 in cash for fuel and other bus expenses. When he's spent this float, he'll turn in the receipts to you, and you'll then give him another $1,000. The driver is essentially always running with $1,000 in float. You can do less than this if you want, but it's a headache for you because he's coming to you for float more often. You will, of course, add these receipts into your accounting each time he cashes in his receipts.

Some bands prefer to give the bus driver a band credit card for fuel, oil, and bus supplies, but this can be a problem because the driver's name isn't on the card. The driver is almost always driving at night while you're sleeping, and he's stopping for fuel in the middle of the night. The last thing you want is to be woken up at 4:00 a.m. because the truck stop won't let the driver use the band credit card because he doesn't have identification matching the name on the card. So you'll have to get up and go into the truck stop and show your identification so he can pay for the fuel. This will be even more unpleasant if the band credit card happens to be in a band member's name and you have to wake up that person.

You don't need to worry about overdrives in the U.K. and Europe; they don't exist. The laws for drivers are becoming stricter there every year. Tour buses in Europe and the U.K. have tachographs installed in them that record the driver's speed, distance and working hours on every drive segment. If the driver is pulled over by the police, he is asked to show his tachograph card, and if he's over on his service hours or he's driven too far in one drive segment, the bus can be shut down, the driver given an expensive traffic ticket, and the bus company can be charged a huge fine.

Because of these stricter laws, the cost of touring in Europe and the U.K. is becoming more expensive, depending on the tour's routing, because double drivers are needed more often. This increases the quote because of the double driver's salary (and the food allowance you must pay him) and the cost to fly him in and out. Sometimes he can catch a train, which is usually less expensive than flying, but he will often have to be flown in. If there's no extra bunk on the bus, you'll have to pay for a hotel for the double-driver. The law says that the double-driver must have a hotel room for his break, but I've never met a bus driver who didn't like a hotel buyout; but that's between you and the double-driver. Some drivers will just take the bunk on the bus and not ask for a hotel buyout.

Double-drivers are not needed as often in the U.K., because the drives between cities aren't as far, kind of like touring on the east coast of America. But if you're doing too many shows back-to-back, you could end up needing a double-driver because of the driver's mandatory rest break. Because these laws are changing so often, it's best that you check with the bus company about the latest rules on every tour you do. The good bus companies will usually give you a sheet listing what you can and cannot do for the tour routing you've sent to them. You have no choice but to follow these rules for the driver's mandatory breaks.

The laws in America are becoming stricter, and eventually the days of overdrives will be over, and double drivers will also be required here. It's also important to remember that overdrives are illegal and bus drivers now have to follow more of the rules that truck drivers have to follow.

If your band is unable to afford a tour bus in Europe or the U.K., there are companies that provide "splitter vans" with cargo space in the back for your gear. Some of these vans are well-equipped with a TV and DVD player, a small refrigerator, and comfortable seats. These companies can provide you with splitter vans that seat six, nine, or eleven people and even offer drivers for hire if there's no one in your entourage who can drive the van. If you're an American band and have no one in your entourage that's used to driving in the U.K. (on the opposite side of the road), you'll probably want to budget for a British driver, for obvious safety reasons. A Google search will list many of the companies that offer splitter vans for hire.

BOOKING HOTELS

One of the things you'll need to do when organizing a tour is book hotels. This process has changed a lot over the years with the advent of the internet. In the old days, a travel agent booked the hotels for you, but today many road managers on smaller tours book the hotels.

There are many websites, such as Expedia, Travelocity, Orbitz, Hotwire, and Priceline, where you can book hotels for your tour. There are advantages and disadvantages to booking your own hotels without a travel agent.

If you're on a smaller tour where you're just booking one room every day for the bus driver and only a shower room on days off for your entourage, you'll be hard-pressed to find a music travel agent who will do the bookings for you unless it's a smaller travel agent who sees some promise in your band and views them as an investment in the future.

Travel agents get a commission from the hotel for bringing them the business, but the commission isn't worth their time if they're only booking one room a day. A travel agent spends just as much time booking one room as they do booking ten rooms, so many of them won't want the band's business until they're buying more rooms. If the band is doing a lot of fly dates and the travel agent is earning a lot of commissions and fees from booking airfares for you, they might book those few rooms for you each week. Anything is possible.

If you don't have a travel agent to book your rooms, you'll most likely end up booking them yourself. This, of course, means more work for you, but at least you can get the hotels booked quicker so you can enter the information into your tour book and get on to the next project.

You'll need a credit card to book the rooms online. Many times a new band won't have their own band credit card and you may have to use the manager's personal credit card to do the bookings. They may suggest that you use your own credit card, but I don't recommend that. A tour could suddenly get canceled and you don't want to be worrying about getting reimbursed for thousands of dollars of hotel rooms that you naively purchased on your credit card. You may never get the money back.

Once you've booked the rooms online, they're pre-paid and you'll usually be charged a cancellation fee if you need to cancel them. Some hotels won't cancel them within twenty-four to seventy-two hours of the check-in date, depending on the hotel's policy. If you're a

Gold member, some sites will credit you for the cancelation if the hotel won't cancel it. Each one of these sites has different cancelation policies, so you'll need to check the rules of the website you use.

Some sites won't give you a refund or have restrictions on refunds should you need to cancel the rooms. For this reason, I don't recommend using those kinds of sites for a music tour. Should your travel plans change because of a canceled show and you have to cancel hotels in a city, you want to be able to cancel the rooms and not lose any money.

Pre-paying rooms on sites like Expedia saves you some trouble when you're booking rooms for the bus driver. If you book a reservation with the hotel directly and use a credit card in your name, the driver will often be unable to check into the hotel without you there because your name is on the card. You don't want to have to go to the driver's hotel each day to check him in when you're at the venue trying to get the show up and running. Some hotels are used to having tour bus drivers in their hotels and will be flexible, as long as the driver has his own credit card to put down for security purposes, but some may not be so flexible.

Pre-paying the room solves this problem. The only thing the driver needs is identification matching the name on the pre-paid reservation and he's allowed to check in. Most of the time he'll need to present his own credit card to guarantee incidentals such as room service, long distance telephone calls, internet, and pay-per-view movies. This is always required at hotels that offer these services. Even the cheap hotels want a credit card in case you damage the room. When you book a shower room for a day off for your entourage, you'll be booking the room in your name and you'll be there to check in.

One of the advantages of using a travel agent is that they have a network of hotels in every city that they're using to dealing with. These hotels are used to accommodating music groups and all of the special requirements they have.

If you've just arrived at the hotel on a day off and your driver is beat because he just finished a six-hundred-mile drive, you don't want the driver to have to wait hours for his room. Providing the hotel wasn't sold out the night before and the rooms are already clean, your travel agent can usually arrange an early check-in for your driver so he can go straight to his room and get to bed. The same goes for the rooms you'll need for your entourage.

Hotels always say there's no check-in before 3:00 p.m., or whatever time is their policy, but most of them will happily check you into the rooms earlier if they have clean rooms available. The only exception would be if the hotel was sold out the night before. Then they will not be able to check you in until housekeeping has cleaned the rooms. There's nothing you can do about this except wait.

Another advantage of using a travel agent is that they'll negotiate a late check-out for you when you need it. On bigger tours, the crew will need to go down to load-in in the morning, but you may not need the band at the venue until it's time for sound check. If the hotel's normal check-out time is 12:00 p.m. and sound check isn't until 4:00 p.m., you'd hope to get the band a 3:00 p.m. late check-out so they don't have to get out of bed so early. If you only have a shower room, the band is probably sleeping on the bus, and they'll go to the venue when the bus goes to the venue for load-in.

Another benefit of using a travel agent is that they will send your rooming list to the hotel ahead of time so when you check the entourage into the hotel, they'll already have packets prepared for each room. The packets will have each guest's name and room number on the front and will normally include the room keys, rooming list, and many times a hotel information sheet that specifies amenities in the hotel and local information about nearby restaurants, shopping malls, movie theaters and other attractions.

This is a great time-saver for you. All you have to do is present your credit card and identification, and they'll hand you all of the packets for your group. You can simply hand them out to each person in your group.

Large travel agencies have relationships with hotel sales managers in every major city. They can negotiate lower group rates that you probably won't be able to get booking rooms online. These travel agents can also get room upgrades that you also usually cannot get online. You can ask for an upgrade at the front desk when you check in, but you may not get it. You must remember that a big travel agent has many clients and is sending that hotel sales manager business all year long, so the sales manager has a lot of incentive to keep that travel agent happy so their clients keeps coming to that hotel.

Travel agents who specialize in entertainment travel are a different breed than your regular travel agent. They're well-schooled in the mechanics and special needs of a music tour. A travel agent working out of a little strip mall who specializes in family vacation travel isn't going to know the ins-and-outs of a music tour, especially big ones.

If you're not using a travel agent, you can always email your blank rooming list to the hotel the day before and ask them to fill in the room numbers and make up the packets for your group ahead of time, but smaller economy hotels may not do this for you.

If they won't prepare for your group before you arrive, then you'll need to just fill in the blank rooming list with the correct room numbers when you check in and ask the front desk attendant to make copies of the rooming list for you. This obviously makes the check-in process longer, but the cheaper the hotel you stay in, the less extra service you can usually expect from them. You get what you pay for.

Always remember that hotel front desk attendants are often music fans or could even be a fan of your group. They may be willing to go the extra mile for you with early check-ins and late check-outs if you can offer them a spot on your guest list. It never hurts to try this approach. They may not be interested in going to the show, but they may have children or friends who might be. It never hurts to dangle that guest list carrot in front of their face when you need some help. It's worked many times for me. If that doesn't work, you can always try offering them a free t-shirt, but that will cost the band some money. A spot on the guest list does not.

Always have a rooming list for your group, even if you only have a driver room and a shower room. I always get at least two copies of the shower room key and take a Sharpie and mark the room number backwards on the key in case someone in the entourage loses it. Be careful with having too many copies of a room key floating around. The hotel may become concerned if you ask for too many room keys. Never leave valuables in a shower room where many people are coming and going all day and night.

On tours where you only have a shower room on a day off, you should make a day sheet that lists the hotel info, the room numbers for the driver room and shower room, and the departure time from the hotel. Post it in the front and back lounges of the bus so everyone knows where to look for it. Stick the room keys to the wall beside the day sheet with some Blu Tack poster adhesive so everyone always knows where to find the keys.

Train everyone to put the keys back on the wall beside the day sheet when they're done using them so the next person has a key to get into the room. The hotel isn't going to give keys to members of your entourage if their name isn't registered to the room. Post a copy of the day sheet in the shower room and make sure to give the bus driver a copy so he knows the departure time.

Remember to ask the hotel for extra towels for your shower room when you check in or there won't be enough for your entourage. Keep in mind that this can open up a big can of worms with the hotel if they're not used to having rock groups in the hotel using the room as a shower room.

I've often encountered hotels that have a big problem when you ask for ten towels because they suddenly realize that there will be many people using the room. Some of the cheaper hotels will freak out and not let you check into the room without paying extra for all of these people, or they'll insist on you buying more rooms, despite the fact that you've told them no one is spending the night in the room and you're only using it for your group to take showers. Some of them will cooperate and some still won't budge. These cheap hotels are only doing this to get more money out of you.

When I'm only booking a few shower rooms for a day off or a midway stop during a long drive so the driver can get his ten-hour break and sleep, I will call the hotel before I book the rooms and tell them the situation and ask them if it's going to be a problem using the rooms as shower rooms for the group. If they say it will be a problem, I go on to the next hotel on the list. If they say it won't be a problem, I ask for that person's name and make a note of it in my tour book, should there be a problem when I check in and that person isn't on duty.

It's important to know how many days you need to book a room for your bus driver. If you're arriving at the hotel in Chicago for a day off on Monday and the show is the next day on Tuesday, the driver will need his room booked for two days because he won't be checking out of the hotel until after the show Tuesday night. Some new tour managers forget about this and only book the driver for one day.

You don't want your bus driver to go back to the hotel after he's driven the bus down to the venue for load-in to find out that the hotel has checked him out of the room and they cannot check him back in because the hotel is sold out that night. You'll then have to go through the trouble of getting online and finding him another room for that day while he sits in the hotel lobby, pissed off, thinking you're the biggest jackass in the music business.

Take a look at the rooming list below. If the entourage all had their own rooms that day, this is what the rooming list would look like. If you only have a band shower room, crew shower room, and bus driver room, you can just name the rooms that way.

Smoking and non-smoking rooms are denoted on the sheet. Smoking rooms in hotels are quickly becoming extinct in the U.S. and most other places around the world. Hotels are charging guests $250, sometimes more, for smoking in non-smoking rooms. Make sure your entourage knows about this. It's an expensive surprise to get when checking out of the hotel.

Many groups make luggage tags for their entourage. These luggage tags usually have the name, address, and telephone number of the management company on one side of them and an identifying number on the other side that is assigned to each member of the entourage. It's also good to have luggage tags on any gear that you check on planes.

When your band is at a point where they can afford hotel rooms for everyone on days off, these luggage tags will be helpful when you have the hotel bellman deliver the band's luggage to their rooms and pick it up the next day when it's time to check out of the hotel.

When you—or your production assistant—have the bellman take the band's luggage out of the bus bay (luggage compartment) and put it onto luggage carts, give him a rooming list so he knows which bags to deliver to which room by matching the luggage tag numbers on the rooming list to the numbers on the luggage tags. Supervising this process is usually a job for the band assistant, but if you don't have one then you'll have to deal with it. The crew can take care of their luggage.

Skinny Girl Riot

Rooming List

Name	Room type	Room #	Luggage Tag #
Stevie Starbright	king, non-smoking	432	1
Frankie Fabulous	king, non-smoking	434	2
Jimmy Giant	king, non-smoking	436	3
Mikey Massive	king, non-smoking	438	4
Tommy Twosticks	king, smoking	622	5
Bobby Blinder	king, smoking	624	6
Lance Loudnoise	king, non-smoking	440	7
Ricky Racket	king, non-smoking	442	8
Jerry Spazo	king, non-smoking	444	9
Kyle Klown	king, non-smoking	446	10
Tony Tonedeaf	king, non-smoking	448	11
Penny Tightpants	king, non-smoking	450	12
Woodrow Pilson	king, non-smoking	452	13
Leadfoot Johnson	king, smoking	640	14

Note: Please call Bobby Blinder (tour manager) with any questions or problems at 555-673-3342.

Whatever you do, don't put the band's name or logo on the luggage tags. Airline baggage handlers, hotel employees, and anyone else who comes in contact with your luggage and gear could be a fan. Most of these people are honest, but some of them may steal the baggage or gear if they know it belongs to a famous band.

It's always good to include your cell phone number at the bottom of the rooming list so the front desk can reach you in case of a problem if you're not in your room. Complaints about the noise and exhaust from the bus's generator are a common problem, especially when the bus is parked too close to the hotel where people are sleeping or another business where people are coming and going. You don't want the front desk calling band member rooms and waking them up looking for you or the bus driver because they don't know which name on the rooming list belongs to you or the driver. I'd rather have the hotel call me about bus problems rather than wake up the driver, who needs his sleep. I can usually solve most problems without waking up the driver. If I can't and it's urgent, then I'll have to wake him up. Think ahead and you'll have fewer problems to solve.

If you're using a travel agent to book hotels, they'll send you a sheet with all of the hotels for you to approve. Ask them to make any changes that you require. When they're done, they'll send you a final sheet with all of the hotel info and the negotiated prices for the rooms.

If you're lucky enough to have a travel agent booking your hotels on a small tour, be sure to send that travel agent a specific list of what you need for each day of the tour. Make sure that you type up a list of the tour dates and the name of the venue, city and state, and include the days off and travel days. Beside each show day, specify what you need for that day. If you only need a room for the driver, type it on the sheet. If it's a day off and you need a driver room and a shower room, state it on the sheet. If you need full rooms for the entire entourage, let them know. Be specific.

You cannot expect a travel agent to read your mind and then be upset with them when they send you a list of hotels that's wrong. Below is an example of what you should send the travel agent to book your hotels. This is foolproof and easy to follow.

You also need to let the travel agent know your budget amount per room and the name of the bus driver so they can book his room under his name. If the shower room is in your name, let them know that. If you will have full rooms for the entourage on days off, make sure to send the travel agent a proper rooming list so they know exactly what they're supposed to book.

Once your band is making money and you're booking rooms for everyone on days off, it will probably be time for the band members to start using an alias. The fans are smart. They go to a lot of concerts in their town, and they've pretty much figured out which hotels the bands stay in. All they have to do is drive by the hotel and see if tour buses are parked in the hotel parking lot and they will know that you're there.

You don't want to book the band's rooms using their real names. The last thing your band members want is to be woken up at 3:00 a.m. by a fan wanting any number of things. If someone calls the hotel front desk and asks to be connected to John Smith's room and there's a John Smith registered in the hotel, they'll put the call through. They won't give out the room number, but they will put the call through unless the person in that room has requested that no calls be put through to the room.

61

Skinny Girl Riot--Hotels--USA 2012		
Date	**Venue/City/State**	**Rooms Needed (see key below)**
Saturday, March 31, 2012	**Travel Day**	2
Sunday, April 01, 2012	Club 1--San Francisco, CA	1
Monday, April 02, 2012	Club 2--Los Angeles, CA	1
Tuesday, April 03, 2012	Club 3--San Diego, CA	1
Wednesday, April 04, 2012	Club 4--Phoenix, AZ	1
Thursday, April 05, 2012	Club 5--Albuquerque, NM	1
Friday, April 06, 2012	**Day Off**	2
Saturday, April 07, 2012	Club 6--El Paso, TX	1
Sunday, April 08, 2012	Club 7--San Antonio, TX	1
Monday, April 09, 2012	Club 8--Houston, TX	1
Tuesday, April 10, 2012	Club 9--Dallas, TX	1
Wednesday, April 11, 2012	Club 10--New Orleans, LA	1
Thursday, April 12, 2012	**Day Off**	2
Friday, April 13, 2012	Club 11--Tallahassee, FL	1
Saturday, April 14, 2012	Club 12--Tampa, FL	1
Sunday, April 15, 2012	Club 13--Orlando, FL	1
Monday, April 16, 2012	Club 14--Atlanta, GA	1
Tuesday, April 17, 2012	Club 15--Raleigh, NC	1
Wednesday, April 18, 2012	**Day Off**	2
Thursday, April 19, 2012	Club 16--Washington, DC	1
Friday, April 20, 2012	Club 17--Philadelphia, PA	1
Saturday, April 21, 2012	Club 18--Hartford, CT	1
Sunday, April 22, 2012	Club 19--Boston, MA	1
Monday, April 23, 2012	Club 20--New York, NY	1
Tuesday, April 24, 2012	**Travel Home**	

Key:
1: 1 king, smoking for Leadfoot Johnson
2: 1 king, smoking for Leadfoot Johnson & 2 double, non-smoking rooms under the name Bobby Blinder

If your band is registered under an alias, the fans won't know what name to ask for. These aliases should probably be changed every tour leg. The hotel employees know who is in that room and hotel employees are also sometimes fans. You never know what they're telling their friends when they go home from work or what they're posting on the internet.

The travel agent can send the hotel a rooming list with aliases for the band members on it, and it will be no problem at check-in time. You'll be the one going to the hotel's front desk to check in the entourage and only you will have to produce your identification and a credit card, so it doesn't matter if the band member aliases don't match their identification, but this can be a problem touring overseas.

Some hotels will insist that each person checking into the room personally present their passport before they can receive a room key, but they will still leave the alias in the computer in case anyone tries to call the room. Check with the hotel before you arrive and you will know what you're faced with at that hotel. The band members can still use their alias, but you will need to let the hotel know that the names on the reservation are not real and are for security purposes. When the reservation for Dick Gozinya doesn't match your singer's passport, you will need to explain why.

If you pre-pay rooms online, the reservation will need to be in the band member's real name because they'll have to produce identification to check into the room. That's a drawback of booking rooms online. Some hotels will let you get away with this if you're polite, say the right things, and you have all of the confirmation numbers, but some hotels that aren't used to dealing with music groups could become highly perplexed and difficult. If they won't change the name on the room in their computer to the band member's alias, you can still block calls to the room. This has never been a problem because we all use our cell phones to communicate most of the time.

If you're booking the hotels online, remember to print out the information for each hotel so you can enter it into the tour book for each city, or copy and paste the information directly from the website and enter it into your tour book right away. Learn to multi-task and do numerous things at the same time.

On sites like Expedia, you can run fantasy trip scenarios to learn more about the cost of hotels and what you can get for your budget. It's a great way to learn more about the hotel industry, and it's free learning.

BOOKING AIR TRAVEL

One of the first things you should do when beginning work with a new client is to send out a "Frequent Flyer Info Sheet" for them to fill out. Once they fill out this spreadsheet and email it back to you, send it to your travel agent if you're using one. If the band has a travel agent but they've never sent her this information, now is the time to do it. You're not only doing this to benefit the people in your entourage, you're doing it to save yourself a lot of headaches when you check them in for flights at the airport.

Skinny Girl Riot

Frequent Flyer Info Sheet

Name:	Stevie Starbright
Seating preference:	Emergency row aisle
Special meal:	vegetarian
Airline Frequent Flyer Numbers	
American (oneworld)	XJ5558383
United (Star Alliance)	838927373
Delta (SkyTeam)	630309773
JetBlue	738387309
Southwest	636878377

You can see that the sheet contains each person's name, their seating preference: aisle or window—no one ever wants a middle seat, any special food requests (vegetarian, gluten-free, diabetic), and the frequent flyer numbers for the major airlines that you'll usually be flying on. Most of the major airlines have all now merged with each other or are a partner with the rest of the majors, so as long as you have frequent flyer numbers for American Airlines (Oneworld), United Continental (Star Alliance), and Delta (SkyTeam), you'll be covered for most of the airlines you'll fly on. If any of your band or crew members frequently use any of the smaller airlines, such as JetBlue or Southwest, suggest that they go online and join their frequent programs, if they haven't already done so, and add their number to the sheet.

It's important for the travel agent to have all of this info for everyone in the entourage. When the travel agent books flights for the group, you want them to be able to get each person their seat of choice. Some people prefer a window seat while some prefer an aisle seat, and this is always a big issue with everyone. No one ever wants a middle seat. It's equivalent to being in a torture chamber in economy class on a long, sold-out flight.

You should also ask everyone if they have any special meal requests. Many people today are vegetarians or gluten-intolerant, and some airlines still offer these special meals if you request them ahead of time. The travel agent will be able to make these special meal requests when they book the flights, and so can you on many of the airlines if you're booking the flights online.

Get all of their frequent flyer numbers that the band members currently have so the travel agent can enter them into the computer when she books the flights. This prevents you from having to worry about this when you check them in online or at the airport.

Frequent flyer numbers are important for more than just building up free miles. If you're doing a lot of flying during the course of an album cycle, it's only a matter of time until your entourage achieves elite status on these airlines. This is important for a number of reasons.

When you receive elite status on most airlines, some of your bags are checked in for free. Excess baggage is becoming an expensive category in the tour budget these days because most of the airlines are now charging you to check bags. It's the band's responsibility not only to pay for everyone's airfare but also for their checked baggage and the band's gear that must be checked on the plane.

If you're flying overseas to do a European/U.K. tour and you have a lot of people in your entourage, excess baggage charges can add up quickly. When you're creating your tour budget, always go to the airline's website to view the charges and size and weight limits for excess, oversize, and overweight baggage. Every dollar you can save by not being charged for these pieces of gear and luggage by having elite status can add up to a big savings over the course of a long album cycle.

If everyone in your entourage has achieved elite status, you can also check in through the business class/first class line or priority access line, depending on that airline's rules. When you have a large group of people and luggage to check in, you'll be happy to be able to check in through the shorter priority access line when the economy check-in line is a mile long. Even if I'm the only person in my entourage who has elite status, I can often drag my group through the priority access line with me. A few polite words to the customer service rep at the check-in desk can go a long way.

There are numerous other perks offered by the airlines when you receive elite status, such as being able to choose better seats and even exit row seats on their website as soon as you buy the ticket. Visit the airline's website, and you'll see the many benefits available to you and your group. When you can, try to be loyal to one airline, and your elite status will come much quicker.

Some airlines have group check-in lines, but they're usually limited to groups of ten people or more. I've often found that if I go up to the counter and politely do the "we're a rock band" thing, many of them will let us check in there if there's no other group in line.

I've also found that if I'm using a few skycaps to help bring the gear and luggage into the airport, they can sometimes work their magic and get my entourage into the group line. Remember that the skycaps are not being helpful because they're the ultimate airport do-gooders; they're hoping for a good tip. If they sort you out, they've earned it. Tip them—a few bucks a bag is just fine—and it's a tour expense.

One of the good things about using a top travel agent is having them deal with your flights. They do a lot of business with the airlines and have connections that you don't have. They can accomplish many things that you won't be able to accomplish, such as getting VIP treatment at check-in, even if you're in economy class. If a travel agent just dealt with some airline rep a week ago for some super group that spent a lot of money on expensive airfares, she might be able to work some magic for a newer client because of her past dealings with this airline rep. Anything is possible when you have powerful people working with your group.

Some airlines have greeters who will meet VIPs at the airport and help them through a speedy check-in and then escort them to the airline's VIP lounge to wait for their flight's boarding time. This probably won't happen with a baby band flying economy, but anything is possible if you have the right travel agent pulling some strings. Things are getting tough with the airlines as they charge for more and more things to stay afloat, so it never hurts to try. All they can say is no.

I've often been able to get out of paying expensive excess baggage charges using a little trick of mine. It doesn't always work, but it saves my clients thousands of dollars over the course of an album cycle when it does work. Once we've checked in all of the baggage and gear and the customer service rep presents me with the excess baggage charges, I immediately say, "No, our promoter has an agreement with the airline that we wouldn't be charged any excess baggage charges. We wouldn't be flying on this airline if we hadn't gotten the waiver. We can't afford it."

Some of these reps simply accept my story and waive the charges, but some of them say, "Sir, I don't see anything about an excess baggage waiver in my computer." I then reply, "Can you please call your manager because we always have the waiver? We wouldn't be flying on this airline without it. We don't have the budget to pay these charges."

Some of them get on the phone and call their manager out to the check-in desk, but some of them look at the long line behind us, knowing full well that they can't hold up the line because the plane is boarding soon, and finally say, "Okay, the charges are waived. Have a good flight, sir."

Sometimes the manager comes out to the desk, and I give them the same story, and they'll dig through the computer while saying they can't find any notes about any waiver, and I will continue insisting that it has to be there. Like the rep before her, the manager will eventually look up at the long line growing behind us and the clock ticking away on the plane's departure and finally waives the charges.

There are some who don't waive the charges but instead give a considerable discount when I do my "struggling band on a tight budget" performance, but some of them will flatly say, "Sir, if you want this luggage checked on the plane, this is what it's going to cost," and we have no choice but to pay it. But I win a lot more than I lose.

No, I don't feel bad about telling my tall tales of promoter baggage waivers. My job is to save the band as much money as I can, and I did that on many occasions. Frankly, I think the airlines are getting out-of-hand with all of these extra charges passengers are now getting hit with.

I'd use this method every time your band flies. Sometimes it will work, and sometimes it won't, but any money you save the band is money that can be used for other expenses in the budget. I'm sure you'd like a raise one day, wouldn't you?

Another thing I do when I can't get out of paying for excess baggage is to say, "Okay, I understand you can find the baggage waiver in your computer, but can we still get the media rate? We always get the media rate."

Some of these customer service reps are inexperienced and have never even heard of the media rate. The media rate does exist, but it's usually only for orchestras with large instruments, photographers, and film and TV crews checking in a lot of camera, film, and TV equipment.

Some of these CSRs know about the media rate, but they don't know the specifics on it. Some of them, after enduring my long drama with the non-existent excess baggage waiver, will just go ahead and give us the cheaper media rate rather than begin a whole new episode as the line behind us grows even longer and the boarding time for the flight grows nearer. This has worked many times for me. Just put on your Robert De Niro mask, be polite, and give it a shot. You've got nothing to lose but the band's money! You really don't need that pay raise, do you?

There's a company called Media On Board that handles media accounts and can get you discounts on excess baggage charges if you're flying on a Star Alliance airline such as United, Lufthansa, Austrian Airlines, Air Canada, or Swiss Airlines. And they do accept music groups as part of the media. They also offer special handling services to make the check-in process for your gear a lot easier. Their website is MediaOnBoard.Com They might be able to save you some money when you're flying on any of those airlines.

Travel agents get their commission from the airline for booking flights, but many travel agents are now charging a fee for each ticket they book for you. These charges average around $50 per ticket but can be higher, depending on the travel agency. Many travel agents started adding these fees because of websites like Expedia taking away a lot of their business. For this reason, many groups have started booking their own air travel online, but you won't get all of that extra attention and service that I've spoken of before. The more popular groups are usually still using travel agents for flights.

There are baby bands represented by big management companies that have the luxury of a travel agent because that agent is working with the manager's other bigger clients. This is good for the band, but the travel agent is probably not making much money from the band. People will only go so far when they're doing favors for little or no return, so it's important to double-check everything they do if you find yourself in this kind of situation.

One of the travel agent's superstar clients might not even consider taking a flight where they're changing planes on a long journey, but your band that is on a tight budget might be happy to do that to save $1,000. These travel agents are mentally programmed to think of their popular band's misery level before their wallet. The last thing a travel agent wants is to lose a big client because they put the band on a hell flight to Europe, but your band may have to do that to make the budget work.

There are smart travel agents out there who've been working with big clients for years and have outlived many managers and tour managers because they know the band and their needs better than they know the bloody bunion on their big toe. These are the top entertainment travel agents that are still doing well despite how the internet and travel websites have changed their industry so much.

Learn to double check everything they do so you can make sure they book what's best for your band. Ask questions; you'll learn a lot this way. If they don't have time to answer your questions, find another travel agent. There are smaller entertainment travel agents out there who may be willing to get on board with a promising new band.

Booking airline travel isn't nuclear science, but there are some important things to know. You won't learn all of it overnight; you learn everything, including this job, by doing it over and over again. I'm going to give you some tips that will greatly reduce your chances of error.

One of the most important things to know about booking airfare is when to buy the tickets. You always want to have at least fourteen days advance purchase when you buy the tickets. The sooner you buy them, the better, in many cases. There's a website called FareCompare.com that will teach you a lot about buying airfares. Just plug in some fantasy flight scenarios, such as Los Angeles to Paris, San Francisco to Auckland, or Miami to Bogota, with different departure and return dates and compare what you see for each one. Los Angeles to Paris is going to cost a lot more than Los Angeles to San Francisco. Some airlines fly certain routes while other ones don't.

The price of each of those trips can also vary depending which day of the week and time of day you depart and return. Tuesday and Wednesday are usually the cheapest days of the week to travel. This is partly because business travel is lower on those days. People flying away for the weekend are flying on Friday and coming back on Sunday. Business travelers are often flying on Sunday so they can be there for their Monday morning meetings. Many times you won't be flying on Tuesday or Wednesday, but if you do it can save you some money. Nothing is carved in stone with the airline business and things are always changing, but you can do a lot of price comparison online with fantasy flights to learn more about how the airline business works.

The earliest flights of the day are usually cheaper than the later flights. Many people don't want to be at the airport at 6:00 a.m., so the airlines may offer cheaper fares on those early flights. A struggling music group doesn't have the luxury of choosing more expensive flights so that they can sleep in longer. Check every flight to find the lowest fares, and if your departure time is flexible, you could save some money.

Many airlines offer group discounts for ten or more passengers when the tickets are all bought at the same time, but right now you won't be able to get a group discount buying the tickets on sites like Expedia. You'd need a travel agent to contact the airline's rep or you'd have to contact them directly for these group fares. Always check the fares online because sometimes you can still get fares online even cheaper than the group discount the airline offers, but restrictions usually apply.

Another thing to remember when booking airfares for your group is to check nearby cities for cheaper fares. If your tour is ending in New York City and you're flying out the next morning, don't just go and buy flights from JFK without checking Newark Liberty International in Newark, New Jersey, or LaGuardia Airport in Queens, New York, or Philadelphia International in Philadelphia, Pennsylvania. LaGuardia airport is only ten miles from New York City, Newark International is only thirteen miles, and Philadelphia International is only one hundred and five miles from New York City.

If you can save $100 each on ten airfares to fly out of Philadelphia as opposed to JFK, that's $1,000 you've saved the band by driving only two hours to that airport. It's worth the drive. If everyone is staying on the bus for the night and the driver is merely pulling up to the airport at the designated time to drop you off for the flight, driving two hours to Philly is no skin off your nose to save that kind of money. Always check nearby cities for cheaper fares.

One of the things that I always try to do for my entourage is check them in online so I can make sure they have the best seats possible and print out their boarding passes for them. On some flights, you aren't able to choose seating assignments when you book the tickets. In this event, you definitely want to always check them in online the day before so you can try to get them the best seats possible. Your options for choosing seats increase, of course, when you have elite status on the airline.

Even if you were able to get good seats when you bought the tickets, sometimes you can get even better seats the day before the flight because other people have canceled their flight. It's worth checking each time.

The airlines will only let you check in twenty-four hours before the flight. If your flight departs at 8:00 p.m. on Friday, get online at 8:00 p.m. on Thursday and check everyone in so you can get them the seats that they want. Don't wait until you show up at the airport the next day because the flight could be full and you may find that your entire entourage is stuck in middle seats if you didn't already have seating assignments.

Even if you know that everyone is in the seats they prefer, I'd still check them in online because you could find out that even though they're in seats that match their preference, they could all be in the back of the plane. There might be better available seats up front so they can get off the plane quicker. If you have only a short amount of time to catch a connecting flight, getting off the plane quickly is a good thing.

There might be emergency row seats with more leg room available for your taller people. Some airlines won't let you choose an emergency row seat online because they insist on seeing the passenger in person to make sure that they're not a child, an elderly person, or someone who is incapacitated and unable to assist in case of an emergency. Some people are simply unwilling to assist in case of an emergency. Some airlines do allow those with elite status to choose an emergency row seat online, but you have to answer certain questions first to qualify.

When I check in my entourage online, I always get them the best seats possible and then print out their boarding passes for them. This saves a little time at the airport, but if you have baggage to check it really doesn't save much time because the CSR will print out the boarding pass when you check in your luggage. If by some lucky chance everyone is flying with only carry-on baggage, then you don't even need to go to the counter, except for some international flights, if you've already printed out boarding passes. You can go straight to the gate. This saves a lot of time if the lines are long at that time of day.

You'll need to make sure that you have the confirmation numbers for each ticket to check in online. If a travel agent booked the flights for you, make sure they sent you a list of the confirmation numbers. If you booked the flights online, make sure you print out the information for each flight as you book them.

Always be at the airport with your group at least two hours before departure for a domestic flight and three hours before departure for an international flight. You'll be in charge of a group that'll probably have a lot of luggage and gear to check in, and that will take much longer than a couple going on vacation with only two bags to check. Don't miss a plane and see a show go down the toilet and your job behind it because you showed up at the airport with your group too late. I'd rather be too early than too late.

Most of the groups I've worked with prefer to get there early so we can be the first in line, get checked in, and go and sit in the restaurant or bar near the gate and relax, knowing that we have no worries about missing the flight and jeopardizing an important show.

Whenever I check my group in at the airport, I always do it myself unless we're overseas in a country where there's a language barrier and we have a promoter rep with us. In that case, I'll let him help me with the check-in and translate if necessary.

Even if we have boarding passes already printed out, we still have to check the luggage. Because of all of the new security rules due to terrorism, you will usually need everyone in the entourage with you to check the luggage.

Some airlines allow a certain number of bags to be checked for free for each person, depending upon your frequent flyer status. Anything beyond that amount will be considered excess baggage, and you can be charged extra for it. Because of this, you certainly wouldn't want to get in line yourself with ten pieces of luggage belonging to the entire entourage, even if the airline would let you, because you'd end up paying for excess baggage on nine pieces of extra luggage beyond the free one they give you. You want to spread the luggage across everyone in your entourage to reduce any potential excess baggage charges.

If you only have ten people and ten pieces of luggage to check in and the airline allows you one free bag per person, you shouldn't be charged for any excess baggage as long as those bags aren't oversize or overweight. Some airlines will charge you for every bag you check in if you don't have elite status. You need to check the airline's website to see their fees for checked baggage. You should do this when you do the tour budget so this expense is covered in your tour budget.

I always get my group in line together and stand at the front of the line. When I get to the check-in desk, I explain to the CSR that I have a group of ten people and we've already checked in online and have our boarding passes printed out, but we need to check the luggage. They will still need to see identification for everyone and match it to a face. You can use a driver's license or state identification card if you're flying domestically in the U.S., but you'll need a passport if you're flying internationally, and that now includes Canada. Everyone must be present when you're checking in. No one can be hanging out in the bar or smoking a cigarette outside, or they will delay the process.

Have everyone's passport in your possession when you get up to the check-in counter. Explain quickly that you're a music group and you need to check everyone in. Hand the CSR the passports for the band so the CSR checks in the band first. If the flight is nearly sold out, you want to make sure that the band has first choice of the remaining seats if you don't already have seating assignments. Don't just hand her a stack of ten passports and let her check in the crew first and have the band end up in the worst seats. Your job, first and foremost, is to look after the band, then the crew. Don't ever disregard the crew's needs or make them feel unimportant, but the band has to come first.

Make sure you specify to the CSR each band member's seating preference so she puts them in the correct kind of seat. Ask them if each band member's frequent flyer number has already been entered into the system if your travel agent booked the flights. If it is, you're golden; if not, you need to give the CSR the band members' frequent flyer numbers. Always have a printout or a memo file on your smart phone handy with your entourage's frequent flyer numbers for that airline so you can hand it to the CSR.

You should always remind everyone to keep their boarding passes until they check their mileage account a few days after the flight—a few weeks for partner airlines—to make sure that their miles were credited to their account. If for some reason they're not, they'll need the ticket number off the boarding pass to get credit. Many airlines allow you to request mileage credit online at their websites. You may need to wait a few weeks before applying for credit with a partner airline. You can't use the ticket confirmation number, also known as the locator number, to request mileage credit. You must have the individual ticket number because the tickets for the entire group could be booked with the same group locator number. If their frequent flyer number is printed on the boarding pass, then it's in the system.

Once you've checked in all of the band members and the CSR has printed out their boarding passes, hand out the boarding passes and passports to the band so they can be on their way to the gate area. Don't let them stand there waiting while you check in five or six crew members, but always ask the CSR if it's now okay to send the band on their way, just to be safe.

Finish checking in yourself and the crew and then you're done with the check-in process. In some airports, you may have to take large oversize items, such as guitars and big gear cases to another location in the airport because they can't go down the baggage conveyor or they need to go through a security scanner. So you don't want to allow all of the crew to go to the gate until you're sure you're completely done.

Make sure you always know what gate your flight is departing from and what time it's boarding. Be sure you've told this to everyone in your entourage as you hand them their boarding pass and passport. Don't just assume they'll read the boarding pass. Say it for the record.

You'd be surprised how many times someone will look at the boarding pass for the wrong leg of the flight and go to the wrong gate at the wrong time and miss the flight because they just quickly glanced at the wrong boarding pass, especially if they're drunk or hung over from the night before. You'll quickly learn which people in your entourage are capable of such mistakes. If it's a crew member, read them the riot act so they never let it happen again. If it's a band member, get used to it. It'll probably never change.

You may think you're treating them like children, but if one of them misses the flight, you'll have to deal with the difficult situation that ensues. Always make sure everyone knows what's going on. As the boarding time for the flight nears, start to count the members of your entourage at the gate and see who is missing. Make sure you know where they are. If they're still nowhere in sight when the flight starts to board, call them or go and find them.

Never be the first person on the plane. Always sit at the gate and count each of your people as they get on the plane. When the last person has gotten on the plane, then you can board.

Always hold the baggage claim checks in case the airline has lost any luggage when you arrive at your destination. You don't want to be chasing everyone all over the airport trying to retrieve baggage claim checks that you should already have in your possession.

Dealing with lost luggage is no great mystery. You simply take the baggage claim tags into your airline's baggage office, which is usually right there in the baggage claim area, give them your baggage claim tags, and fill out a brief form with your contact info, description of your missing bags, and where the bags can be delivered in the next twenty-four hours. Forrest Gump pissed-drunk on absinthe, hallucinating green fairies, could easily handle this simple process.

BACKLINE RENTALS AND ENDORSERS

If you're working with a new band on their first tour overseas, you're probably going to be renting backline for the tour. You can check amplifiers, guitars, and small spares cases on the plane, but things such as guitar cabinets and large drum cases will be too heavy and probably too big. You can separate your drums into individual hard plastic cases that can be checked on the plane, and other smaller items can be checked, but large pieces of gear are impossible to check on a plane.

The airlines have strict rules about overweight and oversize items. Because of this, you'll most likely be renting backline overseas if your band doesn't have gear endorsements that provide them with loaner gear for the tour.

There are some good companies in Europe and the U.K. where you can rent backline for the tour. John Henry's Ltd. and Music Bank, both in London, are the leaders in the United Kingdom. Captured Live in Essen, Germany, is a popular company from which to rent backline in Europe.

If you're starting and ending your tour in the U.K. or flying in and out of London Heathrow because it makes financial and logistical sense, you'll probably want to rent your backline from a company in London. Chances are you've also leased your tour bus or splitter van in the U.K. for the same reasons. If you're using a bus company from Europe and flying in and out of Europe, it will probably make sense to use a European backline company.

No matter what you do, always get quotes from three different vendors on anything you rent for the sake of cost comparison. This is a good learning process for you so you can learn what these things cost to rent.

You'll need to know the dimensions of your trailer or the cargo hold in your splitter van so you can make sure that all of your gear is going to fit. The backline rental company can be helpful in giving you some idea how much space your rental gear is going to take up—even if they have to stack it up in a square block in their shop and measure it—but you must also take into consideration the additional gear you're bringing over on the plane and the amount of merch you're carrying to sell.

I cannot stress enough how much you need to be on top of this situation until you've gained enough experience to make a better assessment of these matters. You don't want the bus and trailer to show up at the backline rental company to pick up your gear and discover it won't all fit into the trailer.

If you're flying into London, the bus driver will usually have no problem picking up the backline for you so it's already in the trailer when the bus picks you up at the airport. They're used to doing this, and the backline companies are also used to having their people load the trailer in your absence. You may have to do some repacking once you load your gear that you brought over on the plane, but at least the gear is in the trailer.

If you're a band coming to tour in America and need to rent backline gear, a popular company here is SIR. They have many locations around the U.S. and also provide audio rentals and many other services.

For an American band touring in Europe and the U.K., anything you rent over there is probably going to cost you more than what it would cost to rent that same gear in the United States because of the exchange rate of the U.S. dollar against the British pound and the Euro. So you'll want to rent only what you need. If your band can afford it, and they expect to tour often overseas, buying duplicate gear and renting a storage unit is always an option. Many of the backline rental companies also offer storage lockers to rent.

Until your band becomes more popular, it will be difficult for them to obtain endorsement agreements that will provide them with free loaner gear. Many companies offer discounts to their new endorsees, but many of them will have to wait until they're more established before they can expect loaner gear for a tour.

The amount of loaner gear available is limited. Depending on the time of year, it can be impossible for even popular acts to obtain loaner gear. Every company is different, and their requirements for endorsements may differ. It's always best for the manager to contact the Artist Relations representative and see what their requirements are for endorsing a new artist.

When your band has an endorsement with an instrument company, you'll often receive your loaner gear from a backline rental company such as John Henry's Ltd. in London or Captured Live in Germany. Even though the gear is being given to you rent-free from your endorser, you will usually still have to rent the road cases for that gear from the backline rental company you're getting the loaner gear from, and there's little chance that they're going to let the gear leave their shop without road cases or allow you to use your own. They have to get something out of being the loaner gear distributor for your endorser. They'll also probably charge you a small preparation fee for their work, but all of this is still much cheaper than having to rent the gear.

Drum risers are impossible to check on planes because of their size, but you can rent one from a backline rental company if you have enough space in your trailer. Most venues will have a drum riser for your band to use if you can't afford to rent one, but you never know what you're going to get. It may not be the exact size that your drummer prefers, or the riser may be in bad condition from too much use and abuse.

If your band is the headliner, you can always add a provision to your rider requiring the promoter to provide a drum riser for each show. As long as you're a little flexible on the specs of the drum riser, the promoter can usually get what you need.

TOUR CREDENTIALS

On December 8, 2004, everything changed.

There was once a day when backstage passes were handed out on tour as if they were invitations to an open party. Back in the old days, if you were a beautiful girl or a guy who brought "gifts" for the band and crew, it was pretty easy to lay your hands on a backstage pass. Then some deranged psycho with a gun walked on stage at the Al Rosa Villa night club in Columbus, Ohio, and killed legendary Damageplan/Pantera guitarist, Darrell "Dimebag" Abbot and four others that night.

From that day forward, I always reminded myself that the real reason those backstage passes were made was to keep the band and crew safe. Most of the fans in the audience are good people, who just want to see their favorite band perform, but there is always the chance of a lunatic being in every audience, and we need to remember that. As road managers, we must do our job to protect the people in our charge.

There are numerous companies that can satisfy your needs for satin passes and laminates. Otto Printing & Entertainment Graphics started it all. They've been around since the mid '70s and are one of the best in the business. They're also credited with being the company that created the satin cloth backstage pass.

Tour Supply is the leader in providing concert tours with every type of supplies you could possibly need. Their sister company is Tour Supply Ink, and they design and manufacture tour passes, as well as custom drum heads and other related printing products.

There are other companies, such as Cube Services, Inc., Bandpasses.com, Backstage Design & Printing, and Band Pass Ltd. in Surrey, England, that make tour credentials.

Satin passes, also known as stick-on passes, are the cloth passes that guests receive. The laminate is the plastic all-access pass that a person normally wears around his neck with a lanyard.

Today, you'll see some band and crew members with their laminate attached to their belt with a lanyard. This bad habit has always been a pet peeve of mine. Your laminate is a security device, not a fashion accessory. It needs to be visible so security can immediately see it; they shouldn't have to visually scan your entire body as if they're on some kind of Easter egg hunt, trying to find a laminate that should be hanging around your neck. It's also much easier for someone to snatch your laminate from you when it's dangling around your knee. They can also be easily torn off on a road case, and you won't even notice it until some stranger has already picked it up from the floor and is running wild backstage. And, no, the satin pass you just gave your new girlfriend of the day doesn't go on her great ass, it goes on her great chest so security can easily see it.

The first thing you need to do before ordering your passes is to create the artwork. If you're skilled with programs such as Photoshop, you can create this artwork yourself. Most of the pass companies have their art submission specs on their website.

If there's no one in your organization skilled at creating artwork, these companies can do it for a reasonable fee. You just need to send them the band's logo, album cover art, or any ideas that you might have, and they'll put together some artwork for your approval.

Once the art is done, you'll need to decide how many satin passes and laminates you'll need for the tour. The first thing I'll always do is calculate the number of satin passes I'll need for my group. If our rider says we get thirty tickets per night on our guest list, then I know that we can potentially have thirty guests every night of the tour. This doesn't mean we'll have that many each night, but if the band has been around a long time, they may have a lot of friends in every city.

The record company will usually send you a guest list for their press people, and many of them will be photographers who will need a photo pass. You might have endorsement companies that send their reps down to the show, and of course, you will want to give them passes to keep them supporting your band.

Let's say you have thirty shows on a six-week tour—five shows a week is usually the norm. Thirty shows times thirty guests each night equals nine hundred satin passes for the tour, but you also have to consider the number of working passes you'll need each day for the local crew, runner, catering people, and other workers at the venue. If you have four stagehands and one runner on call for each show, that's another five passes per show you'll need. The promoter and his immediate staff will also need passes, so I'll add another five passes for each show to cover them. That's another ten passes per show in my calculation. So forty passes a show times thirty shows equals twelve hundred satin passes.

You also need to worry about the support acts. If the first band on the bill is guaranteed five tickets a night and the second band is guaranteed ten tickets per night, I'll add another fifteen tickets times thirty shows, which equals four hundred and fifty passes, to my total count. The grand total now comes out to sixteen hundred and fifty satin passes. To cover myself, so I don't run out before the tour is over, I'll just round this number out to two thousand satin passes. If I have passes left over at the end of the tour, I can use them on the next leg if we don't change the art.

If you're a new band on a tight budget, you might not be able to order this many satin passes. You can only buy what you can afford. Order what you can order, but you get better price breaks the more you order at one time.

In time, you'll be better able to gauge what you'll use on each leg. Many groups don't want a lot of guests backstage. Unless it's family or close friends, many guests will just get a free ticket and that's it. Each band and what they prefer is different.

The next thing we have to do is determine how many laminates we'll need to make. First, I will calculate the total number of people in my touring entourage, including the drivers. Then I will add in the total number of people in the support acts' entourages. I know this number because I've obtained these facts from their road managers.

If my group has a touring entourage of twelve people including the bus driver, and the first act has six and the second act has eight, I know I need twenty-six laminates for the immediate touring entourage. We'll also have band managers, agents, record company people and band wives and girlfriends showing up at one point or another for each band, and we'll need to accommodate those people.

I don't get crazy with the support acts. I'll normally order an additional ten laminates for each support act and that's it. After that, their VIPs get VIP satin passes. My group has to pay for these passes, and there has to be some limit as to how much we can spend on the support acts. If you don't set some limits for them, before you know it, everyone in their family tree is walking around with laminates that your band had to pay for.

For the support acts, I normally limit laminates to their touring entourage, their manager, their agent, the band members' wives or girlfriends, and maybe a top level record label person. The rest of them get a VIP satin pass or maybe a working pass, depending on who they are.

> Headliner: 26 laminates
> Direct support act: 18 laminates (8 for entourage and 10 extras)
> First support act: 16 laminates (6 for entourage and 10 extras)
> Grand total: 60 laminates (five dozen)

Now that I've worked up the number of laminates for my touring entourage and the support acts, I need to add in the extras that I think I'll need for my group. This is always difficult to estimate, and I'm always reordering laminates throughout the tour because everyone seems to be a VIP these days. Depending on my band's budget, I may be carrying a laminator and pouches and make them myself as long as I have the printed passes.

I'll usually calculate the number of all the people connected with my group that will probably show up at one point on the tour (manager, agent, publicist, record company department heads, wives, and girlfriends) and then add another two dozen to that number. So, let's add twenty-four more laminates to our previous grand total of sixty and we have eighty-four, seven dozen laminates to order.

Keep in mind that I almost never use the same laminate for the support acts and their guests that I use for my entourage and our guests. I will normally make an All Access laminate for my group and their guests and a separate Support Act laminate for the support acts and their guests who get a laminate. This way, I can limit what the support acts and their guests can and can't do and where they can and can't go backstage. I'll always make the Support Act laminate with a different background color than our All Access laminate so it's easily distinguishable from our pass.

So now we're going to order two thousand satin passes, fifty all-access laminates for my group, and thirty-six (rounded off to three dozen) support laminates for the two support bands.

Before we can get the quote, we need to decide on a few other things first. We can easily drive up the cost of the satin passes by making separate After Show, VIP, Working, and Photo passes, each printed in four different colors, making it easier for security to quickly tell which pass the guest is wearing, or we can make one combined pass in four different colors to save money.

Most bands are always on a tight budget, so we're going to make one satin pass in two different colors that covers all four passes we'll need. If you look at the pass below—a sheet I made for a tour I did with my longtime client Testament using Excel and the art from the pass company—you'll see that it has a blank box where we can use four rubber stamps made with all four pass designations: After Show, VIP, Working, and Photo. If we want that pass to be a Photo pass, we will stamp it with the Photo rubber stamp. We can use the red pass for the Photo pass and Working pass, and then make the VIP pass and After Show pass blue for this show day.

SECURITY PASS SHEET

ARTIST

Testament All Access Laminate
All access anywhere, any time.
Escort allowed.

SUPPORT

Support Act Laminate
No stage or Testament dressing room access
during Testament show. No escort allowed.

RED
Working: All access. No dressing rooms
VIP: All access, no stage access, no escort.
After show: 30 minutes after show only.
Photo: First 3 songs, no flash.

BLUE
Working: All access. No dressing rooms.
VIP: All access, no stage access, no escort.
After show: 30 minutes after show only.
Photo: First 3 songs, no flash.

We could print this pass in four different colors so each of the four passes has its own color designated for each day, but it would cost more. The passes should be bright colors that can be seen easily by security in low-light situations. I will normally use red, blue, green, and orange, but you can use any colors that suit your group's vibe. Metal bands always seem to make black passes—like everything else they own—but these are difficult for security to see in the dark.

If we had the budget for four different colors, the After Show pass could be red, blue for VIP, green for Working, and orange for Photo. Four different colors will also enable us to rotate them each day should we be in a city today that is very close to the city we played last night. By rotating the colors, we won't have to worry about the people from last night showing up tonight when they're not on the list. The rotation of colors helps security watch out for this sort of thing.

Some bands will just make one pass in one color and have VIP, Photo, Working and After Show printed on the satin pass and use a black Sharpie to black out Photo, Working and After Show to make a VIP pass, for example. Do what you can afford.

You'll always want to stamp each pass with a code and date. I usually use a rubber stamp or a black Sharpie and just put that day's date and a city code on the front of the satin pass. For Los Angeles, I'd just mark "LA" on the pass or "NY" for New York.

Once we've determined how we're going to make our satin passes, we need to determine how we're going to make the laminates. You can order laminates that are cheaper two-color laminates or laminates with full color art from the band's new album cover. Pass companies also offer laminates in different sizes and thickness.

We live in the digital age. Guests can use their cell phone camera to shoot a high resolution picture of your pass in full color and upload it to the internet in a minute. There are some fans that will do anything to get backstage, and it's easy for them to make a bootleg pass. For this reason, many of the pass companies offer security devices, such as holograms embedded in the artwork and identifying watermarks printed on the back of the laminates, to help solve this security problem.

Many groups will put a picture of each person and their name on the back of the laminates. In the end, security has to be efficient in keeping an eye out for bootleg laminates, and it's your job to make sure that they're doing this.

Some bands will also make VIP laminates for their more important guests. These laminates will usually provide them with all access backstage but will come with certain restrictions, such as no stage or dressing room access during the show. It's really up to you what you and your band prefer.

If you're going to put everyone's photo and name on the back of each laminate, you'll need to have a laminating machine so you can laminate the pass after you've attached the photo and name on the back of the laminate. Most pass companies also sell these machines, as well as the plastic pouches that you'll need.

You can use your camera on your cell phone to take a picture of each person and then transfer it to your laptop via email, Bluetooth, or a USB cable. Then you can insert the photo into a Microsoft Word document, resize it, type the person's name underneath it, print it out in color, cut it out, and then use a glue stick to attach it to the back of the laminate insert. Then you simply place the laminate insert into a plastic pouch and run it through the laminating machine. By the way, there are also some Avery labels that are close enough in size for a laminate that you can print the picture on directly and just peel them off and place them on the back of the laminate insert, saving the gluing part of the process. Avery has downloadable templates for Word for all of their labels.

If you don't plan on putting photos and names on the back of the laminates, the pass company can laminate the passes for you so they're ready to be used when you receive them. You can also order other things, such as lanyards and blank security pass sheets, from them, although I usually make my own pass sheet in case I want to change anything on it.

You can use Microsoft Word or Excel to easily make your own pass sheets, which is what I always do. It's easy to take the artwork for each pass and resize it and insert it into a Word or Excel document to make your pass sheets. Then you can type in whatever instructions you desire below each pass on the sheet.

If we take a look at the security pass sheet, we have four satin passes listed on the sheet. The first pass is the Working pass. This pass is given out to the local crew working our show that day. We give these to the stagehands, runner, caterers, promoter's staff, the venue's staff that need to come backstage, and anyone else who's going to be working on stage or backstage during the show day.

It's important for the band members to be able to see a working pass on the caterers when they suddenly walk into the dressing room to set up the band's dressing room catering. Otherwise, they won't know who these people are. We want our crew to be able to quickly determine that some guy standing on stage is one of the stagehands and not some fan that just walked in the back door. Working passes are important so we know who all of the people are that are coming and going backstage.

The next satin pass is the Photo pass. These are given out to photographers that will be shooting the show from the security barricade in front of the stage. The norm is that we allow the photographers to shoot the first three songs with no flash. We have this rule for a number of reasons. Once the show starts, it's usually mania for the security guards in the barricade, especially for a metal show. The crowd begins to go nuts, people are crowd surfing and landing in the barricade, and it's difficult for security to deal with the fans when the barricade is filled with photographers shooting the show. So we limit the photographers to the first three songs.

We don't allow photographers to use flash because it's annoying to the band when they are constantly being blinded by flash for the first three songs of the show. You've been blinded by flash when you've had your picture taken before. Imagine what it's like when you have a dozen cameras going off in your face at one time non-stop for fifteen minutes. It's also a safety issue for the band. They could be blinded by the flash and accidentally step off the front of the stage and fall into the barricade and be seriously injured. The show and the entire tour could be canceled because of it. It also makes the show look horrible with a lot of cameras blowing off bright flash for the first fifteen minutes of the show, especially if the songs call for a dark, moody light show.

If we have any video people shooting the show from the front of the house, we make sure that they have a photo pass so our sound engineer and lighting designer know that they're authorized to be there and are allowed an audio feed from the sound console. We normally only let video people shoot the first song of the show, but this is really up to each individual band and what has been agreed upon.

If a photographer is coming to the venue before the doors open to do a photo shoot with the band, I will usually not give them a photo pass because it's just a waste of passes. I know who the photographer is and that he's leaving the venue when the photo shoot is over. If he's also going to be shooting the show, he'll pick up his photo pass when the box office opens. If it's a photographer I've known for a long time, I might give him his photo pass early so he doesn't have to stand in line to get it.

Next we have the VIP satin pass. The limitations you put on the VIP pass are up to you and will be different for every band, depending on what they want. Normally, a VIP pass will have the same privileges as an all access laminate, except that it doesn't allow the guest to come on stage or go in the dressing room during the show unless they're escorted by someone in our entourage with an all access laminate. The VIP laminate is exactly the same as a VIP stick-on. It's just more of an ego stroke for that person to have a laminate hanging around their neck.

The last satin pass is the After Show pass. This pass has the least amount of access and is often nothing more than a souvenir. I normally don't allow after show passes backstage until thirty minutes after the show is over unless I have a secure area backstage where I can stash them until the band is ready to see them.

Once the show is over, security will immediately start to clear the venue of everyone inside who doesn't have a pass. If you coordinate with security in your security meeting that all after show passes are to be directed to the stage left entrance, for example, they will know to tell each guest with a pass to go to that entrance and wait until it's time for them to be allowed backstage so no one throws them out of the venue.

If the band has after show guests and plans to visit them after the show, I will try to find somewhere backstage to place these guests and let the band know where they can find them. People with after show passes are often people that the band wants to do something special for but not someone that they necessarily want in the dressing room. They may just want to do a quick meet-and-great, say hello, sign an autograph, take a photo, and then go back to the dressing room and do what they do.

When the band is done seeing the after show guests, it's up to you to have these guests escorted out of the venue so they're not running rampant backstage, getting into God knows what. Once they've been walked out the back door, tell security that after show passes are now no longer valid to keep the guests from getting back in.

No matter how specific your security pass sheet is and how much time you spent on a security meeting, some of these security guards will make mistakes. Most security people are pros that know how to do their jobs correctly, but when you're doing small clubs, the security personnel can be inexperienced or badly trained. This situation is never good, but you'll have to make the best of it.

The all access laminate that we use for our entourage is exactly what it says: ALL ACCESS, ANYWHERE, ANY TIME. Our all access laminate usually allows our people to escort, meaning if someone in our entourage wants to bring someone with an after show pass backstage before the show is over, they're allowed to do that. If you decide to suspend the escort privilege for all access laminates, you can merely delete it from the security pass sheet for that day and explain that fact at the security meeting to make sure they understand it.

The support act laminate is an all access laminate just like ours, but it has a few restrictions. We don't allow support act laminates to escort, EVER. We don't allow support act laminates on stage during our show unless they're given the okay by our stage manager. We have this rule because it's distracting for the audience and takes them out of the moment when watching the show. It's also a headache for the backline crew because these guests are in their way while they're trying to do their jobs.

We also don't allow the support act laminates in our dressing room unless they're escorted by an all access laminate or until I tell the security guard that is guarding our dressing room that it's now okay to admit VIP passes and support laminates into the dressing room.

This is why it's always important to have a security guard stationed at the headline band's dressing room. Even though we may say certain things on the security pass sheet, you never know when we may want to momentarily cut off access to the dressing room because the band is having a casual after-show meeting or a knockdown, drag-out fight.

I'll always look after a new support act tour manager if he shows respect, follows my rules to the letter and causes me no headaches. At the beginning of a tour, I'm pretty firm with a new support act tour manager and his band if I don't know what to expect from them. If they act like professionals and prove to me that I can trust them, I will usually give them whatever they need for passes, even beyond their allotted ticket amount. I'll also start to relax a bit on the restrictions for their support act laminates if they're cool, follow the drill, and are becoming friends with my entourage.

I will sometimes give the support act tour manager one of our all access laminates so he can escort guests once he knows the limits and where the line is drawn with me. It's been a rare occurrence that I've ever had any problems with support acts or their crew. They've all been smart enough to tell that I'm not going to put up with any shenanigans from them for a single second, but there's still a certain wall that you must maintain between them. If you don't, they'll try to walk all over you, and you'll have chaos on your hands. Don't ever let this happen.

Once you've gotten your quotes and decided which company you're going to use and figured out how many passes you can afford, you can place your order. You should make sure that you've got enough time to get the passes made and shipped to you before the tour starts. You don't want to get to the first show and find out that your passes aren't going to arrive that day because of some delay at the pass company.

If your band cannot afford any passes, most promoters and major venues have their own generic pass system to use when a tour doesn't have any passes. Just be sure to let the promoter rep know during your advance that you don't have your own pass system; and if you do, tell him that fact during your advance so he knows he doesn't have to prepare passes for your show. Don't waste their time because you weren't thorough in your advance.

Some venues will still insist on you using their wristbands or passes because they want to have more control over the number of people receiving passes. If they won't budge on this, in most cases you can still use your pass system in conjunction with theirs, or just save some of your passes that day and use theirs.

Always remember that your tour credentials are valuable security items that need to be kept under lock and key. They're not items to be left lying around on your desk in the production office because they can be stolen. You don't want your tour credentials given out to people without your knowledge or, even worse, sold to strangers that are capable of anything.

Twenty years ago I was on the road in the U.S. with one of my clients, a heavy metal band that's still very popular today. I still work with them. I didn't have a production case with a lock on it, so I kept all of the band's passes hidden in my bunk on the tour bus. I didn't want to worry about them being stolen from the production office.

As the tour progressed, I began to notice that our stock of passes was dwindling much quicker than it should've been. I was perplexed by this, and finally came to the conclusion that someone in our entourage was taking the passes from my bunk.

My suspicions were finally confirmed when I walked off the tour bus one evening and saw the band's singer in the parking lot selling his own passes to the fans for money to buy weed. And while this was very annoying back then, Testament's singer, Chuck Billy, and I laugh about this old story today.

Lock up your passes!

BACKDROPS, SCRIMS, AND STAGE SETS

It's not necessary for a road manager to know how to design backdrops, scrims, and stage sets. This is something that's usually handled by the band's lighting designer in conjunction with the band. Some bigger bands may hire a stage set designer to work in conjunction with their lighting designer on a stage set design. It's not something that you need to know everything about, but you do need to know some basics on how to get this work done.

The backdrop is the banner that hangs behind the band while they're playing on stage. Many times a backdrop will have the band's logo on it, graphics from the band's latest album or graphics that simply reflect the band's image and genre of music. If you've ever seen a Slayer show, you know that scenes of Satan, war, and destruction are common themes on their backdrops.

Backdrops can be made in any size, but the standard size for most mid-level acts is 40 feet wide by 24 feet tall. Arena acts will make often make backdrops that are 50 feet by 30 feet and even larger than that. It's really up to what your band wants and the size of the venues they're playing in, but the bigger the backdrop, the bigger the price. I usually have backdrops made in 40 feet by 24 feet because I normally fly the rear lighting truss at about 24 feet, and the backdrop is usually connected to the rear truss or hung right at the bottom of the rear truss. I normally make it 40 feet wide because that's the width of the usable area of your average stage.

In the old days, backdrops were hand-painted on sharkstooth scrim (if you wanted to light it from behind) or heavy canvas-type material and were more expensive because of the amount of labor that went into painting them. Today, most of those artists are out of business because of the advent of digital printing. This new process has not only brought the price of backdrops way down, but it's also greatly increased the turnover time of these products. With digital printing, backdrops can now be made in a few days as opposed to a few weeks when they were painted by hand. Digital printing has also cut the cost of backdrops in half, and the material that they use is much lighter and easier to handle.

There are plenty of companies out there that do this kind of work, although I don't recommend using just any digital printer. I always prefer to use a digital printer that has experience in making soft goods for music groups because they know our business and our needs.

Over the past few years, my long-time client, Testament, has used Acre Jean Ltd. in London for some of their backdrops and scrims. They do an excellent job, and their prices are good. For Megadeth in 2010, I used AAA Flag & Banner Manufacturing in Hollywood, California, for their backdrop and scrim needs. Like Acre Jean, they do great work and their prices are good with a quick turnover time. Testament now uses AAA Flag for most of their needs. You can visit either of their websites to view their art submission requirements necessary to have your products made.

Scrims are the banners that you sometimes see in front of the band's backline gear and attached to the front of the drum riser. These are usually attached to a metal scrim frame using Velcro fasteners and placed in front of the band's backline gear to give a more professional look to the band's stage set-up. It's essentially a cheaper type of stage set.

The scrims should match the backdrop's motif so they have a uniform look. Many times a band will also make a drum skirt that's attached to the front of the drum riser and matches the motif of the backdrop and scrims. All of this together makes a great looking stage set and gives the band's lighting designer something interesting to light, making the show look more professional.

The scrims in front of the backline are made on a thinner material than the backdrop because there are usually amps behind the scrims, and the volume of the sound should not be reduced and the quality sacrificed by any material placed in front of them. Most of the backdrops I've had made over the past few years have been made on Celtic cloth, but we're now using a fabric called Prodisplay, which allows brighter colors and a better looking image. This material takes a great digital printing and is lightweight and doesn't wrinkle when you fold it up.

Scrims are made on vinyl-type material that is referred to as 50 percent blow-through mesh. This material allows the sound to pass through it but is not so sheer that you can see what's behind the scrims. If you have no bass or guitar cabinets or monitors behind the scrims or drum skirt, you don't need blow-through mesh and can use the Prodisplay material. It looks much better than blow-through mesh.

Rock City Backdrops is a company that makes backdrops and scrims, and they also make lightweight scrim frames out of PVC material that can be easily taken apart, placed in a duffel bag, and checked on a plane. This is good when you're doing a lot of fly dates.

You can also have your scrim frames fabricated out of aluminum, which is more durable, but they're usually too big and heavy to check on a plane.

I will give you one design tip that is crucial when making soft goods for the stage: avoid using too much black in the design. This smart rule of thumb is violated more by heavy metal bands than any other genre of music because black has always been their color, but as cool as black may be, it doesn't light well.

I can never understand why a band spends thousands of dollars on backdrops and scrims that you cannot light, making them virtually invisible on stage, because the art had too much black in it. I've always explained this situation to a new band using this analogy: what color is the movie screen in a theatre? It's white; and it's white for an important reason.

The white movie screen reflects the light cast upon it by the movie projector and enables you to see the movie. What do you think you'd see if the movie screen were black? You'd see nothing because black absorbs the light; it doesn't reflect it. Most new bands simply don't have an experienced lighting designer to teach them these important things before they waste money making soft goods the wrong way.

Look at some of the Megadeth live photos at MarkWorkman.com. Notice how brightly lit the backdrop and scrims are and how powerful that stage set looks. How powerful do you think it would all look if it were black? It wouldn't look powerful at all. It would look pretty weak, and you wouldn't see much of it.

I had originally wanted to put color live photos into the printed version of this book, but it drove the cost of this book way too high for you. So please view them at my website, and I think you'll get the point of what I'm saying

Bands will often make a backdrop using the art from their latest album cover, even though the artwork contains many dark colors that don't light well. There's nothing wrong with having the artist who designed the album cover replace those dark colors with gray or white for the backdrop version of the art so it produces a backdrop that can be lit properly. Then you have a backdrop that allows the lighting designer maximum control over it.

Let the lighting designer turn the backdrop into red, blue, green, orange, or purple with the light he casts upon it. If you have a backdrop that contains an orange central image, for example, the backdrop will look great when you cast orange or red light upon it, but that image may not look so great when you cast some other contrasting colors on it and the two colors mix to make something that isn't pleasing. Let the lighting designer paint the backdrop.

There are, of course, exceptions to every rule. I've seen some bands make multi-color backdrops for use on outdoor festival tours when the band is playing in broad daylight every day. These backdrops all looked great, but they were only lit in white by the sun, for the most part. I've also seen great looking backdrops that were painted with invisible UV paint that light up in full color in the dark when a UV light (remember black lights) is cast upon them.

I created a backdrop and scrims like this for Mudvayne when I was their tour manager/lighting designer on the Projekt Revolution Tour in 2003. The backdrop was a giant Mudvayne logo and the scrims had a symbol from their album cover on them. When I blacked out the stage and turned on the UV light, the logo and symbols on both sides of the stage glowed in the dark and looked awesome.

If your band has moved up to bigger gigs and wants to carry a stage set, there are numerous companies that can build one for you. All Access Inc., with offices in Los Angeles, New Jersey, London, and Australia, is a great company that has built stage sets for Kiss, Nickelback, Madonna, and many others. They're one of the best. Accurate Staging is also another great stage set company with offices in Los Angeles, San Francisco, and Nashville. Brilliant Stages Ltd., about an hour north of London, is also a great set fabrication company that has been around a long time. They've built stage sets for bands such as Metallica, Iron Maiden, AC/DC, Aerosmith, The Rolling Stones, and Rammstein, to name a few. They're one of the best in the business.

Testament recently rented a stage set from Accurate Staging in San Francisco for American Carnage 2010. Many of these companies will also rent you a staging system for your tour if you don't have the budget to buy one. As you can see from the live photos on MarkWorkman.com, Testament's stage set featured a huge drum riser with a staircase on both sides of the drum riser, enabling the band members to walk up on top of the drum riser and out onto risers above the backline on each side of the stage.

The band had scrims made that attached to the front of the stage set pieces and a matching backdrop behind it. As you can see from the live photo, I had a great stage set to light. You'll notice that all of the gray and white in those soft goods lit up magnificently. The backdrop and scrims were all made by Acre Jean Ltd. in London from a design by Eliran Kantor in Berlin, the artist who designed the cover for Testament's CDs *The Formation of Damnation* and *Dark Roots of Earth*. Eliran also designed the cover of this book.

Always remember what I said about not using too much black in your soft goods design. This also applies to stage sets. There's a reason why the majority of the stage sets you've seen at concerts are made of silver metal grating or are painted with a predominant amount of silver, gray, or white paint.

For a fee, many of these companies can design your stage set for you based upon your design ideas if you don't already have an actual design to send to them. Like any other vendor you're dealing with, it always pays to shop around and get at least three quotes for the sake of price comparison, but always make sure that you're getting the same quality product when comparing prices. Every backdrop and scrim is not the same. Always make sure what kind of material they're using to make your soft goods when comparing quotes. If you get three quotes for a 40 feet x 24 feet backdrop and two of them come in around $3,500.00 and one of them comes in at $2,000.00, you should be asking a lot of questions about the cheaper quote before ordering.

TOUR SUPPLIES

One of the things you must get done when organizing a tour is order the supplies you'll need. This includes everything from gaffer tape, guitar strings, guitar picks, drum sticks, and drum heads to batteries and office supplies.

Some struggling bands live show to show and can't afford to buy all of their supplies at once, but if you can afford to purchase all of your supplies before the tour starts, you'll save money buying them in bulk.

This also saves you the trouble of sending the runner out every day to find the supplies you need. Trying to find guitar strings on Sunday in a small town that has only one music store that's closed is not a problem you want to have.

There are companies that specialize in supplies for music tours. Tour Supply is the leader in this business, and they have locations around the world. Guitar Center is another large company with many locations that can provide you with most of the items that you'll need. Music Bank and John Henry's Ltd., the backline rental companies in London, and Captured Live in Germany also sell tour supplies.

Most of these companies offer discounts for touring artists that are buying supplies in bulk. Buying a gross (twelve dozen) of 9 volt batteries is going to be cheaper than buying a four-pack every day on the road—and will save you the daily chore of finding them. You'll also save money on shipping when buying these supplies before the tour starts, rather than having orders shipped out every few weeks. Some companies offer open accounts for qualified touring artists, and your business manager can pay the bill each month.

Always make sure that the supplies are delivered to you before the tour starts so you know the supplies will be with you when you start the tour. Don't wait until the last minute to place your order just to find out that it won't make it to the first show in time.

If it's your first tour and you've never dealt with any of these companies, you only need to contact them and place your order. Once you start doing business with them, you'll often end up dealing with the same person every time. After a few orders, your company rep will begin to know your band's usual needs and a good working relationship is born.

These companies know that music groups on the road have very tight delivery time constraints and that the packages being shipped to you must arrive on the specified date, or you'll be gone to the next city and the packages will be chasing you across the country.

Always check with different companies and do price comparison before placing large orders. You never know when a company is having a sale on items that are overstocked or being phased out of their inventory. Just because they no longer plan to carry an item, you could have band members who insist on using that product.

If you're an American band going overseas to do a long U.K./European tour, you may want to buy your supplies in the U.S. and check them on the plane. The cost of those supplies will probably be more expensive when you consider the exchange rate of the U.S. dollar against the British pound or the Euro. Get a quote on your list of supplies from Tour Supply in America and Tour Supply in London, for example, and compare the cost of your order by converting the price from Tour Supply London into U.S. dollars.

Find out from Tour Supply USA how many boxes the order will ship in and what the estimated weight and size of those boxes will be. Check with your airline and determine what the charges will be for each piece of excess baggage. After doing those quick calculations, you'll usually find that you're saving money by buying the supplies in the U.S and bringing them on the plane with you and you may be able to talk the airline out of some of those excess baggage charges when you check in at the airport. It's worth the little bit of legwork. Even if the price ends up being the same, at least you can honestly say to your band that you did your job and made sure.

CARRYING SOUND AND LIGHTING

If you're a new tour manager working with a young band, it's highly doubtful that you're going to be carrying any production (sound and lighting), but there are a few things we should cover about this subject.

No manager is going to expect any tour manager to know everything there is to know about sound and lighting. All of that technical knowledge is way beyond the scope of any single book. There are many tour managers, like me, who do double-duty and are also lighting designers or sound engineers. On your first tour carrying some production, you'll most likely have a production manager who possesses a lot of knowledge about sound and lighting. If not, and you must deal with it, at least you'll know some basics after reading this chapter.

One of the first things you must take a close look at is the size of the venues you're going to be playing. This will immediately determine how much sound and lighting you should carry. If you're playing theatres, you don't need to carry enough sound and lighting for an arena tour.

Your first order of business is to send your list of tour dates with the capacity of each venue to three sound companies and three lighting companies. If they're major sound companies that have been around for a while, their people will have a pretty good idea how much audio gear you'll need to do those rooms. And, of course, if the band has an experienced FOH engineer, he'll also know what's needed for a tour of this size.

The same goes with lighting. If your lighting designer has been around the block a few times, he'll also know what size lighting rig you'll need. The lighting budget will often take a back seat to the sound budget. You must have a certain amount of PA to do a venue, but you can always do with less lighting gear if the budget is maxed out. It doesn't matter if the light show is the greatest one ever seen by mankind; if the sound is atrocious because you don't have enough PA, the show will be a failure for the fans. In the end, the band has to sound good before anything else.

It may sound strange to hear that coming from a lighting designer, but my years as a tour manager have taught me that if I'm going to do double-duty, I have to be the road manager first and make decisions with the best interests of the *entire* show in mind and not just the lighting. If you're going to work double-duty, you need to do the same.

There are many great sound companies around the world. Clair Brothers, Eighth Day Sound, and Thunder Audio are three of the leading audio providers in the United States. SSE Audio Group and Britannia Row Productions, both in London, are two of the best sound companies for any U.K. or European tour that you might do.

Some of the top lighting companies in the business are PRG, Bandit Lites, and Upstaging, Inc., but I prefer Gemini Stage Lighting & Sound in Dallas, Texas, because they've always looked after me and my clients very well and do an excellent job. To me, they're one of the very best in the world. Over the years, I've often used Neg Earth in London for the U.K./European tours that I've done. They're a top-notch company that's been around a long time.

Once you have a clearer idea of the size of the sound and lighting systems that you need to carry, you must take a close look at the amount of truck space that you'll need. Truck space will also dictate the size of the sound and lighting systems that you can carry. If you only have a budget for two tractor trailers and you must get sound, lighting, backline gear, and merch into both of these trucks, this already determines how much production you can carry.

If your tour can only afford one truck and you can't fit enough sound and lighting to do the shows into one truck, you'll have to carry what you can fit and have the promoters provide the rest locally. Many bands on smaller tours might only carry sound, monitor, and lighting consoles and maybe a monitor rig and a moving light package. The promoter would then provide the PA and the rest of the lighting rig that's needed. Every tour is different, depending on the budget and what's most important to the band.

I will first find out from the sound company how much truck space that they'll need for sound, then determine how much space we'll need for the band's backline, including any stage set we may be carrying, and that will tell me how much space we have left over for lighting.

Bands will often carry their merch on their trucks, but some of them will require their merch company to provide their own truck before they'll cut sound and lighting just to be able to carry their merch. This is an option to increase more room in the trucks for production, providing the band's merch deal allows it.

As a lighting designer, I'm good at doing a lot with a little. If I'm faced with having to scale down the lighting rig because of limited truck space, I may begin to rethink the types of instruments that I plan to use. I may decide that more powerful moving lights are necessary because I'll have fewer of them due to less truck space.

The trailer on a semi in the U.S. is 53 feet long, but some of the older trailers are 48 feet in length. Check with your trucking company on the exact dimensions of their trailers, and then begin speaking with the sound and lighting company to determine how much space their gear will require. The backline crew may have to measure their gear to determine how much total space you'll need for backline if they don't already know this information.

If you're carrying merch on the trucks, you'll need to find out how many boxes the merch company is planning to send to start the tour. These are usually all the same size boxes, and once you know how many they're sending, calculating the amount of space they take up is easy to do. Sometimes the merch company may have to start out with less merch and ship out additional stock more often if you're tight on space for production, but this, of course, increases merch shipping costs, which may affect the band's merch profits, depending on their deal with the merch company.

I've never done a tour carrying full production where we didn't have to shave down gear a bit to make it all fit into the trucks. This is normal—we always want more than what we really need—and, with some experience, you'll learn how to produce a reasonable "guesstimate" of how much space you'll need.

You'll also need to find out from the sound company and lighting company how many crew members each of them will need to send out to get those rigs up and down each day. This will obviously determine other factors such as how many bunks on the tour buses will be needed for those additional crew members. Once this is determined, you'll need to add their per diems (if negotiated), hotels, and airfares into your tour budget.

Some FOH engineers, monitor engineers, and lighting designers may be willing to do extra work and take the place of one of the sound and lighting crew members to make additional money. I've never met too many experienced sound engineers and lighting directors who would do this extra work for free unless they worked for the company. They'll all usually expect to earn more money for the additional work unless this was negotiated as part of their deal when they were hired. Helping out is one thing, working a second job from load-in to load-out is a whole other financial ballgame.

If they're willing to work on the sound and lighting crew, this will save the band money on hotels, per diems, and airfares, and you'll have fewer bodies on the tour buses, but you need to make sure that your crew members are capable of doing this additional work each day.

You don't want your sound engineer and lighting designer taking on the responsibility of this work and then slacking off. This will only cause resentments with the sound and lighting crew if their job becomes harder when it takes longer to set up and tear down the gear each day because your crew isn't doing the additional duties they've agreed to perform.

If you're going to be carrying sound and lighting, this will change some things in the show day's big picture. If you're only carrying backline on the tour, you'll probably be loading in each day around noon, maybe even later. Many promoters will fight you on this issue because it will cost them more in labor costs and increase their show expenses. If your band is extremely popular and the show is sold out or expected to sell out, anything is possible, but don't ask for time you don't need. I'm sure your crew would like to get some sleep once in a while.

When carrying full production, you may schedule your rigger to come in at 8:00 a.m. to mark his rigging points on the stage and venue floor. Breakfast for the crew would probably start around 8:30 a.m. and then load-in would begin at 9:00 a.m. with lighting coming in first. This is all subject to your show advance, but this is often what happens on a tour that's carrying full production.

Carrying sound and lighting will also increase the labor budget in the show costs because you'll need more stagehands and loaders to set up this equipment on time, and if it's a union hall, the costs will be even greater. Depending on the size of the sound and lighting systems you're carrying, the four stagehands you normally use for a trailer filled with backline gear will quickly go to twelve or sixteen or even more.

If you're not yet experienced in these matters, and you don't have an experienced production manager, the sound and lighting crew chiefs that the companies plan to send out on the tour can give you some advice on the number of stagehands and loaders you'll need each day. Please keep in mind that the promoter is going to have his strong opinion on the labor number you'll need each day because he has to shell out the money to pay for them, including the increased catering costs to feed them.

Another thing to consider is which city your trucks are coming out of and which city your sound and lighting gear is being picked up from. Your trucks will have to go to each of these companies and pick up the sound and lighting systems and bring them to the first city of the tour, and you will have to sort out these logistics.

You'll have to pay for the trucks from the day they start rolling, and you'll have to pay for the sound and lighting systems from the day they leave their respective shops. You'll keep paying for the trucks and both systems until they all get back home, unless you've negotiated something different. Try and negotiate down as much of the deadhead costs at the beginning and end of the tour as possible.

It's in your best financial interest to try and use sound, lighting, and trucking companies that are all in the same city, if possible, or at least in the same region. This will help to cut down on deadhead costs. The cost of fuel is becoming more expensive all the time. You

99

don't want trucks driving all over the country picking up and dropping off gear when you can avoid it. Deadhead costs for the tour buses are also a big expense to analyze, consider, and attempt to reduce.

Even though a band may not be able to afford full production, sometimes they may want to carry a lighting console and some moving lights and strobes or other instruments to give them a better show. The band may want to carry their own FOH and monitor consoles to increase the quality of their audio and so the consoles are for their use only and not shared by the other bands on the bill.

I've never had a problem with a support act lighting designer using my lighting console if he knows what he's doing and takes care of my gear, and I'm sure most FOH engineers feel the same way, but when the support act has an amateur crew that has no idea what they're doing and are drunk or out of their minds or higher than heaven on God knows what at 3:00 p.m., I don't need the stress of worrying if my console is going to be drowned in one of their beers while they're dancing on top of it during their show. In this case, they're using the house console. End of story.

Most sound and lighting companies are more than happy to rent you anything from a small amount of supplemental gear to a full rig, but you need to make sure you have enough space for it if you only have a fifteen-foot trailer on the back of your bus. Depending how much sound or lighting you want to carry, you'll need to make a pre-assessment of each venue so you can make sure that there's enough power in the venue to supply this additional gear. Promoters in small clubs and bars are going to balk at spending $700 to rent a generator to power your additional lighting if the venue doesn't have enough power to run it.

If you're carrying your own sound, monitor, and lighting consoles, you'll also need to make sure there's room in the venue to set them up. If you're doing a small bar or club tour, the venue may only have enough room for their house consoles, and they may not be willing to tear their gear down and worry about where they're going to store it so you can set up your consoles. If you're not allowing the support acts to use your consoles, and the venue has to tear down their consoles to make room for yours, what are the support acts going to use?

Some tour managers seem to think it is okay to turn their backs on the support acts and not care about them, but a good tour manager knows that they're part of the show, and he must solve this problem for the sake of a successful show.

You have to think ahead about these things. You don't want to waste the band's money carrying this additional gear and then find out that you're only going to be using it for two out of five shows a week. There's nothing economical about that, and you'll be the one catching hell from the band for paying for gear that's not being used.

On a club tour that's selling well, the promoter's not going to want to lose floor space in the venue to set up your additional consoles. This will take up space and could force him to reduce the capacity of the room or possibly violate fire and safety laws. If the show is already sold out, there's no way the promoter can reduce the venue's capacity because he's already sold the tickets.

So plan ahead and make sure that you're even going to have room to set up the gear you plan to bring on small club tours, and if you can't do the show without it, be sure to let the promoter know this from the beginning so he can reduce the amount of tickets he plans to sell to make room for your consoles.

This is an issue that should be addressed before the booking agent cuts the deal with the promoter, but your booking agent won't know you're carrying this gear and need the additional venue space unless you tell him. You can't wait until a show is sold out and then go back and tell the booking agent that you need the space of twenty-five customers to set up your sound and lighting consoles. It will too late by then because the promoter has already sold the tickets.

When getting your three quotes from the sound and lighting companies, they may not have the gear you require, but they may be willing to give you a discount on the gear they do have if you're willing to use alternative options. This may be worth considering if it makes the budget work.

No quote is carved in stone; it's just a starting point for negotiation. Don't get three quotes and just choose the lowest one. Go back and negotiate the quotes down with all three companies, and when you feel you've gotten them down as far as they will go, then choose the best company for the tour.

You may find better deals with smaller regional sound and lighting companies that are looking to build up their name by working with popular new acts on the rise. Sometimes it can be hard getting good deals from the bigger companies; they could be too busy with their bigger clients and just don't have any gear available. A smaller company that's willing to make an investment in the band, in hopes of them continuing to use the company in the future, can be a valuable connection, but you must make sure the crew they intend to send out on the tour is experienced and can get the job done on time each day.

It's highly unlikely that any band manager is going to hire an inexperienced tour manager for a tour that's carrying full production. It's just not done that way. But this is the music business and stranger things have happened. If you're working with a band that's suddenly becoming popular and they like you and want to keep you with them, ask a lot of questions of the people you're dealing with. Learn quickly and utilize the experience of the people at the vendor companies.

It's sink or swim time, baby.

There's more work involved when carrying production—but in many ways it makes life easier—and you have to be organized and fully informed to get the job done correctly.

Legendary basketball coach John Wooden once said, "Failing to prepare is preparing to fail." Don't ever forget those words.

FOREIGN ARTIST TAX

Artist tax is deducted from the fees paid to foreign music groups and artists.

The complexities of foreign artist tax are beyond the scope of this book, and no manager will expect you to be an expert on the subject; that's what tax accountants are for. Like the United States tax code, foreign artist tax rules change every year, and it's a job in itself keeping up with them.

If you're working for a new band, foreign artist tax probably won't be something you'll be dealing with that often in the beginning of their career. In many countries, a band's income is not subject to artist tax until they reach a certain income level in a calendar year. A new band might only tour a foreign country once during a calendar year, and their income may be so low that foreign artist tax isn't a factor. If your band is at a point where their income level is subject to foreign artist tax, there are a few things that you'll have to deal with.

If the band is from America, their U.S. business manager may work in conjunction with a U.K. tax specialist to reduce their artist tax deductions in the U.K. and Europe. Some U.S. business managers have offices overseas, in which case their foreign office will deal with these matters for the band. I've worked with Hardy Chandhok at Newman & Company in London many times, and he's one of the best.

The foreign tax specialist will usually require things, such as the band's tour budget and income for each country, to determine their tax liability there. The tax accountant will file the applicable forms with each promoter so he can reduce the artist tax when possible. You'll then be sent a list of those deductions so you know what's being deducted from the band's guarantees in each country.

For American bands touring Canada, the band's business manager will file the necessary artist tax waiver forms. The artist tax for Canada, at the time I'm writing this book, is 15 percent for any amount of income. If your band's only playing one show in Canada during the calendar year and their income is low, it might not even be worth the business manager's time—or the expense to the band—to file for the tax waiver.

If the band's only earning $500 for a show, and the tax deduction is $75, but it costs $200 to hire a tax accountant to file the tax waiver, what's the point in doing it? The band just lost $125. However, if the band is doing an entire Canadian tour and earning a lot of money, it's

Worldwide Artist Taxes For U.S. Bands		
Country	Tax %	Notes
Australia	30%	can be reduced by employing Australian biz accountant
Austria	20%	always email promoter to check to see if fee can be split
Belgium	18%	
Canada	15%	
Czech Republic	25%	
Finland	15%	
Germany	20%	biz accountant may be able to reduce if expenses are more than 40% of earnings
Great Britian	20%	biz accountant can file Reduced Tax application and get amount reduced
Greece	20%	
Holland	20%	tax free with passport info
Iceland	20%	
Israel	5.50%	check with promoter
Italy	30%	tax free for US artists if fee under $12K in 1 year, otherwise split contract 70% prod. costs
Japan	20%	reduced by paying airfares directly to travel agent
Luxembourg	11.11%	Contracts to be split
Mexico	25.00%	can be reduced by biz accountant
New Zealand	30%	same as Australia
Norway	15%	
Portugal	25%	promoter will usually pay some flight costs
Spain	24%	always email promoter to check to see if fee can be split
Sweden	15%	
Switzerland	25%	always email promoter to check to see if fee can be split
Turkey	20%	always email promoter to check to see if fee can be split

worth it to spend the money on the tax waiver. The band will get the deducted money back after they file their tax returns, but the Canadian government will still be holding on to that money in the meantime when the band needs it to pay bills.

Canada usually requires the passport and personal information listed below.

Skinny Girl Riot--Immigration Manifest								
#	Family Name	Given Name	D.O.B.	Citizenship	Place of Residence	Residence Status	Passport #	Social Security #	Artist/Staff
1	Starbright	Stanley	13-Jan-66	USA	California, USA	citizen	8980984058	555-38-8838	artist
2	Fabulous	Francis	30-Jun-62	USA	California, USA	citizen	3509831984	555-23-2324	artist
3	Giant	James	12-Mar-65	USA	California, USA	citizen	980498109	555-84-8302	artist
4	Massive	Michael	21-Apr-66	USA	California, USA	citizen	909840284	555-12-7376	artist
5	Twosticks	Thomas	13-May-69	USA	California, USA	citizen	983405823	555-08-3873	artist
6	Blinder	Robert Mortimer	22-Aug-66	USA	California, USA	citizen	2354647474	555-76-7393	staff
7	Loudnoise	Lancelot	19-Jan-66	USA	Texas, USA	citizen	2389328332	555-38-8390	staff
8	Racket	Richard	30-Apr-69	USA	Texas, USA	citizen	320908932	555-99-0383	staff
9	Spazo	Jeremy	14-Jul-64	USA	Georgia, USA	citizen	3209082308	555-88-5533	staff
10	Klown	Kyle	26-Nov-80	USA	Georgia, USA	citizen	3209808230	555-77-2200	staff
11	Tonedeaf	Anthony	29-Jan-83	USA	California, USA	citizen	4993837333	555-37-3700	staff
12	Tightpants	Penelope	04-Apr-92	USA	California, USA	citizen	9897898798	555-76-1114	staff

You'll also be required to email a PDF copy of the face page of everyone's passport to the promoter. I always compile the information above for each member of the touring entourage and make an Excel spreadsheet listing all of this information. Compile all of this information and store it and the passport scans in a folder in your computer entitled "Passport Info" or something similar. You'll also need this spreadsheet and the passport scans for immigration issues when they arise.

Many promoters will require that you provide them with an original copy of IRS Form 6166 at settlement to complete the artist tax requirements. Form 6166 is a form that your business manager will obtain from the IRS confirming that the band's company is a bona fide United States corporation.

The band's business manager will obtain as many original copies of this form as you'll need for an overseas tour. You'll need to make sure that you have these copies with you when you do settlement for each show. The promoters always require original copies, so you cannot scan one and then expect to print out a copy for each show settlement.

Foreign artist tax is nothing to be afraid of. You just need to make sure that you've received all of the applicable information that you'll need at settlement. Business managers are always swamped with many things to do for many clients. It's your responsibility to make sure that you have the information that you need for each show. If you don't have it as you're getting close to a show where you know an artist tax deduction will apply, be sure to contact the business manager or tax specialist and ask for the information that they've forgotten to send to you.

VISAS AND WORK PERMITS

There will be times when your entourage will require work permits or visas to enter certain countries, and you will need to compile and send off the applicable immigration information to obtain these documents.

As I explained in the chapter on foreign artist tax, compile an immigration spreadsheet that lists all of the information that's required and have passport scans for each member of your entourage in a folder in your computer. This enables you to quickly email a Zip file of that folder to anyone who may require it.

American bands touring the U.K. must apply for work permits to enter that country. This process has now become much easier. In the past, each member of your entourage was required to have an actual hard copy of the work permit when they entered the U.K., and the process to obtain them took weeks to complete.

Now it can be done faster, and you only need to print out a list of the certificates of sponsorship (work permit) codes and give each member of your entourage a copy to keep in their passport.

The band's U.K. booking agent will usually handle the process of obtaining the work permits for your entourage. Your only obligation is to send the booking agency the required information for each member of your entourage, and they will notify you when the process has been completed and send you a list of the C.O.S. codes.

There are some countries where this process can be complicated, so it's usually a good idea to hire an immigration service to help facilitate the process. Global Access Immigration Services in Los Angeles is a company that I've used many times for complicated visa issues. Traffic Control Group in New York City is another good company that I've also used in the past.

When applying for Russian visas for an American band, the passports must be presented to the Russian Embassy after your visa applications are approved by their government so the visas can be attached to the inside of each passport. There are only five Russian Consulates in the U.S.: Seattle, San Francisco, Houston, New York, and Washington, DC.

If your band doesn't live in any of those cities so you can go to the embassy and obtain the visas for your entourage, you'll need an immigration service to handle your visas for you. Even if I lived in one of these cities, I'd still want an immigration service to handle this process for me, as long as the band can afford it.

There are other countries, such as New Zealand and Japan, where your passports will have to be sent off to the applicable consulate so the visas can be attached to each passport. Due to terrorism, immigration laws have become stricter and change all the time. This is another reason using an immigration specialist for certain countries is a good idea and worth every dime that your band pays to them. Please remember that these rules are changing all the time for every country, but your immigration service will always update you on any changes in the application rules and procedures.

Some countries in South America, such as Brazil, Argentina, Peru, and Venezuela, require visas for American bands, and the visa must be attached to each passport by them at their individual consulates. Visas for Chile can be bought at the airport when you land, and they're good for the life of your passport. Visas for some countries, such as Mexico, are handled by the promoter directly. The promoter will send you the visa paperwork so your entourage has a hard copy of it in their passports when they enter the country.

Every country has different visa requirements, but your immigration service will email you the forms that your entourage must complete and walk you through the entire process. They'll tell you everything they need to complete the visa process and how long it will take for them to obtain the visas. This is especially important if your band is on tour and only has a short timeframe to obtain the necessary visas before you have to enter a certain country.

Many of these visa companies offer expedited services for a higher fee and can obtain visas much faster than usual if necessary. They also handle passport renewals, having more pages added to passports, and obtaining second passports for your entourage.

If your group does a lot of international traveling, it's worth the expense to obtain second passports for the band. Any crew members who also do a lot of international touring should consider getting second passports. It's worth the expense.

There have been a few times where I've had to worry about sending my entourage's passports to a visa agency to obtain visas for a future foreign entry at the same time we were about to enter another foreign country, and I had to worry if we'd receive our passports back in time. Having a second passport solves this problem.

It's important that the people in your entourage have no criminal record, especially drug convictions, to obtain visas to enter certain countries. Japan is especially strict in these matters. Your visa company can advise you on what to expect for any band member that might have a drug conviction on his record. If you have a crew member with a prior drug conviction, you may end up having to replace him if he's refused a visa to enter a country.

I never want to see any crew member lose his job, but if he's constantly being refused entry into foreign countries because of criminal convictions, you really have no choice but to replace him. This is why it's important to ask about criminal records before you hire any road crew member.

Obtaining visas for your entourage is an important part of your job. You can't allow any part of this process to fall through the cracks to the point where someone in your entourage wouldn't be allowed into a country and unable to do the show. If this should happen to a band member and an important show had to be canceled, your job with that band would probably come to a quick and sorry end. Stay on top of this important process.

ATA CARNETS AND EQUIPMENT MANIFESTS

A carnet, also known as an ATA carnet, is a passport for your gear. The ATA carnet is an international customs document issued by seventy countries. It's presented when entering a carnet country with equipment that will be re-exported within twelve months.

When presented, the carnet permits the equipment to clear customs without the payment of import duties and import taxes, such as VAT (value added tax) or GST (goods and services tax). Payment isn't necessary because the carnet guarantees that the merchandise or equipment will be re-exported within a year. Thus, the use of a carnet is a way of temporarily importing gear into foreign countries without payment of import duties and taxes.

Carnets also serve as the USA registration of goods so the goods can re-enter the U.S. without payment of duties and taxes. You can go to ATACarnet.com to learn more about ATA carnets.

Whenever we're shipping the band's gear overseas via air cargo or boat or when it's traveling on a truck through European countries, we'll need an ATA carnet for the gear. If your group is an American band and you're shipping gear overseas via air cargo or boat, your cargo company will prepare the necessary ATA carnet for you once you send them an equipment manifest containing all of the information about the gear that they'll require.

Below is an equipment manifest listing all of the information that you'll need to send to the cargo company so they can prepare a carnet for your gear. As you can see, the manifest simply lists each road case by number, what's inside the case, any applicable serial number for the product, the quantity of that item, the item's value, the country of origin, and the case's total weight.

To prepare the equipment manifest, simply list the first road case as item #1. If road case #1 contains two guitars, list the first guitar as item #2 and the second guitar as item #3. Then you'll enter the applicable information for each item in the columns that apply. You should enter the make, model, and serial number of each guitar. Beside each entry, you'll enter the number 1 in the quantity column. Then you'll list the total estimated weight for the road case itself. This weight will be the total weight of the case and the two guitars.

Skinny Girl Riot--Equipment Manifest					
Case #	Description of goods and serial #	# of items	Weight (lbs)	Value (USA)	Origin
1	**Case containing:**	1	25	$ 150.00	US
	Black Gibson Les Paul serial # 123456	1		$ 1,000.00	US
2	**Case containing:**	1	25	$ 150.00	US
	White Gibson Les Paul serial # 856886	1		$ 1,000.00	US
3	**Case containing:**	1	25	$ 150.00	US
	Black Fender Flying V serial # 18348	1		$ 1,000.00	US
4	**Case containing:**	1	10	$ 100.00	US
	Guitar boat, no serial # available	2		$ 300.00	US
5	**Case containing:**	1	150	$ 150.00	US
	Ampeg SVT IV bass amp, no serial # available	2		$ 2,000.00	US
6	**Case containing:**	1	100	$ 150.00	US
	Marshall 4x12 guitar cabinets	2		$ 1,000.00	GB
7	**Case containing:**	1	100	$ 150.00	US
	Marshall 4x12 guitar cabinets	2		$ 1,000.00	GB
8	**Case containing:**	1	150	$ 150.00	US
	Ampeg 8x10 bass cabinets	2		$ 2,000.00	GB
9	**Case containing:**	1	100	$ 150.00	US
	Marshall JCM 2000 guitar amp serial # 83933, 83934	2		$ 2,000.00	GB
10	**Case containing:**	1	100	$ 150.00	US
	Marshall JCM 2000 guitar amp serial # 83935, 83936	2		$ 2,000.00	GB
11	**Case containing:**	1	75	$ 150.00	US
	Yamaha 22" kick drum, no serial # available	2		$ 1,000.00	JP
12	**Case containing:**	1	25	$ 150.00	US
	Yamaha 18" floor tom, no serial # available	1		$ 250.00	JP
13	**Case containing:**	1	25	$ 150.00	US
	Yamaha 16" floor tom, no serial # available	1		$ 250.00	JP
14	**Case containing:**	1	25	$ 150.00	US
	Yamaha 14" floor tom, no serial # available	1		$ 250.00	JP
15	**Case containing:**	1	20	$ 150.00	US
	Yamaha 13" rack tom, no serial # available	1		$ 150.00	JP
16	**Case containing:**	1	20	$ 150.00	US
	Yamaha 12" rack tom, no serial # available	1		$ 150.00	JP
17	**Case containing:**	1	20	$ 150.00	US
	Yamaha 11" rack tom, no serial # available	1		$ 150.00	JP
18	**Case containing:**	1	15	$ 150.00	US
	Yamaha 14" x 5" snare drum, no serial # available	1		$ 150.00	JP
19	**Case containing:**	1	85	$ 200.00	US
	Yamaha hi-hat stand, no serial # available	1		$ 100.00	JP
	Yamaha boom cymbal stands, no serial # available	1		$ 200.00	JP
	Yamaha snare stand, no serial # available	1		$ 50.00	JP
	Kick drum pedals, no serial # available	2		$ 100.00	JP
	Drum throne, no serial # available	1		$ 100.00	JP
	Rack tom hardware, no serial # available	1		$ 50.00	JP
	Floor tom hardware, no serial # available	1		$ 50.00	JP
20	**Case containing:**	1	70	$ 100.00	US
	Paiste cymbals, no serial # available	8		$ 1,000.00	CH
21	**Case containing:**	1	75	$ 100.00	US
	astd backdrops and scrims	5		$ 8,000.00	US
22	**Case containing:**	1	70	$ 100.00	US
	scrim frames	2		$ 1,000.00	US
Total			1310	$ 29,450.00	

If you don't know the exact weight of the road case and its contents, simply estimate it, and the cargo company will obtain the exact weight when they weigh each case. Then you'll list the value of the road case and each of the two guitars inside. Finally, you'll list the country of origin (where the product was manufactured) for each of the three items. You'll do this for every road case that you're shipping.

At the bottom of the carnet, you'll list the total pieces of gear, their total weight and their total value. The cargo company will then have all of the information they'll need to generate an official ATA carnet for your shipment.

Once the gear arrives in an overseas port of entry, the trucking company you'll be using for the tour will require copies of the ATA carnet for the truck driver to present at the applicable border crossings. Your trucking company will let you know how many copies you'll need for your tour. Make sure the driver always has enough copies of the carnet. Your cargo company can supply you with as many copies of the carnet as you'll need.

If you're an American band traveling into Canada with your band gear in a trailer, you don't need an ATA carnet. The rules now say that the band's gear in the trailer is considered "personal possessions," just like your luggage in the bus's luggage bay. In the past, you'd have to stop at the U.S. side of the border, go inside, and present an equipment manifest to be stamped by the U.S. Customs office and then present that same paperwork at the U.S. Customs office when re-entering the United States. That's no longer the case for gear that's traveling inside a trailer attached to the back of your tour bus.

However, it's still a good idea to have an accurate copy of an equipment manifest handy when crossing the Canadian border back into America. Even though this rule has changed, you'd be surprised at how many border guards don't know the rule has changed. Always be prepared for the unexpected, and you'll save yourself a lot of time and trouble.

If your gear is traveling on a truck that's entering Canada, you will need an ATA carnet for that gear, and if your truck contains sound and lighting gear that the band is renting, you'll need a carnet from both the sound and lighting company for their individual amounts of gear. Your truck driver must have these carnets when he crosses the border.

You should always update your equipment manifest whenever the band buys new gear or retires other gear so it's always up-to-date whenever you need to use it.

TRUCKING

If your band has outgrown a trailer for their gear and needs to move up to a truck, you'll have to coordinate trucking for your tour. You'll first need to determine what size truck you need. You can rent Ryder trucks from 16 feet to 26 feet in length, and your driver does not need a CDL (commercial driver's license) to drive these vehicles. Many of these trucks run on diesel fuel, just like your tour bus. You can go to Ryder's website for more information on their trucks and easily get a quote for their weekly rate and mileage costs.

You should also get a comparative quote from other companies, such as Hertz. They offer trucks from 15 feet to 24feet in length. This is the length of the trailer, not the entire vehicle. Budget Truck Rental is also another truck company that you can use.

Renting a truck for a tour from a small local company—unless it's a very short regional run—is usually not a good idea. Even if it's cheaper to rent their vehicle, you'll be in trouble when the truck breaks down at night in the middle of nowhere and you have to load in for a show that morning. The chances of a small local company getting your truck serviced or another one sent out to you right away is probably going to be slim to none.

On the other hand, the major nationwide companies will get you another truck there as soon as possible, and you can't ask for more than that. Trucks are like any other vehicle; sometimes they break down. However, if you're using a large company with a national support network, they'll usually get you back on the road as soon as possible, and the chances of having to cancel an important show are considerably reduced.

Once you've gotten your best quote for the truck you need and made your reservation, you must remember to add the rental fee into your tour budget. If you haven't already done your mileages for the tour, go online and calculate the mileages for the tour and then add 10 percent of that total amount to cover yourself. Next, calculate your mileage charges for the truck using your total tour mileage and the cost per mile that the trucking company is charging you, and add that amount into the tour budget.

Example: 8,000 tour miles x 20 cents a mile = $1,600.00 for mileage charges

You'll also need to add your estimated fuel costs to your tour budget. You can go to AAA's Daily Fuel Gauge Report at FuelGaugeReport.Com to get the current average cost of diesel fuel in America. You can also use PetrolPrices.Com to find current diesel prices in the United Kingdom. Find out from your trucking company how many miles per gallon your truck will get with the trailer fully loaded to its weight capacity. Even if your truck won't be fully loaded, use that mile per gallon estimate anyway to cover yourself in the budget. It's better to come in under budget than over budget.

Divide your total miles for the tour by the amount of miles per gallon (or liter) that your truck gets and then multiply that amount by the current average cost of diesel fuel. This will be your total diesel cost for the tour to plug into your budget.

> *Example: 8,000 total tour miles divided by 8 miles per gallon = 1,000 gallons of diesel needed for the tour*
>
> *1,000 gallons of diesel x $4.50 a gallon = $4,500.00 for total truck diesel costs for the tour*

You must add the driver's salary into your tour budget, as well as any per diem amount that you've agreed upon. There's no sleeping compartment in the cab of a straight truck like there is on a semi, so you'll need to budget a hotel room for the driver each day.

Even if you have an available bunk on the tour bus for the truck driver, I don't recommend this any more than I recommend this for the bus driver. He'll never get any sleep with people coming and going and making noise all day. You don't want the truck driver to fall asleep at the wheel in the middle of the night because your entourage kept him up all day.

Book the truck driver a hotel room, and, no, he can't share a room with the bus driver. Every bus company contract stipulates that the bus driver must have his own private hotel room on a daily basis. I've never met a bus driver who would agree to share a room with another driver.

The truck maintenance category in your tour budget is for things such as motor oil, coolant, and a weekly truck wash. Even though this truck is a rental, you don't want the truck pulling up to the venue looking like it's never been washed. For a twenty-six-foot straight truck, I'd add at least $100 a week to the budget for maintenance costs.

Make sure to add a category for truck tolls into your budget. This is primarily an East Coast thing in the U.S., but toll booths are starting to pop up in more places around the country. If one week of your tour is up and down the East Coast of America, I'd add $250 to the budget for tolls just to cover the truck.

If your band has now graduated to a semi because they're carrying a stage set or supplemental production or a large amount of merchandise that will no longer fit into the largest straight truck, you'll need to hire a trucking company for your tour.

Sometimes you can rent part of the truck to your support act to help pay the bill if they need the space and you have some left over. If you can offer the truck space to them cheaper than the cost of them dragging a trailer or renting a straight truck if they won't fit into a trailer, it might be worth it to them. But if they're doing their own shows on your days off, then it wouldn't work for them.

Upstaging, Inc., is a popular entertainment trucking company in the U.S., about an hour west of Chicago, and they're also a good lighting company. You can sometimes save money by getting both your lighting and trucking from them. S.O.S. Transportation, LLC, is another popular entertainment trucking company whose offices are about thirty minutes southwest of Portland, Oregon. Ozark Mountain Leasing, Inc is an entertainment trucking company about one hundred miles east of Springfield, Missouri. One of the great things about Ozark Mountain Leasing is they also offer a twenty-two-foot straight truck with a driver sleeping compartment up front.

This is a great choice if your band has outgrown a trailer but all of their gear will fit into a twenty-two-foot truck. Since the driver has his own sleeping compartment, you won't need to book a hotel for him each day. In addition to this, you also have the support of a large entertainment trucking company if the truck ever breaks down, and you don't have to worry about hiring a truck driver because you'll be getting an experienced driver from the company.

Having the driver sleep in the cab of your truck is also great for the security of your gear. There have been incidents over the past few years where a band woke up in the morning at their hotel to find their truck and all of their gear stolen. This happened to Iggy Pop in Montreal in August of 2008. This is not the first experience you want to have when you wake up in the morning.

When using a truck like this from Ozark Mountain Leasing, you'd have to consider the deadhead costs involved in bringing a truck all the way from Missouri to the gear pick up location. It's always possible that the company could have a truck in your area around the time you need it, or you can try to negotiate reduced deadhead charges to make the budget work for you. A company will try to work with you on these deadhead costs if they want the business badly enough, and if your tour is happening during the dead season— wintertime—when business is slow, anything is possible.

Most U.S. trucking companies will give you an all-in quote that covers the truck rental, driver salary, per diem, maintenance costs, and fuel. You'll just need to give the driver a hotel buyout on days off and provide him with catering on the show days or include him in the dinner buyout.

Four of the most popular entertainment trucking companies for U.K. and European tours are Transam Trucking, Ltd in Suffolk, England, Fly By Nite in Redditch, England, Stardes in Sheffield, England, and Trucking Service GmbH in Wehnrath, Germany. Most of these companies also offer straight trucks for smaller tours.

All of the things I've said about leasing tour buses in Europe and the U.K. in regards to all-in quotes covering driver salary, fuel, vehicle rental, maintenance supplies, ferries, and double-driver costs also apply to the trucking companies. Make sure you get a quote from at least three trucking companies to compare pricing and all of the extra costs involved.

AIR AND SEA CARGO

Like trucking and bussing, the cost of air cargo continues to rise because of the increasing cost of fuel. If your band requires air cargo to ship your gear, there are companies, such as EFM, Rock It Cargo, SOS Air Cargo, Ltd, and Shockwave Cargo, that provide good service.

Shipping your gear via air cargo is involved, and every scenario and quote is different, depending upon your needs. If you're finishing the last show of your U.S. tour in Chicago and starting your U.K. tour in London four days later and need some of your gear flown over for the tour, air cargo is the only way you'll get it there in time if that gear is too big or heavy to be checked on the plane.

These freight forwarding companies can have your gear picked up at your last gig, flown to your destination, and then delivered directly to your next venue. Their quotes will cover the pickup and delivery charges, the air freight charges, and the carnet and customs clearance charges.

These cargo companies are experts in freight forwarding for the entertainment business just like a music travel agent. It's a highly specialized field, so it's not in your best interest to use a company that isn't experienced with the special needs of a music group.

Most of these companies not only coordinate air cargo but also facilitate land and sea shipments. If you have gear that needs to be shipped overseas for a tour and you're able to send it over at least a month before you need it—and that could be cutting it close depending on where the gear's going—you can save a lot of money by shipping it by sea cargo. Your freight forwarding rep can give you a quote with the estimated delivery date for any shipping scenario that you might be considering.

Your freight forwarding company can also deal with shipments by land for you. If you need a large sound console shipped across country and delivered to the first show of a tour, they can sort this out for you and make sure that it's delivered on time. Certain shipments may be too large or heavy for UPS or FedEx, so you'd need to use a trucking company for the shipment.

If you're using an entertainment freight forwarding company, they'll handle everything from beginning to end in making sure that the shipment is delivered to you on time. If this is a show-crucial shipment, such as a digital sound console, it's worth having a freight forwarding company that you trust making sure that the item arrives at the first show on time.

Your freight forwarding company will guide you through every aspect of freight forwarding and make this process as painless as possible for you.

CATERING COMPANIES

It's rare that you'll see an American band carrying a catering company on tour in the U.S. unless they're an arena act, but it's more common when touring the U.K. and Europe. Many bands, once they reach a certain level, prefer to carry their own catering company on tour.

Many of the venues in Europe are in areas where there are no restaurants within walking distance to buy food using a buyout from the promoter, and it can also be difficult getting food delivered to some venues because of their location. On larger tours where the band is carrying full production, the crew doesn't have time to leave the venue to go walking around trying to find somewhere to eat lunch and dinner, and many successful bands simply prefer the luxury of knowing that they're going to get the same quality catering each day. It's the best way to go if the band can afford it.

Eat to the Beat is a great company, with offices in England, America, Asia, and the Middle East, that has been around for years. They can accommodate your tour's catering needs and are one of the best in the business. Upbeat Food is another good company in Kent, England that can service a tour's catering needs with a strong focus on macrobiotic, vegan, and vegetarian menus using local ingredients. Popcorn Catering, Ltd., in England is also another good catering company worth considering.

Like any vendor you might use on a tour, always get comparison quotes from at least three of them, but remember you're dealing with the food you eat on every show day. Choosing the right one can make the difference between a happy or unhappy band and crew. Choose a quality company with experience doing music tours.

Catering companies carry their own stoves and ovens and everything from pots and pans to dishes and silverware. They load into a venue and immediately turn an empty room into their own kitchen and dining room, and they carry their own catering crew that's skilled in music tour catering and the tight schedules that apply.

They can provide the touring entourage with three meals a day as well as after-show food and bus stock (food and drink) for your tour buses each night. This is usually better for the promoter because he will simply pay the catering company the money that he allotted in his show budget for catering. Like sound and lighting, this saves the promoter the task and worry of having to arrange a local catering company for the tour that your band and crew may not be happy with.

If you plan to carry a catering company on your tour, you must make sure that you have enough truck space for all of their gear and food stock. They shop daily in each city for perishable items, such as meats and fresh vegetables, but will carry some non-perishable items, such as canned goods, in their road cases.

You must also make sure that you have enough bunks on your crew bus for the catering crew. The promoter will usually provide a local catering staff to assist the catering crew in washing dishes and the preparation of meals, but the tour catering crew can be two to four people or even more, depending on how many people they're feeding each day.

The salaries for the catering crew are included in the quote and paid by the catering company. The band will have to pay for their hotels on days off, a per diem if one's been negotiated, and their transportation to and from their home base.

Carrying your own catering company on tour is a nice luxury and saves the tour manager and production manager a lot of worrying about daily catering, but there are numerous aspects that must be organized to make it work.

RIDERS AND CONTRACTS

The band's rider, also known as a contract rider, is a document that *rides* along with the band's legal contract with the promoter. When the booking agent books a concert with a promoter, they agree upon the date of the engagement, the length of the band's performance, the amount of the band's fee (also called a guarantee), the percentage of the profits the band will receive if the show sells enough tickets—unless a flat fee has been negotiated—and the deposit amount that must be paid to the agent up front by a specified date before the band arrives to do the show.

All of these deal points are put into the contract, and it's signed by the promoter and the band's representative, who is legally authorized to sign on their behalf—usually the band's manager. None of the terms of this agreement can be changed without the express permission of both parties; and unless the show sells badly and the promoter and agent—with the manager's permission—agree to a price reduction, these terms never change. The rider, on the other hand, is often changed by the promoter and sent back to the booking agent with revisions and deletions.

You should create a separate rider for different parts of the world and change catering items to common brands that can be found in those countries. Sending your U.S. rider to a festival promoter in Belgrade, Serbia, asking for some microbrew that's only found in Colorado is pointless and will make you look like a schmuck on his first tour of Europe.

It's impossible to create a rider for every type of show you do. Many bands will do tours where they're in a small club one night, a big theatre the next night, supporting a larger band the next week, and performing at a large festival three days later. The contract rider is merely a guide for the promoter rep so he can meet your band's needs as closely as possible within the confines of the show budget.

Put technical specs in your rider for the biggest show you'll probably do on the tour. You need to make sure you include specific lighting and sound specs for venues where the promoter may have to bring in sound and lighting. You could be playing a club but need specific audio and lighting gear to make the production work for your band.

However, just because these items are in your rider doesn't mean the promoter's going to rent them if the venue doesn't have them. If the show's selling well or the promoter expects a sell-out, your chances of him spending money on these additional items is much greater.

If the show is selling badly or he's done a low ticket price to get bodies in the room, there may not be any money in the show budget to pay for this additional gear. In this case, the band would pay for the items out of their own pocket or do without them.

It's common on a club tour for the promoter to cut a deal with the agent specifically stating that the deal is cut based upon the band using house production only. This means that your band will have to use the sound and lighting the venue has to offer and anything that must be rented will have to be paid for by the band, although the promoter may pay for minor extras if there's room in the show budget. Acting like a human being with some manners during the show advance will help with this effort.

If your band's popular in a city and the clubs there are too small, the promoter might put your show into a venue that doesn't have sound and lighting installed in it. The promoter will then have to rent sound and lighting from local companies if you're not carrying full production.

The promoter will try to meet the sound and lighting requirements in your rider as best he can within the confines of the show budget. Promoters can only allocate so much money for production. The show budget is determined by the ticket price and how many tickets the promoter thinks he can sell; it's not a never-ending well of money.

You'll need to be realistic about your production demands and be flexible about what you'll accept. In other words, the specs in your rider are not carved in stone and sometimes you'll need to work with the promoter on alternative choices.

If you're doing a show in a small town and there's only one sound and lighting company there, you'll have no choice but to accept the gear they have. The only other option for the promoter would be to bring this gear in from another city—sometimes another state—and that's usually impossible because of the additional expenses involved.

Another item on your rider that's often a point of contention with the promoter is labor. If you're doing a club tour and only carrying a small amount of backline gear in a trailer, you don't need eight stagehands; and the promoter isn't going to pay for them despite what your rider says. If you're doing a show where the promoter has to bring in full production, he'll have budgeted for more stagehands to get the sound and lighting up in time. Four stagehands will usually be more than enough for a band carrying nothing but backline; but if the show is selling badly, you'll probably end up with two of them, if any at all.

Another costly thing on the rider that's often negotiated when the deal is cut is the amount of guest list tickets required by the band. Your rider may call for a certain number of tickets, but the contract may specify an amount that's significantly lower. For a band that does good business in big clubs, asking for thirty guest list tickets for each show is not unreasonable, but for a new band that's not selling well yet, the promoter may slash this down as far as he can. He wants to sell as many tickets as possible so he reduces his chances of losing money on the show, and a smart band and road manager will work with him on this.

The promoter is trying to build the band's popularity in his city so they'll grow and move up to bigger and better venues, but if he loses money each time you come through town, it could eventually get to where he'll no longer want to book the band. However, if you work with him on show cost reductions and show him that you're feeling his pain when he's losing money, he's more likely to keep the faith and continue booking the band if he believes in them. Being uncooperative about every little thing is a death sentence for the band's future with that promoter. And if he's the only game in town, the band's career could become kaput in that city.

Some road managers don't care if the promoter loses money or if they ever book the band again. These tour managers are a menace to bands and do them no good. Your primary responsibility as a road manager is to look after the band and handle their business on the road in a professional manner—and that includes leaving every promoter with a positive vibe about the band even if he lost money that night.

Concert promoters are some of the biggest gamblers in the world. They know full well that some shows are going to lose money and some will make money. They look at their bottom line at the end of the year. If they're in the black and made money, they had a successful year. If they're in the red and lost money, they're on the way to being out of business.

Another item in your rider that may be reduced is the amount of security on call for the show. Security is another labor cost that can get expensive. If a show's selling badly and the promoter is expecting a small crowd, he'll reduce the amount of security on call for the show to help reduce his loss. Most responsible promoters will only cut security so far, even in the face of a loss, because this could become dangerous for the band and the audience, but there are promoters who'll do anything to reduce their loss on a soft show, even if it risks someone in the audience getting hurt.

Heavy metal concerts can get pretty rowdy. Moshing, crowd-surfing, and stage diving are part of the game. Because of this, a barricade in front of the stage is always mandatory. It's a matter of safety for not only the band but the crowd, too.

Barricades are expensive to rent if the venue doesn't own one, so the promoter will sometimes try to get out of renting one. If your band's just starting out and ticket sales aren't good, this could be something the promoter will try to cut from the rider, but politely fight it as much as you can.

Just because your rider says you require three dressing rooms with a shower and a production office and a forty-foot by twenty-four-foot stage, that doesn't mean you're going to get it. If you a booked a show in a club that has one dressing room, no production office, and a postage stamp for a stage, there's nothing the promoter can do about it. He can't rebuild the venue to suit your rider. You have to deal with it and make it work. Good road managers not only have a plan B but plans X, Y, and Z.

You improvise; you overcome; you adapt.

On some tours, I'll add a clause in the rider that states if the venue has no shower, the promoter must buy the band a shower room at a nearby hotel. If my band's doing good business, I've never had a problem getting the promoter to rent us a shower room, but if your band's just starting out or ticket sales aren't what the promoter had hoped for and he's facing a loss, I'd plan on using the driver's hotel room after the show when he's awake and ready to drive.

The catering budget has always been the biggest headache on most of the tours I've done. Metal bands always tend to have a lot of support acts on the tour so they can give the fans more for their money and draw the biggest possible crowd, but a bigger bill requires a lot more catering for the additional bands, and that makes the catering budget even tighter.

There's only so much money in the show budget. If the promoter's selling $20 tickets and the room holds 1,000 people, this means the promoter will gross $20,000 on a sell-out. If the headliner's getting a $10,000 guarantee, and the three support acts are splitting $2,000 between them, and the promoter spent $3,000 on sound and lighting, and catering cost $1,000 for the four-band bill, he's already spent $16,000 out of the show's gross box office receipts, and that's not even including the money he's spent on advertising, stagehands, security, venue rent, and more.

As you can see, just because the show is sold out, that doesn't mean the promoter's making a lot of money. He could be losing money on a sell-out. Each show has a budget to contend with, no matter how well the show's selling. It's not a bottomless pit of money just because the words "Sold Out" are on the venue's marquee out front.

The only way to increase the show costs without the promoter losing money is to raise the ticket price—not always a good idea in a bad economy—or the band takes a lower guarantee, and that's becoming more difficult as touring grows more expensive.

I've always looked after the support acts. They're part of our show, and they at least deserve to be fed and have some beers after their show. Depending on the catering budget, the promoter may hire a catering company to cook dinner for the bands, or if the club has a kitchen, he might feed the bands from their menu to reduce his costs.

Often the promoters will just give everyone a dinner buyout, which is a specific amount of money per person to pocket or go and eat at a nearby restaurant. This buyout money comes out of the catering budget, and what's left over pays for the bands' dressing room catering. And just because your rider says you're supposed to get $20 per person, that doesn't always mean you're going to get that amount, unless you plan to let the support acts starve. I hope you don't ever do that.

With the catering budget, I always start at the top of the bill and work my way down when determining what the bands get for catering. If it's a buyout, I'll try to make sure that my entourage gets at least $15 per person and the direct support act gets $10 each and the support act below them gets $5 each. It depends how much money is budgeted for catering. A $5 buyout may not sound like much, but it's better than nothing. They can pool their buyout money together and buy pizzas for dinner.

I'll always make sure the support act at the bottom of the bill at least gets a case of water and a case of beer for their dressing room. I'll then try to do the same for the direct support act but maybe give them something extra that's on their rider, such as a bottle of liquor or an extra case of beer. This leaves enough in the budget to supply my headliner's dressing room catering as close to their rider as possible.

In the end, my band's the headliner. They've paid their dues, are selling most of the tickets, and the majority of the crowd's coming to see them, so they deserve more. It's the way it works, but we should never stop trying to look after the bands on the bill below us.

One of the other things that might get cut for the headliner when the catering budget's tight is the after show food. Many bands specify in their rider that their entourage must be fed after the show. This is usually pizzas or sandwiches or something else economical, depending on the size of the tour, but many times this food will have to be cut because of the budget. If you're first on the bill and your band is virtually unknown, don't embarrass yourself by going to the promoter and asking him why you didn't get your after show food that's on your rider. He'll think you've become completely unhinged.

Sometimes the runner will have to be cut because of the budget. The runner is a person with a car who runs errands for you. If you need guitar strings, they'll go and get them for you. If you need laundry taken to a wash-and-fold, they'll get it done for you. If you need band members driven to a hotel shower room, the runner is the person who will drive them there and back. However, the runner's often one of the first things the promoter will try to cut if the budget's too tight or the show's selling badly.

If you're playing a venue that you've been to before and you know there's a large mall and a music store across the street and the venue has a shower and you don't need laundry done, then you'll be more likely to cut the runner to help the promoter out if he's in trouble, but if the venue is in the middle of nowhere and you need many things that day, you're going to resist cutting the runner a lot more.

Again, it's all about the budget and how well the show's selling. With experience, you'll learn to pick your battles and give a little on things you can live without to get something you really need.

Bus and truck parking is often a problem on club tours, especially when you've got four or five bands on the bill and have a lot of vehicles to park. If your rider states that the promoter must provide bus parking for your tour and the club is in the middle of Manhattan, you're probably not going to get any parking for the support acts, if you even get any for your bus. There's very little street parking in Manhattan; that's just the reality of it.

Parking is something you should be dealing with during the show advance, not only for your band but for all of the bands on the bill. You may not be able to arrange any parking for the support acts, but you should at least warn them that there won't be any parking for them and the promoter isn't paying for a space in a nearby parking lot.

As the headliner, you will have more leverage to get the promoter to pay for your bus at a pay parking lot, but this is something you have to work out in the show advance. Just don't expect it to be reality simply because the rider calls for it. The promoter may have crossed that item off the rider, and your agent signed off on it for some bizarre reason. You should always have your agent send you a copy of the rider signed by the promoter with any revisions or deletions that were made.

Always remember that many booking agents have never toured and rarely know what we're faced with every day. The agent's job is to get the band the most amount of money from the promoter, and sometimes they have to make concessions to get that money. Just because something has been crossed off the rider doesn't mean that you still can't talk the promoter into giving it to you. It's all about how you handle people. Treat them with respect, and they'll be more likely to bend over backwards for you and your band.

Many bands will include a copy of their stage plot and input chart in their rider. It never matters to me if these two things aren't in the rider because I always include them in my pre-advance package. Stage plots and input charts have a way of changing often, so I usually don't worry about making sure they're included in the rider.

Some bands will put a clause in their rider that says a promoter must reimburse the band for all excess baggage charges if the show is a fly date. Put it in there if you like, but most promoters are going to refuse to pay for this unless it was agreed upon with the agent when the show was booked, and it's specifically listed on the contract. Even if they agree to it, they're probably going to put a cap on the amount that they'll agree to pay because they have no idea how much luggage and gear you're going to be checking on the plane, much less any control over it. Only an inexperienced or demented promoter would agree to pay for an amount that's unspecified and open-ended.

Read the sample rider below. There are many clauses in the beginning of the rider that are standard for most riders. They cover many things, such as cancellation due to weather and acts of God, the fact that the band controls the production, merchandising rights, reproduction rights of the performance, and other standard things.

Every promoter will expect to receive your rider from the agent to get a clearer picture of your needs, and then he'll mold your rider into his show's reality during the show advance. If your band's a hot act, selling out each night, your chances of getting everything on your rider are much greater.

The rider and contract exists to protect the band and give the promoter a reasonable guide as to what your needs will be for your show, but always remember that your rider isn't carved in stone like the Ten Commandments and will sometimes be amended.

Skinny Girl Riot
Performance Contract Rider
USA 2012

This Rider attached hereto and made part of the contract dated _____, for Artist's appearance on _____ by and between Skinny Girl Riot Inc (hereinafter referred to as "Producer") furnishing the services of (f/s/o) Skinny Girl Riot (hereinafter referred to as "Artist") and _____ (hereinafter referred to as "Purchaser"). Modifications, if any, to this Rider must be agreed to in writing and signed by Purchaser and Producer.

BILLING

Artist shall receive 100% Headline billing in any and all publicity releases and paid advertisements, including but not limited to programs, fliers, signs, lobby boards and marquees. No other name or photograph shall appear in type with respect to size, thickness, boldness and prominence of the type accorded Artist, and no other name or photograph shall appear on the same line or above the name of Artist. If Artist is in support of another performer, Artist shall receive 75% Special Guest Star billing.

CANCELLATION

Purchaser agrees that Artist may cancel the engagement hereunder, at Artist's sole discretion, by giving Purchaser notice thereof at least thirty (30) days prior to the commencement date of the engagement hereunder.

FORCE MAJEURE

Producer's obligation to furnish the entertainment unit referred to herein is subject to the detention or prevention by sickness, inability to perform, accident, means of transportation, Act of God, riots, strikes, labor difficulties, epidemics and any act or order of any public authority or any cause, similar or dissimilar, beyond Producer's control.

Provided Artist is ready, willing and able to perform, Purchaser agrees to compensate Producer in accordance with terms hereof regardless of Act of God, fire, accident, riot, strike or any events of any kind or character whatsoever, whether similar or dissimilar to the foregoing events which would prevent or interfere with the presentation of the show hereunder.

INCLEMENT WEATHER

Notwithstanding anything contained herein, inclement weather shall not be a force majeure occurrence and the Purchaser shall remain liable for payment of the full contract price even if the performance(s) called for herein are prevented by such weather conditions.

Producer shall have the sole right to determine in good faith whether any such weather conditions shall render the performance(s) impossible, hazardous or unsafe, subject to government authorities.

CONTROL OF PRODUCTION

Producer shall have the sole and exclusive control over the production, presentation and performance of Artist in connection with the engagement, including but not limited to, the details, means and methods of the performance of Artist and each member thereof, and persons to be employed by Producer in performing the provisions here on Artist's behalf. Producer shall have the sole right as Producer may see fit to designate and change the performing personnel other than Artist. It is specifically understood and agreed that a representative of the Producer shall have sole and absolute authority in directing personnel operating all lighting and sound equipment during rehearsal and each performance scheduled herein.

APPROVAL OF OTHER PERFORMERS

Producer reserves the approval right of any other performers to appear in conjunction with this performance and the right to determine the length and nature of their performance(s). A violation of this clause shall entitle Producer to refuse to furnish Artist's performance as described herein but Purchaser shall remain obligated to make all payments herein set forth. Purchaser agrees that there will be no intermission except as Producer may direct.

REPRODUCTION OF PERFORMANCE

No portion of the performance rendered hereunder may be broadcast, photographed, recorded, filmed, taped or embodied in any form for any purpose; reproducing such performance without Producer's prior written consent is strictly prohibited. Purchaser will deny entrance to any persons carrying audio or video recording devices without limiting in any way the generality of the foregoing prohibition, and it is understood to include members of the audience, press and Purchaser's staff.

If in the event that the Purchaser, his agents, managers, employees, contractors, etc., reproduce or cause to be reproduced the Producer's performance in the form of films, tapes, or any other means of audio or video reproduction, then upon demand by Artist, Purchaser shall deliver all of the same (together with any and all masters, negatives and other means of reproduction thereof) to Producer at Purchaser's sole cost and expense. In addition, Producer reserves all other legal or equitable remedies that Producer and/or Artist may have.

PURCHASER ASSUMES LIABILITY

Except as otherwise herein specifically provided, Purchaser hereby assumes full liability and responsibility for the payment of any and all cost, expenses, charges, claims, losses, liability, and damages related to or based upon the presentation or production of the show or shows in which Artist is to appear hereunder.

SPONSORSHIP

All forms of sponsorship, whether part of an ongoing series or specifically for Artist's show, must be authorized by Producer. Such authorization may be withheld at Producer's sole discretion.

BOX OFFICE PROVISIONS

In cases where the Artist is being paid on a percentage basis, Purchaser agrees to deliver to the Artist's representative, at least two (2) weeks prior to the date of performance, a plot plan and printer's manifest of the house (notarized, signed statement from the printer of tickets, listing amount of tickets printed at each price). Purchaser further agrees to have on hand at the place of performance the night of the show, for counting and verification by representative of the Producer, all unsold tickets. Producer shall be compensated for the difference between the number of unsold tickets on hand and shown to its representative and the number of tickets printed as shown by the ticket manifest, if any. If Purchaser shall violate any of the preceding provisions of this paragraph, it shall be deemed the Purchaser has sold a ticket for each seat in the house (and any permitted standing room) at the highest ticket price for which the house is scaled. Purchaser further agrees to give said representative the right to enter the box-office at any time (during and after the performance) and to examine and make extracts from the box-office office records of Purchaser relating to the gross receipts of this engagement. A written box-office statement, certified and signed by the Purchaser, will be furnished to Artist within two (2) hours following each performance. Purchaser may not sell tickets to the performance hereunder as part of a subscription or other type of series of other concerts, without written consent of Producer. All tickets printed under the manifest shall be of the one stub, one price variety. There shall be no multiple-price tickets printed. Examples of tickets prohibited under this agreement are:

a) One price for students and a different price for general admissions on the same ticket, or;

b) One price for tickets bought in advance and a different price for tickets bought at the gate on the same ticket.

Further, no tickets can be sold for seats located to the rear of the stage where the stage and equipment on stage is obstructing normal eye-level viewing of Artist's performance, unless the location of the seat is clearly indicated on the ticket. Tickets sold behind bandstand must be marked "impaired vision" or "behind bandstand."

If Purchaser violates the above provision, he shall be liable for the total amount of tickets sold at the highest price printed on the ticket. All tickets shall be printed by a bonded ticket house, such as Ticketmaster, or if the performance is at a college or university, the official printing department of the university or college. Purchaser agrees not to discount tickets or to offer tickets as a premium without first obtaining permission in writing from the Producer. Such authorization may be withheld at Producer's sole discretion. If Purchaser does sell or distribute discount or complimentary tickets without prior approval, or in excess of the number printed, he shall be liable for the full ticket price of each ticket sold or distributed.

SCALING

Purchaser will clearly print the specific capacity, gross potential and ticket price breakdown of the facility where Artist is to perform under this Agreement on the face of the contract to which this Agreement is attached. In the event Producer is to receive a percentage of the gross receipts for this engagement pursuant to the terms hereof, the term "gross receipts" or "gross box-office receipts" or similar phrases, shall mean all box-office receipts computed on the basis of the full retail ticket price for all tickets sold and in no event less that the full retail ticket price for all persons entering the performance with no deductions of any kind, less only federal, state or local admissions taxes and allowable discounts as approved by Producer writing. The Purchaser agrees to scale the ticket prices for this engagement of guaranteed potential gross receipt of no less than $_____.

COMPLIMENTARY TICKETS

Purchaser agrees to distribute no more than five percent (5%) of the official house seating as complimentary tickets relative to this performance. Further Purchaser must supply a representative of Producer with a statement detailing to whom each complimentary ticket was given. Each complimentary ticket will be issued only as a fully punched ticket. Purchaser agrees to supply all radio, television and newspaper personnel, and their guests, with complimentary tickets from above-mentioned allotment.

Purchaser agrees that if **NO ADMISSION** is charged to any part of the audience for engagement hereunder, this condition must be so stated on the face of the attached contract. If, at the engagement, there is evidence that admission <u>was or is</u> being subsequently charged for Artist's performance, Purchaser agrees that Producer must receive 100% of the admissions receipts collected.

In addition, Purchaser must provide Producer with thirty (30) complimentary tickets per show within the first ten (10) rows, the unused portion of which may be placed on sale the day of performance with the permission of Producer. If place of performance is in a theater and/or cabaret style nightclub or seated nightclub, a booth and/or group of tables comprising of eight (8) seats to be called "Star's Booth" or "Reserved Tables" must be available for each performance and if not to be used at said performance will be released by Producer or their representative.

FAILURE TO FULFILL OBLIGATIONS

Each one of the terms and conditions of this contract is of the essence of this Agreement and necessary for Artist's full performance hereunder. In the event Purchaser refuses or neglects to provide any of the items herein stated, and/or fails to make any of the payments as provided herein, Producer shall then have the right to refuse to perform this contract, shall retain any amounts theretofore paid to Producer by Purchaser and Purchaser shall remain liable to Producer for agreed price herein set forth.

MODIFICATION OF CONTRACT

It is understood and agreed that the contract may not be assigned, amended, modified, or altered, except by an instrument in writing, signed by the parties hereto, in accordance with the laws of the State of California. Nothing in this agreement shall require the performance of any act contrary to the law or to the rules or regulations of any union, guild, or similar body having jurisdiction over services of Artist or over the performances hereunder. Whenever there is any conflict between any provisions of this contract and any law, or any such rule or regulation of any such union, guild or similar body, such law, rule or regulation shall prevail, and this contract shall be deemed modified to the extent necessary to eliminate such conflict. This is the sole and complete agreement between the parties hereto. This Agreement shall not be deemed as a partnership or joint venture, and Producer shall not be liable in whole or in part for any obligation that may be incurred by Purchaser in carrying out Purchaser's obligations hereunder.

INDEMNIFICATION

A. Purchaser agrees to indemnify and hold harmless Producer/Artist and its employees, contractors, agents, representatives, heirs, and assigns, from and against any claims, costs (including attorney's fees and court costs), expenses, damages, liabilities, losses or judgments arising out of, or in connection with, any claim, demand or action made by any third party, if such are sustained as a direct or indirect consequence of the Engagement contracted hereunder, or any acts of failure to act on the part of the Purchaser, its employees, representatives, agents or assigns.

B. Purchaser shall also indemnify and hold harmless Producer/Artist and its employees, contractors, agents, representatives, heirs, and assigns from and against any and all loss, damage and/or destruction occurring to its and/or its employees', contractors, or agents' instruments and equipment at the place of the Engagement, including, but not limited to, damage, loss or destruction caused by Act of God.

CHOICE OF LAW/FORUM

This agreement shall be deemed made and entered into in the State of California and shall be governed by all of the laws of such State applicable to agreements wholly to be performed therein. Any action brought to enforce the terms of this agreement, or arising out of or related to the subject matter thereof, shall be brought in the courts of the State of California in San Francisco or Alameda Counties. Producer and Purchaser hereby submit to the jurisdiction of said courts, and agree that service of process in any such action may be served by certified mail, return receipt requested. The prevailing party in any such action shall be entitled to recover its reasonable attorney fees, in addition to any relief awarded by a court of competent jurisdiction.

ANTICIPATORY BREACH

If on or before the date of any scheduled performance hereunder, the financial standing or credit of the Purchaser has been impaired or is unsatisfactory or if Purchaser has failed, neglected, or refused to perform any contract with any other performer for any earlier engagement, in Producer's sole discretion, Producer shall have the right to demand payment forthwith of the guaranteed compensation specified above; and if Promoter fails or refuses to make such payment forthwith, Producer shall then have the right to cancel this Agreement. In the event of such cancellation, Producer shall have no further obligation to Purchaser hereunder, and shall retain any monies theretofore paid to Producer by Purchaser.

INSURANCE

Purchaser agrees to provide comprehensive general liability insurance (including, without limitation, coverage to protect against any and all injury to persons or property as a consequence of the installation and/or operation of the equipment and instruments provided by Producer and/or its employees, contractors and agents) for the contracted engagement and/or any other circumstances that may arise or occur proximate to the performance of the Engagement hereunder. Such liability insurance shall be in the amount required by the venue, but in no event shall have a limit of less than One Million Dollars ($1,000,000.00) combined single incident limit for bodily injury and property damage. Such insurance shall be in full force and effect at all times Producer/Artist or any of Producer's agents or independent contractors are in the place of performance or its proximate property boundaries, including but not limited to any parking areas, walkways, or the like. Producer/ Artist, its agent for the Engagement, and Artist's Personal Management, shall be listed as additionally-named insured under such insurance and this shall be indicated on the pertinent certificate of insurance. Purchaser also agrees to provide a policy of Workman's Compensation covering all of Purchaser's employees or third-party contractors. Purchaser further agrees to provide full all-risk insurance coverage for all equipment and instruments provided by Producer and/or its employees, contractors and agents against fire, vandalizing, theft, riot, or any other type of act or event causing harm or damage to, or loss of, the instruments and equipment so provided. Certificates of insurance relating to the coverage listed above shall be furnished by Purchaser, to Producer at least fourteen (14) days prior to the Engagement. Producer's oversight to request or review such insurance certificates shall not affect Producer's rights or Purchaser's obligations hereunder to provide such insurance coverage. The Purchaser warrants that he has complete and adequate public liability insurance. This certificate must be produced to the Producer upon request.

TAXES

Purchaser shall pay and hold Producer harmless of and from any and all taxes, fees, and the like relating to the engagement hereunder and the sums payable to Producer shall be net and free of such taxes, fees, dues and the like. If and to the extent that taxes of any kind are required by the domestic laws of any country, province, state, county, city or other governmental body, then such Taxes shall be paid according to such laws. However, the Producer Fee stated on the face of the engagement contract to which this rider is attached shall be a NET TO ARTIST SUM, post tax, and indicated as such. For avoidance of doubt, and by way of example but not limitation: if the Producer Gross Fee is $25,000, subject to various governmental taxes totaling 20% Tax (i.e., $5,000) of such Gross Fee, then the contract shall state the Gross Fee, the Tax deductions, and the NET FEE of $20,000. Artist shall also be provided with a certified tax receipt of such taxes deducted from the Gross Fee in Producer's name.

MERCHANDISING

The Purchaser will provide a well-lit secure place to erect a merchandising stall. This shall be in such a position as to be easily visible to the public using the main entrance. This is to be at no cost to the Producer. Purchaser agrees that its arrangement for presenting the engagement provided for herein shall prohibit the sale of Artist souvenirs or similar merchandise on or near the premises in connection with this engagement other than

Producer's official merchandise furnished by Producer. Producer shall retain 100% of all receipts from merchandise unless Artist and their merchandising agency are informed of any scale of charges, commissions or other restrictions on their rights to sell merchandise which shall be specified on the FACE of the Agreement hereof, otherwise the Purchaser will be responsible for all charges levied by the venue or other party.

SECURITY

Purchaser will provide and pay for adequate, responsible and clearly identifiable staff persons to insure the safety of Artist and Artist's staff, equipment, instruments, personal property and vehicles as follows:

A. There must be at least four (4) security persons in front of the stage during the Artist's performance.

B. There must be one (1) security person at each and all band dressing rooms, crew rooms and sound and lighting console positions at all times.

C. There must be a security person or guard at all Artist buses, trucks or other vehicles.

D. There must be a security person within the immediate vicinity of all Artist merchandising displays.

E. There must be a security person at every backstage entrance and stage access to assure the safety of Artist and their property.

DRESSING ROOMS

Purchaser will provide and pay for rooms as follows:

A. Band Dressing Room will be a well-lit, comfortable room with mirror, easy chairs or sofa, etc., for twelve (12) people. This room must be lockable, the key to be given to the Road Manager upon his arrival. The dressing room shall also have hot and cold running water, soap, and bathroom facilities either connected to the dressing room or a private non-public area within a reasonable distance.

B. Production Office at the Venue with electricity, table, chair and functional internet, to include any adaptors to same if international, for use by Artist's Tour Manager/ Production Manager and key personnel. This room must be lockable and the key to be given to the Tour Manager upon his arrival and must be guarded at all times by an identifiable Security person. For International performances where other than 110 Voltage is the standard, power transformers will be provided for Artist and Crew's electrical equipment. If Artist appears as part of a Festival Presentation, or as a support act, Artist's Tour Manager/Production Manager and key personnel shall have shared full access and utilization of the Venue Production Office facilities.

C. Crew/Tuning Room shall also be lockable, the key given to the Tour Manager/ Production Manager upon his arrival. This room shall have electricity, table, and comfortable chairs for twelve (12) people. For International performances where other than 110 Voltage is the standard, power transformers will be provided to Artist/ Crew electrical equipment.

D. If there is no shower in the venue two (2) shower rooms (hotel day-rooms) must be supplied by Purchaser for use by the Artist and crew, complete with a suitable number of towels provided at hotel. Purchaser must also provide for local transportation to and from such nearby hotel so the Artist and Crew may shower. See Runner provisions as set out in Paragraph 26. This will be confirmed during the "advancing" of the show with the Artist's Tour Manager. Purchaser provided hotel day-rooms shall be pre-paid in full and a receipt confirming this shall be provided to Tour Manager upon arrival at Venue confirming same.

E. The Producer will require thirty-six (36) large bath towels at load-in. This number can be reduced to twenty-four (24) if there are no showers at the venue. These towels should be placed in the Artist's Production Office at time of load-in. This does include all towels needed for Skinny Girl Riot, but not the support acts.

F. A massage room and table with a qualified 100% female masseuse for Frankie Fabulous. The masseuse must be between 95 and 105 lbs, blonde, busty and of Polish descent but speaks little to no English. A mute is very desirable if available.

CATERING
LUNCH

Skinny Girl Riot will require lunch for fourteen (14) people. This must be ready at load-in time and should consist of the following:

> Hot soup, French bread and crackers
> One (1) Deli Meat tray (organic Salami, Roast Beef, Turkey, Chicken and Ham)
> One (1) Deli Cheese tray (Swiss, Munster, Pepper Jack and American)
> One (1) Deli Condiments tray (organic Lettuce, Tomato, Pickle and Onion)
> One (1) Fruit tray (Bananas, Oranges, Blueberries and Apples)
> Assorted breads for sandwiches (French Rolls, Sour Rolls and Sliced Bread)
> Condiments for sandwiches (Mayo, Mustard and Butter)
> Assorted desserts (Yogurt, Pudding, Chips and Candies)
> Assorted Beverages (Sodas, Bottled Water, Hot Coffee, Juices, Milk and Tea)
> A never-ending supply of ice

DINNER

Skinny Girl Riot will require a Hot Dinner for fourteen (14) people at 5:00 p.m. This number DOES NOT include any opening acts, local production crews or local stagehands, and the Purchaser should take these other people into account. The people in the Skinny Girl Riot entourage prefer healthy foods. This meal should consist of the following:

Two (2) Hot entrees (Beef, Pork, Chicken, Turkey or Fish)

Two (2) Hot sides (Pasta, Potatoes or Rice)

Two (2) Hot vegetarian entrees

Two (2) Hot vegetables (Corn, Green Beans, Carrots, Peas, etc.)

Hot Soup, Salad, Bread and Butter

Healthy salad bar with assorted fresh vegetables and salad dressings

Assorted Desserts (Chocolate Cakes, Fruit Pies or Pastries)

Assorted Beverages (Sodas, Bottled Waters, Juices, Hot Coffee, Hot Teas and 2% Milk)

Depending on the daily time schedules for the Artist and Crew, some people may elect to eat after the performance or have their dinner wrapped up and taken to the bus for later. The Tour Manager will confirm any special requests.

Please note: In the case of a lunch/dinner buyout, the Purchaser shall provide a $20.00 U.S. equivalent per person for Fourteen (14) people to the Tour Manager of Skinny Girl Riot upon his arrival. This number includes all Skinny Girl Riot personnel.

DRESSING ROOM

The band dressing room must be set with all catering by 3:00 p.m.

One (1) case of Stella Artois beer (24 bottles)

One (1) case of Corona beer (24 bottles)

One Half (1/2) case of Red Bull Energy Drink (12 cans)

One (1) Liter of Jack Daniels Whiskey

One (1) Liter of Grey Goose Vodka

Three (3) cases of 12 ounce Aquafina Water, Seventy-two (72) Bottles.

Four (4) 750 ml bottles of Cabernet Sauvignon or Merlot (Red)

Twelve (12) Bottles of assorted Gatorades

One (1) case of soda (12 COKES, 6 assorted other non diet sodas, 6 Diet Coke)

One (1) gallon of organic Orange Juice

One (1) gallon of organic Cranberry Juice

One (1) gallon of organic Apple juice

One (1) Deli tray with assorted organic meats (turkey, salami, ham, chicken, roast beef, prosciutto) and assorted cheeses (brie, parmesan, Swiss, pepper jack, cheddar).

One (1) small bottle of olive oil

One (1) Large fruit tray (Oranges, Blueberries, Kiwis, Apples, Strawberries and Bananas)

One (1) Large vegetable tray with ranch dip

One (1) Large container of spicy hummus

One (1) bowl of raw cashews and almonds

One (1) plate of flat bread

One (1) bowl of pita-type chips

Four (4) boxes of Fruit Loops cereal, GIANT SIZE

One (1) giant bowl of M&Ms (pink ones only!)

Assorted breads (French, sourdough, white and wheat)

Eating utensils (Forks, Spoons, Knifes and Napkins)

Assorted condiments (Butter, Mayo, Ketchup and Mustard)

Lots of CLEAN ICE in separate bin or cooler

Forty-eight (48) Large Solo Cups

Cork Screw/Wine bottle Opener & a Beer bottle Opener

Thirty-six (36) Full size bath towels

AFTER SHOW FOOD

One (1) Case of Stella Artois beer or local lager (24 bottles)

One (1) Case of 12 ounce Aquafina Water (24) Bottles.

Three (3) Large Pizzas: (1) Cheese, (1) Meat, (1) Vegetarian. The band's after show food must be ready to be given to the tour manager when their performance has ended.

BARRICADE

Purchaser will provide and pay for a professional concert barricade covering the entire length of the stage, (no dinner tables, bicycle racks, etc.) and no farther than five feet (5') from the stage. There must be a barricade around sound and light console platform as well. This is MANDATORY; there can be no show without the proper barricades.

STAGEHANDS/LOADERS

Purchaser will provide and pay for a minimum of six (6) stagehands/loaders to assist Artist with load-in and load-out at venue as well as other tasks relating to the production of the show. Loaders shall not double as security.

RUNNER

Purchaser will provide and pay for one (1) runner with a reliable seven-passenger van that is fully insured and legally registered. The driver must be a sober, legally licensed driver and available from load-in until load-out for the sole use of Producer. Runner/driver shall have a fully operational mobile phone at all times and fully familiar with the local area. For international engagements, said runner/driver shall also be reasonably proficient in speaking English. If and to the extent that Purchaser shall fail to provide said Runner at any time on the day of the Engagement as set forth herein, any and all expenses that Producer may incur, including but not limited to taxi charges, in connection with such failure, shall be reimbursed upon demand to the Producer.

SOUNDCHECK

The Producer shall always be guaranteed a sound check. The Producer shall be notified of any sound level or time restrictions on sound check. The producer's sound check is a closed sound check and unauthorized personnel may not attend. It is the Purchaser's responsibility to assure that the sound check is secure.

PARKING

Purchaser will provide and pay any and all required permits and/or fees, for parking in the immediate vicinity of the venue location(s) for vehicles that Producer may require for the purpose of local and/or touring ground transportation needs. If and to the extent that Purchaser fails to make any and all arrangements with reference to this Parking provision, which results in any tickets, fines, fees, and or penalties assessed to the vehicles utilized by, and, or for Producer for any such Engagement hereunder, Purchaser shall be solely responsible for the payment of any such tickets, fines, fees, and or penalties. The necessity of parking requirements shall be fully determined upon advance of the Engagement(s) contracted hereby. Any inadvertent failure to fully advance such parking requirements shall not relieve Purchaser of the responsibility for Producer's parking needs.

TECHNICAL REQUIREMENTS
    A. SOUND POWER - All sound power shall be on a separate circuit from LIGHTING power.
    B. SHOW POWER - When venue cannot meet Producer's power requirements for sound and lights, Purchaser must provide an acceptable generator to meet power requirements.
    C. STAGE POWER - The specific requirements on stage are as follows:

        1. Three (3) x Twenty (20) ampere 110volt independent circuits for the stage.
        2. One (1) x Twenty (20) ampere 110v circuit for the F.O.H. mix area.

For ALL International performances where voltage is other than 110v, Purchaser shall provide: four (4) step-down power transformers, each with a minimum of two (2) 110v 20A 50/60 Hz circuits per transformers for Producer's exclusive use. We cannot share transformers with any other acts.

D. STAGE - Artist requires a minimum stage size 40' x 20'. Stage should be secure, stable and able to support Producer's equipment and performance.

E. DRUM RISER - Producer requires a minimum drum riser size of 8' (w) x 8' (d) x 2' (h). Riser should be of the rolling type, with wheels, secure, stable and able to roll while still supporting Producer's equipment. This riser is for the exclusive use of Skinny Girl Riot only and needs to be available at time of load-in through time of load-out. Please check with tour manager during show advance to see if this is needed. Sometimes Skinny Girl Riot carries a drum riser.

F. LOAD-IN - Artist will load in at 12:00 p.m. unless otherwise agreed during the show advance. Doors must be open and all loaders and runners must be there on time and ready to work at 11:30 a.m.

G. RIGGING - Purchaser must provide an experienced rigger for venues where lighting and PA are to be flown.

H. HOUSE SOUND SPECS

Purchaser is to supply and pay for, at his sole cost and expense, a concert sound system complete with qualified personnel to install and operate the HOUSE system subject to the following specifications. Producer and or Producer's representative (Sound Mixer) shall have full control over sound system during Producer's sound check and performance. A house electrician will be available and present, from load-in through the entire sound check and performance. In the event that Purchaser engages a Sound System Contractor for the sound provision hereof, Purchaser shall still be accountable for the full compliance herewith. HOUSE SOUND SYSTEM MUST BE FULLY SET-UP AND OPERATIONAL AT TIME OF LOAD-IN.

Purchaser will provide one (1) technically qualified and acceptable FOH System Engineer to assist Producer's traveling Sound Engineer. System shall be capable of providing 120dba clear undistorted sound throughout the listening area, with a bandwidth of not less than 40 Hz to 18 KHz. The drive rack shall contain two (2) one third octave equalizers of professional quality, of the following options: BSS FCS-960. KLARK TEKNIK DN360 or DN 27-A. Following the left and right outputs from the console (not inserted), followed by two (2) DBX compressor/limiters such as DBX 165-A or 160-X, linked for stereo operation followed by the active frequency dividing system.

House Sound Console

Minimum: 40 working channels, minimum 8 VCA group Mixing Console.

The consoles must always be provided with identical number of snake channels to match provided consoles.

<u>Acceptable Console Brands/Models:</u>

Midas Heritage 3000

Yamaha PM-4000

Midas XL-8

Midas XL-4

Midas XL-3

Yamaha PM5D

Yamaha M7CL

Digidesign Profile

Effects

(2) Digital Reverbs; (2) Yamaha SPX 990, (1) Yamaha SPX 1000(1) Eventide Harmonizer

(1) Digital Delay ex: TC Electronics D-2, Roland SDE 3000, TC Electronics 2290

Dynamics

(2) 1/3 Octave EQ, ex: Klark Teknik DN 360, TC Electronics, or White

(16) Compressors ex: DBX-160 A, DBX-1066, BSS

(6) Dramer DS 201

(1) Summit Compressor

(4) Distressor Compressors

Plus: intercom system for talkback from FOH console to stage. This is mandatory.

Playback / Recording

CD Player (Sony or comparable)

DAT Machine (Sony or Panasonic)

<u>House Speaker System and Power Amps</u>

Note: The Front of House speaker system shall be capable of reproducing 120 dba of clear undistorted sound throughout the audience listening area (i.e., including side hangs and or delay systems as required).

Acceptable Speakers include V-dosc, Lacustics, Meyer Milo, d&b, EAW 760/761, EV Line Array, JBL Vertec, etc.

I. MONITOR SOUND SPECS

Purchaser is to supply and pay for, at his sole cost and expense, a professional concert monitor system complete with qualified personnel to install and operate the MONITOR system subject to the following specifications. Producer and or Producer's representative (Sound Engineer) shall have full control over monitor system during Producers sound check and performance. A <u>house electrician</u> will be available through the entire sound check and performance. In the event that Purchaser engages a Sound System Contractor for the sound provision hereof, Purchaser shall still be accountable for the full compliance herewith. The specifications listed below are exact requirements of the Producer, <u>unless notified otherwise in writing</u>, during the Advancing period by Producer's Production Manager and confirmed by Producer's Sound Engineer.

Purchaser will provide one (1) technically qualified, acceptable-to-Producer, English speaking, MONITOR Mixing Engineer. Unless notified otherwise, in advance and in writing, by Producer's Production Manager, the Monitor Mix Engineer shall be supervised by Producer's Sound Engineer.

Monitor Console

    40 (working) channels x 16 console with post graphic EQ soloing system

    <u>Acceptable Console Brands/Models:</u>

        Midas Heritage 3000

        Midas XL-3

        Yamaha PM-4000m

Effects

    (10) 1/3 octave equalizers: Klark Technic, TC Electronics, White

    (10) Noise Gates: Drawmer, BSS

    (2) Digital Reverb/Delay: Yamaha SPX 990, SPX 1000

Speakers

    All monitors must be bi-amp or tri-amplified of the same high quality as House Speaker System.

    Six (6) Double 12" or Single 15" low profile wedges with 2" horn, and an identical wedge for the monitor cue

    Two (2) 18' speaker, w/ (1) 12" speaker with (1) 2" horn for drum fill

    Two (2) 3-way <u>SIDE-FILL</u> cabinets, including additional subs, with same specifications as house system.

    D.I.'s and Snakes, Power Amps & AC Drop Boxes

All direct boxes should be: Countryman, Whirlwind Directors, BSS

300 ft. 40 channel house snake system with 50ft. 40 channel 2-way splitter

(4) 12 channel sub snakes on multi-pin disconnects

(1) 40 channel splitter with ground lifts and multi-pin disconnects

All power amps should be: Crest, QSC or Crown

J. MICROPHONES

Input List shall be available separately with Stage Plot for potential alterations, etc.

Microphones shall be of <u>high</u> quality, as follows:

<u>Condenser microphones:</u>

<u>AKG</u> C414, 451 (451 must have 20db insert).

<u>NEUMAN</u> KM 100/84, <u>BEYER</u> MC 740, <u>SHURE</u> SM 81.

<u>Dynamic microphones:</u>

<u>SHURE</u> SM 57, SM 58, <u>BEYER</u> 201.

<u>SENNHEISER</u> MD 421, 507, M88, (SM Beta 58 for vocals a must)

<u>Direct Injection Boxes:</u>

<u>COUNTRYMAN, BSS</u>

K. BACKLINE

PURCHASER WILL SUPPLY BACKLINE, UNLESS OTHERWISE AGREED IN WRITING. NO SHARING OF <u>ANY</u> BACKLINE EQUIPMENT. ALL EQUIPMENT LISTED HERE IS FOR EXCLUSIVE USE BY SKINNY GIRL RIOT ONLY.

<u>GUITARS & BASS AMPLIFIERS AND CABINETS</u>

4 – MARSHALL JCM 2000 3-channel AMPS w/ FOOT SWITCH & CABLE

8 – MARSHALL 4 X 12 CABINETS (4 SLANTS, 4 STRAIGHTS w/ MATCHING GRILLS)

2 – AMPEG SVT IV (4) PRO BASS AMP or SVT V (5) PRO AMP or SVT VI (6) PRO AMP

2 – AMPEG BASS CABINETS (8X10 SPKRS)

3 – POWER TRANSFORMERS (for international shows only, 3 for stage, 110v 20A 60 Hz output)

<u>NOTE:</u> EACH SPEAKER CABINET SHOULD BE SUPPLIED WITH A SPEAKER CABLE THAT WILL REACH THE AMPLIFIER POSITIONED ON TOP OF THE DOUBLE STACKED CABINETS. EACH AMPLIFIER SHOULD BE SUPPLIED WITH A POWER CABLE THAT REACHES FROM THE STACKED AMPLIFIER TO THE FLOOR.

<u>DRUMS</u>

Yamaha drums – SKINNY GIRL RIOT EXCLUSIVE USE ONLY

PREFER GRAY, SILVER OR WHITE - (NO MIX & MATCHED KITS PLEASE)

2 – 22 x 18 INCH BASS DRUMS (BOTH DRUMS WITH TOM MOUNTS)

ALL RACK TOMS (shallow sizes only, no power toms)

1 – 11 x 8 INCH TOM TOM MOUNTED ON STAND

1 – 12 x 8 INCH TOM TOM MOUNTED ON KICK DRUM

1 – 13 x 10 INCH POWER TOM MOUNTED ON KICK DRUM

1 – 14 x 16 INCH TOM TOM FLOOR, WITH LEGS

1 – 16 x 18 INCH TOM TOM FLOOR, WITH LEGS

1 – 18 x 16 INCH TOM TOM FLOOR, WITH LEGS

1 – 14 X 5 INCH SNARE DRUM

NOTE: REQUIRE NEW EVANS DRUM HEADS ON ALL DRUMS PLEASE

Evans Heads

Tom batters: G2 clear

Tom resonant: G1 clear

Snare batter: onyx

Snare resonant: 300 glass

Kick batter: EQ3

Kick resonant: Yamaha heads

Hardware:

1 – 2 leg hit hat w/ bass drum arm mount system

2 – x-hats w/ arm mounting system (extended ones please)

1 – double Tom stand with mounts

1 – single boom cymbal stand

6 – double boom cymbal stands

2 – snare drum stands

1 – drum throne

1 – DRUM CARPET

2 – 18" FANS

ALL CYMBALS ARE TO BE PAISTE SIGNATURE SERIES

1 – 18" PAISTE CRASH CYMBAL

1 – 19" PAISTE CRASH CYMBAL

2 – 20" PAISTE CRASH CYMBAL

1 – 20" CHINA CYMBAL

1 – 22" POWER BELL RIDE CYMBAL

1 – 10" PAISTE SPLASH CYMBAL

1 – 12" PAISTE SPLASH CYMBAL

2 – PAIR OF 14" HI-HAT CYMBALS

L. LIGHTING REQUIREMENTS

For headline shows each gig will be advanced on an individual basis.

Skinny Girl Riot prefers a fully-automated lighting rig consisting of Mac 2000 or Mac 700 Profiles and Wash lights, Elation Professional LED lights, Atomic 3000 strobes and 8-light DWE moles.

For club shows with house rigs that contain a large amount of par cans, the following gel numbers will be required and no substitutes will be accepted:

Gel List:

Lee 106, Lee 119, Lee 139, Lee 135, Lee 101, Lee 116 and Lee 180.

Skinny Girl Riot will also require two (2) Reel EFX DF-50 hazers with 3-speed fans.

Skinny Girl Riot's optimum lighting requirements for a club performance with par cans are as follows:

a. 60K of front lighting (5 12K washes: Lee 106, Lee 119, Lee 135, Lee 116, & Lee 180)

b. 48K of rear lighting (6 8K washes: Lee 106, Lee 139, Lee 135, Lee 101, Lee 116, & Lee 180)

c. 12K of rear drum lights (6 2K washes: Lee 106, Lee 139, Lee 135, Lee 101, Lee 116, & Lee 180)

d. 4 – 8-light DWE molefays (2 on the front truss, 2 on the back truss)

e. 10 – Martin Atomic 3000 strobes (4 in the rear truss, 4 on the front truss, 2 behind drum riser)

f. 8 – Elation Professional Platinum Wash ZFX PRO LED lights on the floor.

g. If moving lights are provided, Martin Mac 2000 or Mac 700 Profiles and Wash lights are preferred. A fully-automated rig is preferred by Skinny Girl Riot. In this case, a minimum of 12 wash lights and 6 profiles in the front truss are preferred. A minimum of 8 wash lights and 6 profiles in the rear truss are preferred.

h. 1 - Avolites Pearl Expert lighting console. NO Grand MA or Whole Hog!

Skinny Girl Riot has a 40' x 24' backdrop and two blow-up dolls that must be hung.

This is a general guide to follow but each gig will addressed on an individual basis after taking the lighting budget and room limitations into consideration.

SPARE LAMPS

System technician must have sufficient number of spare lamps on hand, to keep all fixtures of house lighting systems in working order.

TECHNICIAN

Competent lighting technician, familiar with current house lighting system, must be provided. Available at time of load-in, through completion of performance, to gel, patch, focus, and assist Producer's LD as needed.

FOCUS

If the lighting system is rigged in a way where it is not possible or safe for a man to climb on, then a ladder must be provided where each fixture can be reached. If any fixtures need to be focused before band gear is loaded onto the stage, Producer's LD must be informed of this during the Advance, before show day.

Opening/Supporting acts may not re-gel or re-focus any lighting.

INTERNATIONAL PERFORMANCES

Visas: When the location of performance(s) is outside the territorial limits of the United States of America, Purchaser agrees to procure, at his sole expense, for Producer and Producer's traveling party, the necessary visas, work permits and other documents of any nature whatsoever necessary or usually obtained to enable Producer to render its services hereunder.

Taxes: Purchaser shall be responsible for, and indemnify and hold Producer harmless from and against, any and all local, county, state, and country or government taxes, fees or levies on all income earned by Producer, or Producer's employees while in the country or countries under this contract. If taxes of any kind are required by the laws of any country, province, state, city, or other governmental body, then such Taxes shall be paid according to such laws. However, the Producer Fee stated on the face of the engagement contract to which this rider is attached shall be a NET TO PRODUCER SUM, post tax, and indicated as such.

Currency/Fees: Purchaser will pay Producer in U.S. Cash Dollars ONLY, prior to public admittance to venue, for any and all Fees and Payments due hereunder. With exception to per diems and/or meal buyouts, if any, which may be in local currency, unless otherwise agreed to in writing. In the event of unauthorized payment in any foreign currency, Purchaser shall assume any and all costs of conversion to actual US Dollars, including but not limited to currency conversion rate adjustments and conversion commissions, such that the Net Sum received in-hand by Producer shall not be less than the contractually agreed amount in US Dollars. Currency conversions will be based upon actual proven transaction percentages, and not upon any bank or government rates, as posted on the internet, any media outlets or newspapers.

Ground Travel: Purchaser agrees to provide Producer any and all ground transportation requirements while on the ground in your country. Producer requires a minimum of two (2) vehicles per trip. One (1) Cargo Van must be provided for transportation of luggage and musical equipment. There will be approximately 30 pieces of gear and luggage total for band and crew. This vehicle must be clear of seats and unobstructed. The production manager will accompany this vehicle at all times with movement of gear and luggage to/

from hotel and venue. Additionally there must be a vehicle capable of carrying 12 persons plus personal carry-on baggage. This vehicle must be comfortable and have a seat for everyone. Both vehicles must be ready simultaneously for all pick-ups and departures. All airport pick-ups will require an airport greeter, or promoter representative, fluent in English, to direct the Producer's entourage at the moment they arrive through customs or baggage. No passenger cars please.

Excess/Oversize Baggage Fees: Purchaser agrees to pay Producer any and all reimbursements, in U.S. Dollars, for costs incurred by the Producer for the shipping of show-related excess baggage. Including but not limited to Producer's professional musical equipment and personal luggage that is needed or associated with the show. These excess baggage fees must be covered for all travel to and from, any performance location, whether by air or ground.

PARAGRAPH HEADINGS

Paragraph headings are inserted in this Rider for convenience only and are not to be used in interpreting this Agreement.

AGREED TO AND ACCEPTED:
PURCHASER

_____

AGREED TO AND ACCEPTED
PRODUCER

_____

SKINNY GIRL RIOT INC.

CREATING YOUR TOUR BOOK

Two of the most important things that you'll need to get done by the time you start a tour is to have at least the first half of the tour advanced and your tour book completed.

The tour book—also called an itinerary—is extremely important. It contains all of the information for each show day: venue info, hotel info, show schedule, promoter info, production contact info, after show travel info, and any other pertinent info that you care to include. It also contains your travel details and hotel info for the days off. It should also contain the entourage's flight info and confirmation numbers for the beginning and end of the tour.

The front part of the tour book should include all of the tour dates and the contact info for the tour-related companies, such as the management company, booking agency, record company, merchandising company, business manager, publicist, travel agent, tour bus company, trucking company, backline rental company, pass company, VIP package company, tour book company, and any other companies involved.

The personnel page lists the names of the band members with their job titles. It also lists all of the crew and their job titles, as well as their cell phone numbers and email addresses. You should never put the band members' contact info in a tour book because it could end up in the wrong hands or even on the internet.

You can use a number of programs to make the tour book. I've sometimes used Microsoft Word or Excel but have also used database software, such as Microsoft Access and Filemaker Pro. Filemaker Pro is a program that many tour book companies use, but this software is a bit expensive and might be out of the price range of a new tour manager. Use whatever program you have to get the job done if you must create the tour book.

Filemaker Pro and other database programs are ideal to use for tour books because once you build your template for the tour book and type in a venue and all of its information, for example, that information is stored in the program's database. So the next time you're playing that venue, you don't need to look up all of the venue's information again. It will already be stored in the database. The same goes for the hotel in that city, should you be staying in the same hotel again.

You'll quickly see that bands of the same genre often play the same venues, so if you continue working in the same genre you'll be seeing the same venues frequently. Once you've stored a venue's info in your database program, it will be in your computer the next time you do a show there and have to enter it into a new tour book. This saves a lot of time and effort.

There are numerous companies that will type the tour book—once you send them the necessary information—and then print and bind them for you, but these completed books can be expensive, depending on the length of the tour and the size of the book. Smart Art Itineraries has been around for years and is the leader in the tour itinerary business. Touring Logistics Itineraries is another good company that does quality work.

If you're working on a tight budget, you may have to create the tour book yourself. If so, once the book is completed, a good place to get the books printed and bound is FedEx Office. They can photocopy and bind your books in only a few hours, and they usually do good work.

If your budget's so tight that you can't afford to have the itineraries printed and bound, try to give everybody one in a cheap binder or just stapled together. If you can't afford to give everyone a hard copy of the tour book, at least make sure you and your driver have one.

Always be sure to email everyone involved with the tour a PDF copy of the book before the tour starts. The manager, booking agent, business manager, record company, publicist, bus company, merchandising company, and anyone else involved with the tour should get a copy of the tour book.

You don't want two dozen people emailing and calling you every day asking you for information they should already have. When you're ready to email everyone a copy of the tour book, the best way not to forget anyone is to think of three groups: the band, the crew, and all of the people in the tour-related companies in the front of the tour book. Once you've covered these three groups of people, you've pretty much covered everyone.

When you print out your tour book, always print each page of the book on one-sided pages. This way, when you're looking at a page in the book, you'll have a blank page on the left to write notes on. I'm always writing notes and guest list names and other things on the blank page for each show day in my tour book. If your budget is hopelessly desperate, you can cut the size of your tour book in half by not doing this, of course.

You can never have enough information in a tour book. If your band wants to know if each show is an all-ages gig, put that information in the book. If there are four bands on your tour and your band is worried if the stage is going to be big enough each day, put the size of each venue's stage in the tour book. If you're on a tight budget and can't afford any shower rooms, let the band know if the venue has a shower or not. Put the information that matters most to your band and crew into your tour book.

Below are the front pages, a show page, and a day off page from a tour book. Let's look at them so you can see what each page contains.

Always make a cover for your tour book so it looks professional. Get a copy of the band's logo and put it on the front of the book, or you could use the artwork from the cover of their new album. Just do something. Below that image, you can put the name of the tour if there is one. If it's a U.S. tour, put something like "U.S. Tour 2012" or whatever applies.

The next page is usually the complete list of dates so everyone can see the tour dates at a glance. Always make the list of dates thorough and include the date, day of the week, venue name, city, and state. Make sure you specify "Day Off" if that day is a day off or type in "Travel Day" if it's a long travel day.

The next page is usually the Personnel page, listing all of the band members' names and what they do. It also lists all of the crew members and their job titles. As I said, always include the crew members' cell phone numbers and email addresses.

After that page is the Personnel page for any support acts. I always like to do a page for the opening acts so we know all of their names, and I also include the contact info for their tour manager. I give the tour manager for each support act a copy of our tour book in case they didn't bother to make one for their band, but I always tell them to keep the book confidential.

Next is the Tour-Related Companies page. Always make sure that this page is accurate and complete. Everyone involved with the tour needs all of the info in the book, and they need to know how to contact everyone else associated with the tour.

On the next page, include any flight info for the entourage that may apply. The band and some of the crew might live in the same city and the bus may be picking everyone up there, but a few of the crew may live in other cities and need to be flown in to start the tour. Put their flight info in the book and make sure you include their confirmation numbers. If everyone flies home at the end of the tour, include all of that flight info. The more info you include in the tour book, the fewer people you'll have coming to you every day asking for info they should already have.

The next page is the first day of the tour when the bus shows up, so the crew can load the gear into the trailer and everyone can load their belongings on the bus and choose their bunks for the trip. Always make sure that the crew waits for the band members to choose their bunks first and then allow the crew to choose from what's left.

In this fantasy scenario, the bus driver will arrive at the band's rehearsal studio at 6:00 p.m. after driving eight hours from Los Angeles to San Francisco. As you can see, we've booked him a hotel room for the night. The band will do a final rehearsal and then the will crew pack the gear into the trailer. We've typed in the driver's hotel info, and we've made sure to put his confirmation number in the book.

The out-of-town crew will spend the night on the bus parked at the driver hotel, and the band and crew members who live locally will go home for the night. The bus will leave for the venue at 11 a.m. the next day for noon load-in.

Print out all of this same info on a day sheet and post it on the wall in the front and back lounges of the bus. Make sure the bus driver gets a copy of the day sheet before he goes to his hotel room. Even though you've already given everyone a copy of the tour book, you still need to do the day sheets.

On the next page, we have our first show day. We've timed the bus's arrival so it's there at the venue before our noon load-in. Look at this page closely and you'll see that we have the driver's hotel info and confirmation number for the day. It's a show day, and there are showers at the venue, so we don't need to worry about shower rooms at a local hotel.

We've also listed all of the venue info, including the address, telephone number, website link, capacity of the venue (how many people it holds), number of dressing rooms and showers, stage size, and the fact that there's wireless internet. These are important bits of info that the entourage will want to know.

Next to the venue info is the show schedule for the day. As you can see, the load-in time is noon and we're going to do a 4:00 p.m. sound check. The promoter's not catering dinner at this venue. Instead, he's giving everyone in our entourage a $15 dinner buyout. If the promoter was doing a catered dinner for the entourage, you'd simply put in the appropriate time that dinner will be up and ready to eat. 5:00 p.m. would make sense because we're doing a 4:00 p.m. sound check and everyone will want to eat dinner shortly after sound check and before the VIP meet-and-greet starts at 5:30 p.m.

Next we have the show schedule. We only have our one support act today with no local bands added to the bill, and we have a strict midnight curfew. We've also added the fact that this is an all-ages gig because the band wants to know this info each show day.

Below is the promoter's contact info, as well as the promoter rep's contact info. The promoter rep is the person with whom you advanced the show and will usually be your contact at the venue on the show day. Sometimes you'll advance the show with the promoter or his rep but will deal with a club representative, such as the club manager, on the show day, but you should be told this when you advance the date.

Finally, at the bottom of the page is the after show travel info. We'll leave town at 2:00 a.m., and we've included where we're going next and the mileage and drive time to that city. I always use fifty miles per hour to determine the drive time for long drives. This compensates for traffic, fuel stops, driver breaks, and usually always works out just fine. In the end, it's better to be early than late.

On a short drive, you don't want to leave too early because it's unlikely the bus driver will be able to check into his hotel in the next city if he arrives too early. Let him sleep whenever you can.

Always check with your promoter rep to make sure how long you can park the bus at the venue after the show. It's always possible that they may have a bigger tour with multiple buses and trucks showing up soon, and they'll need the parking space you're in.

You'll do these same pages for each show day, day off, and travel day for the rest of the tour book. Some of the tour book companies have maps and calendars and all sorts of things that they like to add to the front of the tour book, and while these things are good to have in the book, if you're on a tight budget and doing the book yourself, you can live without them.

Always remember how important this book is to your tour. Never start a tour without one, make sure that it's as accurate and complete as possible, and always be certain that everyone involved receives one. Think of the tour book as your road map through a successful tour.

Skinny Girl Riot

USA Tour 2012

SKINNY GIRL RIOT--USA TOUR 2012	
Date	**Venue/City/State**
Saturday, March 31, 2012	**Travel Day**
Sunday, April 01, 2012	Club 1--San Francisco, CA
Monday, April 02, 2012	Club 2--Los Angeles, CA
Tuesday, April 03, 2012	Club 3--San Diego, CA
Wednesday, April 04, 2012	Club 4--Phoenix, AZ
Thursday, April 05, 2012	Club 5--Albuquerque, NM
Friday, April 06, 2012	**Day Off**
Saturday, April 07, 2012	Club 6--El Paso, TX
Sunday, April 08, 2012	Club 7--San Antonio, TX
Monday, April 09, 2012	Club 8--Houston, TX
Tuesday, April 10, 2012	Club 9--Dallas, TX
Wednesday, April 11, 2012	Club 10--New Orleans, LA
Thursday, April 12, 2012	**Day Off**
Friday, April 13, 2012	Club 11--Tallahassee, FL
Saturday, April 14, 2012	Club 12--Tampa, FL
Sunday, April 15, 2012	Club 13--Orlando, FL
Monday, April 16, 2012	Club 14--Atlanta, GA
Tuesday, April 17, 2012	Club 15--Raleigh, NC
Wednesday, April 18, 2012	**Day Off**
Thursday, April 19, 2012	Club 16--Washington, DC
Friday, April 20, 2012	Club 17--Philadelphia, PA
Saturday, April 21, 2012	Club 18--Hartford, CT
Sunday, April 22, 2012	Club 19--Boston, MA
Monday, April 23, 2012	Club 20--New York, NY
Tuesday, April 24, 2012	**Travel Home**

Skinny Girl Riot--Personnel			
Band			
Stevie Starbright	Vocals		
Frankie Fabulous	Guitar		
Jimmy Giant	Guitar		
Mikey Massive	Bass Guitar		
Tommy Twosticks	Drums		
Crew			
Bobby Blinder	Tour Manager/LD	cell: 555-673-3342	tourmangler@tour.net
Lance Loudnoise	Production Manager/FOH	cell: 555-833-4233	150dBokay@email.com
Ricky Racket	Stage manager/SR guitar	cell: 555-872-4423	stagemgr0@nosend.com
Jerry Spazo	SL Guitar Tech	cell: 555-888-2333	spazinhard@email.com
Kyle Klown	Drum tech	cell: 555-232-3090	klowning@tour.net
Tony Tonedeaf	Monitor Engineer	cell: 555-899-3899	deaddrums@nosend.com
Penny Tightpants	Production Assistant	cell: 555-333-3343	tighterp@email.com
Woodrow Pilson	Merchandiser	cell: 555-422-0393	nocomps@tour.net
Leadfoot Johnson	Bus Driver	cell: 555-434-1130	gofast@nosend.com

The Worst--Personnel			
Band			
Jackson Daniels	Vocals/Guitar		
James Beam	Lead Guitar		
John Walker	Bass Guitar		
Josie Cuervo	Drums		
Crew			
Forrest Dump	Tour Manager/FOH	cell: 555-638-3238	theworsttm@email.com
Hank Krank	Backline Tech	cell: 555-666-2100	doingitall@nosend.com

Skinny Girl Riot--USA Tour 2012	
Tour Related Offices	

Management	**Magnificent Management**	*Booking Agency*	**The Booking Factory Inc**
	8399 Your Dollar Drive		44343 Big Booker Highway
	Los Angeles, CA 90023		Hollywood, CA 90028
Tel	555-323-9973	**Tel**	555-338-8098
Cell	555-323-7373	**Cell**	555-333-3300
Contact	Ronnie Rainmaker	**Contact**	Big Gig Gonzales
Email	raininghard@mmgmt.com	**Email**	bigig@bookingfactory.com
Record Company	**Sadistic Succotash SeeDees**	*Business Management*	**Spot On Numbers**
	8323 Big Star Lane		7676 Bottom Line Drive
	El Segundo, CA 93283		Los Angeles, CA 90028
Tel	555-233-2338	**Tel**	555-233-4234
Cell	555-663-3823	**Cell**	555-663-2383
Contact	L.P. Disc	**Contact**	Jenny Genius
Email	lpd@sadisticsuccotash.com	**Email**	jennyg@numbers.com
Bus Company	**BadAss Busses**	*VIP Tickets*	**Everyone's A VIP Inc**
	323987 Oil Spot Road		7473 Vip Drive
	Los Angeles, CA 90023		Los Angeles, CA 90029
Tel	555-399-9399	**Tel**	555-324-3233
Cell	555-399-3937	**Cell**	555-338-3238
Contact	Connie Crankshaft	**Contact**	Sally Sellout
Email	connie@badassbusses.com	**Email**	sally@priceytix.com

			Skinny Girl Riot--Flight Grid					
			Arriving San Francisco 3/31/12					
Carrier	**Name**	**Flight #**	**Departing**	**Arriving**	**Flight #**	**Departing**	**Arriving**	**Confirmation #**
American	Ricky Racket	AA 2237	DFW 9:00 AM	SFO 10:25 AM				BKLKKS
American	Lance Loudnoise	AA 2237	DFW 9:00 AM	SFO 10:25 AM				BAMPRI
Delta	Jerry Spazo	DL 2049	ATL 8:10 AM	SFO 10:17 AM				GUTRPR
Delta	Kyle Klown	DL 2049	ATL 8:10 AM	SFO 10:17 AM				XRMNB
			Arriving home 4/24/12					
Carrier	**Name**	**Flight #**	**Departing**	**Arriving**	**Flight #**	**Departing**	**Arriving**	**Confirmation #**
American	Ricky Racket	AA 4403	JFK 2:55 PM	RDU 4:40 PM	AA 679	RDU 7:20 PM	DFW 9:15 PM	BKLKKS
American	Lance Loudnoise	AA 4403	JFK 2:55 PM	RDU 4:40 PM	AA 679	RDU 7:20 PM	DFW 9:15 PM	BAMPRI
United	Jerry Spazo	UA 5712	JFK 2:27 PM	IAD 3:52 PM	UA 3769	IAD 4:45 PM	ATL 6:40 PM	GLIHIU
United	Kyle Klown	UA 5712	JFK 2:27 PM	IAD 3:52 PM	UA 3769	IAD 4:45 PM	ATL 6:40 PM	XLKHKL
United	Stevie Starbright	UA 887	JFK 2:40 PM	SFO 6:08 PM				MKEIID
United	Frankie Fabulous	UA 887	JFK 2:40 PM	SFO 6:08 PM				MKEIID
United	Jimmy Giant	UA 887	JFK 2:40 PM	SFO 6:08 PM				MKEIID
United	Mikey Massive	UA 887	JFK 2:40 PM	SFO 6:08 PM				MKEIID
United	Tommy Twosticks	UA 887	JFK 2:40 PM	SFO 6:08 PM				MKEIID
United	Bobby Blinder	UA 887	JFK 2:40 PM	SFO 6:08 PM				MKEIID
United	Penny Tightpants	UA 887	JFK 2:40 PM	SFO 6:08 PM				MKEIID
United	Tony Tonedeaf	UA 887	JFK 2:40 PM	SFO 6:08 PM				MKEIID

Skinny Girl Riot USA Tour 2012	
City/State San Francisco, CA	Saturday, March 31, 2012
Time Zone Pacific	**Travel/Day Off**

Travel

    Band & Crew Entourage arrives in San Francisco. See flight details grid for flight info.

Hotel

The Happy Hotel
838 Happy Drive
San Francisco, CA 94107   **Distance to venue** 15 miles
    Tel 555-674-8383   **Distance to airport** 2 miles
Confirmation # 83873038393
    Amenities free wireless internet, gym, pool, 24-hour room service, restaurant and bar

Notes

    The bus must park across the street in the parking lot in front of the hotel.

Travel/Day Off

Skinny Girl Riot--USA Tour 2012		

Venue	Club 1	Sunday, April 01, 2012
Time Zone	Pacific	**Show Day**

Travel

Band & Crew In San Francisco

Hotel

The Happy Hotel
838 Happy Drive
San Francisco, CA 94107   **Dist. to venue** 15 miles
Tel 555-674-8383   **Dist. to airport** 2 miles
Confirmation # 83873038393
Amenities free WIFI, gym, pool, 24-hour room service, restaurant and bar

Venue	Club 1	**Load-in** 12:00 PM
	666 3rd St	**Sound check** 4:00 PM
	San Francisco, CA 94107	**Meet & greet** 5:00 PM
Tel	555-777-1439	**Dinner** Buyout
Website	www.theclub1.com	**Doors** 7:00 PM
Capacity	1633	**The Worst** 8:00--8:30 PM
Dressing rooms	2 with showers & toilets	**Band X** 9:00--10:30 PM
Internet	wireless backstage	**Curfew** 11:00 PM
All ages	Yes	
Notes	Vile hellhole with a corner stage the size of a bath mat.	

Promoter	Antitrust Suit, Inc.		
Contact	J. Slowhand	**Promoter rep**	Vince Vega
Tel	555-666-1369	**Tel**	666-555-2383
Cell	555-666-3930	**Cell**	666-555-3838
Email	paidbail@email.com	**Email**	vincent@promoter.net

After Show Travel

San Francisco to Los Angeles: 381 miles (8 hours)

Notes

Load-in tomorrow is at 12:00 PM, sharp.

COORDINATING WITH THE SUPPORT ACTS

I've met some tour managers who adopt the "every man for himself" attitude when it comes to the support acts. I've never believed in thinking this way. If you're the tour manager for the headliner, you have to look after the support acts, to a certain degree, if you want the tour to run smoothly; and if it doesn't run smoothly, you're the one who's going to suffer most when the daily chaos ensues.

One of the things I always do when I'm organizing a tour is to obtain from each support act some important information that I'll include in my pre-advance package. The more information you provide the promoter rep about the support acts, the more informed he'll be about the tour as a whole.

There are many tour managers working for new support acts who are inexperienced and untrained and don't know to send the promoter rep any information about their band. They just show up on the show day with the promoter rep completely in the dark about their band, then wonder why their day is so difficult, and you'll be the person they come running to for help when the promoter gets fed up with them.

If I don't know the support act's road manager, I'll contact the band's agent or manager and get his name and email address and then shoot off an email to him to obtain the following information:

1. Cell phone number for the support band's tour manager if I don't already have it.
2. Complete list of names and job titles for everyone in his entourage.
3. How are you and your gear traveling, van and trailer or bus and trailer?
4. Email me the band's rider, stage plot, and input chart.

This is all I need to know about them in the beginning, but it will tell me volumes.

As I said in the chapter on tour books, I always put the names and job titles of the support acts in the front of my tour book. I also include the contact info for the road manager, so I have it handy whenever I need it. I don't worry about contact info for the rest of their crew because it's rare that I'd ever need to contact them; and if any of my crew wanted to speak to them before the tour starts, I'd get their contact info from their road manager.

It's important to know what kind of vehicle each of the support acts are traveling in. You'll want to add this information to your pre-advance sheet so the promoter rep can plan ahead for parking. You'll also want to include the rider, stage plot, and input chart for each support act so the promoter rep has this info. Don't rely on a new support act tour manager to do this; he may not even know to do it. Do it yourself because if the promoter rep can't get this info from the support act, he's going to be calling you for it.

Even though you should request the support band's rider and send it to the promoter for the record, most of what's in their rider will end up being completely irrelevant to your tour. If I have two support acts on the tour, I'll take a look at the catering budgets for each show—and they're all usually in the same range—and determine what I'm going to be able to give each band for dressing room catering.

I don't let the promoter rep fill a support act dressing room rider to the letter, and I certainly don't want the promoter rep to fill their entire dressing room rider after I've gotten the support act used to getting a certain amount, because then they're going to be coming to me constantly asking why they can't get more like they did that night. Don't let that can of worms be opened.

I appreciate a young support act tour manager who's smart enough to at least try to contact the promoter rep and give him some pertinent information about his band, but there's always that one guy who thinks he's smart and can go behind my back and try to supersede my authority and get more than what he's told he can get. But his chances of succeeding at this are worse than starting a snowball stand in hell.

I'm running the tour, not the promoter rep, and if the shows are selling out, my band's paying for 85 percent (or whatever your deal is) of anything the support acts get out of their back end money. So what they get has to be controlled and limited, within reason, so the headliner can earn as much money as possible. Making sure that your band earns every dime possible is your job as the band's road manager and tour accountant.

After taking a close look at the catering budget, I might give the first band on the bill a case of water, a case of soda, and a case of beer. I'll also make sure they're included for dinner each show and get stage towels for their show.

For the second band on the bill, I'll usually give them the same thing the first band received but add something extra, such as a bottle of liquor that's on their rider and a deli tray, because they're our direct support act. I'll find out from their tour manager what they prefer.

I make sure to let each support act tour manager know before the tour starts exactly what to expect each show for dressing room catering so there's no confusion and complaining once the tour begins. If we're on a bigger tour with a bigger budget, I'm always happy to give the support acts more things that are on their rider. If we're on a bigger sold out tour, I'm always happy to try and meet their rider to the letter, as long as their rider isn't bigger than my headliner's rider and doesn't put us over the catering budget.

If we're on a club tour where dressing rooms are going to be limited and there's only one shower in the headliner's dressing room, I'll tell the support acts that they're welcome to use our dressing room shower after all of my people are done at the end of the night. This may seem harsh, but there's no way you can have everyone from the support acts running in and out of your band's dressing room all day to take showers. The bathroom's going to be filthier than a truck stop toilet in no time. How long do you think your band's going to put up with that?

If we're on a club tour and we have three or four support acts and we're going to be faced with small stages, a tight show schedule, and possible early curfews, I'll tell the support acts to get together before the tour starts and figure out how they're going to share a common backline. I don't request this; I tell them that this is what has to happen and for what reasons.

By doing this, you'll be able to shave down the length of the changeovers between each band and solve the Rubik's Cube puzzle of how you're going to get gear for five bands on those small stages. Our direct support act will usually be allowed to set up their own backline in front of ours because they're the most popular support act and deserve a bit more consideration in these matters, but there may come a time in the smallest venue when you may have to make them reduce their amount of gear or also use the common backline.

If you've taken a look at each support band's stage plot, you'll know which of them think sensibly. If the first band on the bill sends you a stage plot that has twenty-four Marshall cabinets and a six-foot-high drum riser on it, you'll immediately know they're new. The same thing goes with a support act's dressing room rider; if they send me one that's bigger than Van Halen's, I'll know it's probably their first tour.

It's up to you to explain to them what they're getting for each show and how things are going to be done. I've always been able to do this respectfully and have never had any problems. It's all in how you deal with them from the beginning, but try to look after them as much as you can.

PREPARING YOUR TOUR ACCOUNTING

Through the years, I've met many people who hear the word *accounting* and suddenly become frightened at the thought of doing this job for a living. I'm not saying you can train a chimp to do accounting for a music tour, but you don't have to be Einstein or a CPA (certified public accountant), either. Although, CPAs—or accounting graduates—who don't want to spend the rest of their lives cooped up in an office are perfect candidates for the tour manager or tour accountant job.

I've never taken a single accounting class; I taught myself how to do it. When I started out as a tour manager back in the '80s, we were still doing our road reports on large envelopes that had a cash ledger printed on the front. You'd enter all of your receipts by hand into the ledger on the envelope and place the expense receipts inside and send it to the business manager every week. Then I bought my first computer in 1987—a Tandy laptop running DOS—and bought an accounting program and taught myself how to use it; and I haven't done any accounting on a printed envelope ever since. Anyone can learn how to do basic accounting.

There are accounting programs, such as Quicken or QuickBooks, which you can use to do your road accounting. Intuit offers various products in the Quicken and QuickBooks series, and each of them offers more features as they become more expensive.

Quicken Deluxe only costs about $60 U.S. and is powerful enough to do your weekly road reports, and it's easy to learn. QuickBooks is more expensive and takes more time to learn, so I don't recommend it for beginners. For new tour managers with little experience, I suggest Quicken Deluxe. It's inexpensive, and you can upgrade to their other products with more features in the future if you feel it's necessary.

Quicken can also convert your accounting ledger into an Excel spreadsheet that you can email to the business manager, or you can email the Quicken qdata file to the business manager if they have Quicken. With two clicks of a mouse, Quicken can formulate a report and graph from your ledger showing all of your expense categories and how much you've spent in each of them, helping you to keep a close eye on your tour budget.

You can also use a Microsoft Excel spreadsheet for your accounting if you know how to build one, but you won't have many of the features that Quicken offers. I have many spreadsheets that I've built over the years—some of them quite complicated—and they do many things, but I still believe that Quicken is the best way to go for the novice tour manager.

I've never met a business manager who insisted I use a certain program for my tour accounting. Most of them only care that what you send them each week is organized, easy to read, and correct down to the penny so they can add these figures into their master accounting for the band and manager.

When you start a tour, you'll most likely be starting off with a small amount of road float (expense money) and that'll be your first entry into your cash ledger. Then on a daily basis you'll add into the ledger the cash receipt for any expenditure that occurs. You'll also enter into the cash ledger any cash that you pick up each night from the promoter.

If your client's a new band, you'll be picking up every dime of your guarantee's balance each night. You'll need it all to pay for road expenses to get you to the next city. If your band's more successful, you'll probably only pick up what you need each night to cover your weekly nut and then take the rest of the balance in a check. Some managers and agents will insist that you pick up cash each night unless the promoter's a big company like Live Nation or AEG Worldwide, so they won't have to worry about the check bouncing.

A check from most established promoters is usually good, but a smaller local promoter could be one show away from going broke. You don't want your break-even tour budget to suddenly turn into a losing situation when a promoter's check bounces because your show happened to be the final loss he could financially bear and he's abruptly gone out of business. He's not going to tell your agent that he's on thin ice; the agent will find that out when the check bounces.

If you look at the Quicken cash ledger below, you'll see how to enter cash transactions. You should only enter cash transactions into this ledger. If you pick up a check from the promoter, you should enter that check into the reconciliation statement that we'll speak about later in this chapter.

The first expense receipt on this spreadsheet is per diems for the band and crew. You'll notice that I've designated that receipt with #101 on the spreadsheet. Next, I've entered the date on which the expenditure occurred, and then I typed a simple description of the receipt. Last, I entered the amount of the expense.

At the bottom of the ledger, you'll see the ending balance change each time you make a debit or credit entry to the account. The ending balance is the amount of cash that you should have when your accounting is current.

			Skinny Girl Riot Cash Ledger--USA 2012				
Date	Receipt #	Payee	Description of Transaction	Category	Payment	Deposit	Balance
3/31/2012			**road float from business manager**	**Float**		$3,000.00	$3,000.00
3/31/2012	101	Per diems	band and crew per diems: 4-1 to 4-7	Per Diems	$2,520.00		$480.00
4/1/2012			**San Francisco, part of balance for float**	**Income**		$1,000.00	$1,480.00
4/1/2012	102	Home Depot	Show supplies: supplies for backdrop	Show supplies	$56.39		$1,423.61
4/1/2012	103	Flying J	bus fuel	Bus fuel	$302.00		$1,121.61
4/1/2012	104	Office Max	office supplies: printer paper & cartridge	Office supplies	$46.75		$1,074.86
4/2/2012	105	Ramada Inn	driver hotel in Los Angeles	Hotels	$152.76		$922.10
4/3/2012	106	Embassy Suites	driver hotel in San Diego	Hotels	$115.16		$806.94
4/3/2012	107	Flying J	bus supplies: oil, coolant, cleaning goods	Bus supplies	$76.32		$730.62
4/3/2012			**San Diego balance of guarantee**	**Income**		$7,500.00	$8,230.62
4/4/2012	108	Home Depot	Show supplies: electrical tape, etc.	Show supplies	$19.38		$8,211.24
4/4/2012			**Phoenix balance of guarantee**	Income		$7,500.00	$15,711.24
4/4/2012	109	Petro	bus fuel	Bus fuel	$287.32		$15,423.92
4/4/2012	110	Hyatt	driver hotel in Phoenix	Hotels	$97.93		$15,325.99
4/5/2012			**Albuquerque balance of guarantee & %**	**Income**		$6,500.00	$21,825.99
4/5/2012	111	Comfort Inn	driver hotel in Albuquerque	Hotels	$79.94		$21,746.05
4/6/2012	112	Flying J	bus fuel	Bus fuel	$199.32		$21,546.73
4/6/2012	113	Blue Beacon	bus wash	Bus Wash	$79.83		$21,466.90
4/6/2012	114	Leadfoot Johnson	paid to driver for 2 generator services	Gen. service	$90.00		$21,376.90
4/6/2012	115	Leadfoot Johnson	paid to driver 1 week salary	Driver salary	$1,505.00		$19,871.90

It's important that you write the receipt number on the actual hard receipt so the business manager can match up the correct receipt to the entry in your ledger. Always circle the expense amount on the receipt so the business manager can quickly see it. Write a short phrase on the receipt, such as "gaffer tape," so the business manager knows what the expenditure was for when it's not specifically stated on the receipt.

After you pick up the balance of the band's guarantee in cash, you'll want to enter that amount into the ledger. Put the date of the cash pick up (show date) and then a short description of the transaction into the ledger. In this case, we've entered "Balance of guarantee for San Diego show" so the business manager will know this cash entry is for the money you picked up from the San Diego show. On the first night in San Francisco, we only picked up $1,000 for float and took the rest of the guarantee balance in a check.

With software like Quicken, you can create reports and graphs that will show you all of your expense categories and how much money you've spent for each of them to help you keep an eye on your tour budget. You can also create a report to show you all of the money you've picked up from the promoters if you suspect that you might have forgotten to enter a show guarantee into your cash ledger. This is quicker and easier than scrolling down through a long ledger trying to find a missing transaction.

If you have a band credit card, always make a separate account for credit card transactions. If you enter them into the cash account, your ending balance is going to be wrong because you didn't pay for those credit card expenses with the cash you're carrying; you paid for them with a credit card. So you must add a new account to your band's Quicken file for credit card expenses.

One of the good things about Quicken is that when you create a credit card account, you can link the account directly to the actual online account for the card. The Quicken credit card account can easily be updated with a click of a button as long as you have internet access. It's a good thing to have in case you should ever lose a credit card receipt. You can simply update your credit card account in Quicken, find the transaction in question, and you have the correct information for your credit card ledger.

Even though the business manager can print out all of the transactions for your band credit card from the card's online account, the business manager still won't know what each expense was for unless you explain it. So, you should still always use a credit card ledger, just like your cash ledger, for your weekly road reports. You really don't want to waste the business manager's time—and yours—when she has to call or email you all the time asking what that credit card receipt was for.

If you look at the bottom line of a Quicken credit card account, you'll see that there's not only an ending balance, like there is on a cash account, but it also shows "credit remaining" amount. However, you need to make sure that you've entered the card's credit limit when you created the account and keep it updated. It's a good tool to have. You'll also notice that the ending balance is always a negative number if you've charged anything on the card. This is the amount that you're essentially "in-the-hole" with the credit lender.

Skinny Girl Riot Credit Card Ledger--USA 2012							
Date	Receipt #	Payee	Description of Transaction	Category	Payment	Deposit	Balance
3/31/2012			Visa credit limit			$20,000.00	$20,000.00
3/31/2012	1001	The Happy Hotel	band and crew rooms in San Francisco	Hotels	$1,439.33		$18,560.67
4/6/2012	1002	Hilton	band and crew rooms in El Paso	Hotels	$1,398.43		$17,162.24
4/6/2012	1003	Steer and Beer	band and crew dinner and drinks	Food	$721.32		$16,440.92

The next thing we'll go over is the reconciliation statement. This statement lists all of your cash and check pickups from the promoter and is pretty much a financial snapshot of each of your show settlements. This is an important statement because it's updated after every show and sent to the manager, booking agent, and business manager so they know what you picked up.

I always like to do a "recon" statement in addition to my cash ledger. The weekly road reports with your cash and credit card ledgers are sent to the business manager. I haven't worked with too many managers who expected to be copied on road reports unless they were also acting as business manager—a major conflict of interest, by the way. Most of them just care that you're sending the reports and receipts to the business manager, you're doing the job correctly, and he's not getting any complaints about your reports.

However, the manager will want to know how each show concluded financially: how many tickets were sold, how much money did you pick up, did the band earn any money on the back end? This is also information that the booking agent will want to know. The agent will usually get a report from the promoter with this information, sooner or later, but it's good for you to send it after the show with your nightly report.

The booking agent doesn't need to know about the band's weekly road expenses, so I do a recon statement that's separate from the cash ledger to show how much cash I picked up, any checks I picked up, and any additional back end money the band earned. This is what the agent cares about knowing most, especially the additional back end earnings, because he also gets a commission from that money. He also wants to make sure that you picked up the correct amount of money because if you didn't, it's going to be his headache to get it from the promoter.

It's best to create your recon statement before the tour starts and enter in all of the show and guarantee information the booking agent has already sent to you. As the promoter deposits come in, you'll also enter those into the recon statement. The booking agent will usually send you and the manager a weekly deposit report, showing you which promoters have paid their deposits and which have not.

Even though the band's contract states that a 50 percent deposit must be paid, some big promoters only pay 10 percent deposits. Some agents may allow a promoter to pay a deposit that's less than 50 percent if they've worked with them for a long time, know their business is stable, and trust them.

Deposits are included in the contract so the agent knows the promoter has made a firm commitment to the show. These deposits are usually not released by the agent and paid to the band until after the band performs the show. If the band should have to cancel the show because a band member is sick or they can't make the show because of bad weather, the deposit would have to be returned to the promoter; but if the promoter cancels the show for any reason that's not the band's fault, the band keeps the deposit as compensation for the lost date.

Even though the contract says the deposit must be paid to the agent by a certain date, many of them are often late paying the deposit, and it's not uncommon for some promoters to wire the deposit into the agent's account the day before the show or even the day of the show. The agent will send you a deposit report informing you that deposits are in before you arrive for the show. Just enter them into your recon report as you receive notification that they've been paid.

An unpaid deposit is the one thing that can turn a show day into complete pandemonium between the agent and promoter, and you're caught right in the middle of it. I've often been in the position where the agent's threatening to cancel the show after we've loaded in because the deposit hasn't been paid. This is especially worrisome if the show's selling badly.

If the agent rolls the dice, hoping for a good walk-up to save the promoter, and allows the band to play, even though the deposit hasn't been paid, the band runs the risk of the promoter skipping out on them if he loses a lot of money. If the band had been paid their deposit and the promoter skipped out on them, at least they would've had half of their money; but with no deposit paid, they just played for free, and now the agent has to worry about getting the money out of a promoter who is going down the financial toilet.

If this happened and the band wasn't made aware of the fact that no deposit had been paid and the promoter skipped out on them, this is the quickest way for the booking agent to get fired. The manager would probably be coming after the agent to at least pay for the lost deposit out of the agency's pocket, and he could even blame the agent—and tour manager—for not getting the balance of the guarantee from the promoter before the band went on stage. If a show's selling badly, you should always consider a promoter to be on shaky ground unless it's a big one that can take the loss.

The next column on the recon statement shows how many tickets were sold for each show. This is for paid attendance and does not include tickets the promoter gave away for promotion or the guest lists. The promoter will give you the paid attendance number at the end of the night when you do settlement.

The next column is for any percentage or overage amount that the band earned on the back end. The Total Fee column automatically adds up the band's guarantee and any overage earned. The recon statement also calculates the agent's 10 percent commission from the Total Fee amount so it includes their 10 percent commission of any percentage earned.

As you can see, all of the band's deposits have been entered into the Deposit column as they've come in. If any guarantee balance is wired straight to the agent, then we enter that amount in the Balance to Agent column. This normally doesn't happen on a U.S. tour for an American band because we're always picking up cash or a check, but it's very common for a U.S. band traveling overseas to have the balance of the guarantee wired straight to the agent after the show is over if it hasn't already been paid in advance by the promoter.

Established promoters in the U.K. and Europe are always wiring the balance of the band's guarantee to the agent after the show has gone down; and in nearly thirty years of doing this for a living, I can only remember a few times when the band didn't get paid. And these few incidents were with promoters that never should've been given the show.

The agents in the U.K. have been working with the same promoters for a long time, and they know which ones they can trust and which ones they can't. Many agents may require smaller and less established promoters in some parts of the world, such as South America and Asia, to pay the band's guarantee in full before they'll allow the band to travel there to perform.

In the Cash Pickup column, we'll enter the cash that we picked up that night; and in the Check Pickup column, we'll enter the amount of any checks we picked up. Notice how the amount in the Balance Due column changes when we enter these figures. If we've picked up all of the band's money that they're owed, the balance due should be zero.

Next is the Tax Deducted column. Enter any U.S. state taxes that may have been deducted from the band's guarantee or any artist taxes that were deducted in foreign countries.

The amount in the Balance Due column constantly changes when you enter deposits paid, overages earned, taxes deducted, and money you've picked up. The formulas in the spreadsheet do all of this for you. You can easily build one of these recon statements once you learn how to use Excel if you don't already know how. It's really not that difficult.

Below the U.S. recon statement, you'll see another recon statement for a U.K./European tour. The only difference between this statement and the U.S. statement is that we've separated the shows that were paid in British Pounds, Euros, and U.S. dollars.

If you're an American band doing a U.K./Euro tour, always convert your expense receipts into U.S. dollars—using the exchange rate you received when you converted your U.S. dollars into that local currency—before entering them into your cash ledger. For expense receipts paid for with a band credit card, you can go into the card's online account and see what the charge amount is in U.S. dollars, and then enter that amount into your credit card ledger. Always write the expense amount in U.S. dollars on the hard receipt for the business manager.

If you're working with a baby band that's only earning a flat guarantee each show and no back end money, you really don't need the recon statement, but you still need to know how to create and use one for when you finally start working with a band that's doing good business. You can just tell the manager, agent, and business manager what you picked up in your nightly email report, but it does make you look more professional when a new tour manager sends them a statement like this. Work hard to impress.

Quicken is also great software for organizing your own personal finances so you can keep track of your checking, savings, credit card, and investment accounts. You can assign tax-related categories to your Quicken transactions and export tax data into TurboTax—another Intuit product—if you do your own taxes.

Skinny Girl Riot Reconciliation Statement--USA 2012

Date	Venue/City	Guarantee	Tickets Sold	% Earned	Total Fee	Agent 10%	Deposit	Balance to Agent	Cash Pickup	Check Pickup	State Tax Deducted	Balance Due
4/1/2012	Club 1--San Francisco	$20,000.00	1633	$ 6,842.44	$ 26,842.44	$ 2,684.24	$ 10,000.00	$ -	$ 1,000.00	$ 15,842.44	$ -	$ -
4/2/2012	Club 2--Los Angeles	$20,000.00	992	$ 1,800.00	$ 21,800.00	$ 2,180.00	$ 10,000.00	$ -	$ -	$ 11,800.00	$ -	$ -
4/3/2012	Club 3--San Diego	$15,000.00	948	$ -	$ 15,000.00	$ 1,500.00	$ 7,500.00	$ -	$ 7,500.00	$ -	$ -	$ -
4/4/2012	Club 4--Phoenix	$15,000.00	939	$ -	$ 15,000.00	$ 1,500.00	$ 7,500.00	$ -	$ 7,500.00	$ -	$ -	$ -
4/5/2012	Club 5--Albuquerque	$10,000.00	1200	$ 1,500.00	$ 11,500.00	$ 1,150.00	$ 5,000.00	$ -	$ 6,500.00	$ -	$ -	$ -
4/7/2012	Club 6--El Paso	$15,000.00	1500	$ 2,250.00	$ 17,250.00	$ 1,725.00	$ 7,500.00	$ -	$ 9,750.00	$ -	$ -	$ -
4/8/2012	Club 7--San Antonio	$10,000.00	1550	$ 2,250.00	$ 12,250.00	$ 1,225.00	$ 6,000.00	$ -	$ 6,250.00	$ -	$ -	$ -
4/9/2012	Club 8--Houston	$15,000.00	991	$ -	$ 15,000.00	$ 1,500.00	$ 7,500.00	$ -	$ 7,500.00	$ -	$ -	$ -
4/10/2012	Club 9--Dallas	$15,000.00	1400	$ 2,000.00	$ 17,000.00	$ 1,700.00	$ 7,500.00	$ -	$ 9,500.00	$ -	$ -	$ -
4/11/2012	Club 10--New Orleans	$10,000.00	1450	$ 1,800.00	$ 11,800.00	$ 1,180.00	$ 5,000.00	$ -	$ 6,800.00	$ -	$ -	$ -
4/13/2012	Club 11--Tallahassee	$12,000.00	1100	$ -	$ 12,000.00	$ 1,200.00	$ 6,000.00	$ -	$ 6,000.00	$ -	$ -	$ -
4/14/2012	Club 12--Tampa	$15,000.00	1053	$ -	$ 15,000.00	$ 1,500.00	$ 7,500.00	$ -	$ 7,500.00	$ -	$ -	$ -
4/15/2012	Club 13--Orlando	$12,000.00	1044	$ -	$ 12,000.00	$ 1,200.00	$ 6,000.00	$ -	$ 6,000.00	$ -	$ -	$ -
4/16/2012	Club 14--Atlanta	$15,000.00	1200	$ -	$ 15,000.00	$ 1,500.00	$ 7,500.00	$ -	$ 7,500.00	$ -	$ -	$ -
4/17/2012	Club 15--Raleigh	$12,000.00	1139	$ -	$ 12,000.00	$ 1,200.00	$ 6,000.00	$ -	$ 5,520.00	$ -	$ 480.00	$ -
4/19/2012	Club 16--Washington, DC	$15,000.00	1412	$ -	$ 15,000.00	$ 1,500.00	$ 7,500.00	$ -	$ 7,500.00	$ -	$ -	$ -
4/20/2012	Club 17--Philadelphia	$13,000.00	1000	$ -	$ 13,000.00	$ 1,300.00	$ 6,500.00	$ -	$ 6,500.00	$ -	$ -	$ -
4/21/2012	Club 18--Hartford	$9,000.00	845	$ -	$ 9,000.00	$ 900.00	$ 4,500.00	$ -	$ 4,050.00	$ -	$ 450.00	$ -
4/22/2012	Club 19--Boston	$12,000.00	900	$ -	$ 12,000.00	$ 1,200.00	$ 6,000.00	$ -	$ 5,364.00	$ -	$ 636.00	$ -
4/23/2012	Club 20--New York	$20,000.00	1000	$ 3,000.00	$ 23,000.00	$ 2,300.00	$ 10,000.00	$ -	$ -	$ 13,000.00	$ -	$ -
Totals		$280,000.00	23296	$21,442.44	$301,442.44	$30,144.24	$141,000.00	$0.00	$118,234.00	$40,642.44	$1,566.00	$0.00

Skinny Girl Riot Reconciliation Statement--U.K./Europe 2012

Date	Venue/City	Guarantee	Tickets Sold	% Earned	Total Fee	Agent 10%	Deposit	Balance to Agent	Cash Pickup	Tax Deducted	Balance Due
5/1/2012	Venue 1--Berlin	€ 15,000.00	1500	€ 2,250.00	€ 17,250.00	€ 1,725.00	€ 7,500.00	€ 7,500.00	€ 2,250.00	€ -	€ -
5/2/2012	Venue 2--Hamburg	€ 15,000.00	1650	€ 2,250.00	€ 17,250.00	€ 1,725.00	€ 7,500.00	€ 9,750.00	€ -	€ -	€ -
5/3/2012	Venue 3--Dortmund	€ 15,000.00	1365	€ -	€ 15,000.00	€ 1,500.00	€ 7,500.00	€ 7,500.00	€ -	€ -	€ -
5/4/2012	Venue 4--Frankfurt	€ 15,000.00	1450	€ 2,250.00	€ 17,250.00	€ 1,725.00	€ 7,500.00	€ 9,750.00	€ -	€ -	€ -
5/5/2012	Venue 5--Munich	€ 15,000.00	1500	€ 2,250.00	€ 17,250.00	€ 1,725.00	€ 7,500.00	€ 7,500.00	€ 2,250.00	€ -	€ -
5/6/2012	Venue 6--Nuremberg	€ 15,000.00	1448	€ -	€ 15,000.00	€ 1,500.00	€ 7,500.00	€ 7,500.00	€ 4,500.00	€ -	€ -
Totals		€ 90,000.00	8913	€ 9,000.00	€ 99,000.00	€ 9,900.00	€ 45,000.00	€ 49,500.00		€ -	€ -
Total in U.S. $ (Euro rate: 1.25)		$112,500.00		$11,250.00	$123,750.00	$12,375.00	$56,250.00	$61,875.00	$5,625.00	$0.00	$0.00
5/8/2012	Venue 7--London	£ 15,000.00	1550	£ 2,250.00	£ 17,250.00	£ 1,725.00	£ 1,500.00	£ 13,500.00	£ 2,250.00	£ -	£ -
5/9/2012	Venue 8--Bristol	£ 10,000.00	942	£ -	£ 10,000.00	£ 1,000.00	£ 5,000.00	£ 5,000.00	£ -	£ -	£ -
5/10/2012	Venue 9--Oxford	£ 10,000.00	1100	£ 1,500.00	£ 11,500.00	£ 1,150.00	£ 5,000.00	£ 6,500.00	£ -	£ -	£ -
5/11/2012	Venue 10--Birmingham	£ 15,000.00	1600	£ 2,250.00	£ 17,250.00	£ 1,725.00	£ 7,500.00	£ 9,750.00	£ -	£ -	£ -
5/12/2012	Venue 11--Nottingham	£ 10,000.00	1000	£ 1,500.00	£ 11,500.00	£ 1,150.00	£ 5,000.00	£ 6,500.00	£ -	£ -	£ -
5/13/2012	Venue 12--Liverpool	£ 10,000.00	931	£ -	£ 10,000.00	£ 1,000.00	£ 5,000.00	£ 5,000.00	£ 2,250.00	£ -	£ -
Totals		£ 70,000.00	7123	£ 7,500.00	£ 77,500.00	£ 7,750.00	£ 29,000.00	£ 46,250.00	£ 2,250.00	£ -	£ -
Total in U.S. $ (GBP rate: 1.55)		$108,500.00		$11,625.00	$120,125.00	$12,012.50	$44,950.00	$71,687.50	$3,487.50	$0.00	$0.00
5/15/2012	Venue 13--Milan	$10,000.00	1000	$ 1,500.00	$ 11,500.00	$ 1,150.00	$ 5,000.00	$ 6,500.00	$ -	$ -	$ -
5/16/2012	Venue 14--Zurich	$10,000.00	1050	$ 1,500.00	$ 11,500.00	$ 1,150.00	$ 5,000.00	$ 6,500.00	$ -	$ -	$ -
5/17/2012	Venue 15--Lausanne	$10,000.00	992	$ -	$ 10,000.00	$ 1,000.00	$ 5,000.00	$ 5,000.00	$ -	$ -	$ -
5/18/2012	Venue 16--Lyon	$10,000.00	948	$ -	$ 10,000.00	$ 1,000.00	$ 5,000.00	$ 5,000.00	$ -	$ -	$ -
5/19/2012	Venue 17--Toulouse	$10,000.00	939	$ -	$ 10,000.00	$ 1,000.00	$ 5,000.00	$ 5,000.00	$ -	$ -	$ -
5/20/2012	Venue 18--San Sebastian	$10,000.00	1200	$ 1,500.00	$ 11,500.00	$ 1,150.00	$ 5,000.00	$ 6,500.00	$ -	$ -	$ -
5/22/2012	Venue 19--Barcelona	$15,000.00	1500	$ 2,250.00	$ 17,250.00	$ 1,725.00	$ 7,500.00	$ 9,750.00	$ -	$ -	$ -
5/23/2012	Venue 20--Madrid	$15,000.00	1550	$ 2,250.00	$ 17,250.00	$ 1,725.00	$ 7,500.00	$ 9,750.00	$ -	$ -	$ -
5/24/2012	Venue 21--Bordeaux	$10,000.00	991	$ -	$ 10,000.00	$ 1,000.00	$ -	$ 10,000.00	$ -	$ -	$ -
5/25/2012	Venue 22--Paris	$15,000.00	1400	$ 2,000.00	$ 17,000.00	$ 1,700.00	$ 7,500.00	$ 9,500.00	$ -	$ -	$ -
5/25/2012	Venue 23--Brussels	$15,000.00	1450	$ 1,800.00	$ 16,800.00	$ 1,680.00	$ 7,500.00	$ 9,300.00	$ -	$ -	$ -
5/26/2012	Venue 24--Amsterdam	$15,000.00	1500	$ 2,000.00	$ 17,000.00	$ 1,700.00	$ 7,500.00	$ 9,500.00	$ -	$ -	$ -
Totals		$145,000.00	14520	$14,800.00	$159,800.00	$ 15,980.00	$ 67,500.00	$ 92,300.00	$ -	$ -	$ -
Totals in U.S. $		$366,000.00	30556	$37,675.00	$403,675.00	$40,367.50	$168,700.00	$225,862.50	$9,112.50	$0.00	$0.00

CREATING SIGNS FOR THE TOUR

You're probably wondering why I've written a chapter on creating signs. Well, do your first show without them and see what happens. I can assure you that your day will be chaotic and you will look sloppy in the eyes of everyone on the tour. You'll waste a lot of time telling people where their dressing rooms are, how to get to catering, how to get to production, where to find the stage, and how to get back out to the buses. If, after all of that, you haven't blown your voice out, you'll probably be thinking of blowing your brains out. Make the signs.

If I go to a rock concert during my time off—something I rarely do—to visit a band or crew friend and I walk in the backstage door and see no signs leading me to the dressing room or production office or the stage, I know right away that somebody's either having a bad day, doesn't care, or is downright incompetent.

Either way, having the people on your tour—especially your band—walking through the maze of some venue like Spinal Tap, lost, trying to find the stage, is something you never want to happen. It really has a way of pissing people off and wasting time that they can't afford to waste. Don't let this happen on your tour. It's amateur-hour all the way.

Design all of your tour signs before the tour starts and print out master copies. Have a certain amount of photocopies made of each sign, so you're ready to use them as soon as you load in for your first show. If you're tight on money and can't have a large amount printed up before the tour starts, you can always print them out as you need them each day, but this is time-consuming. If the venue has a photocopier, always try to get the promoter rep to get copies made for you. Free photocopies are better for your budget.

If the band can afford it, I prefer to laminate about six copies of each of my signs and store them in a plastic file box or in the filing cabinet section of a production case. Laminating the signs looks more professional and you don't have to worry about printing them out each day.

All you—or your production assistant—have to do is go back at the end of each night and take the signs down and use them again the next day. It's important to remember that dressing room signs are a souvenir that guests like to tear down and take home, and laminated signs are more expensive than signs you've printed out from your computer.

Use a product such as Blu Tack adhesive to put up your signs and day sheets. Never use gaffer tape, masking tape, electrical tape, or things like that. It looks horrible and very unprofessional. This is definitely another pet peeve of mine. Blu Tack is also easy to remove from laminated signs and reuse again.

I'm constantly using Blu Tack. I always wear two all access laminates on one lanyard around my neck; and I flatten a ball of Blu Tack and place it between the two laminates so I can easily get to it any time I need it. When you've just walked a hundred yards out to the tour bus to post day sheets and realize that you forgot to bring any Blu Tack to put them up and don't have any on the bus, you'll wish you had some around your neck. This is a good trick that saves time.

Below is a list of the signs that I normally like to make. I've also included a few examples made with Microsoft Word. All you really need to put on the sign is the band's logo, the name of the tour, and the name of the sign: dressing room, production, catering, or whatever applies. You can print them out on white or colored paper, and you can also make signs with full color designs, such as your band's album cover art, if you've got a color printer and money to burn. Make your signs any way you like, as long as they're easy to read and understand.

List of signs:

Headliner dressing room	Toilet/Shower
Support act dressing room	Promoter
Production	Stage
Catering	This Way Out To Buses
Crew Room	This Way In To Everything
Tuning Room	Left Arrow
Hospitality Room	Right Arrow
Toilet	Straight ahead arrow
Shower	

I always prefer to make signs for the support acts because some of them will never think to make their own; and even if they do make their own, I'm still anal about them all looking the same and having our tour's name on them. Be sure to use your band's actual logo and the support act's logo on your signs and not just some Word font. It looks much more professional and shows a strong attention to detail on your part. Consistency is the mark of a professional; always be consistent.

SKINNY GIRL RIOT

USA TOUR 2012

DRESSING ROOM

SKINNY GIRL RIOT

USA TOUR 2012

PRODUCTION

SKINNY GIRL RIOT

USA TOUR 2012

STAGE →

TOUR MANAGEMENT SOFTWARE

Master Tour by Eventric is an online database program that will help to make your job as a tour manager or production manager much easier and more efficient. It allows you to share important tour information with everyone in your entourage on their computer using Master Tour's online database, and there's even an app for your smart phone or tablet, allowing everyone to have quick and easy access to the tour's information.

Master Tour's database contains venue information, such as stage size, load-in access, rigging plot, and more, for thousands of venues around the world. The hotel database provides information on most good hotels you'll encounter on the road. Their database also provides contact info for many promoters around the world. You can even do your accounting, show settlement, guest lists, set lists, rooming lists, and equipment manifests using Master Tour. Day sheets and tour books can be created and shared with your entourage online or using the Master Tour app. More features of this great service are being added all the time.

Master Tour is offered as a flat monthly subscription. You can add or subtract users at any time. Check out Eventric.com for more information on this great service.

Tour manager/FOH engineer Bob Wargo recently used Master Tour on some international runs we did with the heavy metal band Anthrax, and I liked the product a lot. I had already done a trial run with the product to learn more about it for this book and loved it from the beginning, but I don't consider it a substitute for conventional printed tour books and day sheets. I think it's a great addition but not a total substitute yet.

We still need day sheets posted on the bus and in the dressing room and other places around the venue where they normally go. I don't think anyone wants to have to use a laptop or a smart phone every time they want to view info on a day sheet. We don't have time for that. Sometimes I like to just pull a conventional tour book out of my laptop bag and read through it and make notes in it. Maybe I'm just used to doing it the old way for three decades.

When the day comes that we can always get a strong wireless signal everywhere and everyone owns a smart phone or tablet, then I might begin to view a service such as Master Tour as a total replacement for conventional printed information devices, such as tour books, day sheets, press sheets, and memos, and not just a great addition to them. I still believe we're better off to have both for now. Either way, Master Tour is well worth every penny of its subscription cost.

PART THREE

ADVANCING
THE TOUR

GETTING ORGANIZED TO ADVANCE THE TOUR

Now that you've leased the tour bus, hired the road crew, started creating your tour book, and are booking hotels and airfares, you have to start advancing the shows. Don't do these tasks one at a time. You're constantly working on them at the same time, multi-tasking like mad, and this requires good organization and time management skills. You have to stay on schedule and get all of these things done by the time the tour's ready to start.

If your band has a production manager, he's most likely the one who's doing a large part of the show advance. Some production managers will do all of the show advance and just leave the tour manager to advance his cash requirements if the tour doesn't have a tour accountant. Some tour managers and production managers will split the show advance. It's really up to them how they want to do it. It just has to get done.

If you're working with a new band, it's highly doubtful you'll have the luxury of a production manager on your crew—if you have any crew at all—so you'll probably have to do all of the advance work. If so, there are ways of doing the show advance that'll make this process a lot more organized.

When you receive the list of tour dates from the booking agent, it will usually have only the promoter's contact info on the sheets. Sometimes it may list the production contact for each promoter, but these are often out-of-date, so it's always best to send out an email to the promoters that includes your pre-advance package. Ask them to forward the email to their promoter rep with whom you'll be advancing the dates. Once you've received a reply from the promoter rep, you'll have his contact info, and now you are able to begin your show advance.

Down below is a show advance checklist made with Microsoft Excel. I always create an advance checklist so I can see what I've gotten done with a simple glance. I'll make a list of the tour dates and add a column beside it denoting whether or not I've received the contact info for the promoter rep. Then I have another column that tells me if he's returned my advance sheet fully completed. It's important to keep track of which promoter reps are sending you the info you've asked for and which ones you have to keep after to get it.

Skinny Girl Riot--Show Advance Checklist			
Venue/City	Completed advance sheet received	Sound & lighting specs received	Promoter rep contact info
Club 1--San Francisco	x		Vince Vega, 666-555-3838, vincent@promoter.net
Club 2--Los Angeles	x	x	Charles Babbitt, 666-555-1243, charlie@promoter.net
Club 3--San Diego			
Club 4--Phoenix	x	x	Randy McMurphy, 666-555-4333, randle@promoter.net
Club 5--Albuquerque	x	x	R. MacNeil, 666-555-3222, regan@promoter.net
Club 6--El Paso	x	x	Robert Balboa, 666-555-1199, rocky@promoter.net
Club 7--San Antonio			
Club 8--Houston	x	x	William Kilgore, 666-555-1188, bill@promoter.net
Club 9--Dallas		x	Carl Showalter, 666-555-4444, carl@promoter.net
Club 10--New Orleans	x		Luca Brasi, 666-555-9909, gonefishing@promoter.net
Club 11--Tallahassee	x	x	Mike Cheritto, 666-555-7799, michael@promoter.net
Club 12--Tampa	incomplete	x	Honey Bunny, 666-555-1923, honey@promoter.net
Club 13--Orlando	x	x	Trav Bickle, 666-555-9783, travis@promoter.net
Club 14--Atlanta			
Club 15--Raleigh	x	x	Jen Curran, 666-555-6456, jenny@promoter.net
Club 16--Washington, DC	his sheets	x	Donny Corleone, 666-555-7777, donny@promoter.net
Club 17--Philadelphia	x	x	Willie Munny, 666-555-2373, will@promoter.net
Club 18--Hartford			
Club 19--Boston	x	x	Hannah Lechter, 666-555-1110, hannah@promoter.net
Club 20--New York			

You can also use the calendar in your computer or an online version, such as Google Calendar, for your checklist. You can create an event in the calendar for each show on the tour. Use the venue's name and city to name the event, and then use the description box to enter details about the event. You can make simple notes, such as "promoter rep contact info received," "sound and lighting specs received" and "completed advance sheet received." It's another good way to keep track of where you're at in the advance process. There are many ways to do this, but it doesn't matter which one you use, as long as you use something and get the shows advanced.

You can also create different types of calendars for your entourage, such as a show advance calendar or a tour date calendar, that list new tour dates as they're confirmed. You can use the share feature in the calendar to allow the entourage to view the calendar.

Some of the promoter reps in the second half of the tour will take the longest to get back to you with the requested info. Some of these promoter reps are juggling four or five shows a week, and the last thing they want to worry about is a show that's two months away. This is why you only want to get, at this point, preliminary info for your tour book. Then you can finish the show advance as you get closer to each show. However, some of the promoter reps will be show-advancing maniacs who are always ahead of the game and will want to bang out the advance as soon as possible, so go ahead and get it done.

Once you've received the contact info (name, cell phone number, and email address) for your promoter rep, type it in the contact info column. If the promoter has only replied to my email and sent me his rep's info but has not forwarded him my pre-advance package, then I'll go ahead and forward my original email on to the promoter rep so he has it.

When I've received my completed advance sheet from the promoter rep, I'll put a check mark in the column showing that I've received it. Some of these promoter reps may not take the time to fill out your advance sheet but will send you a pre-made advance sheet of their own that contains most of the info you require, or they may send you a website link that contains much of this info.

I still prefer to have my advance sheet filled out so I can print it out and put it into my advance book. If the promoter rep sends me his info sheet, I'll fill in my advance sheet myself. If he's neglected to send me some of the info that I require, I'll email him again and ask for that info. Sometimes it takes some back-and-forth to get all of the info you need.

As you receive your advance sheets from each promoter rep, print them out and put them into a binder in chronological order. You want to have a proper advance book to have with you in the production office each day. This is not only so you can quickly look into the book for information you need, but sometimes the crew will come into the production office asking you about certain aspects of an upcoming show, such as the stage size or number of dressing rooms. If you have all of this info in the advance book, the crew can just look in the book and get the info they require, and save you the time of having to look it up in your computer.

As you're receiving the completed advance sheets from the promoter reps, you'll want to start entering all of the necessary information into your tour book, just as you should be doing with hotels as those are booked. Don't wait until you have all of this info compiled and become overwhelmed at the final hour trying to type up a fifty-page tour book a few days before the tour starts. Work on all of these things at the same time. Be organized and you'll save yourself a lot of headaches in the end.

If you haven't already built the shell of your tour book, you should start doing it. By the time you're ready to start advancing the tour dates, you should already have your tour book created. Once you've built the shell of the book, it's so much easier to type in the show and hotel information as you receive it.

When you first receive your list of tour dates from the booking agent, most agents will have a lot of information on the sheet, such as the promoter's contact info and the venue's name, address, and telephone number. It may also contain other information you need, such as what time the show begins and what time the headliner goes on stage, but you should ignore all of this information and don't put any of it into the tour book until you've double-checked every bit of it online and through your preliminary show advance.

The promoter's contact info will most likely be correct because the agent's dealing with him constantly, and the venue's contact info is usually correct, but you definitely want to double-check that info online. The last thing you want is for the bus to be late for load-in when the driver got lost because the venue address in your tour book was incorrect. Any show schedule on the agent's sheet should also be ignored; these are usually just estimates. The only show schedule you should be concerned with is the one you advance with the promoter rep.

The agent's sheet could say 7:00 p.m. show time on it, but the ticket that's been sold to the fans could say 8:00 p.m. show time. That's the time that counts. You can't start the show at 7:00 p.m. when the fans have bought a ticket that says 8:00 p.m. show. You're going to have a lot of pissed off people showing up for the show when they find out they've missed the first band on the bill that they paid to see. The only schedule that matters is the time on the ticket and the one you've advanced with the promoter rep. He knows what time the ticket says the show is supposed to start.

In this day and age, I only need a promoter's office phone number, cell phone number, and email address. The same goes for his promoter rep. I'm always emailing the promoter rep and sometimes calling him on his cell phone. It's rare that I'll ever have any contact with the promoter himself, except in the beginning when I'm contacting him to get his promoter rep's contact info to advance the show. Although, some smaller promoters may advance the show with you and might even be your promoter rep on the show day. I don't bother getting promoter fax numbers anymore because I rarely use them.

Always do your show advances via email so there's a record of what's been said. If you end up on the phone with a promoter rep over an important issue that you both need to hammer out, ask him to still send you an email about the issue at hand and how it was resolved. You don't want to end up in a situation where what you agreed to on the phone is not reality on the show day.

Some promoter reps have a lot of shows on their calendar and may not remember the phone conversation the way you remember it, and then it's his word against yours. As long as you have an email to produce, proving what was said, you'll never be put in this difficult position.

Tour managers today have it easier than we had it back in the '80s when I started out. Back then, we didn't have cell phones or email or websites; all we had was a landline telephone and a fax machine. Imagine trying to advance thirty shows, faxing back and forth, and spending all of your time on the phone asking dozens of questions and filling in the answers by hand on your printed-out advance sheet.

It was even worse if you were advancing a European tour and you lived in California—nine hours behind Europe—and you had to get a promoter rep on the telephone to advance a show. You had to be up very early every morning to catch them in the office, and quite often the language barrier was a big problem.

Because of the time difference and language barrier that often existed, we did a lot of our advancing via fax back then. To solve these headaches for everyone involved, the European promoters made detailed info sheets to fax to us and save us a lot of faxing and phone calls where we spent a lot of time saying, "What did you say?" because we couldn't understand their broken English. This made the advance process much easier; and I got to the point where I preferred doing European tours over U.S. tours because of it.

Still to this day, there are some U.S. venues that still don't even have basic show advance info sheets to send out to tour managers and production managers, much less a venue website that lists all of this info. European promoters learned long ago how to make the advance process much easier.

183

STAGE PLOTS AND INPUT CHARTS

Two important things that should always be included in your pre-advance package are the band's stage plot and input chart. Some bands will add these documents to their rider, but many times, stage plots and input charts change and are never updated in the rider, or the booking agent's staff will mistakenly send out an outdated version of the rider.

For these reasons, I always include in my pre-advance package the latest version of the band's stage plot and input chart with a revision date in the footer of each document so there's never any confusion.

A stage plot is simply a CAD drawing that shows the layout of the band's gear on stage. If you look at the stage plot below, you'll see that it shows the type of drum kit we have, the type and amount of guitar and bass cabinets, and where we need power drops on stage. It also shows what kind of monitor system we need and how many drum fills, side fills, and downstage wedges are needed. It also shows how many—and what kind—of microphones and DIs (direct input boxes) are needed and where they should be placed.

The input chart lists which channel on the sound console is connected to which kind of device or microphone for each instrument on stage. For example, the singer's vocal microphone, a Sennheiser e945, might be in channel 38 on the sound console or the drum kit's floor tom may be mic'd up using a DPA 4021 and connected into channel 6 on the sound console. All of this info will help the sound crew plan ahead so they can provide you with the microphones, microphone stands, direct boxes, and other audio devices that your sound engineer will need. The input chart tells the house crew which channels these devices should come up in on the sound console. You should also include a description of your monitor mixes on the input chart. Don't forget to include the tour manager and sound engineer's contact info on the stage plot/input chart, although I wouldn't put more than an email address on the version that's on the band's website or anywhere else on the internet.

The input chart and stage plot is often combined into one document and created by the band's sound engineer. If so, make sure he's always updating any changes he makes and copies you on those updates so you're always sending out the most current versions. Always make sure to change the revision date on the stage plot and input chart so you can easily tell if you're looking at the current version. Don't forget to update the stage plot and input chart on the band's website. If you don't have these documents on their website, you really should put them on there. It really is best if the page with these documents is password protected, especially if they have your contact info on them.

For Mac users, StagePlot PRO is a good program for about $40 U.S. to create a stage plot. At this time, there's no PC version of the program, unfortunately. You can use any drawing program, such as Photoshop or Gimp, to create a stage plot.

I used the free drawing program in Google Docs to create the Skinny Girl Riot stage plot below. As you can see, I was able to create a good stage plot, and it didn't cost me a dime. I used Excel to make the input list below with information given to me by Testament's current tour manager/FOH engineer, Rick Diesing; one of my oldest and dearest friends in this business. We've toured together since Keel in the '80s, and he's top-notch all the way.

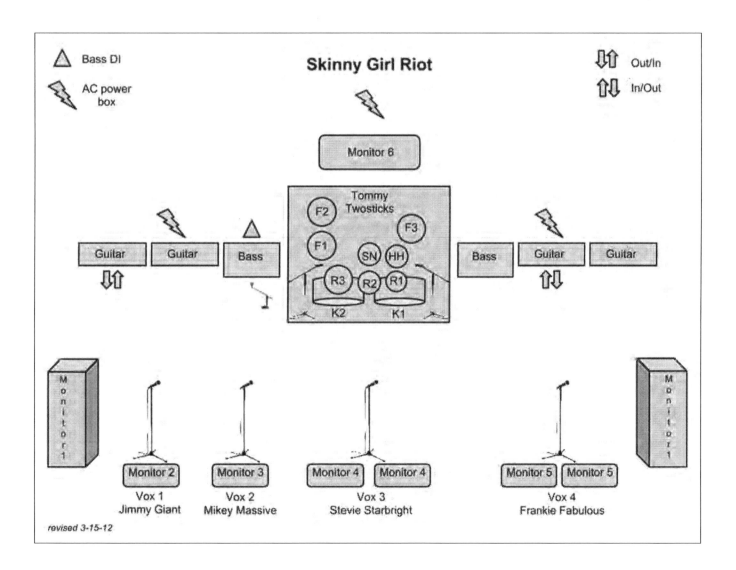

		Skinny Girl Riot--Input List			
Channel	**Input**	**FOH Insert**	**Mic**	**Monitors**	**Monitor Insert**
1	Kick SR	Gate/comp	SM 91	Yes	Gate
2	Kick SL	Gate/comp	SM 91	Yes	Gate
3	Kick trigger		DI	Yes	
4	Snare top	Gate/comp	Beta 57	Yes	Gate
5	Snare bottom	Gate/comp	Beta 57	Yes	Gate
6	Hi-hat 1		Condenser	Yes	
7	Rack tom 1	Gate	Beta 98	Yes	Gate
8	Rack tom 2	Gate	Beta 98	Yes	Gate
9	Floor tom 1	Gate	Beta 98	Yes	Gate
10	Floor tom 2	Gate	Beta 98	Yes	Gate
11	Ride		Condenser		
12	Overhead SR		VP88		
13	Overhead SL		VP88		
14	Bass DI pre	Comp	Active DI	Yes	Comp
15	Bass DI post	Comp	Active DI	Yes	Comp
16	Bass mic	Comp	Beta 52	Yes	Comp
17	SR guitar off stage	Subgroup 1/2 comp	SM 57	Yes	
18	SR guitar on stage	Subgroup 1/2 comp	KSM32	Yes	
19	SL guitar on stage	Subgroup 1/2 comp	KSM32	Yes	
20	SL guitar off stage	Subgroup 1/2 comp	SM 57	Yes	
21	Sample L		Active DI	Yes	
22	Sample R		Active DI	Yes	
23	Vocal SR	Distressor	Beta 58A	Yes	Comp
24	Vocal SR center	Distressor	Beta 58A	Yes	Comp
25	Vocal center	Distressor	Beta 58A	Yes	Comp
26	Vocal SL	Distressor	Beta 58A	Yes	Comp
27	Vocal spare	Distressor	Beta 58A	Yes	Comp
		Monitor Mixes			
Mix 1	Vox 3 100%, delay 100%				
Mix 2	SR guitar 100%, Vox 1 100%, hi-hat 50%, SL guitar 50%, Vox 3 50%, delay 50%				
Mix 3	Kick-snare-hi-hat 100%, Vox 2 100%, Vox 3 50%, Delay 50%				
Mix 4	Vox 3 100%, delay 100%, SR guitar 50%, SL guitar 50%				
Mix 5	Vox 4 100%, SL guitar 100%, kick-snare-hi-hat 100%, Vox 3 50%, delary 50%				
Mix 6	Vox 3 100%, delay 100%, SR guitar 50%, SL guitar 50%, bass 50%, kick 50%				

Contact   Lance Loudnoise--Production manager/FOH engineer
Cell: 555-833-4233
150dBokay@email.com

You should also look at other stage plots and input lists to learn more about how to create them. A Google search for "stage plot and input chart" will result in the stage plots for many professional bands because many of them are putting this info on their websites, which is a really good thing to do, and you should do the same.

Make it easy for the venue's sound crew to get a copy of your stage plot and input chart. They need to have this information so they can plan ahead and make sure they have what you need before you load in. If they don't have this information, they'll be completely in the dark about your band, take longer to get you prepared for sound check, and pretty much consider you an amateur for putting them through a stressful day. Be a pro and make sure the venue's technical staff has the information they need to do their job properly for your band.

MAKING A PROPER ADVANCE SHEET

Another important thing to do before you start advancing the shows is to create an advance sheet. Once you've created your advance sheet, you can email it to your promoter reps so they can fill in the blanks with the required information and then email it back to you. This is the easiest way to obtain the show information you'll need; and not only will you be able to store a copy of this advance sheet in your computer folder for that show, but you'll also be able to print out a copy and put it into your advance book for easy reference by you and your crew.

Always be sure to organize your computer so all of your information can be easily found. Inside the main computer folder for my client, I'll create a subfolder for each tour and give it a name, such as USA 2012, and then I'll create a subfolder inside that one for each show of the tour. Name each of those subfolders with the name of the applicable city on the tour. Store the advance sheet, contract, sound and lighting specs, and any other pertinent info in the folder for that city. You don't want to waste time digging through an unorganized folder containing hundreds of documents each time you need to find something for a show.

The advance sheet below was created using Microsoft Excel. Once you learn how to use Excel, an advance sheet is easy to create. You'll be able to use it for every tour you do, and you'll only have to change the name of the band at the top of the sheet. Depending on the size of the tour, some of the info on the sheet may not apply. For larger tours, you may want to add more information fields to the spreadsheet.

As you can see on the advance sheet, the promoter rep has filled in all of the information that we've requested for that show. If the promoter rep has left any of the fields blank, email him and find out why the information is missing and when he'll have it for you. Once he emails you the missing info, you can type it into the advance sheet if he doesn't send you an updated copy.

Once the advance sheet is complete, print it out on three-hole paper and place it into your advance book. Keep track of any missing info on your advance sheets. Take a yellow highlighter and highlight any areas on the sheet where info is missing. These highlights will remind you that you still need to obtain that info from the promoter rep. Once you

Skinny Girl Riot Show Advance Sheet--USA 2012		
Show date	**Venue name**	**Venue address**
Sunday, April 01, 2012	Club 1	666 3rd St, San Francisco, CA 94107
Venue telephone	**Venue website**	**Venue capacity**
555-777-1439	www.club1.com	1633
All ages show?	**Production office?**	**Production office tel?**
18 & over	yes, 1 small room	555-778-6839
Promoter rep name	**Promoter rep cell**	**Promoter rep email**
Vince Vega	666-555-3838	vincent@promoter.net
Stage size & trim height	**# of dressing rooms**	**Toilet/shower backstage**
20' x 12' x 2', 10' deck to truss	2	There is a shower and toilet in each dressing room.
Internet backstage?	**# of runners provided?**	**# of stagehands/loaders?**
yes, network: theclub1, password: getin7676	1 with 7 passenger van	4 on the in, 2 all day, 6 on the out
Type of barricade	**Sound engineer info**	**Lighting director info**
pro steel blow-through spanning length of stage	Jimmy Parker, 555-692-3838, jim@theclub1.com	Tom Johnson, 555-838-4431, tom@theclub1.com
12:00PM load-in?	**Type of load-in?**	**Bus/truck parking?**
yes	behind venue, ramp straight onto stage	room for 3 buses, ok to run bus generator, no landline
Stage power specs	**Sound power specs**	**Lighting power specs**
100 amp, 3 phase, 20a twist	house: 100 amp, 3 phase, guest: 100 amp, 3 phase	house: 400 amp, 3 phase, guest: 200 amp, 3 phase
Doors open time?	**Show schedule?**	**Curfew?**
7:00PM	The Worst: 8:00--8:30PM, SGR: 9:00--10:30PM	11:00PM
Lunch for 14 @ noon?	**Dinner catered?**	**5PM dinner if catered?**
yes, order from venue menu	$20.00 buyout	$20.00 buyout
Full dressing room rider?	**After show food?**	**# of security on call?**
yes for headliner	yes for headliner	12
Security backstage?	**Security on bus/trucks?**	**Security @ FOH?**
1 on headliner dressing room & back door	1 on buses	1
Security in barricade?	**Merch % & seller info**	**Local wash & fold hours?**
4	80/20, 100% on music, venue sells	Monday - Sunday: 8AM to 6PM, laundromat til 10PM

receive the info from the promoter rep, you can either print out a new advance sheet or hand write the info on the advance sheet, and don't forget to add it to the file in your computer.

Always make a proper advance book. You can purchase a binder at any office supply store that has a clear plastic cover so you can slide in a book cover you've created. The band's logo, the name of the tour, and the words "Advance Book" are all you need for a proper advance book cover. Use tabs for each city so you can easily thumb to the advance sheet you're looking for.

You can also print out the sound and lighting specs—and backline specs for fly dates—and place them in your advance book behind every advance sheet so your crew can see them when necessary. I don't like to put things such as contracts and deal sheets into the advance book. It's not a good idea for others to be viewing the band's private financial information. I'm the only person who needs to be looking at those, so I keep them in my computer.

Don't ever skip making a proper advance sheet and advance book. You'll save yourself a lot of time advancing the shows and save even more time by having an advance book in the production office when one of your crew needs to see info for one of the upcoming shows. And, yes, even though you've already emailed the crew some of this info, they're still going to come into production asking to see it.

PREPARING YOUR PRE-ADVANCE PACKAGE

When you send out your advance sheet to obtain show information from the promoter rep, it's equally important to send him the information about your tour that he'll need to know. Therefore, I always create what I call my pre-advance sheet and include this in my pre-advance package that I send out to all of the promoter reps.

As you can see from my pre-advance sheet below, we've given the promoter rep a lot of information that he needs. Since we're not carrying production, we've told him we need a noon load-in; this is the default time I ask for when doors open at 7:00 p.m. I like to have seven hours to get the show up and ready. If we have early doors for a show, I'll usually request that we come in earlier, under most circumstances.

Some promoter reps will try to get you to come in later because it'll save them money by not having to pay for as many hours of labor for the stagehands and venue techs. If this happens, you'll need to determine if you can come in later and still get the show up in time. I always prefer to give myself some buffer time, should we encounter technical problems.

Sometimes you'll have a show with late doors and can afford to come in later. It could be a bar gig where the local crowd is used to a late show. Going on early in such a venue is never in your best interest because your band could end up playing to a smaller crowd, and you don't want that.

Always negotiate the load-in time that's best for you, but if the show's selling badly, you may find yourself in a position where the promoter's trying to cut every corner to reduce the show costs and his potential loss. In this event, you may have to work with him on the load-in time and probably everything else involved with the show.

We've also let our promoter rep know how many stagehands we need for the show. Labor is usually one of the more expensive show costs, so the promoter will try to hire the fewest number of stagehands possible. Some promoters will even try to use the house techs for stagehands to save some money.

Skinny Girl Riot
USA Tour 2012

Pre-advance Sheet

The following info will answer many of your questions about the Skinny Girl Riot USA 2012 tour.

1. Skinny Girl Riot will require a <u>12:00PM load-in time</u>.
2. Skinny Girl Riot will require a minimum of six stagehands.
3. Skinny Girl Riot is traveling on a forty-five foot bus with a fifteen foot trailer. We will require secure parking for this sixty foot vehicle.
4. Our support act, The Worst, is traveling in a twelve-passenger van with a fifteen foot trailer. Please make every effort possible to provide secure parking for their vehicle.
5. Including our bus driver, there are fourteen people in Skinny Girl Riot's entourage. We prefer a dinner buyout of $20.00 per person.
6. There are six people in The Worst's entourage. They prefer a dinner buyout of $10.00 per person.
7. Skinny Girl Riot is carrying a monitor engineer, but your house monitor engineer will be required to mix The Worst's show.
8. Skinny Girl Riot has a 40' x 24' backdrop that must be hung. In small venues, we have a 20' x 12' backdrop that can be hung. The Worst has a 4' x 4' *backdrop* that must be hung…somehow.
9. Skinny Girl Riot requires that you provide a 10'x10'x2' drum riser for each show. A rolling riser is preferred, if possible.
10. Skinny Girl Riot will require a runner with a passenger van for the entire show day.
11. A professional barricade is MANDATORY for this show. There cannot be a show without a proper barricade. No bicycle racks or homemade match stick barricades, please.
12. If there is no shower in the venue, Skinny Girl Riot will require a shower room at a nearby hotel at the promoter's expense.
13. As we devise a show schedule during the advance, the following information will help you.

    Doors:
    The Worst: 30 minute set
    30 minute changeover
    Skinny Girl Riot: 90 minute set
    Curfew:

    This in no way covers everything as it applies to Skinny Girl Riot but is a brief overview of important information pertinent to our show.

    Please send my completed advance sheet, current sound and lighting specs and a house lighting plot to me as soon as possible. Thank you and we look forward to a successful show at your venue.

    Bobby Blinder—Skinny Girl Riot Tour Manager/Lighting Designer
    Cell: 555-673-3342
    eFax: 555-323-9873
    tourmangler@tour.net

Always try to avoid this whenever possible because once you start load-in, the house techs should be working with your sound engineer and lighting director to start shaping the house systems to your band's specs. They can't be doing this if they're outside unloading your truck or trailer. It slows down the process of getting ready for sound check, and it also slows down the changeovers because the house sound engineer and monitor engineer—sometimes the same overworked poor bastard—can't be getting the next act mic'd up and ready to go on stage on time if they're loading out the previous band's gear.

If you find yourself in a situation where this has to happen, the show may not stay on schedule. You might want to increase the changeover times if that's possible, but if you're faced with a strict curfew, you're going to be even more pressed for time. You don't want the show to get so far behind schedule that your headliner has to cut their show because the support acts didn't go on stage on time and you're caught in a time crunch between a show schedule that's running late and a strict curfew.

Next on our pre-advance sheet, we specify the optimum stage size that we require. If you're doing a club tour, this bit of information is pretty much for informational purposes only. No matter how much space you need, if it doesn't exist in the venue, they can't rebuild the room to make you a bigger stage. You have to make it work.

This is why you should always give a lot of thought to carrying stage sets and too much gear on small club tours. It might not fit on many of the stages you're playing. There's nothing economical about paying for gear that you're only using two out of five shows a week.

If your tour has many support acts and you're playing on a small stage, sometimes you can build the stage out a bit by putting more stage sections in front of the stage to increase the depth, but this decreases the room's capacity. If the show's not expected to sell out, the promoter may not have a problem with you doing this, but if the show's sold out, building the stage out will be nearly impossible because the tickets are already sold, and you can't suddenly decrease the legal capacity of the room for a sold out gig unless you're begging the Fire Marshal to shut down the show.

You can try to put some road cases in front of the stage and put the monitor system wedges on them, but you only have so much room in the barricade, and this gives the security guards less room to work in once the show begins. If you don't have a barricade and the show's sold out, this might not be the smartest way to go because those wedges could end up being destroyed by a rowdy crowd, and the venue may come hounding you to pay for them at the end of the night.

The next item on our pre-advance sheet is bus parking. You always want to be sure to tell the promoter rep what you need for parking, not only for your band but for the support acts, too. Parking's always going to be one of your biggest headaches on a club tour. Some venues won't have enough and some venues won't have any at all, but you must tell the promoter rep what you need so he can warn you about what to expect.

Some venues may only have parking for one bus, so your headliner will be sorted, but it means that there will be no parking for the support acts. They may have to dump their gear at load-in and then park elsewhere. The promoter rep will usually give you options for where they can park if you ask.

The biggest headache involved for a support act bus driver who cannot park his bus at the venue is that he must get out of bed early and come down and move the bus from where it's parked to the venue so the support act can load their trailer once they're done playing. For a support act in a van, this isn't a problem because one of the people in their entourage is most likely doing the driving, and it's much easier to find parking for a van and trailer than it is for a bus and trailer that's nearly sixty feet long. Be sure to have this information in your advance book so you can warn your support acts ahead of time about the parking situation for each show.

Next, inform your promoter rep of the total number of people on the tour. Give him a breakdown of how many people are in each entourage. He'll need to know this number so he can tell the catering staff how many people to expect for dinner. If you don't have your own pass system for the tour, you'll have to use the promoter's passes. Your total entourage number will tell him how many passes he'll need to prepare for your touring personnel.

The next thing to add to your pre-advance sheet is the number of people in your entourage that must be fed lunch at load-in time. Depending on the size of the show and its catering budget, there may not be a budget to feed your people lunch, or the promoter may only be willing to feed your crew because they're the only ones working at that time.

Sometimes on a U.S. club tour a promoter won't provide lunch for anyone in the support acts. They're usually not even loading into the venue until after lunchtime, and the promoter probably won't have the budget for it. It's more common to feed the support acts lunch on a U.K. or European tour if you're carrying catering, providing you've included them in the daily catering numbers. Even if you're not carrying a catering company, the promoter may include the support acts for lunch in his catering numbers. You should always make sure so you can inform the support acts.

It's not a pleasant experience for the support acts to walk into catering on the first day of the tour and be told by the catering staff in front of everyone that they're not included in lunch because you didn't bother to tell them this bit of important information. It can be very embarrassing for them and a really bad way to start the tour.

I always try to get the support acts as much as I can when it comes to catering. Many support acts aren't getting paid very much money, if any at all, and they're struggling to make it to each show. They should at least be fed dinner and have some beer and water for their show. Everyone has to pay their dues, but I also believe that everyone deserves to be fed each day. I hope you'll adopt this same attitude.

Inform your promoter rep of any special dietary needs for the bands on your tour. This information should be in each band's rider, but don't assume that the catering people are going to read the rider if the show's not doing well. Special diets for vegetarians, vegans, and those with gluten-free intolerance are important, and you should make a concerted effort to inform the promoter rep and his catering staff of these needs. It's a bad scene for a vegan or a person with gluten intolerance to walk into catering for dinner and find there's nothing for them to eat. No one can do their job on an empty stomach, and they shouldn't have to, either.

Always tell the promoter rep if you're carrying any production. Even if it's only a small lighting package consisting of a few moving lights, let him know what to expect. If you're carrying no production at all, let him know you're only carrying backline.

If you're not carrying your own monitor engineer—a luxury for many bands—tell the promoter rep you'll need the house monitor engineer to mix all of the bands on the tour. Tell him about any vital monitor needs that your band may have. If you have a singer who requires loud side fills and can't do the show without them, you'd better make sure to stress that fact. You should always go over these things when you advance the house production, but make those vital facts stand out loud and clear by stating it on your pre-advance sheet as crucial needs. This is a time to use **BOLD** and <u>UNDERLINE</u> for maximum effect.

If you're not carrying a sound engineer and lighting director, tell the promoter rep so he can inform the venue's sound engineer and lighting director that they'll be doing your band's show.

If your band has a backdrop to hang, let the promoter rep know about it so the house crew can plan ahead for this. Most of the better venues have the facilities to hang backdrops because they do it so often, but some may not. Don't expect them to be prepared to hang a forty-foot backdrop if you didn't even bother to tell them you're bringing one. If you're allowing the support act to hang a backdrop, inform the promoter rep about it, and don't forget to tell him the size of their backdrop.

Inform him that each band has a manufacturer's fireproof certificate for all of their soft goods. Include PDF copies of every fire certificate in your pre-advance package. Many venues won't allow you to hang a backdrop or set up scrims that aren't fireproof, and you must have a fire certificate to prove it. Save yourself some headaches later on and gather up all of the fire certificates for all of the soft goods you'll be using on your tour and include them in your pre-advance package.

If you're carrying any stage set pieces that'll need to be set up, make sure that info is included on your stage plot and inform the promoter rep in your pre-advance sheet as an extra reminder. A large stage set to erect can make the difference in not only how much labor you'll need but in how much time you'll need to get set up and ready for sound check.

Tell the promoter rep if you're bringing a drum riser, especially if your rider calls for him to provide one and you've slipped up and not changed this fact in the rider. Many clubs have a house drum riser already set up on stage. If you don't need it, let them know that so it can be struck before you load-in. It's a waste of your load-in time when the house crew must suddenly figure out where they're going to store a large drum riser that may not easily come apart. If you're allowing your support act to use the house drum riser, let the promoter rep know that so the house crew doesn't strike it. Be thorough in your advance, and the day will be much smoother for all involved.

I always reiterate in my pre-advance sheet that we'll need a runner with a passenger van for each show. This is always another budget item that may or may not happen, depending on ticket sales. Don't count on it if you don't advance it.

I always make sure to firmly specify in the rider and my pre-advance sheet that a barricade is mandatory for the show. I'm used to doing metal bands for three decades, and a barricade is essential for a metal show—or any show with a large crowd, for that matter. If you think little girls can't get rowdy, buy front row tickets to a Justin Bieber concert; they can make a thrash metal mosh pit seem like a senior citizen ballroom dance when they go berserk.

A barricade is not only to protect the band and their gear from crowd surfers landing on stage, but it's also to protect the security guards posted in front of the stage by giving them room to work. It gives the photographers a safe place to shoot the first three songs of your band's show. It helps to protect the audience members who do come over the barricade because it gives security a clear lane to take them out of the barricade and put them back into the audience or out the back door, depending on the venue's policy.

I always specify that if the venue doesn't have a shower for my entourage, the promoter must buy a shower room at a nearby hotel. Again, this is another budget item that may or may not happen. It all depends on how well the show is selling and whether or not there's room in the show budget. Be polite in your show advance, and you'll be surprised what you can get out of the promoter, even on shows that aren't selling well. No professional promoter with a conscience wants to see his headliner up on stage looking like a bunch of filthy vagrants because he wouldn't buy them a cheap shower room.

Always give the promoter rep the shell of your show schedule so he can send you back a final schedule that makes some sense. If you don't tell him how long each band is playing and how long the changeovers are between each act, how can you expect him to send you a final schedule? In reality, all you really need to know is what time the doors open, what time the show needs to start and what time the show must end. You can fill in the rest. However, if you create the schedule based upon this limited information, be sure to send the promoter rep your final schedule when you've finished it so you're both on the same page.

You should check with your booking agent and find out how long each of your support acts is supposed to play. This is usually agreed upon when they were booked to do the tour. Don't just assume how long they're going to play; confirm it with your agent, and then you should confirm their show length with each support act when you coordinate the tour with them. You'll often find that many of them haven't even been told by their people how long they're supposed to perform each night.

Tell the promoter rep how the schedule will run if any local bands are to be added to the bottom of the bill. This is usually something that's agreed upon between your booking agent and the promoter when the show was originally booked. Most booking agents will specify on their sheet if a show will have any local acts added to the bill, so it shouldn't come as any surprise to you.

Frankly, I usually prefer not to have any local bands added to the bill, especially if we already have two or three support acts on tour with us. There's never any room on stage for them, and I'm not about to make a national act on my tour strike their drum kit for a local band that means very little. So the local band ends up sitting off to the side, crammed into what little space is left on stage.

Sometimes these local bands have been added to the bill because they're not only playing for free but the promoter made them help promote the show by passing out flyers, putting up posters, and selling tickets to their local following, which sometimes only consists of their family and friends. And while this may sound like a great financial benefit to your show, it's not so great when they sound worse than Milli Vanilli on meth trying to sing along to a skipping CD. The audience doesn't always realize that the headliner had nothing to do with them being brutally whipped into submission with such *musical* torture. But there are a lot of great local bands out there.

If a show's selling badly and the promoter can get two local bands—even bad ones—to go out and sell fifty tickets each, that one hundred tickets may reduce his loss significantly or even get him out of the red. If that's the case, then you may have no choice but to endure the headaches of having more bands on the bill.

I have nothing against local bands. After all, every band was once a local band and they are the future of our business, but if we're already in a situation where we can't get our own five-band bill on a stage the size of a Wheat Thin, how are we going to get two more local bands on that small stage? This type of nightmare also makes the show much longer, which has the headliner going on even later, and that's usually not a good idea for your band.

You can add any important bits of information to the pre-advance sheet that you want your promoter rep to focus on. Make this sheet as long and comprehensive as you like. You can never give the promoter rep too much info about your tour, but only tell him what he needs to know.

We've created our pre-advance sheet and completed it with important information that we want our promoter rep to know about. We've also built our advance sheet, stage plot, and input chart. We've made any necessary updates to our band's rider, updated the revision date in the footer, and sent it off to our booking agent so he has it in his files for future bookings. We've also obtained the rider, stage plot, input chart, and other necessary information from our support act. It's now time to combine it all together and send out our pre-advance package to the promoter reps so we can begin to advance the shows.

HOW TO PROPERLY ADVANCE A TOUR

Now that we've compiled our pre-advance package, we're ready to send it out to the promoter reps and advance the shows. Many new tour managers build up this process in their minds to be some complicated nightmare when it really isn't. Only those tour managers who aren't organized feel this way.

Take out the list of tour dates your booking agent sent to you. These sheets should include the contact info for each promoter. Compose a new email and attach your entire pre-advance package to it as a zip file using a program such as 7-Zip or WinZip. 7-Zip is a great tool, and it's free.

Do not send out your pre-advance package as a bunch of separate files attached to the email; it takes too long to download all of those files individually. It's much quicker to download your zip folder and unzip it to view the files. Give the folder a name that helps people to find it easily in their computer. In this case, we'll name our folder SGR advance.

Write a letter such as the one below and address it to each promoter on the tour.

To all promoters for Skinny Girl Riot's U.S. Tour 2012:

Hello everyone. Attached to this email is my pre-advance package for Skinny Girl Riot's U.S. Tour 2012. It contains everything that your promoter rep will need to advance your Skinny Girl Riot show with me. The package includes our current rider, stage plot, input chart, fire certificates for our soft goods, my advance sheet for your promoter rep to fill out and email back to me, and my pre-advance sheet that will answer most of your promoter rep's questions about our tour. The package also includes the same info for our support act.

Please forward this email to your promoter rep that will be advancing your show with me and have him send me his contact info so I know that he has received this package.

I know that some of these dates are weeks away, but if I could just do a preliminary advance and get the information I need for our tour book that must go to print on March 22, 2012, we can do the final show advance as we get closer to the show. My deadline for preliminary information is March 7, 2012.

Preliminary info needed for tour book:
> *Complete venue address, telephone number, and website address*
> *Promoter rep name, cell phone number, and email address*
> *Venue capacity*
> *Stage size*
> *All ages gig?*
> *Dinner catered or buyout?*
> *Wireless internet backstage?*
> *Number of dressing rooms in venue*
> *Number of toilets and showers backstage*
> *Complete show schedule, including load-in time, doors open time, show start time, and any curfew*
> *Venue sound and lighting specs and any available info sheets*

Thank you and we look forward to a successful show with all of you.
Bobby Blinder—Skinny Girl Riot Tour Manager/Lighting Designer
World cell: 555-111-2222
eFax: 555-121-2222
tourmangler@tour.net

Once you've sent out this email containing your pre-advance package, the ball is now rolling, and you'll begin to advance all of the tour dates. It's important to remember that many of these promoter reps are working many shows a week, and sometimes it'll be difficult to get them to fully advance a show that's two months away; but as long as you get the preliminary information you need for your tour book, you can finalize the rest of the advance as you get closer to each actual show date. Advancing a tour is an ongoing process where things have a way of changing, and you must be able to deal with that.

Many of these promoter reps will also stall on a complete show advance if they're not sure how the show's going to sell. They won't want to commit to paying for extras such as additional sound or lighting gear until they're closer to the show and have a better idea if they're going to lose money.

They may also stall on advancing the catering until they know if the show's looking good or bad. Catering will be one of the first things they'll ask you to reduce if the show's selling badly, and the chances of them spending any money on non-critical sound or lighting extras will be slim to forget it. For these reasons, the show advance can often be a process that happens in stages leading up to the show. Be patient; this is how it works.

Some road managers view the promoter rep as some kind of villain, but he has a boss—the promoter—that he has to answer to, just like you have to answer to the band and their manager. He's caught in the middle, too. Even on a sold-out show, the promoter's always looking to keep show expenses in check, and he's relying upon his promoter rep to accomplish this goal.

By the same token, your band members are relying on you to get them all of the things that they ask for in their rider so they can put on the best show and live as comfortable as possible on the road.

I've always appreciated a band that understands how this business works. A professional band realizes that no matter how popular they are or how well their record's selling, sometimes a show may not sell so well. Many times this is due to factors that really have nothing to do with the band. A major sporting event or another much bigger concert could also be happening in town on that day.

Ticket sales could be low if the band's already played a city too many times on an album cycle. Some bands think they're worth X amount of money for every show, and they don't want to hear anything different. What a band is *worth* is determined by how many asses they can put in seats, plain and simple. Any promoter or booking agent will tell you that. Plus, their worth can fluctuate and go down if they've overplayed the market to excess. A band can't expect to play a much smaller venue and be paid the same amount of money unless they're willing to raise the ticket price to pay for it, and that's not a good idea in a bad economy, especially if you've overplayed the market.

The fans can only go see a band so many times before they don't want to—or can't afford to—see them again for a period of time. Therefore, when the band comes back again too soon, they may not pull as many people; and the promoter's going to offer them less money because they're selling fewer tickets this time. Even U2 and The Rolling Stones know that they can only play a city so much over a period of time before they've worn out their welcome there for a few years. This is Band Booking 101.

There are some promoters that may still give you everything you want on a soft show because they have a long history promoting the band, while some others will be begging you to make cuts to reduce their loss.

It makes life a lot easier when the band understands the reasons why you have to make cuts on a show that's not selling well, but it's pretty miserable when a new band doesn't get it or simply doesn't care about the promoter's financial loss and batters the tour manager with the *you failed us* routine.

As you begin to receive replies from the promoter reps, use your advance checklist—in your computer or posted on your wall—and check off the shows where you've received promoter rep contact info and then where you've received completed advance sheets and sound and lighting specs.

Once you've begun to receive this information, don't just store it in your tour folder on your computer; start typing this information in the tour book. You've got to be multi-tasking, working on multiple projects at the same time so you'll get everything done by the time the tour starts.

It's vital that you make sure the promoter reps are also sending you the venue sound and lighting specs. You must forward them to your sound engineer and lighting director so they can make sure they're adequate for your show and get their approval.

It's never a good idea to keep your sound engineer and lighting director in the dark about production. I've seen bands show up with no clue about the venue's gear and then do nothing but complain when it's inadequate and too late for the promoter to do anything about it, but you can be certain that you'll be the one in the hot seat with the band for not sorting it all out in the show advance.

Make sure your sound engineer and lighting director have looked over the venue's sound and lighting specs and signed off on them as adequate, or tell you what you need to advance with the promoter rep to make the gear acceptable.

Some sound and lighting crew guys will ask for everything under the sun, things they don't even really need, just to have plenty of toys to play with out at front-of-house and show everyone how big their dicks are. Unless the band has money to burn and doesn't care, it's a waste of their money renting equipment they don't really need. If the promoter's renting this gear they don't really need, that money could be spent on other things that you do need, and if the show's doing well and into points, the band's paying for 85 percent of these unnecessary expenditures out of their back end money. Sometimes you have to keep your crew's spending in check.

I've seen some sound and lighting crew members go out of their way to wind up the band about how the tour manager isn't doing his job by getting them all of these production extras on the rider, despite the fact that the show's selling so badly you couldn't give a ticket away to a homeless person freezing his ass off outside in a raging blizzard.

Some of them will never change with that shit, and some of them are simply doing it to cause drama. If they're new, explain the reasons why they're not getting the extra gear since the twelve tickets sold in the empty thousand-seat club wasn't a big enough red flashing beacon of reality to alert them to the show's failure. If that doesn't work and they continue doing it, go to the band and explain the reality of things and make them understand the situation. Personally, I'll only tolerate that crap from some crew guy once.

After that, I'm looking for someone's head on a fucking stick and their ass on a Greyhound bus going home.

When your sound engineer and lighting director tell you what needs to be augmented with the house production, go back to the promoter rep and give him a list of your needs. Stay on top of this, and remember that the promoter rep may not commit to renting these extras until you get closer to the show and he sees how the show's going to sell.

I always try to make sure that I have at least the first half of the tour fully advanced by the time we start the tour. You must remember that this will be an ongoing process that you must stay on top of. As I said before, many of these promoter reps are busy with multiple shows. Some of them are incompetent or just don't care, and you'll find that trying to get information out of them can be difficult, but you have to keep riding them until you get what you need from them.

Once in a while, you may end up in a situation where no matter how many emails you send or phone calls you make you just can't get the information you need from a promoter rep. In this event, start copying his boss on your emails, insisting that he send you the info you've requested many times. If that doesn't work, then it's time to get your booking agent involved.

If there's no communication coming back from a promoter rep, I'll send him an email stating how I've sent numerous emails and left many voice messages for him and have gotten no reply. I'll also state how I'm highly concerned because the show's coming up soon and we've advanced absolutely nothing for the show. I'll copy the band's booking agent and the promoter on the email. There's no need to get the band's manager involved unless the booking agent can't or won't get the problem solved.

If this MIA promoter rep is even reading his emails, he's now been put on the spot by me calling him out in front of his boss and the booking agent. This also covers your back by letting your booking agent know that you're doing everything possible to advance the date, but the promoter's people aren't getting back to you. At this point, the booking agent has to fire up the promoter to get the show advanced, and this usually works every time.

There's a lot more to advance when you're doing a bigger tour, such as an arena or stadium tour, but the process remains basically the same. Although on an arena tour, you'll have a production manager doing part or even the entire show advance. As long as you're organized and compile the information for each show as it comes in from the promoter rep and you answer his questions in a timely manner, you'll find that advancing a tour is not the complicated mystery some make it out to be.

As my advance sheets come in completed by the promoter reps, I'll print them out on three-hole paper and put them into my advance book. I always print them on one-sided sheets of paper so that when I have the advance book open, the page to the left is always blank. I do this for the same reason I do it with the tour books: I like to make notes on the blank page to the left. If the promoter emails me and says that a certain brand of beer on the band's rider isn't available in that city, I'll make a note of it so I won't forget about it. I'll then make my substitution with the promoter rep, and then on the show day I'll post a memo in the band's dressing room above the catering table explaining that their brand of beer isn't available in this city, and we've had to make a substitution with their second choice.

This might seem minor to you, but bands have specific things on their rider for a reason. They want their favorite brands of food and booze each night, and some get upset when they don't get it, especially if they think the promoter is just jerking them around to save money. If you explain to them it's simply a case of brand unavailability, most of them will probably understand. However, I'd still go online and do a search to make sure the promoter's telling you the truth, so you don't look like a gullible dumbass when the singer Googles his missing brand of premium vodka and finds out that it's on sale with free delivery at the liquor store right next door to the venue.

I've always made it a point to quickly learn which items the band absolutely must have each night to keep them happy. If I know we're going to a city where any of these items can't be found, I'll send the runner out to stock up on these products and store them in the bay of the tour bus so I can bring them into the dressing room when needed. I have no problem with asking the promoter rep to buy the receipt from me because he would've had to buy the items anyway. This way the band gets what they want, and there's no drama over something as simple as a brand of beer.

If the promoter rep suddenly emails you and says the hot water heater has blown up in the venue and there will be no hot water in the dressing rooms to take showers on the show day because they'll be replacing it, make a note in the advance book that the promoter's going to be buying shower rooms for the entourage at a local hotel. Be sure to make these notes in your advance book and tour book so you don't forget about them because you'll need to add this crucial information to your day sheets so everyone knows about it.

Be thorough when compiling your show information, and always make notes and get into the habit of checking those notes in your advance book and tour book on a daily basis. If a band member emails me a guest list name and I don't have access to my guest list book or computer, I'll write it on the blank page for that city in the tour book. I've always done this for years, so I'm used to checking that page every day for guest list additions when I'm ready to type up the guest list. Use it for anything you need to remember.

By now you're starting to see that it's rare that a long tour is fully advanced by the time the tour starts. Things are always changing, and you have to be able to adapt to those changes if you're going to last in this business, but that's why this job's never dull. As long as you always have a plan B—and C—and can roll with the punches, you'll probably survive.

ADVANCING YOUR CASH REQUIREMENTS

An important thing that you must do is advance your cash requirements for each show. You have to know how much cash you're going to need each week to pay for road expenses.

Some new tour managers forget to do this and then show up in the promoter's office expecting to be paid cash, only to find that the promoter rep just has a check, and the cash has gone home with the promoter. This happened because the tour manager forgot to advance cash, and the promoter rep forgot or didn't care about asking if the tour manager needed any cash. It's your responsibility to advance the cash you need, and you can't blame the promoter rep when he only has a check for you.

Many new bands don't have a band credit card; some band members don't even have personal credit cards yet. Some bands don't have two nickels to rub together and rely upon the cash they receive each night to pay for fuel to get them to the next city. Can you imagine the spot you'd be in if you forgot to advance what little cash you were supposed to pick up and were handed a check at 2:00 a.m., leaving you with no cash to get your band to the next town? Unless you had your own credit card to float the band to the next city, I'd say you'd be in one uncomfortable hot seat with the band.

You don't need to give yourself a brain aneurysm trying to estimate your weekly nut down to the last red cent because you never know what unexpected expenses can come up, but you do need to tally up the regular bills you must pay and establish a number to work with. Look at the simple cash nut budget below.

Skinny Girl Riot--Weekly Cash Nut		
bus driver's salary	$	1,470.00
2 weekly driver overdrives	$	420.00
2 generator services & bus wash	$	165.00
band and crew per diems	$	2,520.00
bus fuel and supplies	$	1,900.00
show and office supplies	$	225.00
miscellaneous expenses	$	300.00
Weekly cash nut	$	**7,000.00**

We have to pay the driver his weekly salary in cash, so we add that to the budget. Let's pretend we're averaging two overdrives a week, and we have to also pay that in cash to the driver. We must pay the driver to wash the bus once a week, and he'll do two bus generator services a week (every one hundred hours), so we've included that amount. We know that the total band and crew per diems each week are $2,520, so we add that to the budget. Bus fuel and supplies are averaging about $1,900 a week. We're spending about $225 a week on show and office supplies, so we throw that into the numbers. We should add about $300 a week for miscellaneous expenses. The total comes out to $7,000 a week for our weekly cash nut.

If you're averaging five shows a week, that's $1,400 a show that you need to pick up in cash each night to meet your weekly $7,000 cash nut. If you're averaging six shows a week, you only need to pick up $1,167 a night—round it off to $1,200. It's not hard to get a clear picture of your weekly cash needs.

Now that you know you must pick up $1,400 a night in cash, you need to email each promoter rep and let him know that you'll need to pick up that amount in cash and the balance of the guarantee in a check. Always remember to email the promoter rep so you have a record of what's been said.

It's possible that your manager and agent may insist that you pick up the entire balance in cash every night because they don't trust the promoters. If this is the case, then you don't need to worry about having enough cash on hand to pay your weekly nut unless you're a new band earning little money.

If you're working for a baby band and they're not even making enough money to pay their weekly road expenses, then that money has to come from somewhere else, but you still need to know the amount of your weekly nut.

Some bands pay some of their bills with their profits from merchandising sales. That may be where your cash is coming from each night to pay most of your weekly nut. The manager may be floating the tour and plans to get reimbursed by the band when they're making more money, if they can find a manager that's willing to do something like that. Needle. Haystack. Good luck. They could also be getting a small amount of tour support from the record company to cover their tour shortfall, although this is becoming extinct quicker than the audio CD.

If a band's guarantees become so large that the band's manager doesn't want you picking up such large amounts of cash for fear of it being lost or stolen, you'll need to take checks from the promoters. So always make sure to advance your cash requirements and inform the promoter rep that you'll take the rest of the guarantee in a check.

If you don't tell the promoter rep what you want to pick up, he may just assume you want the entire guarantee in cash, and you could find yourself carrying around a large amount of cash that you don't need or want. Remember, you're responsible for the band's cash; if you lose it the manager's probably going to deduct it from your salary, if he doesn't fire you first.

When you email the promoter rep your cash requirements, you should also include a completed W-9 form so you don't have to waste time filling one at settlement; you'll only have to sign it. Some promoters require that you send the W-9 form in advance before their accounting department will cut you a check, so it's always a good idea to attach the band's W-9 form to your cash advance email.

The W-9 is an IRS form that certifies the taxpayer identification number of a company or individual. It's simple to complete, and you only need to include the band's company name and address, their tax classification (individual, corporation, LLC), and their taxpayer identification number. This is for American bands only, unless a foreign band has a U.S. company.

You can type in all of the required info and save the completed W-9 PDF file so it's in your computer folder when you need to email it to a promoter rep. You should also complete a W-9 file for yourself and save it in your computer if you accept a gig from a band that wants to treat you as an independent contractor. If you're not incorporated, you'd only use your name and social security number for the form, and your tax classification would be individual/sole proprietor.

Never pick up cash you don't need unless the manager or booking agent insists you do so. Storing cash in the tour bus is never the best idea, even in a bus safe, because buses can be broken into and catch on fire. You never know what could happen. The promoter can stop payment on checks that have been stolen or burnt to a crisp in a bus fire, but cash that's been thieved or converted to ashes is gone forever unless the band has insurance that'll cover the loss.

In 2004, I was on tour with Machine Head in Europe. We were playing at the Markthalle in Hamburg. While the band was on stage, and I was at the lighting console, someone entered our tour bus through a door that someone in our entourage had left unlocked. The thieving little varmint stole my suitcase with every stitch of clothing I had with me. He also stole a suitcase belonging to Machine Head's vocalist, Robb Flynn, which contained some of his stage wardrobe and a lot of his street clothes.

Even though this caused Robb and me some inconvenience, it didn't send us to the poor house, but had the little burgling buffoon not been the dumbest thief in all of Germany, he would've found the merch guy's briefcase containing a small fortune in the top lounge of the bus. Again, never carry too much cash if you can help it, and always make sure the bus is completely secure. You never know when thieving little rodents are crawling around in the darkness.

ONLINE SHOW ADVANCE SYSTEM

For a short time in 2006, I was the road manager for an extremely popular band from Texas called Blue October. Their platinum record *Foiled* was roaring up the charts, thanks to their hit single *Hate Me*, written by their incredible singer/songwriter/guitarist, Justin Furstenfeld, a great artist and one of the nicest people I've ever worked for—a fine man.

When I started working with the band, I decided to implement an idea that I'd been thinking about for a long time: an online show advance system. With the help of the band's webmaster, we created a hidden section on the band's website where promoter reps could fill out an HTML show advance form, click submit, and the server would send me an email with the promoter rep's show advance information. Instantly, I had all of the show info I needed for my tour book, and I'd simply print out the email on three-hole paper and insert it into my advance book. All I had to do was send the promoter rep the address for the hidden website page. It saved us both a lot of time and was very convenient.

Below is a simplified layout of that online advance system. As you can see, it includes the same show advance information fields that are on my Excel advance sheet that I email to all of the promoter reps. The actual page on the website was much more elaborate than this, but that is impossible to recreate in this book. But I'm sure you get my point.

At the top of the page, I also had a number of hyperlinks that enabled the promoter rep to click and download many things, such as the band's rider, my pre-advance sheet answering many of their questions about the tour, stage plot, input chart, our sound and lighting specs, separate catering rider, backline requirements for fly dates, the band's tour dates, and even the band's press schedule that could be viewed by people in our organization. The only thing we hadn't gotten around to doing was password-protecting the system so only those with a password could use the system if they somehow found the hidden web pages.

I had always believed that this would be a great device to advance a tour, and it was very efficient. If we had to update the band's rider or input chart, all we had to do was upload the latest version to the website's server. This ensured that the promoter reps were always downloading the most current version of everything; and anyone in our camp, such as the booking agent or manager, could always go there to download the rider or any other related document and be certain that it was the most current version.

I highly recommend this kind of system for any touring band, and it's easy for a webmaster to build. It will simplify your show advance process in many positive ways.

Skinny Girl Riot Show Advance--USA 2012		
Show date	Venue name	Venue address
Venue telephone	Venue website	Venue capacity
All ages show?	Production office?	Production office tel?
Promoter rep name	Promoter rep cell	Promoter rep email
Stage size & trim height	# of dressing rooms	Toilet/shower backstage
Internet backstage?	# of runners provided?	# of stagehands/loaders?
Type of barricade	Sound engineer info	Lighting director info
12:00PM load-in?	Type of load-in?	Bus/truck parking?
Stage power specs	Sound power specs	Lighting power specs
Doors open time?	Show schedule?	Curfew?
Lunch for 14 @ noon?	Dinner catered?	5PM dinner if catered?
Full dressing room rider?	After show food?	# of security on call?
Security backstage?	Security on bus/trucks?	Security @ FOH?
Security in barricade?	Merch % & seller info	Local wash & fold hours?

PART FOUR

ON THE ROAD

THE FIRST DAY OF THE TOUR

The first day of the tour can often be the most hectic day of the tour; it's really up to you and how well you've prepared for it. However, no matter how organized you are, sometimes the first day is just a living hell, where you begin to think fondly of your previous dreams of ascending to the lofty heights of Subway assistant manager. Slap yourself in the face, wake up, and it will all work out.

The first show can be hard if the band's been off the road for a while. This is why many bands choose to do a low-key warm up gig right before starting a big tour. It gives them a chance to work out any potential problems with their sound and gives them a dry run-through in front of a live audience.

For the tour manager, it's a day of getting the tour up and running and the first show under your belt. On the opening day of the tour, you'll be doing many things that you'll only do on that first day. I'm now going to describe what a typical first day of a tour is like.

Your bus driver should know exactly where to park the tour bus when you arrive because you obtained that information when you did your show advance. You and your crew should be awake at least thirty minutes before load-in so you can get dressed, get some coffee in you, assess the stage, and be ready to load in on time. It really sends a bad message to the local crew when your crew drags-ass into the venue twenty minutes late. If your schedule isn't important to you, then why should it be important to them? Load in on time.

If I've never been to a venue before, the first thing I want to see when I arrive is the stage, and every crew member who works on stage is usually the same way. Even though you've gotten the stage specs from the promoter rep during your show advance, they can sometimes be wrong or involve other factors that make the stage problematic, so our first order of business is to get the crew on stage and make any plan B decisions that might have to be made.

Touring in clubs is often very difficult, despite the fact that you've obtained all of the necessary info in your show advance, so it's important to always have a plan B. Upon seeing the stage, you might decide that it's best to use the smaller twenty-foot by twelve-foot version of your forty-foot by twenty-four-foot backdrop because of the low ceiling, or you may decide to use your alternate scrims that are half the size of the normal ones because the big ones are too wide and won't leave any room for the band to get around them because there's a wall on each side of the stage and the monitor console is taking up a lot of room on stage left. Figure out your game plan quickly and get load in started on time.

Whether it's the first day of the tour or the last, always find the runner the minute you load in and send out any laundry that needs to be done to the local wash-and-fold. If you're loading in at noon, you won't have much time left in the day to get laundry done, and if the laundry is stage clothes that the band needs to wear that night, it must get done.

Always confirm in your advance with the promoter rep if there will be a wash-and-fold open in that town if the show falls on a Sunday or a holiday, and ask him what time the wash-and-fold service ends and not just what time the laundromat closes. If the wash-and-fold service is closed on your show day, but the laundromat is open, plan ahead for that situation. You may need to have the runner go to the laundromat and do the band laundry, but remember that you're now tying up the runner doing laundry and preventing her from doing anything else.

You should hand out a new AAA laminate to everyone in your entourage if you're implementing a new pass system for the tour. You should also pass out a hard copy of the tour book to everyone. By this time, you should've already emailed everyone a PDF copy of tour book. If you're using Master Tour by Eventric, everyone in your entourage should already be signed up and have access to your online information in that database.

Give the bus and truck drivers—if you have any—a hard copy of the tour book and a laminate. You should have already emailed them a PDF copy of the tour book and access to Master Tour when you sent it to the rest of the entourage. You should also give the bus driver his float if you haven't already done so. It's quite possible that you may need to do your cash pick up after the first show before you'll have any float.

If you're using radios on the tour, now is the time to pass them out to everyone in your crew except the bus driver. He's at the hotel all day sleeping, so there's no reason for him to have a radio. If you have a tractor trailer with the truck driver sleeping in the cab up front, it can be helpful for him to have a radio for communication between him and your stage manager for load-in and load-out, although this isn't critical as long as the driver has a cell phone.

Be sure to use a label maker to put each crew member's name on their radio and inform the crew that if they lose the radio, they buy the radio. These devices are expensive. Label one of the radios "Promoter" and give it to your promoter rep each day at load-in so you can communicate with him when necessary. You don't want to waste time running down the promoter rep every time you need him.

Put a radio in the band's dressing room so they can reach you and the crew when they need to. You should also place one in the front lounge of the tour bus for the same reason.

Always be sure to get the radio back from the promoter rep at the end of the night and pack up the radio in the band's dressing room. If they have a wardrobe case, storing it there would be a good idea. Put a Post-it note on the wall in front of your computer if that's what it takes to remind you to retrieve these radios until it becomes second nature to you.

You can rent radios for a tour from AAA Communications. They're one of the leaders in the industry and have been around for a long time. They specialize in Motorola products and also offer radios for sale, but there are also other places online such as MyRadioMall. com where you can buy Motorola products at great discount prices. If the band gets to a level where they're touring often, buying their own radios is probably a good idea.

If it's the first day of the tour with your support acts, you'll want to make sure that you've given each support band's road manager all of the Support laminates he'll need for his entourage. Always make sure to order enough lanyards to take care of the support acts because they never seem to have any. You want to make sure that they're wearing their laminates.

You should also give the support act tour managers at least one hard copy of your tour book so you know that he has all of the venue info. It's important to email them a PDF copy of your tour book, but give them a hard copy, too. If your budget allows it, give them an extra copy for their bus drivers, if they have any. Some of them will not have their own tour book.

It's also a good time to reiterate your *rules of the road* to the support act tour managers, making sure that they know what to expect each day and what you expect from them. I always keep it simple and tell them I'll do anything I can for them as long as they don't cause me any headaches. I tell them that I expect them to be on stage on time and to be off on time. I also tell them that I expect them to show up on time for load-in each day, and I tell them what time I want to see them in the venue each day and not to come in any sooner.

I always make it clear to the support acts that I don't want them running around the venue the minute my crew starts to load in. They have no reason to be there that early. If our sound check is at 4:00 p.m., I'll tell our direct support act to show up at 2:00 p.m. each day and any other bands on the bill to show up at 4:00 p.m. This gives them plenty of time to dump their gear and get it set up near the stage so they're ready to go on stage when my band's done with their sound check. If they're all sharing a common backline, I'll tell them all to be there at 2:00 p.m. Take control of the situation from the beginning, and it will become immediately clear that you're calling the shots on the tour, as you should be.

You and your crew need to concentrate on getting the show up in time for your band's sound check, and it's hard to do that when you've suddenly got three support acts running wild around the venue, getting in everyone's way, going to the promoter rep about things that are low-priority at that time of the day, and pretty much being a nuisance. They're not all that way, but some of the new ones can be because they don't know any better. By the way, don't be this way when your band's a support act.

I always type up the day sheets and press sheets for the first day of the tour before I even arrive in that city. Posting day sheets in the appropriate places around the venue is one of the first things you'll want to do as soon as you load in. Since you probably arrived on the tour bus, you should've already posted day sheets and press sheets in the front and back lounge of your tour bus when you first got on it.

One of the first things you'll do each day at load-in—if you don't have a production assistant—is a walk-through of the backstage area and determine which rooms will be used for your band's dressing rooms, the production office, and which rooms you'll give to the support acts. You can use Post-it Notes to temporarily mark each room as you designate them, and then you can come back later with signs and mark them when you post all of your sheets.

I always post day sheets anywhere the touring entourage might logically look for them, and I try to do it the same way every day so they get used to looking for them in those places. Post one in your production office, every dressing room, the catering room if there is one, and any other rooms backstage such as a tuning room or crew room. Always make sure that there's a day sheet in the support act dressing rooms so they know the show schedule. If you don't post a day sheet for them, it's your fault when they go on stage late. Don't just assume that their green tour manager—if they even have one—is going to do it. You're in charge, so make sure that you make efforts to keep your schedule on time.

I always make sure to post day sheets liberally on the walls in the hallways backstage, near the load-in dock, and the backstage entrance. If someone has to ask where a day sheet's posted, then you haven't done your job correctly.

I'll also give each support act tour manager two copies of the day sheet for their tour bus so they can post it in the front and back lounges of their tour bus. I make sure that there are plenty of day sheets posted on stage but not in a place where they can be seen by the audience.

I always post a day sheet on the side fills on both sides of the stage. I'll make sure that one is posted behind the backline on each side of the stage so my backline guys can easily look at one without having to walk downstage to the side fills. I'll make sure that one is posted at the monitor console so the monitor engineer can easily see it. I'll also post one at the bottom of each staircase or ramp leading onto the stage. Don't ever forget to post a day sheet out at the sound and lighting consoles. The sound engineer and lighting designer for each band needs to know the show schedule. Always remember to give your promoter rep a copy so he can post it in his office or carry it around in his pocket if he doesn't have an office.

As I'm posting day sheets everywhere, I'm also posting signs so everyone knows what rooms are going to be used for dressing rooms, production office, and any other rooms that are needed if I don't have anyone to do it for me.

The production office is usually a dedicated room that's always the production office in that venue. If not, you'll decide which room you're going to use for production. Post a production office sign outside that door so everyone knows where to find you. Don't post the sign on the door; post it on the wall beside the door. If you post it on the door, every time the door is open, no one will see the sign. I'll always post a day sheet right beside the production office sign. It saves you the time of answering the same question every time someone sticks their head in your office asking what time the show starts or the doors open.

Always be sure to post a runner's list on the wall in your production office so anyone in the band and crew can write down things they may need for the runner to pick up. I'll cover more on the runner's list soon.

Make sure you post a dressing room sign for each dressing room so your band and the support acts know which rooms are for them. It's important to do this as soon as you load in. When the support acts show up on the first day, they'll immediately see the sign for their dressing room and a day sheet posted on the wall in their dressing room. You're already training them from minute-one to look for their dressing room sign and the day sheet on their wall when they arrive. If you do things the same way every day, you'll train people to know what to expect, but if everything is inconsistent, no one will know what's going on and each day will be chaos.

If you have other rooms such as a tuning room, crew room, or a catering room, post a sign there so everyone knows what those rooms are for. Always post a stage sign with an arrow below it showing people how to get to the stage. Even if the backstage area's so small that it's a no-brainer on how to get to the stage, post a sign anyway because you'll be getting everyone into the habit of always looking for your signs; and that's what this is really all about. In only a few days, everyone on the tour will be in the habit of following your signs so they know where to go and looking for your day sheets so they know the show schedule.

Post signs showing everyone how to get back out to the buses. Even if it's a no-brainer how to get back out to the buses, post the signs anyway so you train everyone to look for them on the days when they'll have to walk through a virtual maze to get back to the buses. Put a "This Way In To Everything" sign on the door leading into the venue from the bus, even if there's only one door to get in. Again, train your entourage and support acts to look for your signs, and in a few days, they'll have no problem finding their way around the venues. Well, most of them.

Be sure to post your press sheet in the production office and your band's dressing rooms when you're posting day sheets and signs. You also need to post a press sheet in the front and back lounge of your bus. You don't need to post press sheets in public areas such as the backstage hallways and the catering room. Your press sheets are for your band members only, not for everyone else on the tour. The support acts and stagehands don't need to know about your band's interviews that day.

Internet access is vital to your success each day. You can't get too much work done without it in this day and age. It's always in your best interest to have some control over the internet access backstage when possible. Wireless routers are reasonably inexpensive these days, so carry one for your tour if you or the band can afford it. This allows you to connect the venue's internet service to your wireless router in your production office so the internet password is the same every day and you have access to the router. Once you've set up the router the first time, you can email or text the network name and password to the people in your entourage that you want to have it. It saves you a lot of hassle each day.

If I don't have my own wireless router on the tour, I'll post an internet sheet in various places backstage so everyone knows the wireless network and password for the day. Place a copy of the internet sheet on the wall in your production office, dressing rooms, and anywhere else where the tour's entourage may congregate and can get the wireless signal. You don't need to post one on the tour bus if your bus has wireless internet on it.

If you don't post an internet sheet, you'll have the entire tour coming into your production office all day asking you for the wireless password. If there's no wireless internet backstage in the venue, you should still post an internet sheet in the usual places telling the entourage there's no wireless internet today or they can only get a signal out in the house, whatever the case may be, and you'll save yourself the time and exhaustion of repeating "we have no internet backstage today" all day long.

You can always add the wireless network and password to your day sheet, but I prefer not to do this because the day sheet is often seen by people outside our entourage who can sign into the wireless network with their smart phones and suck up the signal. At least you can control this a bit by only posting the internet sheets in specific places. This is another good reason why carrying your own wireless router is a good idea; you won't need to post internet sheets every day.

It's always possible the band's manager may show up on the first day of the tour. Make sure you know if he's coming. If he is, and you've got an extra room backstage, make a sign with the manager's name on it and reserve the room for him. Email or text him and see what time he's arriving. Find out from the band what he likes to drink and eat and have the catering staff set up some drinks and snacks in the room. A bottle of red wine and a fruit and cheese tray is fine, but don't forget some wine glasses and a corkscrew. Be sure to post a day sheet, press sheet, and an internet sheet in the room.

You're probably reading this and saying to yourself, "Wow, this is really sucking up to the manager." Duh! You're fucking-A-right it is. You're a new road manager, and you need all of the supporters you can get. Some of these managers have bigger egos than the band. I'm not telling you to hire the local high school band and choir to perform *For He's a Jolly Good Fellow*, roll out a red carpet, and toss red roses upon his arrival; just give him a room to relax in with something to drink and a snack or two. If for no other reason, it keeps him out of your production office and off your back. Even if you have to pay for it out of your own pocket, I'd do it. It's doubtful you'll ever see him again on the tour—except if you play the town where his office is at—so it's worth the investment, especially if he has other clients that you'd like to work for in the future. Think ahead.

Once you've gotten all of your signs and sheets posted, it's a good thing to walk through parking with the promoter rep for the support act vehicles so you have any potential problems worked out before they arrive. The promoter rep will most certainly have a plan if he's used to doing that venue on a regular basis, but if it's his first time there, you'll definitely want to be there when he figures it out. It's important that you know what's going on with this situation because the support act tour managers will be looking for you when they arrive to ask about their parking if they're unclear about the instructions you've already given them. If you don't know where they're supposed to park, you send a message to them that you're unprepared and don't know what you're doing. Plan ahead for everything, and always try to know the answers to these questions.

Make sure your band's dressing room is properly equipped with the things the band will need to make them comfortable. When you're doing your walk-through with the promoter rep, if the dressing room's nothing but four walls, a floor and a ceiling, ask him to find furniture for the room. If it's a club, then the dressing rooms will probably be equipped as good as they're going to get, but if you're playing in a hotel ballroom the promoter has rented out and the dressing room is an area behind the stage cordoned off with pipe and drape with nothing in it, then you need to make him find some furniture. There needs to be at least enough comfortable seating for the entire band and enough tables for their catering and anything else they set up on a daily basis, such as their laptops, music player, or anything else. A few lamps as opposed to the harsh neon lights will also be a welcome addition.

If your band's carrying wardrobe cases and entertainment centers that need to be set up in the dressing room, make sure they're getting set up on time. If you don't have a production assistant who handles this sort of thing, designate one of the backline guys to handle this chore every day, or you must find the time to do it yourself.

As soon as possible, speak with the person who will be setting up the band's dressing room catering and make absolutely sure they know what time the band's dressing room catering must be set up. Even though you've specified in your show advance that you need the band's dressing catering set up by 3:00 p.m., you still need to confirm this with the catering person or the runner who's going out to buy the catering items. Don't just assume they've been told the correct time by your promoter rep or they've read some advance sheet; tell them yourself.

Always make sure the catering staff is getting your band's dressing room sorted first if they're the headliner. Your band should be able to count on their dressing room catering being set up in the dressing room every day at a designated time. If they're doing a 4:00 p.m. sound check, you should ask that it be set up by 3:00 p.m. in case the band wants some of it before they do sound check. It usually doesn't make sense to expect it in the dressing too much sooner than 3:00 p.m. if you loaded in at noon because the runner will usually go out and buy the catering on the show day, and if you have the runner going out for other things, it'll take a while before they can do all of that shopping and then set it up in the dressing room.

You're probably asking yourself, "Why doesn't the runner just go and buy the band's catering the day before the show so it's already there when we arrive?" Many promoter reps are hoping you'll be overstocked on some items on your rider and willing to cut a few things, saving them some money, and there will be days when you'll probably want to do this. You really don't need seventeen bottles of mustard on your tour bus, so you can probably live without another bottle for a few days.

Some promoters do many shows a month. If they can cut things from the band's rider at every show because you're overstocked on certain items, this ends up being a significant savings for them each month and can save them a lot of money over the course of a year. It all adds up.

If your band's show is sold out, and you're going to be making extra money on the back end, you definitely don't want to be buying things you don't need because the band's paying for 85 percent—or whatever percentage their deal specifies—of those unneeded items out of their back end money.

Some bands don't care about this and demand that their rider be met to the letter every show. If that's the case with your band, tell the promoter rep this fact, and he may be able to buy their catering sooner.

Ask the catering staff to tell you when the catering is set up in the dressing room so you can check it to make sure all of the items are there. Don't just assume it's all there; go and check it. If anything is missing or a brand is wrong, have them fix it before the band shows up.

It's now a good time to have the catering staff ice down the coolers on the tour bus. Most modern tour buses have a full-size refrigerator in them, but like any fridge, it has limited space. Because of this, and the fact that there are usually a large amount of people traveling on the bus, tour buses also have a built-in cooler in the front and back lounges of the bus. These need to be iced down each day so the drinks inside them will be cold for the entourage.

Don't wait until the band is on stage to do this, unless there's still plenty of ice in there from the night before, or everyone will be complaining about having to drink warm drinks. You should do this right before the band's about to wake up so they have cold drinks when they get up. If it's summertime, you'll probably want to top off the coolers a second time later in the evening.

As time ticks by, you want to keep in the back of your mind each and every thing that you must get done that day until it all becomes second nature to you. If your singer's press starts at 2:00 p.m., you must remember to wake him up at 1:00 p.m. so he can get ready in time for his first interview.

If none of the other band members have press that day and usually sleep until sound check, then you must remember to wake them up in time to do sound check. Remember to wake them up, unless they're experienced and reliable enough to get up on time. Don't have your crew standing by on stage, ready to start sound check on time, only to sit and waste thirty minutes waiting on the band because you forgot to wake them up. Always know what time it is, and keep a rolling timeline in your mind of things that must get done.

Check important things in the dressing room, such as the hot water, to make sure they're working. Don't wait until your band members go in there to take a shower to find out the hot water isn't working. You'll find yourself behind schedule when they're not willing to do a thing until they can take a shower. And be sure there are clean towels in the dressing room when the band starts coming in.

Make sure the dressing rooms have been cleaned. If there was a show the night before, you could walk into a disaster zone when you load in that day. If the rooms are upside down, insist on them being cleaned immediately before your band starts waking up. Let's face it, what do most people want when they first wake up? They want a shower, food, and coffee. Make sure these things are sorted out before the band comes off the bus and into the venue.

Another thing that I'll need to know is the latest ticket count for the show. Always ask the promoter rep to get you the latest ticket count because this will be one of the first things that your band members will ask you about when they start coming into the venue. They all want to know if there's a good crowd expected that night. Personally, I prefer for them not to know if a show is selling badly because it blows the vibe for some band members. Nevertheless, you'll still need to tell them, so know the answer to the question.

Get another ticket count right before the doors open so you know where you're at right as the crowd is being let into the venue, but make sure you're getting an official ticket manifest printed out from the ticket system. If you're always getting another ticket count as the day moves along, you'll be better able to detect any promoter shenanigans later on.

If the promoter rep told you at noon load-in that six hundred and fifty tickets were already sold, but the promoter tells you when the doors open at 7:00 p.m. that you only have five hundred and seventy tickets sold, one of them is wrong or lying to you. This is a red flag to me, and I'll politely confront the promoter about this discrepancy and ask for an explanation. If he can't give me a suitable explanation, then I'm going to call the booking agent about the situation.

Your booking agent probably has a lot of experience dealing with this promoter with his other clients, so he'll be able to tell you if he's a promoter you need to keep a close eye on or if he's usually on the up-and-up. Frankly, I always assume they're all mobsters and keep my eyes open for anything they could possibly try to pull. You're better off thinking that way and less likely to get schtupped.

If the promoter's catering dinner, I'll always make sure dinner's going to be on time at 5:00 p.m. so the band and crew can eat as soon as they're done with sound check. This is very important if the band members have meet-and-greets that start at 5:30 p.m.

Many musicians, especially singers, don't like to eat too close to show time because it's hard to go nuts on stage for ninety minutes when they're filled up with a pound of pasta. I know singers who must eat dinner at least four hours before show time or they'll throw it up on stage. Not a pretty sight. Some band members will only have something light, such as soup, after sound check and then eat a full dinner after the show.

If the promoter's doing a dinner buyout for the show, I'll always get the money from the promoter rep before sound check so I can hand it out to everyone; it's one less thing you now have to worry about and they can go eat when sound check is done.

If your band members don't like leaving the venue to go to a restaurant to eat dinner, you'll have to send the runner out for their food or have it delivered. The promoter rep or the venue staff will usually have menus for delivery food in the area because they're used to dealing with this on every show they do.

If the promoter rep's providing after show food, make sure you've decided what you want so he can order it early and have it delivered on time. I always make sure the after show food is delivered right after the show ends so it's still hot for the band and crew. Don't wait until 11:00 p.m. to ask the promoter rep about after show food because everything in the area could be closed by then, and don't rely on him to come running you down asking you what you want for after show food. Some of them are hoping you've forgotten about it so they don't have to pay for it. They're not all that way. Some promoter reps are on top of everything, but they're busy, too. Everyone forgets things sometimes. It's your job to make sure they don't forget to buy the things you agreed upon in the show advance.

While you're running around dealing with all of your daily duties, hopefully you have a stage manager who's keeping things running smoothly on stage for a punctual sound check. On many tours, one of the backline crew often does double-duty as stage manager. It's always been important for me to know I have a rock-solid stage manager with balls and a brain—Gerry "G Money" Millman, where are you—keeping everything on schedule while I'm dealing with so many other things.

After you've gotten your band members through their last interviews of the day and ready to go on stage for sound check, you should make sure that the venue's clear of any spectators if your band prefers a closed sound check. Some bands prefer to not have venue staff, stagehands, local bands on the bill, or any outsiders standing out on the house floor watching when they're doing sound check. If your band prefers a closed sound check, ask the promoter to clear them all out before you bring the band on stage.

Once the band's moving along with sound check, you need to begin working on the guest list and making passes for the guests, members of the press, and photographers coming to shoot the show. This is another job for the production assistant, but if you don't have one, it's up to you.

I always have a guest list book in the production office for everyone to use. It's a simple three-hole binder with a guest list sheet printed out for each show of the tour. It's the same sheet you'll print out each day for the promoter rep. The people in your entourage can write down names for the guest list for any show down the line, and it saves you a lot of time by not having to write down these names every time someone emails and texts you names for the list. Get them trained into using your guest list book. The texts and emails will never stop coming from the band, so looking at your smart phone every five minutes will become habitual.

Let your entourage know that the deadline each day for guest list names is 1:00 p.m. or whatever time is best for you. You don't want to print out a revised guest list three times a day because you haven't set a deadline with your organization. It's inevitable that you'll have to reprint your guest list from time to time, but you'll reduce this by imposing a reasonable deadline.

Give the support act tour managers a similar deadline for passes. Explain to them that if they don't need passes from you, they can give their guest list directly to the promoter rep each day, but if they need passes, you'll have to make them before they can turn in their guest list.

I always try to have my guest list finished, printed out, and passes made at least an hour before doors open. Always print out an extra copy of the guest list and post it on the wall in front of you in the production office so you can refer to it when necessary.

By this time, your sound check is over and the support acts are setting up on stage, and you should be on schedule to open doors on time. Hopefully your stage manager has kept the schedule on track. Once your sound check is finished, the band now has some time to eat dinner and chill out before the show, unless they have more press or meet-and-greets to do.

As you're nearing the time for doors to open, stay in close contact with your stage manager to make sure everything's moving along with the support acts on stage so you can open doors on time. Always be sure to remind the promoter rep not to open the doors until he's checked with you and your stage manager to make sure that you're ready for doors. Experienced promoter reps know to do this.

You don't want the promoter rep to open doors with empty road cases still sitting on the audience floor or the support act standing on stage doing a line check. Sometimes the first band on the bill is happy to continue doing their line check in front of the audience just to get it completed. If they're a band on tour with us, I really don't care if they do their line check in front of the audience. All I care about is making sure that our gear is secure before opening the doors.

An hour before doors are scheduled to open, you should have your guest list turned in to the promoter rep and be conducting your security meeting, if not sooner. We'll cover more about this subject in the chapter on security.

Once the doors are open and the crowd's filing in, make sure your sound engineer has remembered to start playing some house music for the crowd unless the house sound engineer is dealing with this. Many bands prefer to have house music of their own choosing playing before the show starts and during the breaks between bands. This is usually best because you never know what some house sound guy's going to start playing if he's left to deal with it on his own. The last thing you want is for the house sound engineer to start playing Lady Gaga at a Slayer concert; things could get ugly very quickly. Stranger things have happened.

Always be certain that your stage manager announces over the radio that doors are opening so everyone knows that the crowd is about to be let into the venue. If you don't have radios, learn to shout loudly. Don't just assume that your crew is watching the clock or has even looked at the day sheet and know what time doors are opening. Always announce that doors are opening so the crew can secure the gear and any band members on stage or out in the house know it's time to go backstage.

Your stage manager should have sorted out how to kill house lights by the time doors open. If your stage manager is new, make sure he's on top of this situation and getting into the habit of knowing how to kill house lights. It's important for him to know this information when it's time for the show to start. Often the house lighting director or house stage manager will kill house lights and simply wait for the cue from your stage manager at the appropriate time. This must always be sorted out before show time so there's no embarrassing chaos when it's time to put the first band on stage.

Once the doors are open, I'll get the latest ticket count from the promoter and begin looking over his show expenses and receipts and getting prepared for my settlement, which will occur in a few hours. If your band's on a flat guarantee with no back end or bonus negotiated or the ticket sales are so low that there's zero hope of hitting the break point even if the Pope blessed the box office, you don't need to worry about examining the hard receipts for the show expenses. We'll cover more about this subject in the chapter on show settlements.

Keep checking with your stage manager to make sure he's getting the support acts on stage on time. It's important to remember that the headliner's stage manager is also responsible for making sure the support acts get on and off stage on time. Always be conscious of the clock and make sure things are running on time until you have a stage manager that you know is always on the ball.

When the direct support act (the band playing directly before the headliner) goes on stage, it's time to make sure your band is getting ready for show time. Some bands want a one-hour call to remind them that they're on stage in one hour. Some bands want multiple alerts over a two-hour period before they go on stage. Find out what your band prefers and always remember to do this. If your stage manager or production manager is dealing with this chore, watch your clock and make sure they don't forget to do it.

It's important to be sure your band members have heard these alerts; don't just assume they're hearing a radio broadcast in the dressing room or on the bus. You never know what the band is up to; always check on them during the period leading up to show time. If you have a production assistant, make sure she's checking on the band and keeping them aware of the clock.

As bands become more experienced, you don't need to worry about them quite as much, but you still need to worry about them. You never know which one's going to get in their bunk and take a nap and not set an alarm to wake up in time. Always check on them, but do it in a manner that's not annoying.

A crucial thing to remember is to print out set lists for your show if you don't have a production assistant dealing with this chore. If your band does the same set every night, you could type up a set list and make enough copies for the entire tour. This is fewer headaches for you, but many singers like to have the city you're playing in printed at the bottom of the set list. You don't want your singer to walk on stage and say, "Hello, Cleveland!" when you're in Tampa, Florida. It's one of rock and roll's biggest clichés, but it happens all the time. Sometimes I have to think for a second to remember what city we're in. When you print your set lists, use a font type and size that's easy to read in low light situations.

As you're nearing show time, make sure you've checked in with your promoter rep. Have you asked him when he wants to do settlement with you? Does he want to do it during your band's show—if you're not doing double-duty—or after the show? Have you asked him if he needs you to print out your band's W9 tax form that you emailed him with your cash requirements, or has he already printed it out himself? He may have forgotten you emailed it to him since some tour managers don't bother to do this. Remind him of your cash requirements.

Be careful with printed copies of the band's W9 form. Don't print out a copy for the promoter rep and then throw it into the trash can when you discover he's already printed out the one you emailed to him. The band's W9 form has their taxpayer identification number on it; it's equivalent to your social security number. Guard your client's sensitive information well. If you have room in your production case, a paper shredder is a good thing to have.

Make sure you have a copy of the contract and know how much of a deposit has been sent to the agent. Don't rely on the promoter to tell you what the deal is and how much of a deposit he's sent in. He could be wrong or even lying; you never know. The last thing you want to do is pick up a 50 percent balance and then find out the next day the promoter only paid a 10 percent deposit, and you left 40 percent of the band's guarantee behind.

The booking agent will then have to waste his time to get this money from the promoter, and it will definitely not make you look competent. Some of these promoters will take advantage of you being unprepared at settlement and short you on purpose just to make you look bad if you've been a nightmare for him all day. Always know what's going on with the band's deal because this is your most important duty, after taking care of the band.

It's always best to begin settlement during your band's show unless you're performing another job during the performance. Things get hectic after the show is over so it's best to get paid before it's done; but if your band's deal includes back end, you'll probably have to wait until after the show is over to finish settlement.

The box office will usually continue to sell tickets until about midway through the headliner's show, so the promoter rep won't be able to complete his settlement sheet until he has the final number of tickets sold from the box office. Unless he already knows the cost of any final expenses such as after show food, he'll also have to wait and add in those numbers before he can finish his settlement sheet for you. If you have to wait until after the show is over, which is more often the case, you'll simply need to wait.

You should always walk your band to the stage at show time if you're not doing another job during the show. If you're the sound engineer or lighting designer, your stage manager or production assistant should walk them on stage. If you have a production manager and he's not doing double-duty, he may be the person walking the band on stage. Do whatever works best for your situation.

If you're not performing another job during your band's show, you should be checking to make sure everything's going well on stage and there's no problem with security in the barricade and all backstage points. You need to maintain an almost omniscient point of view over everything going on during the show to prevent potential fires from breaking out and becoming roaring conflagrations.

It's always a good thing to check the dressing room while your band's on stage. Check to make sure that all of the coolers and bus trays are still filled with ice and have not melted. If they need refreshing, have the catering people re-ice the coolers, bus trays, and clean ice buckets for their drinks so your band has cold drinks and plenty of clean ice after the show.

Make sure the dressing room and toilets haven't been turned upside down. If they have, have the venue staff tidy it up a bit, but make sure you supervise them doing it. Most venue staff is trustworthy, but you never know when a band member's wallet can suddenly walk off. It's better to be safe than sorry. If there's no venue staff available, do it yourself.

Always make sure to be at the stage when your band's done playing so you can lead them to the dressing room. Have the key to the dressing room in your hand and ready to open the door for the band—and I hope you remembered to lock the dressing room while the band was on stage. You don't want to be standing there digging through your pockets trying to find a dressing room key while your band's dripping with sweat and worn out after a long show. This only makes you look like an amateur; be prepared. And don't lose the key.

Make sure there are enough towels for your band members when they walk off stage. You don't want the band asking for towels as they walk off the stage; their crew should already be handing them towels. Just make sure that they haven't run out of them by the time the show's over. If so, bring more from the dressing room and give them to the stage manager before the show's finished.

Be sure there are more towels waiting for them in the dressing room to take showers. Towels seem to be an item that's always in short supply, no matter how many you ask for in the rider. Early in the day, I always hide a certain amount of towels so I know we'll have enough left over for the band and crew to take showers after the show.

Some band and crew sometimes seem to think there's a towel factory in the venue. Some of them will use six towels to take one shower and then wonder why there's none left at the end of the night. This may seem like a minor issue to you, but wait until you have a bunch of upset people who can't take a shower because there are no towels left. Always find a solution to the problem before it becomes a problem.

After the show ends, you should start packing up any production cases you don't need for settlement so they're ready to go on the truck when they're called for by your stage manager. During this time, the band may be calling you for everything under the sun. You might even have a formal meet-and-greet scheduled after the show, although this is best avoided when possible.

Always check security points backstage after the show is over. Everyone will be trying to get back to the dressing room at this time. Do a verbal recap with the security guards posted at important security points, such as the backstage door, the entrances on each side of the stage, and anywhere else that people can get backstage.

Even if your VIP passes allow people backstage as soon as the show's over, remind the security guard on your dressing room door not to let anyone into the dressing room until you've given the okay. You don't want guests walking in on naked band members. If you think it's going to be more than thirty minutes before the band will be ready to receive guests with after show passes, tell the security guards at the stage entrances not to let after show passes backstage until you've given them the okay. By the way, security should never let after show passes backstage until you give the okay, anyway, but some of them will open the flood gates exactly thirty minutes after the show regardless of what you tell them.

If your band's going to meet with the after show guests but they don't want them in the dressing room, make sure you've determined a place where the band will receive them and that security is directing them to this place when they allow them backstage. Also remember to have a security guard at this predetermined place to make sure that those with after show passes stay in that area and don't go wandering on stage or into the dressing room.

As your crew's packing up the gear, you need to remain conscious of the clock and what time you've scheduled the bus to depart for the next city. You must remind your band how much time they have left before you have to leave so they're packing up their personal items and getting ready to leave.

If you didn't get your expense receipts and any remaining float from the runner during settlement, you'd better do it now so you don't forget it. Make sure the runner has remembered what time to pick up your bus driver if he's not coming in a taxi. You don't want the bus driver to be late for bus call. If he's late, it just gives the entourage an excuse to head to the local bar at the last minute, and then you've got to worry about rounding them all up when the driver shows up.

If your band makes a habit of going to local bars after the show, making sure that they're back in time for bus call is also one of your nightly chores. Having your entourage back on time for bus call is something that you really need to train them well on. You don't want the bus driver sitting there in his seat getting tired before a four-hundred-mile drive because he's waiting on people in your entourage who should've already been on the bus. This isn't safe for anyone involved, and if the driver's kept waiting too long, it could turn the drive into an overdrive.

Once the gear's packed up, the crew's taken their showers and everyone's on the bus, you must ALWAYS remember to do a head count before the bus departs. Don't leave this responsibility to someone else in the entourage; do it yourself. It will be on your head if you go to sleep and wake up the next morning and find that you've left someone behind. Make it clear to the bus driver from day one that he's never to move that bus unless *you* tell him that everyone is on board and he can leave.

I've only left one person behind in my long career, and he was the last person that I'd ever want to leave behind. Sometime in the early '90s, I was on tour with Testament somewhere in America. I didn't do a proper head count, fucked up out of my mind, and I left Alex Skolnick, the lead guitarist of Testament, at a truck stop in the middle of the night. No one on the bus even knew we'd left him behind. We were mental back then.

Alex was always the person who went to bed at a respectable hour and didn't stay up all night bombed out of his mind like the rest of us. It wasn't a pleasant experience for me, and it certainly wasn't for Al, one of the nicest guys you'll ever meet. Even today, he'll keep a close eye on the tour bus whenever we stop at a truck stop, and I'm always looking around to see if he's on the bus when it's about to roll. To this day, I'm just glad that nothing bad happened to Al that night. Don't be an idiot like I was and leave a musical genius at a truck stop in the middle of nowhere. Count everyone!

Once the bus is moving, you should post tomorrow's day sheets and press sheets in the front and back lounge so everyone knows what they're faced with the next day. Of course, you made time earlier in the evening to type them up and print them out.

229

Some tour managers will put up tomorrow's sheets much earlier in the evening. I never like to do this because you'd be surprised how many times people in your entourage will simply look at a show schedule and not see at the top of the sheet that it's for tomorrow's show. This could lead to people not being where they're supposed to be on time. Because of this, I prefer to post the sheets for tomorrow right after the bus leaves town so everyone can check the sheets before they go to bed.

You must remember to do all of these things every day. Consistency is the mark of a professional. If you have a bad memory, stick Post-it notes all over the production office if that's what it takes to make sure you don't forget anything until you form an internal alarm clock called *experience* inside you that reminds you of these things. You can also set recurring daily alerts in the calendar in your laptop or smart phone if that's what it takes to prevent you from forgetting things that must get done. If you have a production assistant, get them to help you remember important things. Do whatever it takes.

You can't let it get to the point where you keep hearing the words *we've told you fifty times* from the band because you continue forgetting to do things that must be done every day. They'll just become convinced that you don't care, and before you know it, the most important aspect of your new career will be mindlessly repeating the haunting refrain, *Do you prefer paper or plastic bags, ma'am?*

Every day is different, and anything can happen, and on the worst days when nothing is going right and you're hiding in the production office ordering a thick rope and a blindfold from HangYourself.com, try to remember that it's just a concert. It's not going to change the course of history—no matter what some musicians think—and it's definitely not worth an extended stay at the funny farm. Just take a deep breath and deal with it.

I hope you're starting to see that a good road manager is the closest thing to Nostradamus: always predicting the worst but hoping for the best and planning for both.

DAY SHEETS, PRESS SHEETS, AND THE FLOW OF INFORMATION

One of the most important parts of your job as a road manager is maintaining a constant flow of information to your organization. It can make the difference in everyone despising you or thinking you're the greatest thing since Fruit Loops.

You must always keep the flow of information moving constantly and accurately. Nobody wants to be on a tour where no one knows what's going on. I've been on a few tours where I was the road manager for the direct support act and getting information from the headliner's tour manager or production manager was nearly impossible. Doors would be opening, and there'd still be no day sheets anywhere, and if there were any, you needed a bloodhound to find them.

Even if you're only the first band on the bill and the headliner's tour manager isn't posting information properly, it's still your job to make sure your entourage is fully informed. You can still get the info you need and make your own sheets and post them.

However, be careful when you're the support act. Don't go posting your sheets all over the venue. This could ruffle some feathers with the headliner's people because it makes it seem as if you're blatantly pointing out the fact that they're not doing their job.

As long as your day sheets are posted on your bus, in your band's dressing room, and on stage where only your crew can see them, you've done your job. I don't care if my client is at the bottom of the bill; I always do my own sheets for my entourage, and you should, too. Be careful where you put your sheets on stage if you're the support act. Put them on your workboxes for your backline crew and give your FOH engineer and lighting designer each a copy to put in their pockets. In situations like this, Master Tour comes in handy.

Below is a copy of a day sheet. Some tour managers will put every bit of information under the sun on their day sheet, but I don't like putting certain information, such as the band's hotel, on a day sheet that's going to be posted around the venue. I disseminate information on a need-to-know basis and separate my sheets accordingly, but every tour manager does things differently.

SKINNY GIRL RIOT

DATE:	SUNDAY, APRIL 1, 2012
VENUE:	CLUB 1--SAN FRANCISCO, CA
CREW LOBBY CALL:	11:30 AM
LOAD-IN:	12:00 PM
BAND LOBBY CALL:	3:30 PM
SOUND CHECK:	4:00 PM
DINNER:	BUYOUT
DOORS:	7:00 PM
THE WORST:	8:00--8:30 PM
Skinny Girl Riot:	9:00--10:30 PM
CURFEW:	11:00 PM
BUS CALL:	2:00 AM, sharp!

SAN FRANCISCO TO LOS ANGELES: 381 MILES (8 HRS)

LOAD-IN TOMORROW:	12:00 PM

As you can see, the day sheet has the date, venue, city, and state. If the band and crew is checking out of a hotel, coming off a day off, be sure to put their hotel lobby call times on the sheet. Next on the day sheet is the schedule for the day, including the load-in time, dinner time if the show is catered or showing that it's a buyout if it's not, and the complete show schedule. Also be sure to include any curfew times that may apply.

At the bottom of the sheet, the next thing to be included is the time for your bus call, the time your tour bus or van is leaving town. If your band's headlining the tour and you're coming off stage around 11:30 p.m., a 2:00 a.m. bus call will usually be the norm. If you're only pulling a trailer with nothing but backline gear, there's no reason why you can't be packed up and everyone showered and ready to leave by this time.

Some nights, you'll have to leave as soon as possible because you have a long drive. If the drive's only a few hours and the next day's load-in isn't until noon, I'll often set bus call for a time early the next morning so the driver can get some rest.

There's no point in leaving at 2:00 a.m. when you have a two-hour drive. You'll arrive at the next venue at 4:00 a.m., and the driver won't be able to check into his hotel room unless you've blocked his room out from the night before, which is usually cost-prohibitive. You'd essentially be paying for two driver rooms in one day, and most new bands don't have the budget for that.

Blocking the room out from the night before simply means you've paid for the hotel room but you're checking in near the end of day you've paid for. If the driver was checking in the blocked room at 4:00 a.m. and check-out was at 11:00 a.m., then he'd have to check out in seven hours. However, since he's not leaving town until after your show that night, you now have to pay for two days on that room after you've already paid for the room he just checked out of at 2:00 a.m. in the last city. This is why it's best to let the driver leave the next morning on short drives. If you do decide to block out a driver room, and he's arriving late the next morning, always call the hotel and tell them that he's coming in near the end of the day you paid for because they could release the room to someone else, thinking he's not coming.

Some drivers won't care about leaving right away on a short drive and not being able to check into their hotel when they arrive. Many drivers prefer to drive at night when there's no traffic and are happy to sleep on the couch in the front lounge until they can check into their hotel.

The bad thing about setting bus call for the next morning is that you'll have to worry about the band and crew running wild around town and not being on the bus at bus call. You can always set your alarm to wake you up and make sure everyone's on the bus before it leaves, but that doesn't help you get much sleep. But it comes with the job, and you'll have to get up and do a head count if you have band members who are in the habit of going out to bars and then going home with the newest *friend* they've just met.

After you put your bus call time on the day sheet, you need to list the trip's mileage and where you're going. This information should be in your tour book, and therefore, it's easy to obtain. On the day sheet above, we're driving from San Francisco to Los Angeles, and the drive mileage is 381 miles. Then you need to add the estimated drive time. I always use 50 mph to calculate the drive time; so for this sheet, we'll round that off to an eight-hour drive and put that on the day sheet. The drive time almost always averages out to this amount when you take into consideration traffic and the driver's stops for fuel and his breaks. On short drives, it usually won't take that long if he doesn't need to stop for anything and there's no traffic, but still use 50 mph to calculate your drive time, so you're never late. It's always better to be early than late.

Always include at the bottom of the day sheet the load-in time for the next gig. Even if load-in is noon almost every day of the tour, still list the load-in time so everyone gets into the habit of looking there for it. At some point on the tour, there's certain to be a day when you'll have to load in earlier because of early doors due to an early curfew or load in later when you have late doors.

You can add anything else you want to the day sheet; that's really up to you. I always include the band's logo on the sheets to make them look professional. Always make sure that your font sizes are large enough so they can be read easily. Avoid font types that are hard to read. You don't want a day sheet that's harder to decipher than a wall of Egyptian hieroglyphics or, even worse, a death metal band's logo.

You can use Microsoft Word or Excel to make your day sheets. I've always used either Word or Excel. You'll quickly find that once you've made your first day sheet, it's easily edited for the next show day. You'll only have to change the date, city, and venue. You'll often find that the show schedule will be the same or may just require a few little tweaks. Your bus call will often be the same time every night, and changing the travel info at the bottom of the day sheet is easy to do.

Always save a copy of your day sheet in the computer subfolder for that show because you'll often find yourself printing out more copies as the day goes on. You never know when the promoter rep will come to you and say, "I screwed up on the show schedule. We need to change it on your sheet." Then you'll have to repost the day sheets. It happens.

Next is the press sheet. Always put the date, venue, and city at the top of the sheet. I'll usually just copy and paste the day's press from the sheet the record company's press team or the independent publicist sent to me. This is the easiest thing to do and saves you a lot of typing, although it often requires a bit of quick clean-up to make it look neat on your sheet.

Skinny Girl Riot

Press Sheet

Club 1--San Francisco, CA
Sunday, April 01, 2012

3:00--3:20 PM (PST) - Press Phoner (confirmed)
For: Stevie Starbright
Submitted by: Patty the publicist
Submitted on: 3/15/12
Interview with Dead Rotten from Stinky Metal Magazine
Dead Rotten will call tour manager to connect.
Dead Rotten's cell number is 555-666-2399

3:30--3:50 PM (PST) - In person video interview (confirmed)
For: Frankie Fabulous
Submitted by: Ronnie the record company rep
Submitted on: 3/16/12
Interview with Dark Tulip from Metal Horticulture TV
Dark Tulip will find tour manager when he arrives at the venue.
Dark Tulip's cell phone number is 555-666-1385

Make sure to be specific about what's booked, and if you need to add information to it, do so. You need to make sure that each band member is clear on whom the interview is for, what time it's scheduled, where it's happening, and what publication, website, TV show, or radio station it's with. The more detailed the info—without turning it into *War and Peace*—the fewer questions you'll have to answer about it. If the press details are lacking in some critical info, email the publicist and obtain the necessary info so your sheet's complete.

The internet sheet below is pretty straight-forward; a chimp could figure it out. You're listing the name of the venue's wireless network and any password that may apply. If there's no password, put "No password required" on the sheet or you'll have people coming into production all day asking for the password. If there are any signal limitations, such as only being able to get the wireless signal in the catering room, note them on the sheet.

Skinny Girl Riot

Internet Sheet

The wireless network for today is **everybodysurfin**.

The password is **surfinforrockbabes666**.

The runner's list is a sheet that allows people in your entourage to write down things that they need the runner to pick up. As you can see, the runner's list is pretty simple. You have a column for your entourage to write down the item they need. There's a column that lists which person the item is for and a column for how much cash has been left if it's a personal item and not a tour expense.

	Skinny Girl Riot--Runner's List		
#	Item	Ordered by	Cash given
1	2 rolls of pink gaffer tape	Ricky the stage mgr	
2	12 pairs of white socks (size 15)	Lance the FOH guy	$20.00
3	1 bottle of canola oil	Jerry the guitar tech	
4	band laundry--5 bags	tour manager	
5	crew laundry--1 bag	Kyle the drum tech	$20.00
6	144 Magnum condoms	Mikey Massive	show cost
7	4 cans of corn flavored whipped cream	Tommy Twosticks	show cost
8	1 pair of pink velvet-covered handcuffs	Stevie Starbright	show cost
9	4 bottles of RID (URGENT!)	confidential	show cost
10	12 cans of bacon flavored whipped cream	Mikey Massive	show cost
11	6 cans of Aquanet hairspray	Frankie Fabulous	show cost
12	2 pairs of shoe elevator insoles (size 7)	Jimmy Giant	show cost
13			
14	**Take bus driver to hotel @ 2:00 PM.**	tour manager	
15			
16			
17			
18			
19			
20			
21			
22			
23			
24			
25			

Runner:	Jenny Runfast
Runner cell:	555-232-6278
Cash given to runner:	$500.00

If the item is a tour expense, such as gaffer tape, ordered by the stage manager, he's not going to leave any cash because you'll be paying for it out of the float you've given the runner. However, if the drum tech needs a carton of cigarettes, you'll expect him to leave money for them. You don't want to be mounting a big accounting expedition at the end of the night trying to get reimbursed for personal items bought with the band's money. Have your people put their personal money in an envelope and write their name, item needed, and amount of cash enclosed on the front of it and give it to the runner. And, yes, add envelopes to the runner's list as a tour expense if you don't have any.

Down at the bottom of the runner's list; always put the runner's name, cell phone number and how much float you've given her that day. Remember to list how much cash you've given the runner so you don't forget this number at the end of the night when it's time for you to settle up with her.

Don't forget to settle up with the runner, or your books will come up short and you'll have no receipts to show for that money. In which case, it'll end up coming out of your pocket. Get into the habit of settling with the runner right after you settle with the promoter or beforehand. It's a good memory jogger so you won't forget to do it until you've done it so many times that it's become a natural reflex. Put a Post-it Note on the wall in front of your laptop to remind you if that's what you have to do.

You'll often find yourself posting a Memo sheet that explains any new information that the entourage needs to know about. Post it with the day sheet, press sheet, and internet sheet in your band's dressing room and the lounges of your tour bus. You don't want to put memos up in public places such as the catering room or on stage. Keep private info that's meant only for your entourage in places where only they'll see it.

Skinny Girl Riot

Memo

Hotel
The Country Castle
323 Hillbilly Highway
Wichita, KS 67201

Tel: 555-838-1238

Note: Free wing dings and Bud Lite in lobby from 5-7PM.

Driver room: 686
Band shower room: 738
Crew shower room: 740

Bus call: 2:00 AM. Be here!

Wichita to Kansas City, MO: 442 miles (9 hrs)

Load-in tomorrow: 12:00 PM

THE POWER OF THE PRESS

If you ask any tour manager which of his daily duties he dislikes most, many of them will invariably answer, "dealing with press and meet-and-greets." I usually don't mind doing this part of my job because it's vital to the band's success, but I don't like it when my schedule falls apart after interviewers show up late.

By the first day of the tour, you've coordinated with the record company and the independent publicist and conveyed how you want the daily press to be scheduled. You've posted a press sheet in the appropriate places, such as the tour bus and dressing room, and the band knows what they're faced with that day. You're all set to get your day's press done so you can get on with the major reason you're in that city: to perform a concert.

I always make sure that I'm given a cell phone number and email address for every press person. I'll always call them a few hours before they're scheduled to arrive at the venue for their interview to make sure they're going to be on time. If for no other reason, this immediately lets them know that I'm on a tight schedule and cannot afford for them to be late. Don't get on the phone talking to them like they're your long-lost friend; be polite but keep the tone of your voice and your demeanor strictly-business, and remind them that they must be on time.

I also call them for another reason. You'd be surprised how many times I've called an interviewer just to hear them say, "That interview was cancelled a week ago, Mark." Sometimes an interview is cancelled, and the record company or publicist forgets to take it off the press sheet, but at least I found out about it a few hours ahead of time so we're not waiting on an interviewer who isn't coming.

If a phone interview doesn't happen for any reason, always be sure to notify the record company press team or publicist that booked the interview. If you don't, it could cause a deadline to be missed and an important article to go down the drain. If you rescheduled the missed phoner yourself, you should still notify the press team so they know what's going on with the interview they booked.

Sometimes your press sheet from the record label won't list which band member is supposed to do the interview. They've just left it open, allowing you to choose the band member on your own. If the singer's slammed with a lot of interviews that day, as usual, I'll give it to a band member who has no press scheduled. I'll tell the interviewer when I call her which band member she'll be doing the interview with.

But they might tell me, "I need to do my interview with the singer because all of my questions are planned for him." This happens a lot; they always want to interview the singer or leader of the band. In this case, revise your sheet, re-post it and explain to your singer why he's now got another interview to do when he's already got six of them to do. Hey, it's rough, but the band should be glad people want to interview them. If no one wants to interview them, it usually means they couldn't draw flies if they were covered in horse shit.

I also call the journalists to tell them where to meet me if we're playing at a venue where they can't get inside unless I walk them in. We could be playing in an arena where security is tight, and they won't allow the press into the venue without an escort. If this is the case, then you need to tell the journalists where to meet you and to call you on your cell phone when they arrive. You can always send them a text message, of course, but then they won't hear the *tone* of your serious, all-business voice. Trust me; it has a way of helping them get there on time.

It's often impossible to leave passes for journalists to get into the venue to do interviews because the box office often isn't open during the early afternoon when you're doing press, and I don't leave passes for journalists anyway, unless it's someone important and the publicist has specifically requested that they receive a pass. If they're only getting a photo pass, they don't need it until show time, when they'll shoot the first three songs of the show from the barricade. They don't need a photo pass if they're doing a photo shoot backstage long before doors open. Once they're done with the photo shoot, they're leaving the venue, and I don't need to worry about them anymore.

It's important to predetermine where you're doing your interviews. It needs to be a quiet place where the interview won't be disturbed. A journalist can't do an interview with your singer beside the stage while your sound engineer's tuning the PA louder than an AC/DC concert unless they're both telepathic or can read lips.

Some band members prefer to do the press on the tour bus, maybe in the back lounge. Some will prefer to do it in the dressing room. If you only have one dressing room, this may not work, because other band members may be in there trying to take a shower. You need to plan for this and find the best place to do the interviews.

I always make a sign that says, "Quiet, please. Interview in progress." If the interview's happening in the back lounge of the bus, I'll post the sheet on the door so the others on the bus know to keep it quiet and not enter the back lounge. If it has to happen in the dressing room or my production office, God forbid, I'll post the sign on the door. The others in your entourage will quickly get used to seeing this sign and know not to enter the room while the interview's in progress or to be quiet if they must.

I always make sure to keep an eye on my watch while the interviews are in progress to make sure they're not going over time. I'll remind the journalists how much time they have before the interview begins, but they'll go over if I let them. Five minutes before the interview's supposed to end, I'll quietly enter the room and give them the five-minute sign with my hand. They know what it means. If you don't stay on top of this, you'll get behind schedule and cause sound check to run late. Your band member doesn't want to be the bad guy who cuts off the journalist when their time's up; that's your job.

If you have a record company rep with you at that venue to supervise the press, the only thing you have to worry about is delivering your band members when it's time for the interview, and if the publicist has been working with the band for a long time and knows them well, you don't even need to do that. They'll probably take a load from your shoulders that day.

Always make sure you're checking on your band members when the time for press is near so you know where to find them. Definitely make sure they know they have press that day, despite the fact that your press sheet is posted where they can see it. Train your band members to check the press sheet and day sheet when they get up in the morning, but always assume they haven't.

Most journalists are professionals who do their interview and leave when they're done. They're experienced enough to know that hanging out isn't appropriate unless they're friends with the band, but once in a while you'll get a new one who doesn't understand that.

Escort the journalists out of the venue when they're done, thank them for the interview, and say goodbye. Most of them get it. If they don't, and you find them hanging out backstage, have your promoter rep politely tell them it's time to leave so they think it's coming from the venue. If you have a rep from the label there at the venue helping you with press that day, ask them to do it. They booked the interview; let them deal with their journalist.

Try to avoid doing this yourself so you don't alienate the journalist. No matter how polite you are when asking them to leave, some of them may be offended and start complaining, perplexed as to why they can't hang out. These are the new ones. Don't put yourself in this time-wasting situation. Let someone else do it so it doesn't seem as if it's coming from your organization. You don't need a green journalist trashing the band in their article because you asked them to leave and things got weird. Believe me; it won't be an unbiased account of the events that took place.

It's always best not to let journalists hang out backstage unless they're good friends of the band and can be trusted. I always cringe when there's a request from the record label to allow a journalist to travel on the bus with us to do an on-the-road report. While this may provide a great article for the magazine, the entourage has to spend the next two or three days of their lives watching what they say and do so the wrong things don't end up in some rock magazine.

In the spring of 2004, I was on tour with the mighty Machine Head in the U.K. The band was playing on the main stage with Metallica at the Download Festival at Castle Donington. It was an important event for Machine Head because their popularity in the U.K. was growing rapidly. The band's record label, Roadrunner Records, had convinced the band to allow a journalist from one of the big metal magazines to travel with us and write an on-the-road report. No one was overly thrilled with the idea, but they had to do it.

After we finished the show, we had a brief amount of time for the band's singer, Robb Flynn, to do a post-show interview with the journalist, and then we had to drive to London's Heathrow airport and fly home to the U.S. It's an easy drive to Heathrow airport from Donington Park, but it can take up to four hours to get there with heavy traffic. We had a long thirteen-hour flight to San Francisco ahead of us, and I had no intention of missing that flight.

The post-show interview was important and needed to be done, but Robb Flynn was nowhere to be found. Donington Park is a massive complex, and the tour buses were parked a great distance from the main stage area. It was a very long walk, and you had to wait for shuttle buses to take you from the bus park to the main stage. As the clock started to tick away and Robb was still nowhere to be found, I started to get tense, worrying about missing our flight.

As my English friends will tell you, some people in the U.K. drop the word *cunt* like they say hello. Here in America, on the other hand, even whispering that diabolical word will provoke enraged responses, such as *off with his head, burn him at the stake,* and *castrate the motherfucker!,* by the entire female population. The scene from *Frankenstein* where the angry mob, fiery torches in hand, chases the frightened monster through the town immediately comes to mind.

I've toured the U.K. more times than I could ever remember, and there was a time when I immediately morphed into an English alien replicant the minute I entered England. I ate wonderful cholesterol-packed English breakfasts and greasy fish and chips, drank me some of the finest English ales, puffed me some lovely Dunhill cigarettes, honored Her Majesty the Queen, and said the word *cunt* with every breath I could muster. Sorry, Mom.

While I stood outside Machine Head's tour bus waiting for Robb Flynn, the journalist from the metal magazine chatted away incessantly. He could sense that I was becoming highly annoyed and very worried about missing our flight. He continued asking me trivial questions while I basically ignored him. Looking off into the distance towards the main stage area, I said to myself, "Where *is* this fucking cunt?"

Now, I've known Robb Flynn since the late '80s when he and Phil Demmel (Machine Head guitarist) were both in Vio-lence, and at the time I had already done three records with Machine Head. The band was an old client, and the guys in the band are wonderful people. I consider them dear friends. Robb Flynn wasn't a cunt, nor did I feel he was a cunt.

However, when this magnificent on-the-road *report* finally came out in the magazine, there it was in black and white: the tour manager calling the singer of the band a cunt. Robb was far from pleased, and neither was I. And Machine Head's long-time manager, Joseph Huston, a good and honest man, didn't think too much of it, either.

Only a complete and utter mongoloid idiot would call his employer a cunt in a magazine that's distributed around the world. While there's a tiny, infinitesimal part of me that wants to believe the journalist meant no harm and was merely repeating a harmless phrase that he'd blabbered countless times himself, I no longer believe in Santa Claus, the Tooth Fairy, or the Easter Bunny.

Do I regret saying what I said? Hell, no. They're just words, and my friends, including Robb, have heard my colorful expressions many times. Do I regret dropping my guard and muttering those words in front of a journalist that I didn't know and trust? Abso-fucking-lutely.

Lesson learned.

If your band has a radio or TV station visit on the press sheet, you'll need to coordinate getting the band to and from the station. I always try to get the record company to provide transportation and send a local record company rep along for these visits. It's not a good idea for the bus to take the band to these events because the driver needs to be in bed sleeping so he can drive that night; and if you're hauling your gear in a trailer on the back of the bus, the crew can't unload it at the venue it if it's sitting at a radio station. You can always drop the trailer at the venue and have the bus driver become completely convinced that you're the Marquis de Sade reincarnated. Using the bus doesn't make sense, and you certainly don't want to use a vehicle that gets six miles to the gallon as a taxi.

I've always found that the label's usually willing to pay for a black van from a car service to take the band to station visits. If it's a larger record company, they'll usually have a rep in that town who can accompany the band so you can stay at the venue and get the show up in time.

There are times when station visits are more than just an interview, and they want the band to perform a few songs. This turns into a much bigger ordeal because some of the band's gear will have to go with them so they can perform. If the performance is on a show day, the band might have to do it without their backline techs because the crew can't be at the venue setting up for the show and doing a live radio performance at the same time.

Most of the time, the band will only need minimal gear to do a radio show and might even be able to set up their own gear, depending on the band. If the band's popular, it's doubtful they're going to be willing to set up their own gear; so it's unlikely that this kind of show would happen on a show day if too much of their gear's required. If you're in a major city, there's always the possibility that you might be able to hire some local techs that are off the road if there's a budget for it. If the opportunity presents itself, the label will talk the band into doing something like this on your day off. Hey, you wanted to work in the music business.

I've done radio shows where our crew loaded in at 9:00 a.m.; the band banged out the performance, packed up the gear, and then we went straight to the venue to load in at noon to do a show that night. This can be a logistical nightmare and a tiring day, but sometimes it's just too important for the band to turn down. You have no choice but to deal with it.

It's never ceased to amaze me how some bands have this personal war with the press and refuse to do interviews. You can't make it without the press. I'm not saying that there aren't some jackasses in the press, but most of them are just trying to do their jobs. Many of them are fans and want to help build up a band they love. They want to feel like they're part of it all, and they're willing to help spread the word to the fans. They're not your enemies—most of them—but you still need to keep them at a polite distance.

I've seen some tour managers treat journalists like dirt when they come to the venue to do an interview. Don't misunderstand me; some of them can't be trusted as far as you can dropkick them. But most of them are good people and deserve to be treated with respect.

Do your band a favor and look after the press, but always be firm and let them know how things are going to be done. Most of them will appreciate your professionalism and be on their way once their interview's done.

Have journalists leave after an interview feeling as if they're part of the band's team. If you can do that, many of them will support your band until the last day of their career, and that's one of the most valuable things you can contribute to your band's success as their road manager.

Meet-and-greets are usually quick and painless if you've advanced everything with the appropriate person. Sometimes the local radio station that's sponsoring the show will have a contest, and the winners get to meet the band. Having the radio station constantly plugging the show on the air is great promotion, so meet-and-greets are a fair exchange for their support.

Some bands prefer to do their meet-and-greets right after sound check is finished so the band can do what they want until show time. Some groups prefer to eat dinner after sound check and then do the meet-and-greets. Sometimes the people in the meet-and-greet are allowed to watch sound check, while some bands don't allow any outsiders in the venue during this time. Do what works best for your band.

Coordinate with the person who is handling the meet-and-greet and ask them to have all of their people at the venue on time and explain where you'll meet them. If there are any restrictions about the meet-and-greet, go over them with your contact person.

It's important to put some limitations on meet-and-greets, or they'll take forever to get done. Some fans will show up with the band's entire discography, expecting them to stand there and autograph a dozen CDs and every picture they've ever cut out of a magazine. No band has time to do that; there could be dozens of people in the meet-and-greet. I'll usually limit the guests to one or two items, such as the band's latest CD and sometimes a special poster or photo that's been printed specifically for the meet-and-greet. It's really up to you and the band to decide, but there has to be a limit. The show's today, remember.

Plan ahead and find a proper place to do the meet-and-greet. You don't want to do one right in front of the stage if the support act's getting ready to do their line check. It's kind of hard for the band to chat with contest winners when the support act's sound checking at Motorhead, bone-crushing volume.

Do the meet-and-greet in an organized manner. Have the venue set up a long table and enough chairs for your band members. Form a line so the guests can walk down the table, meet the band, and get their items signed like they would at an in-store appearance. Instead of shooting a photo with each person in the meet-and-greet—which will take forever—you can do a group shot with everyone at the end of the meet-and-greet and have the rep from the radio station email the photo to everyone at a later date. This speeds up the meet-and-greet.

Be creative and plan ahead. Make the meet-and-greets as organized and painless as possible for the band, and they won't dislike doing them. Always make sure you have a Sharpie and something to drink for each band member.

Always be sure to have a small bottle of hand sanitizer in your pocket to squirt in each band member's hand once the meet-and-greet is done. You never know if any of the fans are sick. Shaking hands with a lot of people is an easy way for your band members to get sick. Be prepared with hand sanitizer, but don't start squirting this stuff in their hands in front of the fans; it could be misconstrued and taken as very rude.

Sometimes meet-and-greets are difficult to get done right after sound check because some of the guests are students or have jobs and can't make it to the venue that early. If this is the case, you may have to schedule it for later that evening, possibly after doors are open. Be flexible and anything is possible.

VIP packages were once something that was mostly reserved for only the biggest acts, but today smaller mid-level acts are now doing them and opening up another revenue stream to earn more money, increase profits, and help pay for tour expenses.

There are companies, such as SLO VIP Services and I Love All Access, which sell VIP packages to fans. Some of these packages can be pricey, but most of them offer a meet-and-greet where the fans can obtain autographs and a personal photo with the band. The packages may include special items, such as a VIP laminate, special seating close to the stage or even on stage, a pre-show party and early entrance to the venue before the rest of the audience. Prices vary, and the more expensive the package, the more it offers.

If demand is high for VIP packages with your band, the company will send out one of their representatives to travel with the tour and coordinate the meet-and-greets every day. This rep will usually travel on the crew bus if you have two buses. If not, they'll have to travel on the only bus you have, if there's an available bunk for them. Not having a bunk for them could mean the company will have to find someone locally in each city to deal with the daily coordination, which means things could be good or bad each day depending on the quality of the rep—or it could all just end up in your lap.

It's always best if they're sending out a rep to coordinate the VIP meet-and-greet every day. If you have a production assistant, you both can probably handle it, but it'll be virtually impossible for a road manager to deal with VIP packages in addition to his own daily duties without some help. I wouldn't even consider it, especially if the band's selling a lot of them.

For you, VIP package meet-and-greets are handled just like any other meet-and-greet. You should always plan ahead with the VIP company rep so you know what you're doing and where you're doing it each day. The VIP rep coordinates with the fans who have bought the VIP packages and tells them what time to be at the venue and where to meet up. Like regular meet-and-greets, the VIP meet-and-greets are usually best done after sound check or after dinner following sound check. It's up to you and the band.

Bands are usually more enthusiastic about doing VIP packages because they can make a lot of money doing them, but they can become a tiring experience if your band's popular and a lot of people are buying the packages every show.

The VIP package companies have been given a maximum number that they're allowed to sell each day based upon their agreement with the band. There, obviously, has to be a limit on the number of packages sold, or the band could be there all night doing the meet-and-greet.

If your band's a bit new, always remind them that the fans are recording away with their cell phone video cameras during meet-and-greets, and anything they say is being caught on video. It's now become a YouTube world where anything you say and do can be caught on camera and uploaded to the internet in only a matter of minutes. Most of the fans are pretty cool and love the band, but don't think that just because they spent $150 on a VIP package that you can trust all of them. Watch what you and your band says and does, unless you don't mind being the stars of your own embarrassing *Jackass* episode.

In-stores are appearances that the band makes at brick-and-mortar record stores. If the band's willing to do them, the record company or promoter will set up in-stores because it helps to sell CDs and concert tickets, but since record stores are quickly becoming extinct, in-stores will inevitably become the same.

While they still can, some bands like to do in-stores. Fans are more compelled to buy a copy of the band's new CD if they can actually meet the band and get it signed by them; and it doesn't cost them anything like a VIP package.

The record store will promote the in-store and usually put the CD on sale at a reduced price to further entice the fans to buy it. Some stores will only allow fans to meet the band if they buy a copy of their new CD, and many bands insist on this.

When doing an in-store, limit the number of items that the band will sign. Frankly, I believe they should only sign the band's new CD because that's why we're doing the in-store: to sell the new CD. Let an employee of the record store stand at the front of the line and be the bad guy to enforce this rule with the fans. Make sure the store prints on all advertising that the band will only sign their new CD and nothing else, and if a fan isn't holding a copy of the band's new CD, they shouldn't even be in the line.

Use the in-store as a way to sell copies of the band's new CD. In the old days, we didn't have rules like this, but back then, we didn't have the internet where anyone and their mother could become a virtual shoplifter and steal the band's music. Make decisions to help the band sell every CD they possibly can. Some bands don't want to impose these kinds of rules on their fans because they're giving up on the concept of selling their music to their fans. Many new bands now view their music as merely a vehicle to get them on the road where they can sell merchandise. I suppose this is a topic that could be debated heavily. I certainly don't know the answer to the dilemma. It's just the state of affairs in the music business today.

It's important that you advance security with the record store and make sure they'll have enough security to handle the number of fans they're expecting. In-store appearance can get out of hand if a lot of fans show up and there's no security presence.

Many of the record stores promote in-stores all the time and know what they're doing. They're also experienced enough to know how many fans to expect for your in-store based upon how well the band's new CD is selling and how well their show's selling. They can easily find out how well your show's selling by calling the promoter or by checking in their computer if they also sell concert tickets in the store. Many promoters are also working hand-in-hand with a popular local record store and promoting in-stores because it can help the band sell more concert tickets.

I always make sure to get the record label to provide transportation to in-stores and have a record company rep accompany us when possible to act as a liaison between our entourage and the store; every bit of extra help is always useful.

Advancing an in-store is a bit like advancing a show. I'll make sure they have some sandwiches and drinks for the band so they can have a bite to eat before or after the in-store. I'll try and get some idea how many people they think they're going to expect that day, and I'll always inform them of our absolute cut-off time. We can only stay for so long because we have a sound check and a show to do. There has to be an end to it. I always make it clear to the store that when I say it has to end and we have to get back to the venue, it's over and we have to go.

It's always a drag to end an in-store when there are still many fans in line, and right when you say, "Okay, we'll do those last ten people and then we're done," ten more people show up behind them. When you're done, you're done. Call it a day and head back to the venue. The show's not next month.

VENUE SECURITY

You can't expect the venue's security team to follow your pass system if you don't explain it to them thoroughly in a security meeting before the doors open. It's also vital that you post a security pass sheet at every access point where a security guard will be posted. Some people have a short memory and can't remember everything on your pass sheet or what you said in a security meeting. You need to post it all on the wall beside them so they can refer to it when necessary.

Always post your security pass sheet at every backstage entrance, including all entry points on either side of the stage. If you have a security guard posted on the band's dressing room, like you should, put up a security sheet on the wall outside the door. Make sure any security personnel who are guarding any stage access points have a security pass sheet.

There may be some access points where you don't want to post a security sheet because the audience can get their hands on it. You don't want someone to make fraudulent copies of your passes. Anything is possible with Photoshop and a color printer. In this situation, just give the security guard a copy of your pass sheet to keep in his pocket so he can refer to it when needed. This won't prevent bootlegging of your passes, but it will help to curtail it.

The promoter will usually have the full security team come on duty about an hour before the doors open, sometimes a little sooner. Your promoter rep can tell you when they're coming on duty. You must remember that the promoter's paying the security team an hourly wage—unless they're permanent employees of the venue—so he's not going to want them on duty until absolutely necessary to save money.

Once the security team's on duty, it's time for you to have your security meeting and explain your pass system and tell them what you expect from them. Most venues have professional security guards. You don't need to tell them how to do their jobs; they know how to do them. You only need to explain to them your particular dos and don'ts.

You only need to have a meeting with the security personnel who are going to be working areas that are critical to your entourage. This includes security personnel who are working at all backstage entry points, any areas outside the immediate backstage area that your entourage will travel through to get to the tour buses and trucks, security guards working in the barricade, and those guarding the front of the house where your sound engineer and lighting designer work.

You don't need to have a security meeting with ushers who are guiding people to their seats. The head of security can inform them of anything they might need to know after your security meeting is completed.

Print out enough copies of your pass sheet so every security person in the meeting has a copy. It's also important to have a sheet that lists all of your specific dos and don'ts to hand out to them. Don't expect the security team to have a photographic memory.

If you're working with a band that attracts a rowdy crowd, such as a metal band, you'll probably be playing in a venue that does a lot of metal shows. Some of the venues may have strict rules against moshing, crowd surfing, and stage diving; and some of them may have signs posted that specifically state that these activities aren't allowed and that anyone caught doing them will be ejected from the venue. In this case, whether your band allows this sort of thing or not, you probably won't have any say in it. The venue may have had incidents in the past where fans or security guards were injured, and they were sued because of it. You have no choice but to follow their rules, regardless of what your band wants.

The security guard's job is easier without these activities, and the chaos level is reduced, but it's impossible to prevent moshing at a metal concert. When a thousand kids start a massive circle pit, there aren't enough security guards in town to stop that. It's what the crowd does; it's almost part of the show. However, I don't like to see kids get injured by stage divers and crowd surfers when all they want is to watch the show without getting their head kicked in by someone flying through the air.

Stage diving isn't safe for the band. The audience doesn't realize that the band members can't see things flying through the air at them—and that includes people—because the stage lighting and spotlights are blinding them. No musician wants his front teeth knocked out when someone in the audience flies through the air and crashes into his microphone stand and rams a microphone halfway down his throat because he didn't see the stage diver coming at him until it's too late.

To be frank, ever since Dimebag was killed, I don't like seeing anyone coming on stage. You never know what someone is capable of anymore. It's better to be safe than sorry. The band belongs on stage, and the crowd belongs out on the venue floor.

Even if the venue doesn't allow stage diving or crowd surfing, there's still no excuse for a security guard beating up a fan unless the guard was attacked and had no choice but to defend himself, but I've rarely seen this in all of my years on the road. Most of the fans just want to have a good time.

Make a list of what you expect from security on a security information sheet, and pass it out to everyone in your security meeting. Some of the points I might put on the sheet are listed below as an example:

1. Please don't physically abuse the audience, or the band will stop the show.
2. If the venue has a strict policy against crowd surfing or stage diving and violators are subject to ejection from the venue, please eject them in a civil manner.
3. If anyone in the audience does get on stage, the band's crew will remove them and hand them to a security guard so they can be put back into the audience or ejected from the venue, depending on venue policy. Do not run on stage after them.
4. Please exercise special care during the first three songs when photographers are in the barricade shooting the show. Try to help them do their job and avoid injury.
5. All security guards in the barricade should be looking at the audience at all times, not watching the show.
6. There is NO smoking in the barricade or anywhere near the stage, even if the venue is a smoking venue.
7. Do not shine flashlights into the audience unless absolutely necessary during a blackout. Not only is this annoying to the audience, but the band's sound engineer and lighting designer can't do their jobs when they're being blinded by your flashlight.
8. Do not stand in front of the PA fills as this affects the quality of the audio.
9. While the band permits fans to photograph and video the show with non-professional cameras and cell phones, they do not allow the show to be recorded with professional audio or video devices. These devices should be confiscated and given to the band's production manager so the media can be confiscated. Please tell the person caught with these devices that their equipment will be returned to them once the media has been destroyed.

It's important that you read everything on the security information sheet and thoroughly explain it to the security team. Answer all of their questions so they're clear on all points. Go over every pass and laminate on your security pass sheet, one by one, and explain to them in detail the restrictions and limitations of every pass. Answer any questions about each pass.

If the band can afford it, always try to print your pass sheets in full color so security can see what each pass actually looks like. If you can't afford to print pass sheets in color, add a line to your sheet below each pass so you can write in the color of the day for each pass, and be sure to explain this information to security.

Never assume that security guards know everything; they don't. They only know what you explain to them. Every show is different, and every band does things a different way. And while the security team may seem professional, you never know how many of them may be experiencing their first day on the job. Be thorough with your security meeting, and you'll get the best possible results from the security team.

However, despite how well you conducted your security meeting and assuming you posted pass sheets at the required places, there will be some nights when security is your torment of the day. There are venues that have some of the best security personnel you'll ever deal with—total pros that are there to protect your entourage and the audience; and then there are venues that hire amateurs who work for free beer. These people are a menace and are usually only there to see the show for free, get drunk, and kick someone's ass. In venues like these, anything is possible. If your band has to play in a joint like this, you can only keep a close eye on things throughout the evening and try to correct problems as they arise.

I've done sold out shows where I've caught backstage security taking money from fans who couldn't buy tickets and walking them in the back door. Security personnel like this need to be replaced immediately because they're capable of anything. Don't put yourself in a position where you could end up in a fight with some unethical security guard. Get your promoter rep and the head of security, explain to them what you've witnessed, and tell them you want this person removed and sent home immediately and another security guard put in his place. Don't just have him sent to guard the men's toilets; have him sent home. I'd also have the head of security confiscate the money he's stolen from the band and promoter.

Some clubs will hire anyone to be a security guard as long as he's big and strong and looks intimidating, but some of these people have no experience or training and their first reaction to a situation is to beat somebody up. These are the worst kind of security people to have on a show.

Any real promoter will avoid having a security guard like this on a show because he knows they could cause him to get hit with a financially-crippling lawsuit and put him out of business.

The smaller clubs and bars that are struggling to keep their heads above water are the ones that usually hire people like this to save money. Venues like this don't last and are always one step away from being shut down. No responsible club owner is going to hire a security staff that's going out of their way to beat up and injure his customers, but it happens sometimes.

The best venue security guards and band bodyguards defuse a situation with their brains, not their fists, but are still capable of going to DEFCON 1 when left with no other choice.

GUEST LISTS AND PASSES

You're probably saying to yourself, "What's the big deal about guest lists and passes? You just type up the names, make some passes, and take it all to the box office." You can think of it that way if you want your day to be crazier than a horde of hysterical housewives running amok at a Kmart Black Friday sale, but I prefer to row my boat with both oars in the ocean.

Depending on the popularity of your band, doing your guest list can be your easiest or most difficult and time-consuming chore, but it's one of the most important things you'll have to do each day. You need to make sure your entourage's guests get the passes they're supposed to receive, and you also need to make sure the journalists on your list get into the show. Photographers that are coming to shoot the show can't do their job if you've forgotten to give them a photo pass.

Wait until the day inevitably comes when the promoter rep screws up and your guest list and passes don't make it to the box office somehow, and your band starts raising hell because their guests are calling them and saying their name's not on the list, and your phone begins to ring off the hook with nonstop calls from the record company, publicist, and manager wondering if you've forgotten how to do your job or just gone cuckoo on a kaleidoscope clusterfuck of an acid trip. Then you'll truly understand what I'm trying to tell you.

Some bands think the guest list is a never-ending well of free tickets for them to give away; it's not. There are a negotiated amount of guest list tickets in the band's contract for a reason. The promoter can't let the bands give away all of the tickets and expect to break even, much less make any money.

I've always found that if you've built a good rapport with your promoter rep during the advance and are not excessive in going over on the number of tickets you require, many of them will give you a few extra tickets if the show isn't already sold out. However, if the show's sold out, he's only going to have what he's held back for your guest list, and that amount will be what's been agreed upon in the band's contract.

When you're doing major markets such as New York, Los Angeles, or, even worse, the band's hometown, you'll generally need more tickets. Everyone is a VIP in your band's hometown, Los Angeles, New York, Nashville, or any other big music industry city around the world.

Most managers will attempt to get the record label to do a ticket-buy for these major markets so their industry guests don't use up all of the band's tickets, but sometimes the record label just doesn't have the budget for ticket-buys. This is a situation that your manager has to sort out with the label, and you're left to deal with the resultant decision.

I always tell the record company press team there's a limit to how many people I can have running around backstage. If I'm in a small club that only has one dressing room for the band and it's the size of my bedroom, how can I give out fifty VIP passes to people on the label's guest list? In addition, I still have to accommodate the band's guests.

On major shows where you have very little room backstage, you have no choice but to insist the record company only send you pass requests for the most important guests. You could also set up a system with the promoter rep where you give out VIP passes, but those guests are directed to an area in the balcony, for example. After the show is over, they'll be allowed to stay there when security clears the house. Then your band can go there and greet the guests once they've had a minute to rest and get dressed.

Many times when a band's playing in their hometown, their guest list will greatly exceed the amount of tickets agreed upon in their contract. Some promoters will agree to give the band extra tickets, knowing it's their hometown show and they'll have a lot more guests, but beyond that amount, the band will usually have to buy tickets for their additional guests.

I can understand the band buying tickets for their family and close friends, people who have supported them as they paid their dues to get where they are, but some bands fill their guest list with people who just want everything they can get out of the band for free. Like I always say, "This is the music *business*, not the music *charity*." Let some of them buy a ticket for once. When a band becomes more experienced, they start to realize what I'm saying is true. Constantly giving away concert tickets, CDs, and merchandise doesn't earn the band any money; it just drains them of it. There has to be a limit, or they could end up with nothing when it's all over one day, but that's just my point of view.

If you don't have separate support act satin passes, always be sure to mark the passes you give to your support acts so you can immediately tell the difference between your band's guests and the support act's guests. If your support band's called Shocker, use a black Sharpie to mark a big S in the middle of the pass. This will allow you and security to determine which band the guest is there to see. You don't want your support act's guests walking into your band's dressing room because you and the security guard don't know who they are.

If you have specific stick-on passes for the support acts, then you'll easily know who that guest belongs to, but if you can't afford separate stick-on passes for the support acts, simply mark them with the initials of the band's name.

If I give out stick-on passes to my crew for girls they've just met at the show or for girls they're looking to meet, I always mark the stick-on pass with that crew member's initials. I do this for a reason. It's not a good idea in this day and age to be giving backstage passes to strangers unless your people are going to supervise them at all times.

Most crew members are good about this sort of thing, but if I suddenly walk into the band's dressing room and find some strange girl going through the band's wardrobe case, all I have to do is look at her stick-on pass and see the initials I've marked on it to find out which one of my crew members has let me down and won't be getting another pass until the end of time.

Many professional crew members will only ask for passes for their family or close friends because most of them don't have time to babysit guests; they're just too busy.

It's often the band members who are the worst offenders in allowing guests to run wild backstage. They don't want to say no to them, but they also don't want to be saddled with babysitting them all night, so it's inevitable their guests end up in areas they're not supposed to be in. All you can do is try to teach your band the best way you can and hope they'll finally learn that not every guest on their list has to have a VIP pass, giving them way more access than they should have.

When I have band wives or family members coming to a show, especially if I've never met them before, I always prefer to give them an all access laminate so I know they're a band family member. The last thing you ever want to do is to be rude to a band member's family, no matter what they do backstage. It's the quickest way to get fired. If they do something that causes trouble, let the band member to whom they belong handle it.

Putting yourself into a position where you could end up in a shouting match with your singer's drunken sister is probably not the best way to keep your job. And, unfortunately, there are a lot of family members who show up at a venue and don't know how to act and think they can do whatever they like just because they're related to someone in the band.

Frankly, you're better off to let them do what they want and hang themselves with their own bad behavior. I'll usually wait until the next day when things have calmed down and speak to the band member about what happened. Some will deal with it, while some won't do a thing about it, but at least you'll know what to expect from that family member the next time they show up. It's a hard position to be in, but you have to deal with it, or you can go and find a job with a band that has family members who know how to act like human beings.

If your band's manager, booking agent, business manager, record producer, or any high-level person from the record company comes to a show, make them an all access laminate.

People like this are easily offended when receiving a pass they feel is beneath them. Don't make yourself look like an amateur by giving the band's manager a working pass that you'd give to the stagehands; and telling him that you're sorry but you've run out of laminates will only make you look even more incompetent. Always stash away a dozen laminates, if you have the budget for it, to cover yourself in situations like this.

As you can see from the guest list below, it's pretty simple and straightforward. A sheet like this can be easily made using Microsoft Excel. I usually add thirty lines to the sheet because thirty tickets is usually the amount on my band's rider. If the number is higher, add more lines. Add a copy of the band's logo at the top of the sheet to give it a professional look. Be sure to type in the show's date and the venue's name and city.

Skinny Girl Riot

Guest List

Date	Sunday, April 01, 2012			**Venue**	Club 1		**City**	San Francisco, CA	

#	Name	# of Tix	AAA lam	VIP lam	Working	VIP	After Show	Photo	Guest of
1	Hooters, Helen	2			2				FF
2	Connie from Little Rock	2			2				MM
3	Munrow, Marilyn	1			1				TT
4	Sweettarts, Sara	2			2				JG
5	Upton, K.	2	2						SS
6	Anderson, Annie	0						1	SGR
7	Flash, Johnny	0						1	SGR
8									
9									
10									
11									
12									
13									
14									
15									
16									
17									
18									
19									
20									
21									
22									
23									
24									
25									
26									
27									
28									
29									
30									
Totals		9	2	0	7	0	0	2	

Please call Bobby Blinder (tour manager) with any questions or problems at 555-673-3342.

You'll notice that we have a column for the guest's name. Always put the last name first, then a comma, and then the guest's first name. This will make it easier for the person in the box office to find a guest's name. Don't make things hard and cause them to miss a name on the list and turn away an important guest.

The next column is where you type in the number of tickets the guest will receive. If they're getting passes only, leave that field blank. Next we have columns for all of our different passes. Enter the amount of the passes that the guest will receive under the appropriate column. In the last column type in the initials of the name of the person who gave you that guest list name.

Knowing to whom the guest belongs is important. If after you've finished your list, you realize you're ten tickets over and you have to cut someone, you need to know to whom the guest belongs so you can decide which one to cut. If you had to choose between cutting a band member's mother or a girl your drum tech picked up at the mall yesterday on the day off, it should be a no-brainer as to who gets cut, but you need to know whose guest it is to be able to do that.

When you're done typing your guest list, select the rows and columns of names, tickets, passes, and ID initials, and use Excel's data sort function to rearrange them all in alphabetical order. This makes it easier for the person in the box office to find a guest name and less likely to turn someone away.

If you've built the Excel spreadsheet correctly, the total number of tickets and passes at the bottom of the page should add up automatically, so you can easily see the total number of tickets and passes needed.

I always add my name and cell phone number to the bottom of the guest list so the person in the box office can call me should there be any problems with the list, such as someone saying they're supposed to be on the list but are not. Sometimes we all forget to put someone on the list. Include your contact info so you can be reached to solve these problems.

Make a concerted effort to do your guest list properly and your show day will run much better. Always remember that passes are much more than souvenirs; they're important security devices used to protect your band, crew, and valuable gear.

DOING YOUR DAILY ROAD ACCOUNTING

One of your duties that you must find time for every day is your tour accounting because you don't want to get behind on it. Some tour managers will wait and do their books on their day off, but those may be few and far between on many tours. Experienced road managers know how to get a lot of expense receipts done quickly, but it's never a good idea for a new tour manager to get backed up on accounting.

The business manager will expect to receive road reports from you every week on the same day. Since the weekend is often when we have our biggest shows, I normally end my accounting week on Saturday, do my weekly road reports on Sunday, and get them shipped off to the business manager on Monday for arrival on Tuesday.

It's up to you to decide when to end your accounting week, unless the business manager requests something specific, but it's important that you're consistent in whatever you do, so the business manager knows what to expect. You don't want her complaining to the manager because she's not getting road reports from you on time. Road reports that don't arrive consistently not only get the accountant backed up on her work but will start to send up red flags that you're not doing the job right.

Find the time every day to enter your expense receipts into your accounting; try to do it at the same time every day so you get into the habit of doing it. If you let yourself get backed up, you're more likely to lose a receipt that could cost you money or make mistakes that could have your numbers come out wrong. It's a lot easier to find a mistake when you only have a day's worth of receipts in front of you as opposed to two weeks' worth piled up in a large heap.

On many tours, the biggest expenses on the road will come from the tour bus expenses. You should always keep the bus driver running with a certain amount of road float so he can buy necessary things for the bus, such as fuel, oil, generator service supplies and bus cleaning products.

I'll usually keep the driver running with $1,000 in float on a U.S. tour; anything less and he runs out of float too quickly. Once the driver's spent that money, he'll turn in the receipts, and I'll give him another $1,000 in float. It's never a good idea to keep giving the driver money without having him turn in his receipts. He'll start to get backed up on his accounting, which will cause you to get backed up on yours.

Once in a while, if you're in the middle of a lot of back-to-back long drives and the driver's barely getting enough time to sleep, you'll have no choice but to be patient because he hasn't had time to do his receipts. This is understandable. However, if the drives are short and he's just being lazy, insist that he does his accounting before you give him any more float.

You'll also need to pay the driver his salary and overdrives on a weekly basis, unless the band has him on payroll like the crew. Make the last day of the driver's pay week the same as the last day of your accounting week. If the last day of your accounting week is Saturday and the tour started on Wednesday, pay him for four days that first week.

You'll need to create a receipt on your computer, like the one below, for the driver's salary and overdrives each week. You can use a receipt book from any office supply store, but I prefer to make my own receipt. It looks more professional, and it's easy to edit for each week's salary. I always save each receipt in my computer in case I need to refer back to them for any reason.

Some drivers like to pay themselves their overdrives out of float. I don't like to do this because if there are a lot of overdrives on the tour, he'll be running out of float quicker and turning in his receipts to me more often. I also want to go over each overdrive before I pay the driver to make sure he's not charging the band an overdrive for only going five miles over the limit.

I don't have a problem with the bus driver paying himself for the weekly generator services, as long as he makes a proper receipt and adds it into his accounting. Generator services are done every one hundred hours and are usually around $45 to $50 each, depending on the bus company. If the driver's doing the weekly bus wash himself, I also have no problem with him paying himself for this service out of float. The bus wash charge is usually $50 to $75, depending on whether you're pulling a trailer or not.

You should also pay the band and crew their per diems on a weekly basis. If the last day of your accounting week is Saturday and the tour started on Wednesday, pay each of them four days of per diem the first week. I always prefer to make a separate sheet for the band and crew per diems if the band's getting a higher amount than the crew.

You normally won't be paying the band or crew any salary on the road. This is almost always paid by the business manager each week or every two weeks. Most business managers will do direct deposit for you as long as you provide them with the proper banking information. Some bands from overseas may pay American crew members cash on the road if they don't have a U.S. business manager to handle payroll for them.

SKINNY GIRL RIOT

USA Tour 2012

Receipt

Friday, April 06, 2012

To:	Leadfoot Johnson (bus driver)		
For:	7 days salary ($215.00/day) from March 31 to April 6	$	1,505.00
For:	1 overdrive from Phoenix to Albuquerque	$	215.00
Amount:	**$**	**1,720.00**	

Signature: _____

Skinny Girl Riot --Per Diem Sheet		
Week ending:	Friday, April 06, 2012	
Name	**Amount**	**Signature**
Stevie Starbright	$210.00	
Frankie Fabulous	$210.00	
Jimmy Giant	$210.00	
Mikey Massive	$210.00	
Tommy Twosticks	$210.00	
Bobby Blinder	$210.00	
Lance Loudnoise	$210.00	
Ricky Racket	$210.00	
Jerry Spazo	$210.00	
Kyle Klown	$210.00	
Tony Tonedeaf	$210.00	
Penny Tightpants	$210.00	
Total	**$2,520.00**	

If that's the case, make a salary receipt, like the bus driver's salary receipt, for each crew member you have to pay. Whatever you do, don't make one receipt, like your per diem receipt, listing all of the crew salaries on it; it will only lead to arguments when one person sees that another person is making more money than him. A crew member's salary is no one else's business.

When I'm doing accounting, I'll always do it in a secure area where my expense receipts will be safe. If you lose an expense receipt, it's the same as losing the band's cash, and you'll have to replace this money out of your own pocket if you can't obtain a duplicate copy of the receipt. If you're taking in a lot of expense receipts each week, you may not even know which receipt you've lost when your numbers come out wrong.

I'll never lay out thousands of dollars worth of expense receipts in the production office if I can't lock that door when I have to leave. Always guard receipts like they are cash that belongs to you.

I always lay out my cash receipts in one pile and my credit card receipts in a separate pile. I prefer to get my cash receipts done first. Always remember to mark each receipt with an identifying number, circle the amount of the expense, and write a description on it if the receipt doesn't clearly state what the expense was for. If you're using an accounting program, such as Quicken, the program will arrange your expense receipts in chronological order as long as you enter the purchase date from each receipt. Always be careful and enter the correct receipt amount into your cash ledger. Rushing through your accounting and entering incorrect receipt amounts is almost always the reason why someone's bottom line comes out wrong. Take your time and do it right.

As you're entering your expenses, be sure to enter any cash pick-ups that you haven't already entered into your computer, but you should enter your cash pick-ups into your accounting each night after settlement. Don't forget to enter your cash pick-ups into your cash ledger or your numbers will come out wrong. If you're using Quicken, you can enter in all of your cash pick-ups at one time, and the program will rearrange them in chronological order on the cash ledger, as long as you put the correct date of the cash pick-up in your entry.

Always remember not to enter credit card receipts into your cash ledger or your numbers will come out wrong. You didn't pay for a credit card expense with cash, so you certainly don't want to enter that expense into your cash ledger. Always make a separate ledger for credit card receipts.

As you number and enter all of your expense receipts into your ledger, add them to your stack of hard expense receipts in sequential order because you'll have to send these with your road reports to the business manager. You don't want to send the business manager a big envelope filled with expense receipts that aren't in proper order unless you want her to make a voodoo doll of you and jam sharp pins into its eyes.

The accountant needs to be able to go down your ledgers and see each expense and at the same time be able to go through a stack of hard receipts that match each of the entries in your reports. Once you're done with your weekly report, use binder clips to secure your stack of hard expense receipts. Print out a copy of your cash ledger and attach it to the top of your stack of cash receipts. Do the same thing with your credit card receipts and credit card ledger.

If you're carrying any checks you picked up from the promoters that week, you must include them in the weekly package you send to the business manager. If the band's on a tight budget and living week-to-week, the business manager may insist that you FedEx checks to her as soon as you receive them. This, of course, increases the weekly FedEx bill, but the business manager may not be able to pay the band's bills, such as payroll and the bus lease payments, without them. Just do what she asks you to do, and do it on time. FedEx will come down to the venue for a pick up whenever you need it. You don't have to worry about going out and finding a FedEx drop box. It's easy to go to FedEx.com or call their 800 number to schedule a pick up.

Once I'm done with my weekly reports, I always email a copy of my cash and credit card ledgers to the business manager and manager, and I include the FedEx tracking number. I also include in the email a list of the checks that I'm sending to the business manager so they know what to expect in the package. In addition, I let them know if there's a cashier's check included for any surplus cash I'm sending to them.

Never pick up cash you don't need unless the manager and agent insist upon it. If you must pick up large amounts of cash, try to turn this cash into a cashier's check or money orders as soon as possible so you don't have to worry about it getting lost or stolen. If a cashier's check or money order is stolen or lost, at least it can be replaced.

Use a locking money bag to secure all of your cash, checks, and expense receipts. You can buy one at most office supply stores or from the band's bank. Always be sure to use a bag that's made of heavy-duty canvas material and has a durable lock on it.

If your bus doesn't have a safe on it, you could ask the bus company to install one underneath a couch in the back lounge. They may do it. If they won't pay for it, the band always has the option of paying for it. The band could buy a safe and install it in your production case, although I'm not a big fan of doing this, because production cases can be wheeled away and stolen very easily. If you don't have a production case, find a place on the bus to hide your money bag. I'm always reluctant to use a safe on a tour bus because you never know who else has a copy of the key or knows the combination. Most bus drivers are honest guys, but you never know. Of course, the bus can always be broken into or catch on fire. Nothing is foolproof.

I always try to carry as little cash as possible, and what I do carry, I keep it close to me at all times so I don't have to worry about it getting stolen. You should do the same. You can wear a money belt or a fanny pack, if you don't mind the fashion misstatement.

In this day and age, it's nearly impossible to go into any bank and get a cashier's check if you don't have an account with the bank. Banks simply won't do it because they have no way of knowing if you're laundering drug money or funding a terrorist organization.

It's always good for an American band to have an account at a large national bank such as Chase Bank, Bank of America, or Citibank that have branch locations all over the country. Even if one of the three largest banks in the U.S. doesn't have a branch in the city you're in, you usually won't go more than a few days before you get to a city that has one.

When you need to go to the band's bank to buy a cashier's check, print out a simple sheet with the band's company name, address, telephone number, taxpayer ID number, their account numbers and routing information, and the address of the band's branch where they opened the account. This will save you time when the bank teller asks for this information.

Inform the bank teller from the start that you're the road manager for the band and that they're playing in town—name the venue—and you need to convert the cash you've picked up from the promoters into a cashier's check so you can FedEx it to the band's accountant. Telling them this information as soon as you get up to the counter puts them at ease. They won't be wondering what you're up to and giving you the third degree. It's always possible that they have heard of the club and maybe even your band, which will immediately put them even more at ease and get the transaction completed for you as quickly as possible.

You should always be careful when walking around any town with a lot of cash on you. Try to get the runner to take you to the bank. You never know what can happen. Don't put yourself in a situation where you can get hurt or killed over some band's money. Guarding the band's money is one thing, risking your life for it is a whole other matter. If someone sticks a gun in your face, give them the money. There aren't too many managers and business managers—with a conscience—who would fault you for doing so. It's not worth getting killed over; and the band's insurance—if they have any—should cover the loss.

HOW TO DO SHOW SETTLEMENTS CORRECTLY

Completing your show settlement is your most important financial duty each day. In the end, the band is a business, even if they don't like to look at it that way. They can't stay on the road for long if they don't get paid; and if they're a new band, they're probably not selling much merchandise to help pay the bills. Every dime they earn will help pay for road expenses and keep them rolling to the next city.

If your band's just starting out and they're supporting a bigger group, chances are they're not getting paid much at all, and you're picking up a flat guarantee each night. If this is the case, there's not much of a settlement for you to do. You're simply picking up the balance of their guarantee, or the entire balance, if the promoter hasn't paid a deposit.

If your band's starting to become popular, and their deal includes money on the back end, you need to know how to settle a show correctly. Most of the good promoters want the band to earn as much money as possible; it makes the promoter look good when he's able to report to the band's agent that he made the band extra money. It shows that the promoter did his job well. However, there are promoters who will rob your band blind if you give them the chance to do so. It's your job to make sure this doesn't happen during settlement.

You need to obtain updated ticket counts from the promoter throughout the day so you know how many tickets have been sold up until the time the box office is closed. Not asking for updated ticket counts sends a message to the promoter that either you don't know what you're doing or you simply don't care. Either way, you set yourself up to be taken advantage of.

The band's booking agent will send out a weekly ticket count so you'll know how each show is selling. This helps you to determine where you stand with the promoter when you're advancing the shows. If the show's dying, you'll already know that you're going to have a hard time getting extras from him, and he'll even try to get you to cut many things. However, if the show's selling well, you'll have a much easier time getting what you want. Below is a ticket count sheet that you can expect to receive from your booking agent.

Skinny Girl Riot Ticket Counts--USA 2012

Date	Venue/City	Capacity	On Sale	2/22/2012	2/29/2012	3/7/2012	3/14/2012	3/21/2012	3/28/2012	4/4/2012	4/11/2012	4/18/2022
4/1/2012	Club 1--San Francisco	1633	2/15/2012	459	689	1002	1445	1633				
4/2/2012	Club 2--Los Angeles	992	2/15/2012	202	306	455	683	992				
4/3/2012	Club 3--San Diego	1100	2/15/2012	155	226	345	499	753	799			
4/4/2012	Club 4--Phoenix	1100	2/15/2012	142	243	369	488	742	802	848		
4/5/2012	Club 5--Albuquerque	1200	2/15/2012	169	296	379	499	783	822	899		
4/7/2012	Club 6--El Paso	1500	2/22/2012	388	499	587	689	788	992	1102		
4/8/2012	Club 7--San Antonio	1550	2/22/2012	399	488	525	699	801	1003	1344		
4/9/2012	Club 8--Houston	1000	2/22/2012	204	300	449	583	799	893	943		
4/10/2012	Club 9--Dallas	1400	2/22/2012	399	498	589	684	777	953	1296		
4/11/2012	Club 10--New Orleans	1450	2/22/2012	388	434	586	633	742	902	1236		
4/13/2012	Club 11--Tallahassee	1200	2/29/2012	163	288	386	483	644	803	899	983	
4/14/2012	Club 12--Tampa	1200	2/29/2012	153	234	355	488	633	788	833	943	
4/15/2012	Club 13--Orlando	1200	2/29/2012	143	236	388	433	623	732	899	999	
4/16/2012	Club 14--Atlanta	1300	2/29/2012	188	299	383	493	588	692	901	1002	
4/17/2012	Club 15--Raleigh	1400	2/29/2012	193	282	399	484	578	639	912	1018	
4/19/2012	Club 16--Washington, DC	1500	3/7/2012	203	399	450	599	748	985	1208	1301	1398
4/20/2012	Club 17--Philadelphia	1200	3/7/2012	153	238	332	433	599	744	843	899	944
4/21/2012	Club 18--Hartford	1000	3/7/2012	133	199	301	399	488	603	744	801	822
4/22/2012	Club 19--Boston	1000	3/7/2012	122	188	293	354	487	593	743	812	844
4/23/2012	Club 20--New York	1000	3/7/2012	133	199	287	366	493	591	801	902	1000
Totals		24925		4489	6541	8860	11434	14691	14336	16451	9660	5008

In the past, some bands would hire a person to work the front door with a clicker and count each person that came in to prevent the promoter from lying about how many tickets he'd sold. Today, it's impossible to carry more bodies on tour just to perform this function, and you never know what you're going to get when hiring people locally. Hiring someone to click the door can also be insulting to your promoter. It's unnecessary today because the ticket outlets are computerized, and most established promoters aren't willing to destroy their reputation with every booking agent in the business by getting caught robbing your band. Although, you still need to keep an eye on them; you never know when a smaller promoter could have one foot in bankruptcy court and the other in his financial grave.

If the tickets are only being sold through a company such as Ticketmaster, you're going to get a ticket audit at the end of the night showing exactly how many tickets were sold. The promoter cannot modify this printout because it comes directly from Ticketmaster's system, but this does not prevent him from selling other tickets directly to the fans at the box office.

Twenty years ago, I was on the road with my long-time client, Testament. We were doing a sold-out headline show at a venue in the Midwest that's still open and doing business today. I had strong reasons to believe that the dodgy promoter—a person I won't name because he'd definitely sue me to make a buck—had been selling tickets to the fans after the show had sold out and was pocketing the money, robbing the band of their back-end earnings.

After the show was over, Testament's vocalist Chuck Billy and I dragged the promoter into my production office and held him at gunpoint with Chuck's sawed-off shotgun and a 9mm pistol belonging to our sound crew chief—who shall remain nameless because he's a big promoter rep today—in an effort to get the money he stole from the band. He denied selling the tickets and stealing from the band.

We finally had to take the venue's sound console and load it on our semi. Our friend, Ricky Dynamite from Chicago, set off a half a stick of dynamite in the venue parking lot, as our crew confiscated the venue's sound console and put it on the truck.

As things started to get really out of control, we finally got the money that was coming to the band, but it was a ridiculous affair that probably wouldn't happen in this day and age. We didn't take shit from anyone back then, and we weren't about to let some scumbag promoter rip off Testament. The band's managers, Elliot Cahn and Jeff Saltzman—who also happened to be entertainment attorneys—were far from impressed.

The gross potential of the show is the total amount of money the show can earn. It's simple to calculate. You multiply the number of tickets that can be sold by the price of the ticket. If the venue's legal capacity is one thousand people and the ticket price is $20, then the gross potential of the show is $20,000.

There was once a day when a promoter could get away with selling tickets beyond the legal capacity of a venue, but that's a dangerous game to play today. Local Fire Marshals are much stricter about violations and will shut a concert down in two seconds if the promoter exceeds the legal capacity. They have been vigilant ever since one hundred people were burned alive and more than two hundred were injured at a 2003 Great White concert at The Station nightclub in Rhode Island when the band's idiot *road manager* ignited pyrotechnics and burned the club to the ground.

While I believe that the band's inexperienced road manager was a scapegoat hung out to dry by the band members—who should have also gone to prison—he was still the one who ignited open flame in a packed club with low ceilings and no permit from the Fire Marshal allowing the band to use pyrotechnics.

In thirty years on the road, I've never met a crew guy who was dumb enough to set up pyro on stage and set it off without the band's full knowledge and consent. He'd have to be more ignorant than Lloyd Christmas and doing more coke than Tony Montana to even think of such a thing. It doesn't work that way. Any crew guy that was crazy enough to do such a thing without the band's permission would be fired on the spot, arrested, and banned from the road forever. He wouldn't be able to get a job as a trained chimp holding a tin cup for an organ grinder.

The Great White band members knew about the pyro and told him to use it, and he was dumb enough to do what the band—his employer—told him to do. James Hetfield, the singer and guitarist from Metallica, nearly lost his arm and his career when he stood in the wrong place at the wrong time on stage and was burned by exploding pyro. Pyro has to be perfectly choreographed with the band so no one on stage is killed, and it's set up and discharged by highly-trained professional pyro technicians whose first priority is the safety of everyone in the venue. A fire permit granted by the Fire Marshal must first be obtained—after the pyro to be used is demonstrated and approved—before the pyro can be used in the show. And this usually only permitted in large venues with high ceilings, not in little clubs.

You don't allow some inexperienced road manager to set up and discharge dangerous pyrotechnics to save the costs of paying for a pyro technician and the fire permits. That's like hiring a flight attendant to pilot a Boeing 747 and then wondering why the plane has crashed into a residential neighborhood with a hundred people incinerated beneath the wreckage.

One hundred people burned alive. Just writing that sentence makes me disgusted to know that the tour manager who started the fire only spent two years in prison and that TWO VERSIONS of Great White are on the road today doing shows and earning money while one hundred families are devastated forever. And that doesn't include the more than two hundred people who were injured and barely escaped with their lives.

Sure, there were others involved who deserved to wear the Scarlet letter G of guilt. Everyone and their mother got sued over this tragedy, but the buck stops with the band members who decided to use pyro that night. The poor dumb bastard masquerading as a reputable road manager didn't just pull that idea—and the pyro—out of his ass at that one moment in time and start a roaring conflagration. He did it because he was told to do it by the band, and they know it. They will always know it.

The road manager was in charge of the tour and should have known better than to do something as psychotic as firing open-flame pyro in a small club. If he didn't know better, he was too stupid to be in the job in the first place. Yes, the road manager works for the band, but a responsible and experienced road manager would've told the band to go to hell when they told him to do something as incredibly dumb, irresponsible, and dangerous as that. Don't ever let yourself be put into a situation like that. There are plenty of gigs out there. No one in their right mind would take a chance of killing people and going to prison over some rock band's silly little club show.

As I finish this book, Great White is fighting with their singer, Jack Russell, over the rights to the band's name. That band doesn't deserve to play any venue in the world. The guilty ones got off scot-free. The families of the dead got paid, but where was the justice for the one hundred dead people? When that band sent one hundred people to their graves, they should've sent the Great White name to the grave right behind them; anything less dishonors the dead.

When a promoter books a show with a band's booking agent, he'll first determine the ticket price based upon the band's popularity and what the local market will bear. He then estimates how many tickets he thinks he'll sell, and that will determine the size of venue he'll rent for the show if it won't fit into a club he works out of or owns.

Once the promoter has determined the ticket price and the size of the venue, he can easily determine his show's gross potential. Once he knows his gross potential, he'll have a better idea how much money he can pay the headliner once he takes into account his other show expenses.

If the promoter's working out of a club where he does many shows, he already has a pretty good idea what his show expenses are going to be, giving him a clearer picture of what he can afford to pay the headliner.

A promoter who owns his own club is in a much better position than an outside promoter who is renting the venue. The owner of the club is going to profit from liquor sales, and those can help to cushion the financial blow of a show that doesn't sell well. Outside promoters are sometimes able to negotiate a cut of the liquor sales to help cushion their potential losses, but they may pay a higher rental fee to the club for that right.

Show expenses are simpler to analyze when it's a club gig, and the band's only using house production. When using only house production, the promoter doesn't have to pay to bring in sound and lights, except for any small extras he might agree to rent if the club doesn't have them. If the club has their own kitchen that sells food to the public, the promoter will also save money feeding the bands. Many clubs have their own staff of technicians, stagehands, and security, so the promoter wouldn't have to hire these workers in such a venue.

The outside promoter can usually negotiate an all-in rental fee that includes these essential workers and the cost of renting the venue. He might also be able to include the catering needed to feed the bands if the club has their own kitchen. He might even be able to include booze for the band's rider if the venue sells beer, wine, and liquor.

If you look at the settlement sheet below, you'll see the show expenses for this fantasy show. Venue rent, catering, stagehands, house techs, security, advertising, and some other minor expenses are listed on the sheet.

Show costs will vary, depending on the size of the show and whether or not the promoter has to bring in production. If the show's happening in a town where there's only one sound and lighting company, the cost of sound and lighting could be higher than a city where there are multiple sound and lighting companies competing against each other. I've seen situations where promoters are being bent over and raped on sound and lighting because there's only one company in town, and they have no choice but to pay the charges. Their only recourse is to bring in production from another town, which would usually be cost-prohibitive because the other town is far away. Anything that has to be shipped from another location is always going to cost more because of the cost of transporting it.

During settlement, compare the final show costs on the promoter's final settlement sheet to the show cost estimates that are on the promoter's show budget that was sent to the agent when the show was booked. This estimated show budget is usually attached to the deal sheet. The booking agent has probably done many shows with the promoter in that venue, and he'll know if the estimated expenses in the budget are realistic, inflated, or downright fantastical. It's important for you to compare these estimated expenses with the final costs to make sure there's nothing dramatically different. If the estimated show expenses included $1,000 for security and the final security bill was $2,500, you know you have questions that need to be answered. If the sound and lighting estimate was $5,000 and the final bill was $8,000, red flags should be going up in your head.

Club 1				TIX SOLD	PRICE	TOTAL
Skinny Girl Riot						
The Worst			Advance Ticketmaster	1633	$30.00	$48,990.00
Sunday, April 01, 2012			Advance Venue	0	$30.00	$0.00
			DOS Ticketmaster	0	$30.00	$0.00
			Box Office	0	$30.00	$0.00
	Total Paid	1,633		0	$0.00	$0.00
	Guest/Promo	0		0	$0.00	$0.00
	Total In	1,633		0	$0.00	$0.00
				0	$0.00	$0.00
			TOTAL	1633		
Talent	**Deposit**	**Balance**	**Bonus**	**Total**	**GROSS**	**$48,990.00**
Skinny Girl Riot	$10,000.00	$10,000.00	$0.00	$20,000.00		
The Worst	$100.00	$100.00	$0.00	$200.00	**VARIABLES**	
	$0.00	$0.00	$0.00	$0.00	Insurance	$816.50
	$0.00	$0.00	$0.00	$0.00	Ticket Comm	$1,333.75
				$0.00	ASCAP/BMI	$576.00
			Total Talent	$20,200.00	**Total Variable**	**$2,726.25**
Advertising Expenses	**Predicted Exp.**	**Actual Expense**	**Misc**	**Total**	**EXPENSES**	
Admats/Art Production	$3,000.00	$40.00	$0.00	$40.00		
Billboards	$0.00	$220.00	$0.00	$220.00	Talent	$20,200.00
Color Poster/Flyers	$0.00	$250.00	$0.00	$250.00	Fixed Expenses	$8,733.31
Print Ads	$0.00	$675.00	$0.00	$675.00	Variable	$2,726.25
Radio	$0.00	$1,175.00	$0.00	$1,175.00	Show Expenses	$31,659.56
Street Team	$0.00	$200.00	$0.00	$200.00	Promoter Profit	$4,748.93
Internet	$0.00	$250.00	$0.00	$250.00	**Split Point**	$36,408.50
			Total Advertising	$2,810.00		
Catering Expenses	**Predicted Exp.**	**Actual Expense**	**Misc**	**Total**	**FINAL FIGURES**	
Catering In-House	$1,000.00	$108.00	$0.00	$108.00	Total Attend.	1633
Dinner Buy-Outs	$0.00	$340.00	$0.00	$340.00	**Gross**	**$48,990.00**
Groceries	$0.00	$475.31	$0.00	$475.31		
Lunch	$0.00	$0.00	$0.00	$0.00		
Aftershow	$0.00	$0.00	$0.00	$0.00	Tax %	9.25%
	$0.00	$0.00	$0.00	$0.00	Total Tax	$4,531.58
					NET	$44,458.43
			Total Catering	$923.31	Show Expenses	$31,659.56
General Prod. Expenses	**Predicted Exp.**	**Actual Expense**	**Misc**	**Total**	Promoter Profit	$4,748.93
Barricade	$400.00	$400.00	$0.00	$400.00	Split Point	$36,408.50
Box Office	$200.00	$200.00	$0.00	$200.00	% over split	85%
Catering Coordinator	$0.00	$0.00	$0.00	$0.00	Amount to share	$8,049.93
Local Production	$1,750.00	$1,750.00	$0.00	$1,750.00	**Artist overage**	**$6,842.44**
Production Manager	$150.00	$150.00	$0.00	$150.00		
Rent	$1,000.00	$1,000.00	$0.00	$1,000.00		
Runner	$150.00	$150.00	$0.00	$150.00		
Security	$900.00	$700.00	$0.00	$700.00		
Stagehands/Loaders	$600.00	$600.00	$0.00	$600.00		
Towels	$50.00	$50.00	$0.00	$50.00		
			Total General	$5,000.00		
			Total Advertising	$2,810.00		
			Total Catering	$923.31		
			Total Fixed Exp.	**$8,733.31**		

There are shows that go over budget all the time, but they usually go over budget because of the band's demands. If the promoter had a PA and lighting system budgeted for the show, but you demanded a lot more gear in your show advance—and the promoter agreed to it against his better judgment—then, of course, the final bill's going to be higher.

Always examine the original receipts for every show expense; don't look at photocopies, because they could be altered. However, you also have to keep in mind that a vendor could do a lot of business with the promoter and may be providing him with a receipt that's bogus so the promoter can inflate the show costs, thereby reducing the band's back-end earnings; you never know. Nevertheless, after doing your due diligence, there comes a point where you have to trust the promoter and accept his expense receipts as legitimate.

Once all of the show costs have been calculated, the promoter will add the bands' guarantees to those costs, and this will give him the total show costs. This next step, calculating the split point, is what confuses so many new tour managers most, but it isn't hard to do. Once you've determined the total show costs, you must next calculate 15 percent of the total show costs to give you the promoter's 15 percent promoter profit, and then you must add that 15 percent promoter profit to the total show costs. That gives you your split point. If your band's supposed to receive 85 percent of the profits, then they would receive 85 percent of the net profits beyond the split point.

Look at the example below:

> Show's gross potential: $20,000 (1,000 tickets sold at $20 each)
> Gross box office receipts: **$20,000 (sold out)**
> Total show costs: $15,000
> 15% promoter profit: $2,250
> Split point: $17,250
> Money to be split between band and promoter: $2,750
> **85% of profit to band: $2,337.50**
> Band's guarantee: $7,500
> Total earnings for band: **$9,837.50**
> Deposit paid to agent: $3,750
> **Amount picked up by band's road manager: $6,087.50**

The calculations above were simplified for the sake of the example. Tax is usually deducted from the gross box office receipts, and the split point is derived from the gross after tax amount, but the tax amount will always be listed on the promoter's settlement sheet.

The promoter's 15 percent profit is always added into the settlement so the promoter gets paid for promoting the show, but that doesn't always mean that he'll earn the money; sometimes his 15 percent promoter profit will be a negative number because the show lost money. In this case, there won't be any money left over to be split by the band and promoter. It may be possible that the promoter didn't lose any money, but he didn't make any money, either.

Look at the next example below:

Show's gross potential: $20,000 (1,000 tickets sold at $20 each)

Gross box office receipts: **$15,000 (750 tickets sold)**

Total show costs: $15,000

15% promoter profit: $2,250

Split point: $17,250

Money to be split between band and promoter: $0.00

85% of profit to band: $0.00

Band's guarantee: $7,500

Total earnings for band: **$7,500**

Deposit paid to agent: $3,750

Amount picked up by band's road manager: $3,750

As you can see from this example, the promoter didn't make a dime for all of his work. He grossed $15,000 and the total show costs were $15,000. He didn't even earn his 15 percent promoter profit, much less any extra money on the back end; and the band only made their $7,500 guarantee—no money on the back end.

Now look at the next example below:

Show's gross potential: $20,000 (1,000 tickets sold at $20 each)

Gross box office receipts: **$10,000 (500 tickets sold)**

Total show costs: $15,000

15% promoter profit: $2,250

Split point: $17,250

Money to be split between band and promoter: $0.00

85% of profit to band: $0.00

Band's guarantee: $7,500

Total earnings for band: **$7,500**

Deposit paid to agent: $3,750

Amount picked up by band's road manager: $3,750

Loss to promoter: $7,250

With this example, the promoter lost $7,250. This is what the settlement sheet would probably show. In reality, he actually lost $5,000, and he didn't earn his 15 percent promoter profit. He didn't get paid for his work, and he lost $5,000 on top of it. Many promoters—unless they're a big company with deep pockets—can't withstand losses like this for long until they go out of business; and that's not good for the promoter, the bands, or the music business as a whole.

When a promoter finds himself in this kind of situation, he may call the band's booking agent and ask for a reduction in the band's guarantee to help reduce some or all of his loss. If your booking agent does a lot of business with this promoter and has made money on other shows with the booking agent's other bands, he may talk the promoter into taking the hit, promising him that he'll "make it up to him" on the next show they do together.

If the promoter has endured a lot of losing shows recently and is on the verge of going down the financial drain, your booking agent may ask the band's manager if he'll authorize a fee reduction to help the promoter.

It's difficult for a band to take a reduction these days because of the high cost of touring, but this could be a promoter who has worked hard building the band's popularity in that market, and the manager may feel he deserves some help. It's a difficult decision to make, especially if it's a lot of money.

Giving the promoter a reduction could mean that the band's tour budget will now show a much bigger shortfall number, and that's never good, but if it's a promoter in a major market that's important to the band, the manager may decide to help him out to keep the relationship alive. It's always possible that the promoter could decide never to book the band again if the manager chose not to help him, completely disregarding his financial loss.

Take a look at the next example below:

Show's gross potential: $20,000 (1,000 tickets sold at $20 each)
Gross box office receipts: **$10,000 (500 tickets sold)**
Total show costs: $15,000
15% promoter profit: $2,250
Split point: $17,250
Money to be split between band and promoter: $0.00
85% of profit to band: $0.00
Band's guarantee: $7,500
Total earnings for band: **$7,500**
Deposit paid to agent: $3,750

275

Amount picked up by band's road manager: $0
Reduction given to promoter by band: $3,750
Loss to promoter: $3,500

As you can see from this example, the band gave the promoter a $3,750 reduction—half of the band's guarantee—to cover part of his loss. In reality, the promoter only lost $1,250 and he didn't make a dime of his 15 percent promoter profit. Essentially, he promoted the show for free and lost $1,250. Managers usually won't agree to a reduction unless the band's doing great business and can afford it. Sometimes a manager will agree to split the promoter's loss, in which case he'll still lose money, but his loss is less.

Some venues, such as the House of Blues chain in America, will have a flat "house nut" amount on the contract with no breakdown of show expenses. The house nut includes venue rent, sound and lighting, labor costs, advertising, and catering. This house nut amount is usually always the same for every show, and every booking agent knows it.

The House of Blues owns the venue, has an in-house restaurant that handles all of the catering, has a permanent staff for labor and house techs, and spreads their advertising budget across all of their shows by doing strip ads that list all or many of their upcoming shows. This house nut makes it easier for you at settlement because there aren't a lot of expense categories and hard receipts to examine.

Some show settlements will have many expense categories, while other shows will have much fewer expenses. As the band becomes more popular, they'll play larger venues, the show expenses will increase, and the settlement will become more complicated. At this point, a major act will often hire a tour accountant to deal with show settlements and the tour's daily accounting.

There are different kinds of deals that are sometimes negotiated between the promoter and booking agent. The promoter may cut a deal with the agent where the band receives a guarantee versus a percentage of the net box office receipts after expenses. This means that the band will get whichever one is greater. Sometimes the deal's cut so the band will receive a guarantee versus the gross box office box receipts, but this usually means that the guarantee will be lower. Some promoters will cut a door deal with the agent. This is a deal where the band's working for a percentage of the box office receipts with no guarantee at all. Unless the band's agent is extremely confident the show's going to sell well, this is never a good idea. The band could end up playing for free if no one comes to the show, and there's no guarantee negotiated.

You've now finished doing your show settlement, and it's time to send off your nightly report. Unless you've been told otherwise, this report should be sent to the manager, booking agent, and business manager. The leader of the band may also ask to be included in this report.

I always make sure the promoter emails me a copy of his settlement sheet as soon as we finish settlement. I'll enter the settlement figures into my reconciliation statement, showing paid attendance, any back end money earned, and what cash or checks, or both, I picked up for that show. Next, I'll add any cash that I picked up to the cash ledger in my accounting.

My nightly report is an email that includes the promoter's settlement sheet and my updated reconciliation statement. I don't bother sending a copy of the cash ledger because everyone will see what I picked up that night on the reconciliation statement, and the booking agent doesn't need to see the band's road accounting. The business manager—and the manager if he requests it—will get an updated copy of the cash ledger when I send her my weekly road reports.

After I attach the two files to my email, I'll type a short note telling them how much cash I picked up, the amount of any check I picked up and the final paid attendance. I'll also tell them how the show went and if the promoter took care of us and did his job well or not.

It's important, especially for the manager and agent, to know how the show went and whether or not the promoter did a good job. It keeps them informed about what's going on, they feel more connected to the tour, and they relax and worry less. The business manager's usually only concerned about the financial result of the show.

Always remember to send your nightly report. If for some reason you can't send it, be sure to at least send an email explaining why it's not coming that night and when you'll be sending it.

You won't have to worry about complicated show settlements in the beginning of your career, and you'll learn how to do them with more confidence and ease as you do more of them.

ADVANCING YOUR HOTELS

If your entourage is living on the bus, there's not as much to worry about when advancing your upcoming hotels, but if you do have hotel rooms on your days off, there are a few things you can do that will make it easier and more organized when you check in.

If I have a day off and my entourage has hotel rooms booked, I'll call the night before to advance the hotel. It's usually better to wait until after 6:00 p.m. to call them because they'll be able to better assess if they're going to be sold out that night, which will help to determine what time you'll be able to check into the rooms the next day. Two of the most important things I want to know when I call the hotel are where we'll be able to park the tour bus and what time we'll be able to check into the rooms.

You already know the hotel has bus parking because you confirmed that fact before you booked the hotel. If they didn't have bus parking, you wouldn't have booked rooms there unless it was your only option, but you do need to know exactly where to tell the driver to park when he arrives. Don't just go to bed after the bus leaves town and tell the driver nothing. He needs specific details (behind the hotel, in the lot across the street, in the space in front of the hotel reserved with orange cones) about where to park the bus at the hotel.

Call the hotel and tell them your name and that your group has reservations at the hotel the next day. Tell them that you're a musical group and will be arriving on a forty-five-foot tour bus with a fifteen-foot trailer attached—a sixty-foot-long vehicle. Ask the person on the phone to give you specific details about where your driver will park the bus. Is there a parking lot out back where they park buses and trucks? Is there a parking lot across the street? Will they reserve a space? Find out exactly where the bus is supposed to go. Be sure to remind them how big the bus is and that your driver will need to be able to enter and exit the parking area with no problems. You don't want your driver to drive into something he can't get out of.

Tell the front desk attendant on the phone your estimated time of arrival and ask if there's any reason that the driver wouldn't be able to park at that time. Ask them if they can reserve a space for the bus, blocking it off using orange street cones or sawhorses. Ask them if there's any kind of city parking permit that you'll need to get from the hotel and place on the windshield of the bus. This is sometimes the case when the bus is parking on the street, taking up multiple parking meters.

Build a rapport with the person on the phone. Tell them the bus driver will be ending a long drive when he arrives, and you just want to make sure that he'll have no problems with parking. Ask his or her name and make a note of it in your tour book below the hotel's contact info. Be polite, and you'll be surprised how accommodating the hotel will be most of the time.

After you've determined exactly where to park the bus, ask the attendant if he or she thinks your rooms will be ready at the time you're expected to arrive. Hotels always have an official check-in and check-out time. Most hotels will "officially" say that you can't check in until after 3:00 p.m. Hotels say this because they never know if the previous night's guests will check out early or stay in the rooms until the last minute before check-out time. Because of this, they don't know how early their housekeeping staff will get the rooms cleaned for the next guests.

If the hotel isn't sold out that night, the chances are more likely that you'll be able to check into the rooms earlier than their official check-in time. If the hotel's half full, and they know that they'll have clean rooms when you arrive, the hotel will have no problem checking your entourage into the hotel hours before their official check-in time, as long as you're not showing up at 4:00 a.m. If that's the case, they may expect you to pay for two days on the rooms. It never hurts to ask, but don't count on it.

If the hotel says they're sold out that night, it's unlikely that you're going to get into the rooms too early. If they're full that night, ask the hotel attendant if they can try to clean your rooms first so you can get your entourage checked in as soon as possible. Explain to them that your group hasn't had a day off in a few weeks and is really looking forward to a day off in their hotel. They'll probably give you some idea when you can expect to get your rooms, but nothing is guaranteed except the 3:00 p.m. official check-in time. Always ask the attendant to have the bus driver's room cleaned first since he's been driving all night and needs to get to bed. Then ask them to clean the band members' rooms next and then the rooms for you and the crew last. You'll have to specify which reservations are for the band members.

If you had a travel agent book the hotels for you, ask the hotel clerk if the travel agent has sent them your rooming list and special requests, such as no rooms near the elevators or on the ground floor. If they don't have the rooming list and special requests, ask them for their business email address so you can send them a copy. Unless you have more special requests than Elvis Presley, put them at the bottom of the rooming list so it's all on one sheet. Keeping it together on one sheet prevents your important special requests from being lost.

If you're staying at an economy hotel like the Econolodge, don't walk in there acting like you're Richard Cole with Led Zeppelin outside on the tour bus, acting pissed off because they forgot your red carpet, free champagne, and twenty-one gun salute. They don't give a damn that your band just won the Emo Battle of the Bands competition. You get what you pay for. If you expect to be treated like royalty, you need to buy rooms at hotels that have at least a one star rating.

Ask the front desk attendant if he'll be on duty the next day when you arrive. If he is, tell him that you'll ask for him when you arrive so you can get an update on what time you'll be able to check in. If he's not on duty, ask him the name of the front desk attendant who will be on duty and make a note of their name in your tour book.

Request that he give a copy of your rooming list to the attendant who will be on duty and tell him what time you're expected to arrive. Ask the attendant to fill out the rooming list with the appropriate room numbers and place a copy of the rooming list, any available hotel info sheets, and two copies of the room key in an envelope marked with each person's name and room number.

If the hotel's sold out, you may have to wait until they clean each room before they'll know what the room numbers will be. By that time, you'll probably be there waiting patiently in the lobby and helping them along with this process, possibly filling in the room numbers yourself as your entourage checks into each room.

Once you've obtained this information, be sure to tell the bus driver the specifics on where to park the bus when he arrives. If the hotel's sold out, tell him what time they think the rooms will be ready. If your estimated arrival time is 8:00 a.m. but the rooms aren't expected to be ready until noon, tell the driver that fact. If he's in no hurry to get to the hotel because the rooms won't be ready until noon, he may want to take his time and pace himself getting to the hotel. He may decide to find a truck stop along the way and stop for a nap since he won't have a room to check into when he arrives at 8:00 a.m. If he can't have his parking space until a certain time, he definitely doesn't want to show up early, because he won't have anywhere to park.

You should be awake when the bus arrives at the hotel so you can help the driver park the bus. You never know when the parking space the hotel has reserved for the bus is going to be a tight squeeze for the driver to get into, especially if he's pulling a trailer. He may need your help backing into it if you don't have a crew member who's capable of helping him.

Once the bus is parked, go and check in with the hotel's front desk attendant that you spoke with on the phone and politely introduce yourself. Explain to them that you realize the rooms probably aren't ready yet, but you just want to check and see how things are coming along. You never know when guests may have checked out early, and the housekeeping staff is ahead of the game and cleaning rooms fast. Your rooms could be ready much earlier than expected.

Tell the attendant you'll be sitting near the front desk and to let you know when each room is cleaned and ready so you can get your entourage into their rooms. Many times you can get into the rooms sooner if you are willing to accept double rooms with two beds instead of king singles with one bed.

Advancing your hotels properly will make your hotel check-in experience a lot easier and much more organized for you.

MERCHANDISING

It's all about merchandising now. When I first started in the music business nearly three decades ago, selling records was the name of the game. Today, with file-sharing and illegal downloading so prevalent, merchandising is how many music groups earn their living.

There are many "merch" companies that manufacture band merchandising. 11345.com, a division of HiFidelity Entertainment, produces official merchandise for Santana, Machine Head, Testament, and many others. FEA Merch and Global Merchandising Services are two other popular companies. FEA Merch provides merchandising services for bands such as Megadeth, Van Halen, and The Smashing Pumpkins. Global Merchandising Services has clients in all genres of music, including Slayer, Alice Cooper, Judas Priest, Bon Jovi, and Motorhead.

Unless you're doing double-duty as the merch guy on a tour, your involvement with merchandising sales will probably be minimal. In all of my years working as a tour manager, I've rarely had too much to do with it directly, and that's the way I prefer it. Often doing double-duty, the last thing I needed was another job to deal with.

Traditionally, a band will sign a merchandising deal with a merch company, and that company will design, manufacture, and sell the band's merch at shows, online, and in retail stores. They pay the band a royalty for each item sold, much like a recording contract.

The merch company's art department will create merch designs based upon ideas from the band. Once that art is approved by the band's organization, the merch company will print up what they think they'll sell on a tour. The merch company will then choose a merch guy from their company to go out on the road and sell the merch for the band.

The merch seller is employed by the merchandising company, but he also works for the band. If the band doesn't like the merch seller, or they don't feel he's doing a good job, they can have him replaced. No merchandising company is going to risk losing a band's account over a merch seller the band doesn't want to use.

The merch company pays for the merch seller's salary, per diem, plane tickets, and hotel. The band doesn't pay for any of those expenses, which is why you don't see them in the tour budget. However, unless the merch seller is driving the merch in a truck on the tour and staying in a hotel each day, you'll need to provide a bunk for him on the tour bus and make room for merch in your truck or trailer. So it's always important to find out how much merch stock your company is sending out at the beginning of the tour and make sure that you have enough room for it in your truck or trailer.

Most merch companies will send out an experienced merch seller who will always make sure the band's merchandising area is set up in a professional manner and do their best to sell as much merch as possible. The seller will complete their nightly paperwork detailing how much merch they sold, how much of a percentage they paid to the venue, and any taxes deducted.

They'll order more stock as it's needed, and have it sent out to venues down the line so it's waiting when you arrive in that city. The merch seller will email nightly reports to the merch company and the band's manager. They'll also copy you and the band on the report if you require it.

The tour manager's job in relation to the merch company is to provide them with the logistical information they need so they can perform their job. Always send them a copy of the tour book before the tour starts so they have the information needed to send out merch stock when necessary.

Always obtain in your show advance the venue merch percentages (the cut of your sales the venue receives) and find out if the venue merch personnel or your merch seller will sell the band's merch at the show. You merch seller will need to know this information. Some merch sellers will call the venues and do their own merch advance if they don't already have the info from previous shows they've done in that venue.

Your merch seller may sometimes come to you for help if he's having trouble with the venue. It's usually best if you get the promoter rep to deal with these issues when possible. Take yourself out of the equation when it comes to these things, if you can. The promoter's renting the venue, so ask him to deal with any problems relating to the venue.

Unless the band's not getting their nightly report from the merch seller or they feel he's not doing a good job or he's impossible to live with on the bus, you'll probably never hear too much about him.

There are some bands that do their own merchandising so they can make more money. I've worked with a few bands that do so. Some of them were painless and not much different from a conventional merch deal, and some of them were constant headaches for me because the band didn't have their act together. They were always running out of merch because they were placing orders for new stock too late, and the shipments didn't show up at the venue until after we'd already left for the next city because it shipped out too late. It can be challenging when a band tries to run a merchandising company.

When the band does their own merchandise, they'll usually hire a freelance merch seller for each tour. It's rarely someone who works full-time for the band unless the band's always on the road. Most of the groups I've worked with that do their own merch will have an American seller for their U.S. tours and a U.K. or European seller for those tours.

For short fly dates overseas, some American bands that do their own merch will simply bring the merch with them on the plane and have the venue provide someone to sell the merch for them. If the band has a merchandising deal with a merch company, the merch company will sort out who is going to sell the merch in those situations. It's not your worry.

If the band handles their merchandising, going into Canada is usually the biggest merch headache of the tour. If you plan to bring merch into Canada, you need to declare it at the border and pay duty. Like any government, Canada wants their cut of your sales. Some bands have been known to try and smuggle merch into Canada, hiding it in road cases so they don't have to pay the taxes. This is never a good idea. If the band gets caught, it will always be in the customs office's computer and they'll search you thoroughly every time you come back to Canada in the future. Plus, you run the risk of the band's merch being confiscated, the entourage denied entry into the country, and your shows canceled.

Some bands have been known to take what they think they'll sell on the Canadian shows into Canada and leave the rest of their stock in a hotel room on the U.S. side of the border and pick it up when they come back through into the U.S. However, this only works out when you're coming in and out of the same border. If you're playing shows across Canada and coming back into the U.S. through a different border, bands have been known to ship the rest of their merch on to the next U.S. city that they'll play after coming out of Canada.

As you can see, working with a band that runs a merch business can be problematic. If the band has a deal with a merch company, all of these headaches and logistics are the merch company's problem to deal with, not yours.

Some bands that do their own merch will sometimes hire a Canadian company to manufacture the merch they need for a Canadian tour, and they'll send it to the first venue and have the band's merch seller vend it at the shows. Or if it's a long Canadian tour and the band's not doing any U.S. shows, they may have the Canadian merch company manufacture the merch and send out one of their merch sellers to vend on the tour. There are various options that will work.

Forget about bootleggers. If you see them outside the venue in the U.S., have the promoter's security run them off or call the police. Don't get stabbed or shot over people selling t-shirts. It's not worth it. In places like Mexico and Italy, the cops don't even care. They'd probably arrest you for trying to stop bootleggers. It's the merch company's headache, anyway. And if your band's doing their own merch, it's not worth you or your band members getting hurt over.

If your band is new, you could find yourself having to deal with merchandising until they become popular enough that a merchandising company will want to sign a deal with them. Hey, don't expect the load to be a light one in the beginning when you're trying to build a career.

UNION VENUES

If your band's a new one on their first club tour, it's doubtful you'll be playing in too many union venues; but there are some things to know about them when you finally do.

IATSE is the International Alliance of Theatrical Stage Employees, Moving Picture Technicians, Artists and Allied Crafts of the United States, Its Territories and Canada. With a membership of over 110,000 members, they're the largest labor union in the entertainment and related industries and were formed more than a century ago.

On a music tour, IATSE members are the stagehands who help set up the show each day. This includes the loaders in the trucks, the stagehands who work on stage, the electrician who ties in your sound and lighting power, and the spotlight operators who run the spotlights during the show.

For IATSE members, being in the union is a good thing, but it may not always be a good thing for you. In strict union cities such as New York and Cleveland, your crew can't unload anything from your truck; only the union loaders can do it. Your crew can only direct where the cases go on stage. The stagehands will then set up the gear per your crew members' instructions.

The union crew only sets up equipment, such as stage sets, drum risers, and backline cabinets, anything that requires labor. The drum tech and guitar techs do their jobs stringing guitars and tuning drums. The union crew members don't do that. They union crew also assembles and stacks the PA and assembles the lighting rig under the direction of the sound and lighting crew. In many union cities it's not as strict, and your crew is able to be more hands-on, but they're usually all pretty firm about their union breaks and overtime.

Have you ever heard the one about how the band's production assistant couldn't plug in the singer's blow dryer because the union electrician had to do it? While I've never seen a union venue that was this ridiculous, I've had my fair share of union problems through the years. Almost all of these problems involved union spot operators.

During my years as Slayer's lighting designer, I'd call more spotlight cues in the first two songs than most lighting designers called in an entire show. The color of the spotlights had to match the color of the front lighting. When I changed cues and the front truss changed color, the spotlights had to do the same thing. It looked awesome and had a lot of impact, but it also wore out the older union spot operators who couldn't keep up with the fast pace.

Three hundred spotlight cues is a very large amount in a ninety-minute show. Plus, many of the union operators were older gentlemen with less than perfect hearing, and they simply couldn't deal with the monstrous volume of Slayer's sound. Some of them simply hated the music and just went into mental shutdown and flubbed cues constantly while feeling besieged and pinned to the back wall by Slayer's sonic attack. Hey, it ain't no fucking Dolly Parton show.

Today, I'd rather not even use spotlights. There are other options to utilize. Putting the success or failure of my show into the hands of others isn't the right way to go for me. If I'm in control of the entire lighting performance, I know what the final outcome will be. If I put part of it into the hands of others, it's a nightly crap shoot. Don't misunderstand me, some of the best spotlight operators I've ever used were union guys and gals, but I do metal bands and that's a whole other angry animal from Taylor Swift.

In Europe and the U.K., there's no stage workers union to deal with. Your bus and truck drivers can make extra money each night running the spotlights for your lighting designer. As a lighting designer for three decades, I've always loved this because I have the same spotlight operators each night. In a few shows, they know the cues before I call them. This isn't done in the U.S. because it wouldn't be allowed in union venues.

In the U.S., the show almost always ends by 11:00 p.m. in union venues because this is the union curfew. If the show goes beyond the union curfew, expensive union overtime charges can start to accrue. There are union breaks during the day where you'll have to go to a "dark stage," meaning no work at all can be done on stage. This can be a headache when you're behind schedule, but there's nothing you can do except deal with it.

There's always a union steward who's in charge of the local union crew, and he's the supervisor to go to with any problems or complaints. However, you're always better off to let your promoter rep deal with these situations because he probably works in that venue often and has a relationship with the union steward. He's more likely to get a problem solved to your satisfaction.

All you can do in a union venue is follow their rules and schedule, be polite and professional and do your job. More often than not, the union crew will do the same.

SURVIVING FLY DATES

Doing a string of fly dates can be one of the most exhausting things you'll ever do. You'll rarely do a lot of fly dates on a U.S. tour unless it's an important show you can't turn down and the tour buses can't make it in time. Fly dates happen more on tours of Europe, South America, or Australia, where some of the drives are so long that you must fly to make the show in time.

If a European tour is routed properly, you shouldn't have to do any fly dates, but sometimes during the spring and summer, there may be big festivals booked that can't be driven on the tour bus because the drives are too long. If this happens, you'll have to fly in for those shows, and the tour bus will pick you up down the line when the fly dates are done.

I've done Australian tours where we did five shows in a row, having to fly to each city on a show day after getting little sleep the night before and going straight to the next venue after we landed. Trying to do five shows in a row on three or four hours of sleep each night can be exhausting.

South American tours are always fly dates because there are no real tour buses over there, and the drives are impossible to do anyway because of the mountains and the long distances. Some bands can afford to do a South American tour where there's always a travel day between shows so they're never flying on a show day; but many groups are on a tight budget and need to work every day, so they fly on show days every day.

I've done some brutal South American tours where I never got any sleep and felt like a zombie the entire time I was there, but I've also done some great ones like Megadeth's four-week South American tour in the spring of 2010 where we always flew on a travel day. That's the best way to do it, if the band has the budget for it.

When you have to do fly dates on very little sleep, the more you prepare, the better off you'll be. If you're finishing a show and flying out early the next morning, you should have the tour bus take you to the airport so the entourage can get some sleep before you have to check in at the airport. Time it so the bus driver arrives at the airport about an hour before you have to check in—not an hour before the flight leaves!—so you have enough time to get your fly gear and luggage onto baggage carts and make it to the check-in desk on time.

You should be there to check in three hours before the flight departs for an international flight and two hours before a domestic flight departs, especially if you have a lot of gear and luggage to check in. The sooner, the better; it's always best to be early than late. You don't want an important show to go down the drain because you missed the flight. The road manager will be the person the manager blames if this happens.

Obviously, on fly dates, you'll be using rental gear the promoter provides. If backline isn't part of the deal the booking agent cut, then the band will have to rent it if their endorsers aren't providing it. However, you'll still have to take things, such as the band's guitars, cymbals, backdrop, scrims, and anything else that can't be rented that the band must have to do their show.

Some brands of gear can be hard to find in certain parts of the world, and you may have to make concessions in these situations. Always have an alternate choice for the gear you use. I always add a section to the tour rider listing the gear needed for fly dates, and I also list an alternate choice for each item if that gear isn't available.

If your band uses Marshall guitar cabinets and amps and Ampeg bass amps and SVT cabinets, you'll be fine most all of the time; it's some of the most common gear found around the world. However, your drummer may need to be flexible in the brand of drum kit he'll use when doing fly dates in certain parts of the world. Sometimes he might need to make concessions in the sizes of certain drums if he uses a large kit. Even the color he prefers may not be available sometimes. You should carry your own cymbals, or you run the risk of showing up and discovering that every cymbal on the drum kit has more cracks than the San Andreas Fault. Many drummers also prefer to carry their own kick drum pedals and a good snare drum. Always include in your rider a stipulation that says the drum kit must have new drum heads on every drum, and specify which heads your drummer prefers. You should also remember to advance a drum riser, and you must include this requirement in your fly gear specs in the rider.

Don't forget to advance any power transformers your band may need for gear you're bringing with you if the power in that country is different from your own. These devices should also be included in the fly gear requirements in the band's rider.

I also add to the rider a clause that says all of this gear is for my band's use only and not to be used by anyone else on the show. The promoter may not agree to this if your band isn't headlining the show, but it never hurts to try. This is important because if you're doing a show where ten other bands are using the gear before your group, the drum kit's going to be beat up worse than some poor bum who just went twelve rounds with Mike Tyson, and the blown up speakers in the guitar cabinets are going to sound worse than the distasteful fart scene in *Blazing Saddles*.

Always be certain that you've redone your truck or trailer pack the night before so everything you're taking with you on the plane is on the back of the vehicle. You want to be able to unload this gear quickly when you arrive at the airport so you can get to the check-in desk quickly. The bus may have to dump you in an area at the airport where it can't sit too long before the airport police are crawling all over it.

The promoter rep will usually arrange local transportation to pick up your entourage at the airport, providing the booking agent has included this as part of the deal, but this is usually the case. With most of the bands I've worked with, the booking agent will negotiate hotels, local transportation, and backline rental as part of the deal—many times airfare is included. Nevertheless, you'll still have to coordinate all of these things with the promoter rep and make sure he's done it all correctly. You must also get him to send you the applicable information for your tour book.

Many times the promoter will do his own tour book. The Japanese promoters almost always do this. If this is the case, then you can send him any pertinent info that you'd like to have included in his tour book. Make sure that he emails you a PDF copy of the tour book before you fly so you can forward it to the appropriate people in your organization.

When I'm working as a tour manager, I rarely get any sleep when doing fly dates. I'm just too afraid to go to sleep for fear of not hearing the alarm go off and missing the plane. I'd rather stay awake and get what little sleep I can on the plane. I've done fly dates before where I sat in the hotel lobby while the band and crew got a few hours sleep in their rooms. I'd sit in a chair near the front desk and ask the hotel front desk attendant to wake me up when it was time for me to wake up the entourage, if I fell asleep in the chair. However, you should still always set the alarm on your smart phone.

No matter what you do on a fly date, don't rely on the band and crew to wake up to an alarm clock or a hotel wakeup call; they'll sleep right through it if they're beat up from no sleep. You need to call each room and make sure they're awake when they're supposed to be up. If they don't answer the phone in the hotel room or their cell phone, then you need to go and start beating on their door.

When you're on tour in Australia, for example, you'll usually have the promoter rep traveling with you from city to city. This is a great help, and the promoter rep will handle many things for you, such as paying the hotel bill, coordinating the local transportation and helping you check in the entourage at the airport. The same goes for touring in Japan. You'll almost always travel on the bullet train—Japan's high speed train that links all of their major cities—and the promoter rep (also called the promoter tour manager) also acts as your interpreter. Depending on the size of the show, the Japanese promoter will often provide each band with their own "minder," who also acts as their interpreter.

Depending on the size of the tour and whether or not it's the same promoter handling all of the shows, you may or may not have the same promoter rep traveling with you throughout a South American tour, but there will always be a promoter rep taking you to the airport when you leave a city and another promoter rep meeting you when you land in the next city.

You can make fly dates much less painful for you and your entourage by making sure you've covered every base and coordinated well with your promoter rep. Strong coffee will be your best friend.

FOREIGN CURRENCIES

On January 1, 2002, the Euro went into circulation in Europe.

American tour managers today have it easier than we had it back in the '80s and '90s when doing a European tour. Back then there was no Euro; every country had a different currency and accounting was a lot more complicated. You spent a lot of time going through expense receipts and recalculating the German mark, French franc, Dutch guilder, Italian lira, Spanish peseta—to name only a few—into U.S. dollars so your road accounting made sense.

Scandinavia is home to Denmark, Sweden, Norway, Finland, and Iceland. Scandinavian countries, such as Sweden (krona), Denmark (krone), Iceland (krona), and Norway (krone), still use their own currency—Finland now uses the Euro—but a tour manager's accounting duties are much easier since the Euro came to be.

There's nothing to be afraid of when dealing with expense receipts that were paid for with foreign currencies. If you did a show in Stockholm, Sweden, and you exchanged one hundred U.S. dollars into Swedish kronas to buy guitar strings and you had to add that expense receipt into your road accounting, you would simply convert the expense amount from kronas into U.S. dollars using the exchange rate that you received when you exchanged the money.

Frankly, it makes life a lot easier when you can pay for things like this with a band credit card so you don't have to worry about exchanging money, and you'll usually get the better exchange rate and not have to pay any exchange fees. You can always go into your credit card's online account and see what the expense amount became, after it was converted into your home currency, when you're ready to enter that receipt into your credit card accounting.

If you exchange cash to pay for these expenses, you may have foreign currency left over when you leave the country. Then you have to worry about exchanging that money back into your home currency later on, and you'll lose money with the exchange fees. You should only exchange what you think you're going to use. This is another reason why using a band credit card is always the best option.

When exchanging the band's money into foreign currency, always try to find a major bank. You'll usually get the best rates there, while exchanging money at airport exchange kiosks gives you a lower rate and the commission can be very high at some of them. The hotels are usually even worse. If you have an ATM card for the band's bank account, always use that if you need emergency cash because you'll get the best exchange rate, and the same goes for you and your ATM card.

CROSSING CRAZY BORDERS

In the fall of 2006, I decided to try something I'd wanted to attempt for a long time: I got my CDL (commercial driver's license) and began to drive a tour bus for my old friend Sandy Stein at Coast to Coast Coach in Lancaster, California. I drove many of Sandy's buses for almost two years, and I had a great time doing it, with the exception of a nasty confrontation with a hotel's brick wall and a telephone pole, and two difficult tours that were run by new road managers.

Near the end of my driving career, I had an *interesting* experience that will drive home the sharp point of this chapter. It was November 2008, and I had pretty much stopped driving a tour bus and was back doing the tour manager/lighting designer gig for my long-time client Testament. I was at home enjoying some time off the road when Sandy Stein called me up and asked me if I'd be willing to fly into Chicago, Illinois, and do a double-drive up to Saskatoon, Canada, with his bus driver, who was driving a popular heavy metal band that shall remain nameless to protect the guilty.

The bus driver had to drive thirteen-hundred and fifty miles across one travel day from Chicago to the band's next show in Saskatoon, a small city out in the middle of nowhere between Winnipeg and Edmonton. Now, that's not an impossible journey for one driver to do, but a bad snowstorm was expected along the route. I had already driven the Long Beach Dub Allstars—the living remnants of Sublime—nine hundred and thirty-five miles from Vail, Colorado, through a blizzard to Long Beach, California, in twenty hours on my own, so I wasn't afraid of this long double-drive in bad weather.

I was getting bored sitting at home in Richmond, Virginia, so I agreed to fly in and do the double-drive. I also wanted to do it because one of my best friends was the band's new road manager. This was his first time doing the job, but he'd done many tours with me in another capacity, so I was very curious to see how he'd do on his first tour as a road manager.

Once we'd begun our journey, and I was behind the wheel doing my first shift of the drive, my friend sat with me and we spoke of old times while I drove. At one point in the conversation, after remembering how much my friend loved his weed, I reminded him that we'd soon be crossing the Canadian border. I asked him how many people on the bus did drugs. He promptly replied, "No one does any drugs at all, except for me; but I'll get rid of my weed before we reach the border."

We drove north as the snow began to fall.

Before we reached the Canadian border crossing at Pembina, North Dakota, I stopped at a truck stop to get fuel because the cost of diesel was lower in the U.S. It also gave me a chance to take a short break and allow the entourage to get some food before we resumed our long drive, which was becoming more difficult as the bad weather grew worse.

Once I got back on the highway, I asked my friend if he'd remembered to get rid of his weed. He replied, "Yes, sir. As much as it pained me, I tossed it in the garbage can at the truck stop." I reminded him to do a good cleaning of the bus to remove any possible weed residue or anything else that a border drug dog could detect. He promised me that he'd complete this important chore.

The snowstorm began to worsen, and driving became more dangerous. I needed to get the entourage to Saskatoon in time for noon load-in the next day, but the bad weather was slowing me down considerably. By the time we reached the Canadian border, we were in the midst of a full-blown blizzard.

Driving in bad weather wears you out a lot quicker than driving on clear roads. I looked at my watch and realized it was almost midnight. Knowing full well that some of these smaller Canadian border crossings are not open twenty-four hours, I asked my friend if he'd checked to make sure the border crossing was open all night. He hadn't remembered to do it.

My stress level increased two notches. Driving on iced earth is one thing; but hauling ass through the creepy Dean Koontz darkness of the night while worrying about slamming into a dumb Canadian moose stupidly hanging out in the middle of the road and careening over a high cliff to a fiery, pig-squealing death is a whole other matter.

If the border was closed from midnight to 8:00 a.m., there'd be no chance of us making a noon load-in the following day, since we still had another six hundred miles to drive through what was turning into a very scary snowstorm. We wouldn't have made it to the venue until 9:00 p.m., in which case the first show of the Canadian tour would've been canceled.

I finally pulled up to the Canadian border crossing a few minutes past midnight, and my friend and I walked inside the office to begin processing the entourage into Canada. The border guards were not happy to see us, because they were about to close the office until 8:00 a.m. and go home for the night. My friend knew he was going to be in deep trouble with the band if we had to sit there at the border for the next eight hours and miss the Saskatoon show. He pleaded with the border guards to process us into Canada so we could continue our journey. After a bit of tense complaining, the border guards begrudgingly agreed to process the entourage into Canada. The tour manager was told to get the entourage off the bus and bring them inside for processing; and that's when the trouble began.

When your tour bus or van attempts to cross into Canada, you can almost always be assured they're going to check your vehicle for drugs. A music group should always assume this is going to happen every time and prepare for it. Clean your tour bus from top to bottom—no, the bus driver won't do it for you—if anyone has been doing drugs of any kind in the vehicle, and don't smoke weed right before you arrive at the border because you'll never get rid of the smell in time. You'd have to be completely paralyzed from that shit and have fuzzy fruit salad for a brain to think otherwise. Wake up.

While the entourage waited in the immigration office and the border guards checked us out for criminal records in their computers, the rest of the guards searched our bus for drugs and other contraband. As I looked at my watch, realizing that their search was taking a lot longer than it normally does, I turned to my tour manager friend sitting beside me and said, "Bro, this is taking a long time, and that's happening for a reason. Are you sure you got everything off that bus?" He looked at me with worried eyes and replied, "To be honest with you, when I cleaned the bus, I couldn't find my pipe."

Just as he said those words, a female border guard walked into the office carrying my friend's pipe in her hand. Slowly shaking my head, I looked at him and said, "Well, they just found it for you." My friend was far from happy. What happened after that was one of the worst Canadian border crossings of my entire career, and I've done more than I could ever hope to remember.

For the next four hours, we sat in the immigration office while they turned our bus upside down; and we were told we had to wait for the *canine* to arrive. They said the drug dog and the border guard who took him home every night would arrive in about ninety minutes, delayed by the storm, of course. None of us were allowed to use the restroom because they believed some of us probably had drugs shoved down our pants and would flush them down the toilet if given the chance.

Once the drug dog—a frightening beast of German descent that I could easily see terrorizing prisoners at Stalag 13—and his handler arrived, we were all told to form a long line so the canine could walk down it and sniff each of us for drugs. Before doing so, the border guard warned us that the dog would also be sniffing our crotches, and if he smelled drugs, he could get very excited and possibly bite us in our happy parts, so if we had any drugs hidden in our underwear, it would be a smart idea to hand them over now. I thought of Mike Tyson dropping Michael Spinks, slowly clenched my fist, and tried to imagine what part of my living room wall I was going to hang this dog's jaw on after it came back from the taxidermist … after I got out of a Canadian prison, of course.

I knew I didn't have any drugs on me—hell, I hadn't done cocaine in two years—but the thought of going back home to Richmond without my testicles because they'd been gnashed off at the bloody roots by Canadian Cujo had me slightly concerned. Since we'd all been deprived of using the toilet for quite some time, I had to piss desperately and was in a lot of pain. If the little four-legged fucker had bit my precious prick, a tsunami of piss would've blown him back to the fatherland.

The canine snitch went down the line and sniffed everyone in the entourage and found nothing, although he seemed to have a special fondness for the sound engineer's genitals. Still determined to find the massive cache of drugs that we had to be smuggling into Canada, the border guards then made us empty every piece of luggage from the tour bus and take it into a nearby building where they thoroughly searched it all. That was a first.

Finally coming to grips with the agony of defeat, the Canadian border guards threw in the towel and said to us, "At this point, we have enough with the pipe to refuse you entry into Canada." The band became very agitated, knowing full well that being denied entry into Canada would force the cancelation of four sold-out Canadian shows and cost them a small fortune in lost income. One of the border guards held up the pipe and said, "Whoever this belongs to had better own up to it now."

The entire entourage turned and looked at my tour manager friend, and he knew then and there that he had no choice but to confess to being the owner of the pipe. Now hours into the ordeal, he'd become more unwelcome on the tour than Hamas in a synagogue.

My young tour manager friend confessed to being the owner of the pipe, and we were finally allowed to enter Canada as the snowstorm continued to come down on us hard. My friend was very lucky that night. He could've been arrested. He also set himself up to be thoroughly searched and harassed every time he comes into Canada in the future.

Do I need to speak anymore about how it's extremely important to make sure your vehicle is cleaned spotless before crossing any border? Have you gotten the sharp point?

In case you're wondering, we arrived in Saskatoon five hours late for load-in. To say the crew had to do a quick "throw-and-go" was an understatement, and the vibe amongst the entourage was not a good one. I got paid, said goodbye to my friend, and went to my hotel to spend the night and fly home the next morning.

That was the last run I ever did as a tour bus driver. I decided to just stick with doing my gig as a tour manager and lighting designer. Since then, I've been in and out of Canada many times with Megadeth, Anthrax, and Testament with no problems.

It's important to make sure your paperwork is in order before you arrive at the Canadian border. The Canadian promoter rep will send your immigration paperwork to the border so it's there when you arrive. He'll usually send an immigration manifest, like the one I've taught you how to create, and a letter explaining that your group's coming into the country to do shows promoted by his company. He'll also include copies of the show contracts as further proof of your performances in the country.

You should always have a copy of the promoter's paperwork and the gig contracts with you just in case you show up at the border and the immigration officer says they didn't receive the paperwork from the promoter. It's rare that this happens, but it's better to be prepared than have to waste hours sitting at the border trying to run down the promoter so he can send over the paperwork again, especially if you're crossing the border in the middle of the night. If you come into their office acting like you own the place, they can lie and say they don't have your paperwork just to cause you some pain.

Always be polite at any border crossing and act like a professional. You'll almost always have to bring your entourage off the bus when crossing in and out of Canada, but there have been times in recent years when I've been able to talk the border guards out of doing this in the middle of the night. I'll just tell the border guard the band had a bad show tonight and they're dead-tired and ask him if there's any way that I can just show him their passports without waking them all up. I've been able to get away with this a few times. It's becoming practically impossible now due to terrorism, but it never hurts to try. Your chances of doing this are greatly increased if you're an American band coming back into America, but don't count on it.

Now that the borders in most of Europe have opened up and you no longer have to stop the tour bus to cross them, it's a lot easier touring Europe. While I certainly don't recommend that anyone carry drugs on a tour bus, some bands still do it; and many times the rest of the people on the bus don't know they're doing it. I'm not a preacher or a drug counselor; do your thing, but watch where you do it.

Back in the late '90s, I was the tour manager and lighting designer for a very popular metal band, and we'd just ended a long European tour and were driving to England to fly back home to the U.S.

When we arrived at the border in Dover, England, after crossing over on the ferry from Calais, France—you now go through immigration on the French side of the English Channel at Calais—the singer refused to come out of the back lounge of the band's tour bus and into the immigration office to be processed into the U.K. He was drunk and thought he could get away with this rock star silliness. If he'd been Robert Plant or Mick Jagger, he might have had an eency weency spider's chance in hell of accomplishing this impossible mission, but the U.K. border patrol wasn't having it.

The border guards then proceeded to make every person—band and crew—on both tour buses sit outside on the curb while they tore each bus apart. They brought on the drug dogs, put cameras down into the toilets, and even pulled the panels off the walls to see if we were hiding drugs in the walls.

Now, it didn't matter if they truly thought we were carrying drugs or not; they were doing this to cause us extreme pain because our singer had decided to have his drunken diva moment. In the end, they found nothing in their search, but that entire affair could've caused us to miss our flight back home, and it could've snowballed into a painful ordeal for all involved if the next flights out had no available seating for us.

You can't arrive at any international border acting the fool and making a spectacle of yourself, thinking you can do whatever you want because you're in some band. Believe me, these immigration people have seen the biggest and the best come through their gates, and they're not impressed by anything except good manners.

WORKING DOUBLE-DUTY ON A TOUR

For a large part of my career, I've worked double-duty as both a tour manager and lighting designer. I started out as a lighting designer in 1983, and five years later, I decided I also wanted to work as a tour manager so I could earn additional money and get more tours.

Not only do you make more money by doing two jobs on a tour but you increase your options for more work. Many bands are always looking for people who can do double-duty because it saves them money. If you work as a tour manager/lighting designer or tour manager/sound engineer, the band usually isn't paying you two salaries for doing two jobs; they're paying a salary and a half, sometimes less, depending on your negotiating skills and their budget. Hiring someone who can do double-duty also benefits them because they only have to pay for the travel expenses of one person, not two. Someone who can do double-duty effectively is a valuable employee to the band, especially in this day and age when the costs of touring are always increasing.

Even though a sound engineer, lighting designer, or backline tech with a desire to do double-duty may be working on the road and seeing a tour manager do his job every day, that doesn't necessarily mean they have a complete understanding of what the road manager's job really entails. Oh, some of them think they do, until they jump into the hot seat and quickly realize they've taken a job they're not yet qualified for; and then they either lose confidence in themselves and fail miserably or just get fired. I've probably done five thousand rock concerts with sound engineers over the past three decades, and I have limited knowledge of how they do their jobs each day, but I have no interest in being a sound engineer, so I only know what I need to know to operate effectively with them each day. Don't ever take on a job without first getting some knowledge and training, unless you're a glutton for pain and ridicule.

One of the first things I learned when I started doing double-duty was how organized I needed to be every day. I had to implement a daily system that helped me get all of my duties completed on time. Eventually, an internal clock grew inside me that helped me get everything done on time each day, and that internal clock grew from on-the-job training and experience.

299

No book is going to teach you everything you need to know to become a tour manager, sound engineer, or lighting designer, but an informative book is a damn good start. However, your best training comes from doing the job on the road every day once you've gained some knowledge. I truly believe there's no substitute for on-the-job training.

I spent the first few years of my career as a tour manager conning people into believing I knew what I was doing while I struggled to learn how to do the job. I wish I had had a book like this back in the '80s; at least I would've started that first tour doing double-duty with a lot more knowledge and confidence. If you study the information in this book, it will give you a rock-solid foundation from which to start that I never had when I began my career, and that's a valuable thing to have.

If you're about to do double-duty on your first tour, sit down and make a detailed checklist in your computer of all the duties you must perform each day for both of your jobs. Separate your things to do by an exact timeline that shows the specific time of day when each of those duties must be completed. The checklist should be divided by four important daily milestones:

1. sound check
2. time for doors to open
3. show time
4. bus call (time to leave for the next city)

List all of the important tasks you must get done by the time each of these important milestones occurs. Be specific on your list, but don't make the list so detailed that it's too difficult to read at a glance. Make it more of a list of important things to do.

Below is an example that will help you to create your own list. It's by no means a complete list of everything you'll have to do each day, but it is a list of the usual important daily milestones to give you an idea of how to create a list for you.

Print out a copy of the checklist and refer to it until you've done these daily tasks enough times that the internal clock has grown inside you, guides you, and you get your daily duties done without even thinking about them. This will come through on-the-job training and experience.

Don't ever start doing double-duty on a tour until you've learned what a tour manager's job entails and you've worked out a plan for accomplishing all of your daily duties on time each day. Without this, you're destined to fail, and what's the point in starting something if you know it's going to end badly? Doing double-duty shouldn't be like rolling dice at a craps table in Las Vegas, hoping you're going to win. Hedge your bets for success by doing your homework and formulating a smart, solid plan so you won't fail.

12:00 PM	Load-in
	check out stage
	set up production office
	send out laundry to wash and fold
	order lunch for entourage
	sort vehicle parking for support acts
	assign dressing rooms
	post signs and sheets
	make sure dressing room catering will be set up on time
	have bus coolers iced down
	do your duties for second job: tune PA, program lighting console
	get ticket count from promoter rep
	get band ready to do press
	start guest list and passes
	answer emails
	get dinner buyout from promoter rep and disperse
	start band press
	do your duties for second job: do line check or focus lighting rig
	clear room for sound check
	finish press and bring band in for sound check
4:00 PM	**Sound Check**
	finish sound check
	do meet-and-greets
	have runner get band dinner if show is a buyout
	answer emails
	finish guest list and passes and give to promoter rep
	get ticket count from promoter rep
	make sure venue is clear and announce doors opening
7:00 PM	**Doors Open**
	begin to examine promoter expense receipts
	have bus coolers iced down again
	do your daily accounting
	make sure stage manager gets support act started on time
	check on band
	answer emails
	give band one-hour to showtime call
9:30 PM	**Showtime**
	check on band after show is over
	do show settlement
	give security okay to let guests back stage
	pack up production cases
	receive after show food and take to bus
	pack up dressing room cases
	round up entourage to leave town
	do a head count before bus leaves
2:00 AM	**Bus call**
	post tomorrow's sheets in front and back lounge of bus

Performing two jobs on a music tour can be a stressful thing for anyone. Believe me; I've got the gray hairs to prove it. However, I've learned through the years that being unprepared is what causes stress most often. Trying to do a your job while knowing deep inside that you haven't advanced the show properly and you're not sure what to expect causes fear, and fear breeds stress.

If I have my act wired tight, there's not much that's going to rattle me, but if I've let things slip through the cracks and I'm uninformed about certain aspects of a show, I'm going to be stressed out and possibly take it out on those around me. That's never a good thing, and you shouldn't let that happen. Again, I speak from experience.

Waking up hung over from too much hell-raising the night before also has a way of making you feel like you're not in control of yourself and your job, and that loss of control breeds stress. You must do things to ensure your success, not guarantee your failure. Performing one job on a tour is hard enough; you don't need to tie one hand behind your back when trying to do two jobs by doing things that stress you out and cause you to not be in control of you and your duties because you feel as if you're on your deathbed. Remember, you're supposed to be in charge.

Possessing the ability to perform two jobs on a tour can elevate your career, make you more money, and keep you working more often. Take advantage of this opportunity for advancement by being highly organized and learning what you need to know to do both jobs successfully.

SUPPORTING A BIGGER BAND

I started in the music business as a lighting designer in 1983. My first client was a heavy metal band called Steeler, featuring singer/guitarist Ron Keel and Swedish guitar whiz Yngwie Malmsteen. We all lived together in a roach-infested warehouse we called Steeler Mansion that was converted into a rehearsal studio and living quarters on the corner of South Palm Grove Avenue and Washington Boulevard in a rough Los Angeles neighborhood that became scarier than *Night of the Living Dead* once the sun went down. Just walking two blocks to the liquor store for beer—cloaked in denim and leather with sky-high hair—made you feel as unpopular as Osama bin Laden sitting down for soup in a New York deli.

They don't sell no goddamn Aquanet in this liquor store, punk rock muthafuckahs!

Before I met Ron Keel, I used to photograph rock bands playing in Hollywood, California; shooting rock concerts was fun to me. I finally met Ron at The Roxy Theatre on the Sunset Strip when he realized I was the guy in the crowd shooting Steeler every time they performed. We became friends, and my live photos became three of the four live shots on the cover of Steeler's self-titled debut album. The band recorded one record, Ingwie left the group to join Graham Bonnet's band Alcatraz, and Ron disbanded Steeler and started a new band called Keel.

Keel released their debut album, *Lay Down the Law*, on Shrapnel Records, and then signed a major label deal with A&M Records. They released their debut record, *The Right to Rock*, produced by Gene Simmons of Kiss, in March of 1985. Practically overnight, Keel became the opening act to the stars, supporting major bands such as Dio, Bon Jovi, Motley Crue, Krokus, Accept, Van Halen, Aerosmith, and Quiet Riot.

I got lucky when I first started out. I didn't have to spend years traveling in stinky vans and overcrowded motor homes with struggling baby bands playing every shithole in America. Keel took off from the get-go, and we were playing big gigs around the world in a very short time. Believe me when I say that I've never forgotten how lucky I was. It's part of the reason why I wrote this book to help to new guys—and gals—starting out at the bottom, traveling across the country in a rickshaw, playing to three people a night trying to build a career. However, even though I was lucky and my career took off quickly, I had the immense pressure of having to learn how to do the job much faster than most people had to—rise to the occasion or be replaced and left behind. And I wasn't about to be left behind. There was no way in hell I was going back to West Virginia to work in a coal mine.

One day I was performing the light show for Keel in popular L.A. clubs, and the next day I was standing in front of lighting consoles in arenas all over the world, trying to figure out what the fuck I was doing; but that was the fast track on-the-job training that started my career and taught me what I needed to know. Luckily for me, I also had a talent for it. I'll never forget that crazy, yet wonderful, time in my life, but I made a lot of mistakes in the beginning and learned the job the hard way because I had no one to teach me the right way to do things.

Back in the early '80s, I was the King Kong of heavy metal posers gone bananas, and I cut a path of fashion destruction down the Sunset Strip like no other. I wore white leather Lemmy boots, black stretch jeans, a black leather jacket, and enough silver studded belts and wrist bands to fill a rock shop on Melrose Avenue. Hell, I even had a big, curly perm. Oh, piss off; I was making a fashion…something.

One of the first *lessons* I learned in the beginning of my career happened at the Hollywood Palladium in 1985. Keel had built a loyal following in Hollywood, and the band Dokken had done the same but were more popular than Keel. They were already a touring act and were becoming bigger every day, selling a lot of records. A promoter in L.A. asked Keel to do a co-headline show with Dokken at the Hollywood Palladium, and Dokken would close the show.

Keel's two managers, Tim Heyne and Ray Chambers, made an agreement with the promoter stipulating that Keel would have full use of the sound and lighting system with no restrictions, co-headline all the way. The Keel entourage and I arrived at the venue on the day of the big show, ready to blow Dokken off the stage and show everyone in Hollywood who was the better band with the better show; or so we thought.

It was a big show for Keel. I was nervous that day, and I'd put a lot of pressure on my shoulders to do the best job I could that night. I had never met Dokken's lighting designer Paul Dexter, but I knew of him; he was one of the best lighting designers in the business. I stood near the lighting console in that famous venue, where I'd seen many great shows, while Paul finished programming Dokken's show. At some point, I'm sure he realized that the sad fashion-misguided bastard sweltering in the silver stud-covered walking leather sauna who'd been watching him for the past hour was the *lighting designer* for Keel.

Once Paul was done programming Dokken's show, I introduced myself. Even though Paul was polite to me, I could sense that he knew right away that I didn't know too much. He began to show me on the lighting console what Keel was allowed to use, but what he was showing me was not the entire lighting rig. I immediately became indignant and explained to him the agreement that had been made, which allowed Keel to use all of the lighting and PA with no restrictions. Paul smiled at me and said, "The agreement said that you could use all of the lighting that the promoter paid to bring to bring in. The rest of this lighting gear was paid for by Dokken out of their pocket, and you're not allowed to use that."

I wasn't very happy with this scandalous revelation, so I walked backstage to the promoter's office and began to complain as my shiny metal outfit blinded everyone who dared gaze upon it. While the promoter rep tried to muster every ounce of diplomacy and patience possible, I could tell he was becoming exasperated with dealing with some amateur who didn't understand how things worked, but he did his best to explain the reality of the sorry situation to me.

Right about then, an angry-looking man walked into the production office and began to listen to our conversation. Suddenly he said to me, "Listen, you poser, this is how it is, and that's all there is to it. Get over it," and he walked out of the room. I soon learned that the man was Rick Sales, Dokken's tour manager.

I stood outside the backstage door of the Palladium and debated the simple pros and cons of putting that rude cocksucker in an L.A.P.D. chokehold and strangling him to death, but I decided it wouldn't be a good start to the evening, so I let it go. At that point, I knew that I wasn't going to get anywhere with my futile argument—we'd been fucked—but I learned a big lesson in how to handle the bigger acts above us and the nefarious shit they can pull on you.

On paper, the Hollywood Palladium gig was a co-headline show, but in reality Dokken was more popular and had money to spend on extra production. Even though Keel had a great show that night, I drove home never wanting to be in such a predicament ever again.

A few months later, Keel was offered their first tour of Europe and the U.K. supporting the heavy metal band Dio. Fronted by the legendary Ronnie James Dio, Dio was touring in support of their *Sacred Heart* record. We were thrilled to be going to Europe for the first time; and to be going there opening up for a true legend like Ronnie Dio was the greatest news Keel could've received.

When we landed in Helsinki, Finland, to start the tour, the Chernobyl nuclear disaster had just happened. The media was full-bore in winding up the public all over Europe, and every news broadcast was about nothing but nuclear fallout blowing across Europe: don't drink the contaminated milk; only eat canned vegetables; the end is finally near. Keel didn't care about nuclear fallout and contaminated milk and vegetables. As long as they had beer, hairspray, and a show to do, we weren't leaving Europe. Everyone was worried the tour would be cancelled, but Ronnie Dio didn't want to let his fans down, so we did the tour and rocked it hard across Europe and the U.K., gonorrhea notwithstanding.

On the first show day, I walked out to the lighting console to introduce myself to Dio's lighting designer and see what I'd be allowed to use in the lighting rig each day. What I saw sucked every ounce of enthusiasm from the bottom of my desolate soul.

Standing behind the lighting console, programming the light show for Dio, was none other than Dokken's lighting designer Paul Dexter. I just stood there in the darkness of the arena, shaking my head, knowing full well that I was completely and utterly fucked for the next four weeks. The only thing that would've made that day even worse would be to see Dokken's rude-ass road manager Rick Sales walking across the venue floor.

Can someone sprinkle a little nuclear fallout on my perm?

But that incident at the Hollywood Palladium had happened months ago; maybe Paul Dexter wouldn't remember me. So, I rolled the dice and walked up to him and said, "Hey, Paul. I'm Mark Workman, Keel's lighting designer." He smiled at me and replied, "Hollywood Palladium."

Not good.

However, Paul accepted my sincere apology, knowing full well that I was as greener than Johnny Rotten's teeth. He was fair with me, gave me enough gear to do a good show, and never mentioned the Hollywood Palladium calamity ever again.

Through the years, I've always said the only lighting designer who ever had any real influence on me as a lighting designer in my formative years was Paul Dexter. I learned a lot about creating big theatrical looks from watching him light Dio's castle and dragon stage set and seamlessly linking them all together with clockwork timing to create a real rock and roll light show. Ten years later, I worked for Ronnie Dio as his lighting designer on a U.S. tour in support of his *Strange Highways* record.

The real king of rock and roll, Ronnie James Dio, died of stomach cancer on May 16, 2010.

Five years after the Dokken debacle at the Hollywood Palladium, I went after the Slayer lighting designer gig right as their *South of Heaven* record was about to be released. I loved the band's music, and I wanted that gig badly.

Eager to land the client, I did my research and found out who managed the band and was instantly depressed to learn that it was Rick Sales, Dokken's road manager, who had treated me like dirt at the Hollywood Palladium.

Can I get another dose of radioactive fallout, please?

Luckily for me, Rick Sales didn't remember the Dokken show at the Hollywood Palladium. I had toned down my wardrobe a bit, and my perm had long since been ensconced in the Horrible Hairdo Hall of Fame. He hired me as Slayer's lighting designer, and I worked for the band for many years.

The smartest words a manager ever said to me came from Rick Sales more than twenty years ago. It was during a night of partying at Kerry King's bachelor party—the guitarist for Slayer.

Rick said to me, "Mark, what do you think is the most important part of my job as Slayer's manager?"

More interested in the two porn stars I'd hired for Kerry's party, I said, "I don't know, Rick."

"The most important part of my job as Slayer's manager is to keep the illusion alive that they're much bigger than they really are."

I've never forgotten those words. They came from a smart man who can be the biggest son of a bitch on the planet when he wants to be, but he's a manager to be respected.

Those words, more than twenty years later, became a self-fulfilling prophecy now that Slayer has become a 100 percent bona fide heavy metal legend. Nothing annoys me more than writers who use the words *legend* and *legendary* like dice thrown across a craps table, but the legendary Slayer is the real fucking deal.

Believe me, when this world is about to implode and someone sends a spacecraft to another world with the remnants of what once was from this hopeless ball of shit, media with *Angel of Death* will be on that spacecraft to show the world the greatest example of thrash metal. There is no better example. And Rick Sales will always be written in the history books when it comes to this genre of music.

Twenty-five years later, Rick Sales is still the manager of Slayer. Unless he has compromising photos of the four Slayer band members in a drunken Satanic hot tub orgy with a gaggle of midget porn stars locked up in his safety deposit box, he must be doing a damn good job. It's rare for a band to have the same manager for that long. Most groups will go through half a dozen or more managers in that length of time, but most bands don't survive for twenty-five years like the kings of thrash metal, Slayer, has done.

You can learn a lot from the headliner's crew: the right way to do things from the good ones and the wrong way to do things from the bad ones; but they're good lessons to learn, nonetheless. Some of them treat the support acts like they were family, and some of them treat every opening band like they were dirt; but I've always found that by using a vanishing concept called manners and conducting myself like a professional, I can usually get whatever I need for my client.

I've explained to you how it's important to coordinate with the support acts on your tour. By the same token, it's important for you to coordinate with the headliner's production manager when your band is the support act. I've always found that a polite email requesting the information that I need will usually get me what I require.

It's sometimes our knee-jerk reaction to expect a new band and their crew to be a headache because of their lack of experience. Show them from the beginning that this won't be the case with you and your band. First impressions count a lot and will make the difference in how they respond to you and work with you from the very beginning.

Do the things I've told you about how to coordinate with the support acts. But instead of you asking for support act information, you're the one sending that information. Send off a polite email to the headliner's production manager introducing yourself as the band's tour manager. Tell the production manager that you've included your band's stage plot and input chart and ask him if he'd be kind enough to forward it on to the sound company that will be doing the tour.

Tell him you've also included your band's rider but that you know the entire dressing room catering rider probably won't happen. Ask him if there's a predetermined amount of dressing room catering that your band will get each night, and if there is, what it consists of.

Tell him how your band's traveling and how your gear's being moved. If you're in a bus and trailer, tell him that. If you're in a van and trailer, tell him so. Send him a personnel sheet for your entourage that lists each person's full name and job title. Ask him if your band and crew will be included for lunch each day.

You'll also want to ask the production manager what time he'd like for you and your entourage to show up on the first day. If he tells you to show up at 2:00 p.m., don't come rolling in at noon. He said 2:00 p.m. for a reason. Ask him about his protocol for your guest list: what time would he like it presented to him each day, or would he prefer that you give it directly to the promoter rep and just come to him for passes? Ask him about his policy and any restrictions on passes for your group.

Attach a PDF copy of your tour book if it's already finished and ask him if you can obtain a copy of his tour book. He may refuse to send you one if he doesn't have a separate tour book for the band because he probably won't want to send you a tour book that contains his band's hotel info, but it never hurts to ask.

If your band's carrying a lighting director, ask him if he can send you a lighting plot specifying which parts of the rig will be available for your band to use. You'll also want to ask him what kind of lighting console your L.D. will be using. If your band hopes to use spotlights in their show, ask him if it will be possible to have any of the spotlight operators on call for your show. If so, he'll tell you how many spots you can use. If you're on a U.K. or European tour, you may have to pay some of the bus and truck drivers to run spotlights for you if the promoter doesn't have any operators for you to use. The production manager may just send you his lighting designer's contact info and ask you to contact him directly about lighting issues.

Ask him if there will be any sound restrictions for your band that you need to know about. Ask him if he has any idea how much time your band will have on stage each day for at least a line check. Keep in mind that if your band's first on the bill, you'll probably have all of the time left before doors open for a sound check unless you're told you must be done by a certain time due to any union dark stage restrictions that might apply.

If your band is in the middle slot on the tour, it is doubtful there will be enough time for anything more than a quick line check unless your band's popular and a full sound check has been negotiated. The production manager may just refer you to his FOH engineer or send you directly to their sound company for any answers to specific questions about audio.

If your band's first on the bill, there may be some shows when your band won't get a dressing room. The headliner may need a minimum amount of rooms, and then the direct support act's dressing room needs will come next, and then yours last. If it's a smaller venue or a venue that has limited dressing room space, you may need to use your bus for a dressing room that day. If you're in a van, then you'll have to find whatever crack in the wall you can and make it work.

When you walk into the venue on a show day and all of the dressing rooms are marked with signs for the headliner and the direct support act, then that's probably a good sign that your band won't be getting a dressing room that day. Don't go into the production office every day when you arrive and ask where your dressing room is, because that'll get old quickly. Be proactive and fend for yourself whenever you can.

Make your email to the headliner's production manager as brief as possible. He's got enough things to do and doesn't have time to read an email from the support act's tour manager that's longer than a preacher's sermon. Make it brief, get to the point, tell him what he needs to know and end it. *Adios.*

Once you've started the tour, don't be the type of person who's rolling into his production office every five minutes asking for something. You'll start to wear out your welcome right away, and they'll start to use the word *no* more frequently because they're getting sick of you. So unless you look like Kate Upton or have one helluva personality, try to gets things done on your own.

Have you noticed I've never suggested that you contact the headliner's tour manager? On bigger tours, where the headliner has a production manager, you'll usually only be dealing with him. The headliner's tour manager is there to take care of his band, and he's also sometimes the tour accountant. He's a very busy person. There's nothing you'll ever need from him unless you have some problem with getting paid by the promoter and you need him to intervene on your behalf. Even then, go through the headliner's production manager first. If he can't solve your problem, then let him go to his tour manager for you.

One of the other important things that you should ask for in your email to the headliner's production manager is the name of their stage manager and his contact information. This will be the person that your crew deals with each day on stage when setting up your band's gear. After you quickly introduce yourself to the production manager on the first day of the tour, the stage manager should be the next person you meet.

Start off on the right foot with the stage manager. Be polite and professional and remember that he's in charge of that stage, even when your band's performing. Ask him how he'd like for your crew to proceed each day. Ask him when and where he'd like for your crew to dump their gear. Ask him if he'll be on stage each day to call house lights in conjunction with you or your stage manager when it's time for your band to go on.

The best way to send your relationship with the stage manager down the drain is not to go on stage on time. Do what he says when he says to do it. Get him on your side, and your life every day will be much easier and run a lot smoother.

Make sure your stage manager's there when you introduce yourself to the headliner's stage manager. Always make sure your crew remembers that this isn't one of their headline shows where they can take forever to get their gear off stage. When your show's over, your crew needs to have a rock-solid plan to get their gear off stage in record time each night. If you want to impress these people and suddenly have them wishing you were their support act for life, get your gear on and off stage in record time. If you want them wishing you'd marry their sister, help their crew with their changeover. Do anything you can to make their day easier, and most of them won't forget it.

You should always look for the promoter's office when you show up each day. The headliner's production manager will usually post a sign up showing which room the promoter is in. Look for the promoter's office first before bothering the production manager. If the promoter's office is marked on the first day, then it's highly likely that it will be marked every day. If there's not a room designated for the promoter's office, then ask the production manager where you can find the promoter rep.

Introduce yourself to the promoter rep when you arrive and hand him your W9 tax form in case he forgot to print out the one you emailed to him. Even on a tour where your band's the support act, you should have already advanced your cash requirements with the promoter rep and emailed him your band's tax form. It's highly likely that he's forgotten you sent it to him, so he'll appreciate the fact that you're thinking ahead and brought him a copy. Remember, his first priority that day is the headliner. Some booking agents will put the band's company info and taxpayer ID number on the contract, so the promoter may have already prepared a W9 tax form if he needs one, but be prepared with one just in case he hasn't.

Promoter reps are busy people. Make his life easier by being prepared and cause him as little grief as possible. Ask him what time is best for you to come and get paid. Be there when he says to be there. It's important to have the promoter rep ending the night with a positive vibe when it comes to your band.

If your band's brand new and has never been on a major tour before, you'll do them a great service by reading them the polite "riot act" before you arrive for the first show. Many new bands are often big fans of the headliner and can let their enthusiasm get them into trouble from the beginning.

Remind your band and crew how important it is to build a good relationship with the headliner's crew so they're on your side and doing what they can to help you. Stress how important it is for your entourage to cause them zero grief and to respect their pass system and not violate it.

Remind everyone that they should never enter the headliner's dressing room unless invited by someone in their camp. No one in your band or crew should be going to the headliner's production office for anything. If they need something or have a problem, they should come to you and let you deal with it.

Never allow your entourage to hang in the hallway outside the headliner's dressing rooms or production office, raising hell and being loud and annoying, and don't let your guests do this, either. Your guests should always be kept in your dressing room, and when they're not, they should be accompanied by someone in your camp and never allowed to run around unattended backstage. The last thing you need is one of your guests walking into the headliner's dressing room just as their singer is getting undressed to get into his stage clothes. Police your people, and you'll keep the peace.

Never leave the venue after the show with your guests running wild backstage. Always clear them out and send them home before you leave. If you're worried about any of them returning after you leave, speak to the backstage security guards and tell them that the passes designated for your band are no longer valid. You don't want to show up at the venue the next day and discover that one of your guests caused mayhem backstage after you left last night. You could quickly find that your guest list is now nothing but a distant memory that once was.

There's nothing more important than dealing with the headliner's people in a professional manner. You always want to end the tour with their people hoping to see you in the future. This is good for your band, and it's good for you. Always leave a tour having made the best impression you possibly can.

TAKING CARE OF YOUR CLIENT

Someone once asked my ex-wife, Nicolette, what I did for a living, and she immediately replied, "He's the highest-paid babysitter in the world." While those words were meant to be a cynical joke from a beautiful woman who'd grown tired of having a husband who was never at home, there is a bit of truth in the statement. First and foremost, a road manager gets paid to take care of the band. And, yes, some musicians can be more hellish than Regan in *The Exorcist*—bile-spewing, backwards-speaking, rotating heads and all.

Father Karras, will you please bless my crucifix-shaped, Jack Daniels-flavored pacifier?

Even though taking care of the band has sometimes been the most difficult part of my job as a road manager, that's not been the case with the majority of my clients. Although, whether I'm working for the band as their road manager, lighting designer, or both, there can be times when dealing with the artist is an unpleasant experience, to say the least.

With the exception of one demonic, hypocrite, lunatic motherfucker whose biggest accomplishment doesn't come anywhere near justifying his grotesque ego—and his minuscule bloodsucking, worm-like creature of a manager—most of my clients through the years have been pretty good human beings, and many of them are still dear friends of mine today.

What do you have to do to take good care of the band? Well, for some road managers that's about as hard as trying to properly score a boxing match, but it's really not that complicated. You just have to spend the time to get to know your client and find out what makes them tick and, more importantly, what ticks them off.

I once had a client who would flip out if the promoter gave him the wrong brand of his favorite canned drink, convinced that the promoter was trying to screw him over. There was another client who believed everyone in the music business was out to rob him blind, and you never heard the end of it. While there are a lot of shysters running around the music business, out to rob any unsuspecting band that they can con into a signing a contract, there are a lot of good people out there. Sooner or later, a band has to trust someone to handle their business, though there's something to be said for sleeping with one eye open.

One of my past clients was so hooked on prescription medication that I literally worried every night when I went to sleep if he'd be alive when I woke up the next morning. It can be a scary situation when someone you care about is abusing prescription medication or using hard drugs, especially when you're in charge of taking care of them.

I don't believe it's the tour manager's job to play wet nurse to a musician who's abusing drugs or alcohol, but it usually ends up in the tour manager's lap whether he likes it or not. You deal with it or you find another gig. Of course, you also have grounds to ask the manager for more money. The more high-maintenance the client, the more money you deserve to earn. However, not every manager sees it that way.

As I'm writing this book, an old client of mine from the '80s, Jani Lane, the singer of Warrant, has been found dead in a Woodland Hills, California hotel. It was discovered that he died of acute alcohol poisoning. Jani had fought alcohol addiction for many years.

I worked for the band as their lighting designer around the time their first hit record, *Dirty Rotten Filthy Stinking Rich*, was released. It hit a bit hard when I learned of his death. He'd always been a nice guy to me, and he was one helluva singer. He was another casualty of alcohol and drug abuse like Kevin Dubrow, the singer of Quiet Riot, who died in 2007 from a cocaine overdose. One of the first U.S. tours I ever did with Keel was supporting Quiet Riot back in the mid-80s when they were touring in support of their multi-platinum record, *Metal Health*. Poison was the opening band on the tour, and their first record was soon to go right through the roof. I can still remember that tour like it was yesterday.

I've worked with bands that fought like cats and dogs every day, and I ended up being the reluctant referee through every battle and the emotional tampon that had to soak up the blood and tears between every round. It's not something I like doing, but when you're in charge, you have to keep the train rolling for the sake of the entire operation so everyone keeps earning a living.

I've been in situations where the leader of the band expected me to spy on his band members and report to him about their drinking or drug use. I've never liked doing this and always refuse to do it. I've never believed that my job entails being an informant for someone who spends too much time worrying about how others live their lives and how it's going to affect his. Doing this kind of thing is a great way to get caught in the middle and have people hating your guts. I'm not a drug and alcohol counselor or a snitch. My job is to get the band from A to B and handle their business along the way, although I've always been willing to help anyone who asks for my help.

I think any road manager should be honest up front about what he is and is not willing to do before he's hired. Never assume anything when it comes to the duties a band expects you to perform for them. They could be used to having certain things done for them because the tour manager you replaced did those things. You might not feel the same way. However, if you're in the beginning of your career and need the job, you might not be in a position to give the client a list of things you won't do.

No responsible road manager wants to see a tour go down the drain, leaving everyone without a job, because the band won't sit down and iron out their personal and professional problems. It's a drag being on a tour where everyone hates each other's guts. I've only experienced this a few times in my career, and that was a few times too much. Here in the twilight of my road career, I choose my clients very carefully. Life's too short to be miserable every day.

I've worked with musicians who didn't have two nickels to rub together but they acted like they were Prince, expecting to be treated like royalty. I always try to give each of my clients the *star treatment*, whether they've earned it or not, but that star treatment can backfire when they start demanding Cristal champagne on an MD 20/20 budget. You can only remind them of their financial reality when they lose touch of it and hope they come back down to planet earth.

There are musicians who have highly successful careers and are some of the most *real* and grounded people you'll ever meet, and there are those who are more high-maintenance than General George S. Patton, four stars and all. While I truly believe that anyone who has worked hard to achieve great success deserves all of the luxuries he can possibly afford, there's something to be said for always being a humble human being, utilizing good manners, and never forgetting where you came from. I speak bluntly, but I never forget how lucky I've been and the great and talented friends I've made in this business.

I firmly believe that no successful person is without an ego, but I also believe that ego can be a positive force or a destructive force. It's all in how you use it. It can propel you to greater heights and happiness or destroy you in the end. We should always treat everyone with respect and kindness because you never know when you're going to meet those people again on the way back down. Nothing lasts forever, and that couldn't be truer than in the music business.

One of the hardest gigs a road manager can have is working with a veteran band that was once much bigger than they are now. It can be hard for them to adapt to playing clubs when they once headlined arenas, getting picked up at the airport by passenger vans instead of limousines, and staying at the Holiday Inn instead of The Ritz-Carlton across the street like they once did.

It's an even harder job when the band still expects the luxuries that they were once accustomed to but can no longer afford them. Adapting to a lower level of touring can often be difficult for them. Some of them refuse to accept the reality of where their career is presently and take it out on everyone in sight, convinced that the music business is screwing them over once again. It's hard to work with a band like that. They come to believe that there's always a conspiracy against them, and no one's doing their job for them, but no manager or agent can make the big crowds come back if they no longer care. I prefer to view my shot glass half full than half empty.

Every client is different from the last. Each one of them is a different personality with different needs and expectations. To last with any band, you must learn what makes them happy and content and, even more so, what does not. With some musicians, figuring this out can seem more impossible than solving the mystery of the Bermuda Triangle. But if you give a damn about the band, you'll keep trying. And, in the end, I think the good ones will see that you care and are trying.

I've been lucky through the years. For the most part, all of my clients have been great people and a pleasure to work with, despite some of their little quirks and difficult moments, but that comes with the job. And God knows I've not always been a walking carnival, but I always gave a damn. Artists of every type are unusual people and quite unlike the average person you deal with in normal everyday life. There's no list that I can create to tell you what you need to do each day to *take care* of your band. They're all different, but that's what makes them all unique.

A good tour manager is not only a problem solver but a problem detective. You must try to know a client better than he knows himself so you can detect when a problem is brewing inside him long before it manifests itself in an ugly manner.

Don't be a road manager who is always waiting for the band to tell you what they need. Figure out what their personal needs are on your own and make sure those needs are always attended to, big or small. Neglected needs that you might think are trivial can turn a client into an ex-client because you're not attending to them.

You must learn quickly how the band wants to live their daily life on the road and make that a reasonable reality if you want to last. Even the most amicable and easy-going musicians have minimum expectations as to how they want their life on the road to be. It's your job to make this happen for them—within the confines of their budget, of course. However, many of them will still expect you to be a miracle maker; and you have to become one to a certain degree. Be creative. Figure it out. Do what you have to do. You don't do the big tours, earning thousands a week, if you can't think outside the box and solve problems that the average guy says are impossible. Nothing is impossible.

I've always told my clients that if I don't know the answer to a question, give me a minute, and I'll come back with the answer. No one can ask for more than that, but you have to get them a satisfactory answer.

Being a tour manager for a music group can sometimes be a difficult job with a new catastrophe waiting to rear its ugly head at every turn you make, but that's what makes the job so painfully exciting. You never know what's going to happen next. If a person can't deal with pressure and solve unexpected problems, there are less demanding careers out there, such as a Walmart greeter or envelope stuffer.

Which do you prefer?

THE LAST DAY OF THE TOUR

The last day of the tour can be the most frantic day because you have so many things to get done, but whether or not it becomes the worst day of the tour depends on how well you've prepared for it.

In the final week leading up to the last day of the tour, you should be doing various things to make that last day go as smoothly as possible. The last day of the tour is the last impression you're going to make on the band and their manager. Make the last day the best day of the tour. You're only as good as the last thing you've done.

If you've listened to what I've said about doing your road accounting on a regular basis, you shouldn't be backed up on your receipts, but if you are, start multi-tasking in the midst of everything else and get caught up on your expense receipts. You don't want to wait until the last day of the tour to find out there's a problem in your cash ledger and your numbers are adding up incorrectly.

I don't like to end a tour with road reports left undone. It's always possible you're heading straight into another tour, and you don't want to start a new tour with another band and still have unfinished work from the tour you just ended. That's a good way to get behind in your work with your next client.

Unless you're on the most brutal tour ever, booked with no days off and not a single second to spare, there's no reason you should be ending a tour with a bag full of expense receipts. There has to be a time management problem somewhere, and you need to solve it. Maybe you need to ask yourself what's more important: staying on top of your duties or Facebooking your friends all day and showing them what a big-time tour manager you've become.

Let me give you a hot tip. If you get Facebook friend requests from your band members and their manager, they probably don't really give a shit about being your Facebook friend. They're more interested in seeing how much time you're spending doing trivial personal things on their time clock.

Frankly, if I were managing a band and the road manager was always late on his road reports, and other important things were always falling through the cracks, and I suddenly saw a new Facebook picture of the road manager dancing on the beach with a beer bong attached to his face like a sleep apnea mask, I'm going to want his ass roasted alive on a barbecue spit.

Even if you're doing a great job, don't give people bullets to put in their gun to use against you in the future because when you finally do screw up—and we all do, sooner or later—they will use that ammo against you. Second hot tip: resist the urge to put your moments of personal lunacy on the internet.

I always pay the bus drivers any salary they're owed the day before the last day of the tour so it's one less thing to deal with on the final day. Have your bus driver make up a list of his final payments, such as his salary, any overdrives he may be owed, generator services, and bus linen cleaning fees.

You'll also need to give him fuel money to drive the bus back home. You can easily estimate what that number should be by calculating the mileage for his drive back to the company shop or wherever he's going. Once you've done this, double-check the number with the bus company so you know it's the correct number they're expecting you to pay the driver. This amount should have been determined when you first leased the bus.

Pay the driver everything you owe him, have him sign the receipts, and then enter them into your cash ledger. Also, have the driver turn in his float receipts that day so you can enter all of the bus expense receipts into your cash ledger. If the driver has been using a band credit card for bus expenses, get any credit card receipts he might possess and enter them into your credit card ledger.

If he still needs to fuel up that night for the final drive to the last show, give him the estimated amount of float he thinks he'll need, and then you'll only need to enter that final fuel receipt into your accounting on the last day. If the bus driver's using a band credit card for fuel and he needs it for that last night, remember to get it back from him on the final day of the tour.

If there are any per diems that need to be paid to the band and crew, pay those to them before the last day of the tour. If the last week of the tour was only two days long, I would've paid everyone nine days of per diem the previous week so I didn't have to make receipts again for just two days of per diem.

If any of the crew members are getting paid their salary in cash, pay them off and enter those receipts into your accounting. Get as far ahead of the game on your road reports as you can before you reach the final day of the tour. If you do this, then the only things you'll need to enter into your accounting on the last day are receipts for things the runner had to pick up for you. Plus, you'll need to enter your final show settlement into your cash report and reconciliation statement.

If you're only picking up a flat guarantee on the last night, or you're absolutely certain you won't be going into overage and picking up any back end money, you can go ahead and enter the cash or check you know you're going to receive at settlement. If you've advanced your cash pick up like you should have, you'll know what you're receiving from the promoter rep.

I'll usually wait until after doors have opened before I start printing out road reports. By that time, the runner will have picked up any final things that I might need. It's also a good time to have the runner come into the production office and turn in his receipts so you can enter them into your cash ledger. Don't forget to settle up with the runner on that last hectic night.

Print out your cash ledger. Place it on top of your stack of cash receipts and bind them together with a binder clip. Do the same thing with your credit card receipts, just as you've done every week of the tour. Now print out your final reconciliation statement. Stack the cash and credit card reports in a neat pile and place the final reconciliation statement on top of it all. Place it all into a FedEx envelope.

You should also include in the package any checks you've picked up since you sent in your last road reports. If you have any cash left over, and you usually will, you'll need to convert that cash into a money order or cashier's check so you can include that money in the package. Never send cash to the accountant in your road report package.

If you've been estimating your cash requirements properly, you shouldn't have too much cash left over on the final day unless the manager and agent have been insisting that you pick up cash from every promoter. If you have only a few hundred dollars left over, you can send the runner out to a 7-Eleven or a U.S. Post Office to convert the cash into a money order. Don't forget to add the money order fee receipt into your accounting before you print out your cash ledger. You can always call ahead and see what the fee will be if you don't already know. Make the money order out to the band's company and add it to your package along with any checks you might have, just as you've done every week of the tour.

If you should have a large amount of cash left over, you can do what you've done every week on the tour and find a branch location of the band's bank and buy a cashier's check. If you don't have time to do that on the last day of the tour, or there's no branch of the band's bank in that town, you can send the runner to a 7-Eleven or the U.S. Post Office to buy multiple money orders for the total amount. The largest money order you can buy from 7-Eleven at this time is $500, and the largest money order you can purchase from the U.S. Post Office is $1,000. I wouldn't trust the runner with too much of the band's money. Nothing against the runner, but if they lose the money, you're still responsible for it. Try to make time to go with the runner and do it yourself.

If you're carrying a large amount of cash, you should've done this banking chore the day before the last day of the tour. Pick up a check at your last settlement, unless you need the cash to pay final bills or the manager or agent are insisting that you pick up cash. If you're an American band on tour overseas, you're most likely not picking up any cash from the promoter—unless you need float—because it's all being wired to the booking agent after each performance is completed.

If you're a foreign band on tour in America, you're probably doing the same thing, but if you have any cash left over that you need to take back overseas with you, it's probably best to wait and deposit this cash into the band's bank account in your home country so you get the best exchange rate and avoid any exchange fees. However, there is the risk of losing the cash or having it stolen from you on the journey home. Of course, there are also limits to how much cash you can bring into most countries without declaring it. Declare it or it can be confiscated if you get caught.

If I've done all of my accounting and have it all packed up before the last FedEx pick up occurs, and I'm picking up a check that night because there's zero chance of any overage, I'll ask the promoter rep if he'll give me the check early so I can include it in my package and get it sent off to the business manager. If you haven't driven the promoter rep off his mental cliff that day, he may give you the check early. Some will do it; some won't.

If you can't get your package sent out that day, wait until the next day when the tour's over, but make sure you let the accountant know when the package will arrive when you send your final nightly report. Be sure to include in your nightly report the FedEx tracking number and a list of any checks inside the package, just as you've done the entire tour.

On the last day of the tour, go online and check everyone in for their flight the next day. Some tour managers don't do this, but always try to do it. You can't check in online any sooner than twenty-four hours before the flight. If everyone's on the same flight, checking them in will be much easier. If they're all on different flights, wait until twenty-four hours before the earliest flight out to start checking everyone in.

Make sure that you go around and ask each person how many bags they'll be checking in at the airport. Make a list of how many bags each person is checking in. Don't just assume that they're checking in one bag because they started the tour with one bag. People have a way of accumulating a lot of stuff on a long tour.

Don't wait until late that night to check people in online if you're trying to get them better seats than what they already have or if they have no seating assignments at all. You want to be the first person online trying to check in your group, just as you should be the first person in line when you're checking in your group at the airport. The longer you wait, the fewer the good seats available.

Even if you can't check them in online because you have excess and oversize luggage and gear, you can still go online with many airlines and change seating assignments, so at least do that. If someone's on a sold-out flight and seating assignments were impossible to get when the tickets were bought, make sure you warn that person in advance if he's stuck in a middle seat. This can sometimes happen when buying cheap tickets, but at least you've warned the person involved.

If everyone's on the same flight, check and see who's in the bad seats and who's in the good seats using the online seating chart. You can ask some crew members to swap seats with band members who got stuck in bad seats. It's better than having Armageddon fought on the plane over a middle seat.

Don't forget to plan how you're getting everyone to the airport the next morning. If the cheapest and most sensible option is for everyone to spend the night on the tour bus and have the driver drop the entourage off at the airport the next morning, make sure you carefully decide your departure time for the airport. If it's a weekday morning, plan for traffic, and always remember to be at the airport at least three hours before your departure time for an international flight and at least two hours before a domestic flight departs. Always make sure you're up and awake at least thirty minutes before the bus driver is supposed to arrive from the hotel so you can make sure he hasn't overslept and cause you to miss your flight. Have him send you a text message when he's leaving the hotel so you know he's on the way.

On the bottom of your last day sheet, always thank everyone for a job well done. This might sound minor to some people, but I think it's important. Even if it's been the worst tour you've ever done and you can't wait until it's over so you never have to see any of them ever again, do it anyway. End it on a positive note. There has to be at least one person on the tour who worked hard, gave a damn, and deserves to hear it.

PART FIVE

BUILDING YOUR SUCCESSFUL CAREER

NETWORKING AND SELF-PROMOTION

You should always be planning ahead for your next gig, especially if your current client's touring cycle is coming to an end. You don't want to wait until your tour is over to start looking for another gig, unless you want to take some time off. Most tour managers are self-employed, and it's up to them to find their own work. You can help to keep the phone ringing by promoting yourself in the beginning of your career until you're more well-known.

When a band releases a new CD, they can tour off that record for a few years if they're popular or a new band building a lot of steam fast. On Testament's last album cycle for *The Formation of Damnation*, we toured for almost four years off that record. It was a long and successful run, but not every band enjoys that kind of success, especially if they're a new band just starting out.

If you're a new road manager who hasn't built a reputation yet, you'll need to spend more time planning ahead for future work. Networking and self-promotion is the most important thing for you to do in the beginning of your career.

I've had an email address since 1995, and I built the first version of my website, MarkWorkman.com, in 1997. I knew early on that being able to put my resume and pictures of my work as a lighting designer on my website was a valuable thing to promote my business. Today, there are social media sites such as Facebook, Myspace, Crewspace, Linkedin, Twitter, and even YouTube, to promote our careers in the music business; and more of them are being developed every day.

You must continue to promote yourself and make connections in the music business to further your career. This is something you should never stop doing, even if you don't need a gig. You never know when a band member could get sick and a tour gets canceled, leaving you without a gig on short notice. Anything can happen.

I built my website fifteen years ago. Once I built it, all I had to do was tell a manager my website address so he could view my resume and a photo gallery of my lighting design work. You must have a strong presence on the internet. Build yourself a website, even if it's only a simple two-page website with a home page and a resume page. If you're also a lighting designer, make sure you have a photo gallery page with pictures and video clips of your work. Websites are easy and cheap to build these days, and some are even free. A quick Google search will yield many options.

Go into the settings of your email account and add a signature to the bottom of your email that includes your name, cell phone number, eFax number, and your website address. Make sure the website address is a hyperlink that anyone can click on to go to your website. Don't make people type your domain name into an address bar. No one wants to jump through hoops to give you a job, and it really doesn't send a message to potential employers that you're a very thorough tour manager.

If you don't have a business card, have one made. If you're short on funds, there is cheap software available that allows you to make business cards on your computer and print them out on real card stock. Both of these items can be bought online or in most office supply stores. Always include your cell phone number, eFax number, email address, website address, and job title on your business card. If you have a P.O. Box, you can also add that to your business card, but I wouldn't put your home address on a business card, especially if you live alone and spend a lot of time on the road.

We have to be careful in this day and age what personal information we give to people and post on the internet. If you're going to advertise to the world that you're single, live alone, and are about to go on the road for six weeks, you might as well just put a sign on your front door that says, *come steal all of my shit.*

Always ask for a business card from everyone you meet in the music business and enter their contact info into your smart phone. Build a large email address book as you go along. We're always hearing about some band suddenly in need of crew members because somebody quit or got fired. If you have the contact info for the right person at the right time, you're much more able to be the person to get the gig when you need one most.

Get contact info from managers you meet. You can always send off a brief email to them when you're looking for a gig and tell them you've just finished a tour and are now available and to please keep you in mind should they find themselves in need of a tour manager. Even if they're not in need, they're often speaking to other managers who might be. The right email at the right time could land you a gig. Everyone likes to be the person who helps to solve someone else's problem.

And for God's sake, don't ever refer to yourself or anyone else who works in this industry as a roadie, because no one in this business will ever take you seriously again. Only the general public that doesn't know any better, or watches too many badly made movies, uses this worn-out, idiotic term.

HOW TO FIND YOUR FIRST GIG

It's hard to believe that it's been thirty-three years since I left West Virginia and moved to Los Angeles to pursue a career in the music business. It seems like only yesterday that I got on that Trailways bus and traveled twenty-four hundred miles to follow a dream that everyone I knew thought was more like an insane nightmare. It's been a long ride with a lot of ups and downs, but I have few regrets. I've seen the world more times than I'll ever remember, and I've made a lot of money doing it.

Now that I've shown you the fundamentals of how to be a music tour manager, I want to give you some ideas on how to find your first gig and begin to build a resume that'll lead to bigger clients and establish a successful career.

You may want to become a band manager one day. I've always believed that the best managers are the ones who were once tour managers. I honestly believe that you can't effectively manage a band unless you really know how a concert tour is run, especially in this day and age. With the music business now going through more dramatic changes than a middle-aged woman enduring menopause, touring is the primary way that many bands now earn a living, and all of those bands will need competent road managers to run their tours. A career as a road manager is a good and logical path to band management.

I've worked with some new managers who didn't know the first thing about how a concert tour is run, and it made my job as a tour manager more difficult. I spent a lot of time teaching those managers things they should've already known, but, like new tour managers, new band managers have to start learning somewhere.

There are good managers who were once record company executives and know the mechanics of producing, releasing, and promoting a record, but the success of a band's career now hinges more upon their success on the road. Every manager needs to know more about concert tours and how to maximize the success of those tours. For many bands, a new CD release has now become more of a vehicle for going on the road, playing live, and selling merchandise than actually selling CDs.

The writing's on the wall. It's been there for some time now, but the record companies kept trying to remove it like subversive political graffiti so no one could read it. CDs and DVDs and all other forms of physical media will soon be extinct. It's a digital, wireless world and we need to accept it, embrace it, and look to the future, and the record companies that won't let go of their old ways of operating will also become extinct. For artists with balls and vision, I often wonder if they even need record companies anymore. These are exciting times for an artist who wants more control over his creative output and future, but promoting music takes a lot of time, effort and money to do it right.

If I've learned nothing during my thirty years in the music business, I've learned not to sign slave contracts that give away all of my rights to my creative output for little return. I'm also of the mind that conventional publishers are becoming less important if an author's willing to expend the effort and spend the money to produce and promote their work. This is the reason why I chose to self-publish this book and not seek a conventional publishing deal in the beginning. I'm not saying there aren't any good publishers out there offering fair deals—there are—but I'd rather do my own thing if I can, at least in the beginning, and see what I can do on my own. Having total control over your work is a good thing.

I've heard many artists complain how the internet fucked them, but the internet didn't hurt their business; the thieves who use the internet to steal their work fucked them. The best thing that ever happened to creative artists is the internet. It's just difficult for some people to adjust to this quickly changing business and its new ways when they've been used to the old ways for so long.

I'm a college dropout. I was studying Electronics Technology at Los Angeles City College, with plans to move on to UCLA, when I met Ron Keel and Steeler in 1983. I had originally planned to become a recording engineer until I met Ron and my path took a surprising turn into concert lighting. I'm glad that happened; I accidentally found what I was best at and truly had a talent for. Had I known at the time that I'd also become a music tour manager, I probably would've studied business administration and accounting in college instead of electronics.

There are college students around the world who are studying business administration and accounting who aren't looking forward to using those hard-earned skills cooped up in some claustrophobic office for the rest of their lives. Those business and accounting skills would serve you well in a career as a music tour manager and band manager.

For three decades, people all over the world have asked me what they have to do to become a tour manager in the music business. It was hard to give them a real answer until now because there were no real books on the subject. Reading this book is a good first step. Then you must find your first talented band that's going somewhere in their career. After all, you can't be a tour manager for a local band that doesn't tour.

There may be up-and-coming bands in your town with a lot of talent that are starting to create a big buzz. Those are the acts you need to meet. Find those bands with talent and offer your services for free so you can show them what you can do and prove yourself to them. Tell them what your goals are, explain to them what you know—or what you're learning—and how you can be valuable to them. Show them loyalty and support, but most of all, show them that your goals are the same as theirs. Make an investment in their future, and you'll be making an investment in your own future.

You must prove to your band that you're serious about your goals for the future. If the band finally gets signed to a record deal, and you've proven yourself to them, you could find yourself embarking upon the beginning of your career and working with your first signed act. This is how it all begins.

If you live in a small town where there aren't any talented local bands, you may have to consider moving to a bigger city like I did. There wasn't much hope of me starting a career in the music business living deep in the mountains of West Virginia. That's why I packed up my life and moved to Los Angeles. You may need to do the same thing if you truly want to make your career a reality.

I don't believe you need to live in Los Angeles, New York, or Nashville to begin a career as a tour manager, but it will certainly give you a big advantage over those who don't. And living in the heart of the music business will certainly increase your chances of success in a major way. There are other cities, such as Austin, Chicago, Seattle, Boston, San Francisco, Washington, DC, or Dallas with thriving local music scenes that are producing talented bands. The same can be said for other cities around the world, such as London, Toronto, Montreal, and Copenhagen. You won't find your first act living in the middle of nowhere; you have to go where the talent is. You have to get out there and start meeting that talent, building a name for yourself, and showing those bands how you can be valuable to them.

If they already have a manager, build a relationship with him or her. Let the manager know what your goals are and explain how you can be a valuable asset in helping him realize his goals. You could suddenly find yourself on board for the ride, if he gets the band signed to a record deal.

Even if your first client eventually fails, there's still a lot of value in having a signed band on your resume and a good reference that you can count on from their manager. Most managers have had an act that just didn't succeed, for one reason or another. That's just the way it goes sometimes in the music business: some acts make it and some don't. However, it has nothing to do with the road manager. Band managers only care that you have experience and do your job well.

Start taking business management and accounting classes at night; most community colleges offer these classes, and there are many available online. If you're not computer literate, start taking computer classes so you know how to use a computer. You must learn Microsoft Office and a good accounting program, such as Quicken. Every community college offers classes on Microsoft Word, Excel, and Access; and if you're not the classroom type, there are online classes and tutorials all over the internet that can teach you this information.

Put these accomplishments in the education section of your resume. If you have sound or lighting skills, include this information in your resume. Managers are always looking for people who can perform double-duty because it saves the band money.

Read other music business books, such as *All You Need to Know about the Music Business*, *This Business of Music*, and *Artist Management for the Music Business*. These books contain some information that has nothing to do with the job of a road manager but are geared more towards band managers. However, there's no downside in knowing as much about the music business as possible. If your ultimate goal is to one day move up from road manager to personal manager, then you'll need to know this information.

Do the things I've said about self-promoting and networking when you're looking for your first gig. Build a website and make business cards to let managers know you exist. The popular touring industry website Pollstar.com releases a series of directories every year, and a valuable one for you to utilize is the *Artist Management Directory*. This directory isn't cheap, but it's a valuable resource for you to use.

Create a resume and write a straightforward cover letter stating that you're an aspiring tour manager looking to get started in the music business. Find management companies in the *Artist Management Directory* that represent artists in the genre of music you prefer to work in, and send your letter and resume to them. Be honest and tell them you have no experience but that you possess a lot of knowledge from the books you've studied and the classes you've taken. Tell them you're working at a local club and continuing to learn every day. Explain to them that you're looking for a shot to prove yourself and get that first notch on your resume. Make it crystal clear to them that you're even willing to work with one of their new baby bands for per diem—or even for free if necessary—just to get a chance to prove yourself. A manager with an impossible tour budget may respond to an offer like this if you've convinced him of your ambition and sincerity. Anything is possible, if you're willing to go after it.

Don't just send one letter and resume to these managers and then never contact them again, but don't hound them into the ground until they become sick of you, either. Make a list of the management companies that represent the kind of acts you want to work with and send them a letter and updated resume every four months, at the beginning of January, May, and September, to keep your name in their minds. Some will admire your persistence and start to remember you, and some will think you're annoying and throw your resume in the garbage can every time, but you never know when your resume might show up at the right time and some manager decides to give that "persistent person who never stops contacting me" a shot. It's all about timing.

Find yourself a job at a club where local bands perform and national acts play when they come through town. This is a great way to meet people and learn the mechanics of how a rock concert works. Even if it's only a job as a stagehand, loading and unloading the band's gear, it is still valuable training and offers a chance to meet people who can help you. If you're a sound engineer, lighting director, or backline tech and plan to tour for a living, you're already on the right path to working your way up to becoming a tour manager. Plus, you can also start working double-duty one day to earn more money and get more tours.

Working for sound and lighting companies is another way to get started in the music business. Even if you're only packing road cases in their warehouse, it's a place to begin learning how to be a sound engineer or lighting director. There are also schools where you can learn the technical skills necessary to start working on a sound or lighting crew so you can work your way up to mixing the band's live sound or running the light show. This is a good route to go if you want to do double-duty in your career in the future.

If you have an accounting degree and live in a major music business city, you can always go to work for a music business manager. The business manager is one of the first people to know when the band needs a tour manager or tour accountant. This is a good launching pad if you don't want to work in an office the rest of your life.

You can also look for a start as an intern at a music management company. You may have to work for free in the beginning—like most interns—but you'll learn a lot about managing a music group. Plus, it's a good way to get your foot in the door with that management company. Let them know your goal is to become a tour manager and that you're willing to start with their baby bands to prove yourself. They'll be a lot more likely to give you a shot if you work in their office every day and they can see how hard you work and how motivated you are. This same route could be followed by starting out as an intern at a booking agency, record company, or even for a concert promoter. You just have to position yourself where you can meet the bands, their managers, and others who have the power to give you a chance. Where it goes from there is up to you.

Do anything and everything it takes to learn what you need to know to do the job, and go where you have to go to meet the people who can be instrumental in helping you find your first gig and start your career. Do whatever it takes to make it happen.

There are no secret formulas or tried-and-true methods to become a tour manager in the music business any more than there are cryptic formulas or proven methods to become a famous actor or musician. This book, and every book about any aspect of the entertainment business, teaches you the fundamentals of the business, but none of them contain any mysterious secrets about how to start a career. The only big secret is you must work your ass off and never stop believing in yourself.

If you ask any famous musician or actor how they made it in the entertainment business, every single one of them will tell you a different story about how they got started and what it took to make it, but what they all had in common was the relentless drive to learn everything they could, an unshakeable belief in themselves, balls the size of Godzilla's, and the indestructible will to never give up and succeed.

I've given you some knowledge and advice; now the rest is up to you. You can do it, just like I did.

ROAD HAZARDS UP AHEAD

A close friend of mine kindly suggested that I remove this final chapter from my book because it was much too personal, but I never considered doing that for more than a nanosecond. While I appreciate my friend trying to protect me, my life—and its mistakes—has always been an open book, unfortunately. It's a small world. I've usually found that I learn more from the mistakes of others—personal and professional—than from their accomplishments.

You don't know the power of the dark side.

I've given up trying to understand that baffling brain twister; I merely accept it and live with it like I do my undying urge to pull up a comfortable seat in a dark, moody bar, fire up a nectarous Marlboro Red, and slam shots of fine Russian vodka while pondering the meaning of all life that only I can see cryptically written across the barmaid's beautiful bottom. But with each passing day, my force field grows stronger, my light saber shines deadlier, and the *Urge* is more easily fought off, yet never completely destroyed.

The Force is strong with this one.

When I started in the music business back in the early '80s, it was Friday every night. You'd walk into the dressing room after the show and nearly everyone in the room—the manager, agent, producer, promoter, record company reps, business manager, you name it—was cutting lines of coke on the table, slamming shots, and drinking beer on a hell-bent mission to stick their dicks into every female in the room who dared show the slightest sign of life.

Today, things are a little different. Oh, there are those who still think we're in 1983—including me sometimes—and try to keep up that same pace. Believe me, I drove that pace car proudly for quite some time, but it gets harder to lead the race as you get older. It's a task better left to younger men and women.

I've always told every crew guy who ever worked under me that I didn't care what they did as long as they performed their job well and didn't cause me or the band any headaches. Even though I refuse to lecture or judge anyone who does their job to the best of their abilities, I hate seeing anyone destroy themselves with drinking and drugging. Fun is one thing; self-destruction is a whole other matter. It's okay to come out of the darkness and sit in the sun again.

I got into the music business for four reasons: money, wine, women, and song. I make no bones about that. Why else would I do a job this hard for thirty years? Today, I'm trying to take the wine out of the equation and am beginning to be a happier and healthier person because of it. God knows I grapple with the cigarettes more than anything. Beautiful women will probably always be my greatest weakness, but I guess there are much worse things in life to succumb to.

The money, the music, and the company of old friends is what's left now; and even though traveling the world becomes more painful every day—thanks to terrorist idiots—it's nice to see something more than the hotel bar when in Paris.

A music group is a business, but it's also meant to be a fun. That's what rock and roll is all about. It amazes me how many musicians have forgotten that. I come from the old school where a little rock and roll chaos every now and then keeps things interesting; and I'm not really into working with musicians who refuse to remove the guitar that's firmly planted in their ass and can't enjoy life so others can do the same. Working for a music group is a hard job, but it doesn't have to be a miserable job. Have your fun, but never let that fun become the reason you do the job or you'll become a miserable mouse on a treadmill chasing something you'll never catch.

Nothing lasts forever, and that includes a career in the music business. Save as much money as you blow, at the least. If you do that, you'll be okay when it's all over one day; and it will be over one day. It's tough traveling the world for a living, and it eventually takes a toll on you. Set yourself up so you're financially secure when it's all over. Become disciplined enough from the very beginning of your career to put money into a retirement account and never touch it for any reason.

Watch and protect your credit score like it was your only child, and buy your first property as soon as you possibly can. If you live alone, buy a duplex so you can rent out the other side, and let your tenant pay your mortgage for you every month while you build personal wealth and financial security for the future. Even if you buy a house or a condo, you can still rent some of the rooms to other road crew friends or other people who will pay your mortgage for you and keep an eye on your property while you're on the road. Treat yourself as a business.

Start your own LLC (limited liability company) so you can take advantage of the tax benefits it allows you. If you don't have the time to stay on top of the necessary paperwork and bookkeeping for your company's taxes, hire an accountant to do it for you, but just don't ever let yourself get into trouble with the tax man. It's not a fun place to be, and tax liens on your credit report will destroy your FICO score and never go away until you pay them. And then they'll stay on your credit report for seven years after you pay them. Handle your personal business correctly.

If you don't own your own company, don't let bands pay you as an independent contractor and send you a 1099 form at the end of the year if you can avoid it. This is never good for you because you don't want to end up with a big tax bill to pay at the end of the year. The winter is our slow time of year, and work can sometimes be scarce during this period. After enduring a slow winter, you don't want to start back to work in the spring knowing that every dime you make for the next two months has to go to the government for taxes.

You're better off having the band take taxes from your check each week and get a refund in the winter. Businesses in the U.S. must send out W2 tax forms by the end of January. If you're ready to do your taxes as soon as you receive your W2 forms—and you should be—you can file electronically and get a tax refund by the first week of March, sometimes sooner. You'll be glad to receive that money if you're hurting for work in the wintertime.

Some of the best people I know in the music business are managers. The good ones do their job well, try to look after the crew as best they can, and actually give a damn. However, there are managers in this business that I wouldn't piss a hot beer on if they were self-combusting in front of me. You'll eventually learn that some of them don't care about you or anyone else in the crew. Hell, some of them don't even care about the band. You're nothing more than a necessary evil in their mind, but they'd have zero chance of sending their band on the road without people like us.

Strangely enough, some of these managers were once road managers, but I guess some of them think if they pretend they're better than us, it'll make them forget what they once were, where they came from, but it won't. They spend their lives treating people like dirt, but when they finally leave this earth, there will be no one there who gives a damn except the poor bastard shoveling dirt in their face. That's a sad thought, but money and power is all that matters to some of them.

For most of 2010, I was the lighting designer for the heavy metal band Megadeth. I had worked with the band twenty years earlier when I designed the Clash of the Titans. In the fall of 2010, while we were in the midst of the American Carnage tour, my younger brother Thomas Ray Workman died of a terminal illness at the age of forty-eight after a three-year battle for his life. I had designed a large, complicated lighting rig with a lot of moving lights for that tour, and it was a big show with a lot of cues.

I never left that tour to be there for my family when my brother died because I didn't want to let Dave Mustaine down by leaving him without a lighting designer on such a big tour. Don't ever let misguided loyalties confuse your priorities. I come from the old school where the adage "the show must go on" is serious business. Maybe it always will be with me; but business and family are two totally different things.

I wasn't there to hold my brother's hand when he faded away, and I wasn't there for my mother when she suffered the loss of her second son. And that wasn't the first family funeral I missed because of a music tour. I will always regret not being there for my brother and mother because of some insignificant rock concert that no one even remembered a month later.

Always be there for your family. There's nothing more important than that, and don't ever let anyone tell you differently. They'll be your family long after some band is dead and buried at the bottom of the 99 percent off bin, and they all end up there sooner or later.

I sometimes think of how I've seen and done it all, but I have so much left to see and do. A clear mind is a powerful thing. I have no real regrets in life except for not being a better husband to my ex-wife Nicolette and for not being there for my family when they've needed me most. People can be crushed beneath the massive burden called guilt if they don't allow themselves to set it down and walk away from it once and for all.

"You will never, ever stop this," my wife once said to me, crying on the phone, wanting me to come home, when she knew that I couldn't. Maybe she's right. This is what I do. Except for writing a word or two, maybe it's what I was born to do; or maybe that's just what I've always told myself to keep this crazy crutch under me.

It's not easy keeping a relationship alive and healthy when you live the majority of your life on the road. You should try to always remember the effect that your absence has on those who love you, and try to be patient with them. They deserve it, and they're worth the effort.

I've made many mistakes in my life because of the Three Deadly B's: broads, blow, and booze; but that's a whole other book. I've always tried to make good on every mistake I've ever made, but even then, there are some people who won't let me forget yesterday. Well, I can't change yesterday, and I'm tired of trying.

Start off on the right foot and keep it together, and one day you could be doing stadium acts, earning thousands of dollars a week. If you want to get ahead in this business, you have to learn everything you can about the job and act and look the part. People will remember you by the good job you do and the professional way in which you conduct yourself, not by the purple pentagram you tattooed on your forehead and the six pounds of metal shit you pierced into your face.

The desperate manager for some no-hoper band called Satan's Anal Holocaust might hire you looking like that, but no real manager is going to trust his important client with you. So unless you have a strange affinity for putrid twelve-passenger Ford vehicles, little sleep, and low pay, try to act like a professional and look the part. If you don't, there's not much hope of you ever making it in the music business unless Jesus gets drunk and decides to miracle you to success.

Keep your chin up and never lose your sense of humor. There are poor, miserable bastards in this business who will try to suck it right out of you, if you let them. If you don't have a sense of humor, you might want to consider a more serious profession, such as mortuary work. Without comedy, we have nothing.

I will never forget my old friend Ron Keel for believing in me and giving me a shot back in 1983. And while I truly believe I would've still made it without him because I would've never given up, he gave me my start; and for that, I will always be profoundly grateful to him.

I will always love Ron's ex-wife, DeeDee Keel, for keeping us going back then during the starving Steeler and Keel days with her money, love, and undying support and belief in us. I often wonder if either of those two bands would've gone anywhere without DeeDee. There are many people in the music business who owe their starts to her, but how quickly some forget.

I hate hearing the term The Big Four; it should be The Big Five. And the uncrowned king of thrash metal that is Number Five is the legendary Testament. I will never forget how they gave my life and career a restart in 1988 when the hair band explosion of the '80s came to a sad end (props, Kurt Cobain, R.I.P.).

I will always love and be eternally grateful to my brothers Chuck Billy, Eric Peterson, Alex Skolnick, Greg Christian, and Louie Clemente for giving me a second chance. I don't know where I'd be without them. It's been a long twenty-five years.

If you read this book because you had nothing better to do, I hope you were entertained. If you really want to be a road manager in the music business, I hope it gave you some confidence, optimism, and knowledge. If you're a new tour manager already out there on the road, I hope it taught you a thing or two. I did the best I could.

May the Force be with you.

ABOUT THE AUTHOR

Mark Workman lives near the ocean in southern California. He's a former boxing writer whose feature articles have appeared on Boxingscene.com and Foxsports.com. He loves to write, read novels and watch great movies. Mark is also an avid cryptocurrency and blockchain enthusiast.

If you liked this book please go to your favorite online retailer where you bought it and leave a review or rating. Please support your favorite books by spreading the word on social media. Thank you.

Made in the USA
San Bernardino, CA
23 January 2020